THE EPIC IN THE MAKING

THE EPIC IN
THE MAKING

SVETOZAR KOLJEVIĆ

CLARENDON PRESS · OXFORD
1980

Oxford University Press, Walton Street, Oxford OX2 6DP

OXFORD LONDON GLASGOW
NEW YORK TORONTO MELBOURNE WELLINGTON
KUALA LUMPUR SINGAPORE JAKARTA HONG KONG TOKYO
DELHI BOMBAY CALCUTTA MADRAS KARACHI
NAIROBI DAR ES SALAAM CAPE TOWN

Published in the United States
by Oxford University Press
New York

British Library Cataloguing in Publication Data

Koljević, Svetozar
  The epic in the making.
  1. Folk poetry, Serbian—History and criticism
  2. Folk poetry, Croatian—History and criticism
  I. Title
  891.8'2'103   PG1452   79-41149

  ISBN 0-19-815759-2

Printed in Great Britain by
Western Printing Services Ltd, Bristol

For Đorđe

Preface

Vuk Stefanović Karadžić, the author of the first modern Serbian dictionary, grammar, and reformed alphabet, wrote down and published hundreds of oral epic poems during the Serbian struggle for independence from Turkish rule in the first half of the nineteenth century. These oral epics tell the story of Serbian medieval grandeur, the Turkish conquests in the fourteenth and fifteenth centuries, the subsequent life in vassalage and slavery, the outlaws' and the rebels' fight for freedom. Even if they never achieve the form of a unified oral epic, they are closely linked together in the historical awareness shared by many singers and in this sense they reflect one of the last stages of an oral epic in the making. This body of material was recorded in largely illiterate communities in which it was a major form of flourishing oral culture. This is what makes it different—in the immediacy of its heroic tone and the liveliness of its epic colours —from the later epic poems in the same tradition, which has survived to the present day.

In the course of the nineteenth and twentieth centuries many oral poems in the same epic tradition were discovered in older manuscripts and books, the earliest of them dating from the end of the fifteenth century. In spite of considerable range in versification this body of epic material contains many common traditional themes and heroes, dozens of standard narrative and stylistic devices, many universal formulas and hundreds of phrases based on common traditional formulaic patterns. Thus it enables us to study the life of an oral epic diction through several centuries of changing historical circumstances, to observe its formulaic and formulopoeic aspects in time, to trace the development and the interplay of its basic moral concepts which belong to the different social and spiritual settings of pagan and Christian, feudal, and village life. This is what gives the Serbo-Croat oral epic material its unique interest.

This material reveals the ways in which the older layers in an epic tradition are exposed to the pressures of contemporary history. It suggests that the oral epic singer has to create in what often is, and must be, both a living and an anachronistic medium. The traditional language often imposes the patterns of a dead past on a living present; the inertia of the singer, which makes him persist in what is already dead or dying, is often as strong as his creative urge to adapt and respond to the burning issues of actual history. This is why the singer is often a mechanical reciter of formulaic chronicles, even if he is also sometimes a visionary witness who brings together the past and the present, whose own experience finds a way into his traditional stories and gives a dramatic colour to his awareness of history. But there are also occasions when his spiritual needs make him step beyond history and push through the limits of existing social morality. It is not surprising that in such instances his basic formulas sometimes fail him: his utterance has to be unique, or formulopoeic, not because he cares for originality, but because he has to compel the language to do what it has never done before.

This book is an attempt to study the genesis and the achievement of the Serbo-Croat oral epic poems in their specific linguistic, social, and historical context. If many comparative issues are involved, they can be only touched upon: their proper study would demand not only another book and another author, but also a completely different context. However, the richest oral epic material in any single European language, comprising a continuous tradition of more than three and a half centuries of epic singing, can be fully appreciated in its comparative aspects only after it has been properly understood in its own context and studied in its own right.

Acknowledgements

While teaching Yugoslav literature in translation in Blooming-ton, Indiana, USA, in 1963/64 I realized that Serbo-Croat oral epic poetry could give foreign students some insight into the social and historical background of a little-known literature. Some of my American students appeared to be enlightened by this approach; this is perhaps what made the subject more and more puzzling for me in the ensuing years.

I tried to work out my bewilderment in several articles, but these led to further confusion and endless discussions with my brother Nikola Koljević and my friends Novica Petković and Rajko Nogo. This tempted me to write a book on the subject. The temptation might have been resisted—had it not been for the encouragement of the late Professor Vladan Nedić of the University of Belgrade. His careful reading of the manuscript spared me—within the bounds of my obstinacy—some mistaken notions and several errors of judgement. After this book was published (*Naš junački ep*, Belgrade, 1974), I was led on, imperceptibly, by Anne Pennington and Peter Levi to produce an English version of it. In 1975/76 a visiting fellow-ship at All Souls College, Oxford, provided me with an opportunity to do so. But even with many useful suggestions from Professor Desanka Kovačević-Kojić it took some years to find out about the historical background which had to be introduced for a foreign audience—although it could be, and was, assumed as common knowledge in the initial Serbo-Croat version of this study.

I am grateful to Professor M. Pantić for many favours, not least for putting at my disposal a manuscript copy of his article about an unknown *bugarštica* from the fifteenth century. I should also like to express my thanks to Asim Abdurahmanović for his work on the maps, to Dušan Tasić for his photographs of the fresco paintings of St Sava, Tsar Uroš and King Vukašin, to Tomislav Ladan for providing the photograph of the portrait of Stojan Janković and to Vera Han for her permission to use some of her illustrations earlier published in an article. I am indebted to the editorial staff of the Oxford University Press, particularly for many helpful suggestions in the course of the copy-editing of my manuscript.

I am grateful to my friends Andrew Harvey, Gojko Subotić, Ljubomir Zuković, Omer Hadžiselimović, Bogdan Rakić, Zoran Mutić, Mirko Ljubojević, William Tribe, Samir Busovača, and, particularly, Ivo Šoljan for their generous help with too many things to be noted here. Finally, my thanks are due to my wife and children for putting up with almost everything that the writing of this book involved.

Contents

PART SIX: THE STRUGGLE FOR INDEPENDENCE

PART SEVEN: THE EPIC SETTING

Illustrations

Photograph for Pl. 4 supplied by T. Ladan; drawing and
photographs for Pls. 5 and 6 supplied by V. Han.

Maps

Maps drawn by Asim Abdurahmanović

Abbreviations

Balović–Pantić   Professor M. Pantić's copy of his edition of 'Balović's Manuscript', forthcoming.

Banašević   'Beleške i objašnjenja' in V. S. Karadžić, *Srpske narodne pjesme*, iii, ed. N. Banašević, Belgrade, 1954 (rpt. 1958).

Bogišić   V. Bogišić, ed., *Narodne pjesme iz starijih, najviše primorskih zapisa* (*Glasnik srpskog učenog društva*, x, 1), Belgrade, 1878.

Gesemann   G. Gezeman, *Erlangenski rukopis starih srpskohrvatskih narodnih pesama*, Sremski Karlovci, 1925.

Karadžić   V. S. Karadžić, *Srpske narodne pejsme*, i–iv, ed. V. Nedić, Belgrade, 1969 (rpt. 1976).

Latković   'Beleške i objašnjenja' in V. S. Karadžić, *Srpske narodne pjesme*, iv, ed. V. Latković, Belgrade, 1954 (rpt. 1958).

Matić   'Beleške i objašnjenja' in V. S. Karadžić, *Srpske narodne pjesme*, ii, ed. S. Matić, Belgrade, 1953 (rpt. 1958).

Mazarović–Pantić   Professor M. Pantić's manuscript copy of his edition of 'Mazarović Manuscript', forthcoming.

PS   'Popjévke slovínské', Nacionalna i sveučilišna biblioteka, Zagreb, R 4091.

All quotations are given in English translation in the text. Verse quotations are also given in Serbo-Croat in footnotes (those from *Gesemann* in slightly modernized transliteration).

All verse quotations have been translated into English by Anne Pennington and Peter Levi.

Note

The nearest equivalents in English to the Serbo-Croat consonants printed with diacritical marks are as follows:

Ć, ć; Č, č: ch *as in* chair

Đ, đ; Dž, dž: j *as in* journey

Š, š: sh *as in* shadow

Ž, ž: s *as in* treasure

Also:

J, j: y *as in* yard

Introduction

Oral epic singing was in the history of the Slav population in the central Balkans what the Pharoahs' tombs were in ancient Egypt, *The Iliad* and *The Odyssey* in the Hellenic world, the cathedrals in medieval Europe—not so much a specific form of art as a complex expressive medium, reflecting in great depth a long cultural history, summing up—as it were in retrospect—several centuries of the imaginative response of a civilization to its historical realities and spiritual needs. In a largely illiterate society this oral epic singing also had a function roughly corresponding to that of the modern mass media—it spread the political news, much more slowly but perhaps not less reliably than the modern press, radio, and television. But it interpreted the significance of the historical events in a formulaic language sometimes charged with the highest communal moral concepts and coloured as much by a deep awareness of the past as an intense expectation of the future. Besides, the medium combined the expressive powers of poetic language, singing, and *gusle*, the one-stringed (in some regions often two-stringed) musical instrument, ideally made of maple wood. As this wood was also used for coffins, it came to symbolize the cult of the ancestors and was often evoked as the Muse of the epic song.[1]

---

[1] See V. Čajkanović, *Mit i religija u Srba*, Belgrade, 1973, p. 5. In fact, however, maple wood is rare, in some areas unknown, so that the *gusle* is often made of pine, ash, alder, olive, walnut, plane, poplar or other kinds of wood. The Moslem epic singers in Serbo-Croat used the *tambura* instead of the *gusle*; the *tambura* has usually two strings and looks like a mandoline (for further details about the *gusle*, the *tambura* and other instruments see M. Murko, *Tragom srpsko-hrvatske narodne epike*, Zagreb, 1951, i, pp. 322–39). There were also 'singers', however, who only 'spoke' their poems instead of singing them and accompanying them on a musical instrument. This was, for instance, the distinctive feature of Karadžić's best 'singer' Tešan Podrugović. Karadžić believed that there was some connection between Podrugović's achievement and his manner of oral delivery (see below p. 322). He also pointed out that 'speaking' was a frequent, 'homely' manner of performance—used, for instance, by old men addressing the audience of children (see note 3, p. 322). But the *gusle* has remained the emblem of oral epic singing and, for the Serbs at least, a great symbol of national identity.

The voice of the song lived above all on the struggle between the Cross and the Crescent which went on from the fourteenth to the nineteenth century in the central Balkans. But the growth of this epic tradition can be partly followed from the Middle Ages. In the predominantly monastic medieval literature there are several clear references to and reflections of oral epic singing. Besides, some of the major epic concepts in the songs which were written down much later can be traced back, sometimes in their actual phrasing, to medieval sources. But the embedding of occasional medieval elements in the epic poetry is only a small part of the rich and fascinating interplay of literary and oral culture in the central Balkans. The early ecclesiastical animosity to all forms of popular lay singing— coupled with the translations of Latin hymns into vernacular oral poetic forms in which they are sung to this day as 'folk' Christmas carols[2]—was only one of the first paradoxical chapters in this long story. A little later oral folk forms provided some of the models for the most successful lyrical literary compositions in Renaissance Dubrovnik,[3] whereas Gundulić's *Osman*, the greatest seventeenth-century literary epic in the language, inspired by Italian models, particularly by Tasso, was 'translated' into oral folk epic idiom and sung in the neighbouring area of the Bay of Kotor![4] This story of a complex give-and-take relationship between oral and literary culture is certainly one of the major features in the history of the expressive modes in the Serbo-Croatian language.

This interplay is also mirrored in the circumstances of the recording of epic songs. From the end of the fifteenth century— many years before the age of Kirsha Danilov, Percy, Macpherson, and Herder—different learned people, in diverse social settings and for very different reasons, began to write down

The invocation of 'the *gusle* made of maple wood' ('gusle moje, drvo javorovo') can be heard at the opening of the performance from many singers today (see M. Murko, op. cit., pp. 324, 329); the earlier collectors left this out probably because they assumed that the line did not belong to any particular song.

[2] See M. Kombol, *Poviest hrvatske književnosti*, Zagreb, 1945, p. 40.

[3] Such were, for example, some of the best poems by Džore Držić. See M. Kombol, op. cit., pp. 93–4.

[4] See M. Pavić, *Istorija srpske književnosti baroknog doba*, Belgrade, 1970, pp. 425–6.

these epics, independently and unaware of each other: at first in the so-called 'long lines' (usually varying from fourteen to sixteen syllables) and later in the shorter octosyllabic and decasyllabic lines. The latter had a far less feudal and a far more peasant imprint, but on the whole all these oral epics shared a common epic language. Some of the recorded poems combine lines of varying length and this also suggests the comparative unity of the whole tradition.[5]

Among the earliest collectors we find an Italian court poet, grand Renaissance literary noblemen inspired by pastoral interests, Dubrovnik and other merchants and soldiers moved by patriotic zeal, educated Dalmatian and Montenegrin diplomats and statesmen, an occasional Franciscan monk devoted to the art of the people with whom he often shared his social origin and historical experience, a German clerk or officer far better versed in the art of the Habsburg Cyrillic calligraphy than in the phonetics of the Serbo-Croatian language. However, much of this treasure—and chaff—was buried in the dust of oblivion for a very long time. Admittedly, there is an English reference to these oral epics at the time when they were hardly known even if two or three of them had been written down. As early as 1603 Richard Knolles—in his classic *Generall Historie of the Turkes*—invoked Serbo-Croat 'countrey songs' to support the then popular European explanation of

[5] See, for instance, V. Bogišić, *Narodne pjesme iz starijih, najviše primorskih zapisa* (*Glasnik Srpskog učenog društva*, X, 1)., Belgrade, 1878, No. 108. See also below pp. 71–2. Bogišić's collection will henceforth be referred to as *Bogišić*. All quotations from *Bogišić* have been checked against the manuscript of 'Slav Songs' in the National and University Library in Zagreb ('Popjévke slovínské', Nacionalna i sveučilišna biblioteka, Zagreb, R 4091—henceforth referred to as PS), the manuscripts in the Yugoslav Academy of Sciences and Arts in Zagreb (Jugoslavenska akademija znanosti i umjetnosti, Zagreb, IV. a. 30, previously No. 638, and I. b. 80, previously No. 641) and M. Pantić, ed., *Narodne pesme u zapisima xv–xviii veka*, Belgrade, 1964, henceforth referred to as *Pantić*. Quotations from poems which Bogišić printed from Balović's and Mazarović's manuscripts have been checked, by the kindness of Professor M. Pantić, against a manuscript copy of his forthcoming edition of these texts; these are henceforth referred to as Balović–Pantić and Mazarović–Pantić respectively. Corrections to Bogišić's text and his line numbers have been duly noted, except when Bogišić simply miscounts the lines—in such cases the correct line number is given in square brackets without any explanation.

the disaster of medieval Serbia—which, it was claimed, was due to the treacheries of some of its despots who failed to defend not only themselves but also the rest of Christendom.[6] But it was only in the second half of the eighteenth century and the first half of the nineteenth century that the work of Alberto Fortis and Vuk Stefanović Karadžić aroused considerable international interest in the Serbo-Croat oral epic songs.

Fortis was an Italian explorer and scholar, a friend of Cesarotti and an admirer of his Italian translations of Ossian. His accounts of his visits to the Dalmatian islands and coast, almost immediately translated into German and English, contained his Italian translations of two epic songs—one in fact written in the manner of oral epic poetry, but the other a genuine gem of oral composition. This soon attracted international attention to the 'Ossianic' significance of Serbo-Croat oral epic poetry.[7]

---

[6] See R. Knolles, *The Generall Historie of the Turkes*, London, 1603, p. 365. Knolles supports his account of the double dealing of Đurađ Branković, George Despot of Serbia, by claiming that 'the people of that countrey even at this day in their countrey songs still tearme him the faithlesse and gracelesse Despot'. At least one of these terms ('faithless') has stuck to the name of this fifteenth-century historical figure as a heroic epithet in the oral epics recorded in the eighteenth century. Thus within one single poem—which describes how Đurađ Branković put John Hunyadi into prison—he is six times called 'nevjera' (*Bogišić*, No. 10, ll. 34, 39, 56, 80, 93, 98). This is a standard epic term denoting a faithless person (see below pp. 21, 28–30, 164–5, 191–2).

[7] In 1771 Alberto Fortis published his Italian translation of what he believed to be a genuine Serbo-Croat (or 'Morlacchian') oral folk poem ('Canto di Milos Cobilich e di Vuko Brancovich', *Saggi d'osservazioni sopra l'isola di Cherso ed Osero, Venice, 1771* pp. 162–8). In fact this was a poem written by Andrija Kačić Miošić, a Dalmatian Franciscan monk, who published a collection of epic poems covering the whole of South Slav history and mostly written in the manner of oral folk poetry (*Razgovor ugodni naroda slovinskoga*, Venice 1756, second enlarged edn., Venice, 1759). Some of these poems were so well adapted to the folk idiom that they were absorbed later into the oral tradition. But it was not long before Fortis published the genuine folk poem 'Xalostna Pjesanza Plemenite Asan-Aghinize', together with his Italian version of it in his *Viaggio in Dalmazia*, Venice, 1774, pp. 98–105. Both these poems, the latter one in Goethe's translation, together with two more poems translated from Serbo-Croat, found their way into Herder's *Folksongs* ('Ein Gesang von Milos Kobilich und Vuko Brankowich', 'Klaggesang von der edlen Frauen des Asan-Aga', *Volkslieder*, Leipzig, 1778, pp. 130–8, 309–14; 'Radoslaus', 'Die Schöne Dolmetscherin', *Volkslieder*, Leipzig, 1779, pp. 161–6, 167–71). This was the

Moreover, Fortis's observations about the 'Morlacchians'—as he called the inhabitants of the mountains near the Dalmatian littoral—helped to build up the image of some wild Slav tribes as the noble savages of south-east Europe. Of course, the spontaneous oral compositions of the illiterate, noble, and formidable 'Morlacchians' fitted perfectly the Romantic concept of 'natural' poetry,[8] and they soon found their way into Herder's *Folksongs* (*Volkslieder*, 1778, 1779). 'The Wife of Asan-aga', an excellent song, rendered in Goethe's impressive translation, inspired Madame de Staël to write to the great Goethe that she was 'ravie de la femme morlaque'.[9] The young Walter Scott produced his highly poeticized, Augustan version of Goethe's version of Fortis's version of 'The Wife of Asan-aga' —but it remained, until the twentieth century, deservedly unpublished.[10] When Karadžić's collections appeared in print,[11] Jacob Grimm, the greatest German comparative scholar of the time, contrasted the Serbian and the German heroic songs, stressing the 'pure' and 'noble' language of the

beginning of the international literary history of Serbo-Croat oral epic singing, which can be followed in detail in M. Ćurčin's *Das serbische Volkslied in der deutschen Literatur* (Leipzig, 1905) and D. Subotić's *Yugoslav Popular Ballads* (Cambridge, 1932). There are also good shorter accounts in D. H. Low's introduction to his *Ballads of Marko Kraljević* (Cambridge, 1913, second edn. 1922) and in D. Wilson's *The Life and Times of Vuk Stefanović Karadžić 1787–1864* (Oxford, 1970), pp. 192–207. This last book also contains much excellent information about the general background of the golden age of Serbo-Croat oral epic singing.

[8] In his review of the classic German translation of *The Folksongs of the Serbs* (*Volkslieder der Serben*, trans. Therese Albertine Luise von Jakob (Talvj), 1825; second vol. 1826) Jacob Grimm referred specifically to 'diese serbische naturpoesie' (see '*Volkslieder der Serben*', *Kleinere Schriften*, iv, Berlin, 1869, p. 419). This review was first published in *Göttingische gelehrte Anzeigen*, 1826, No. 192, pp. 1910–14.

[9] See D. H. Low, 'Introduction', *The Ballads of Marko Kraljević*, Cambridge, 1922, p. 15.

[10] For a full and reliable discussion of Scott's interest in Serbo-Croat oral epic poetry see D. H. Low, 'The First Link Between English and Serbo-Croat Literature', *Slavonic Review*, iii (1924), pp. 362–9.

[11] V. Nedić, ed., *Srpske narodne pjesme*, i–iv, Belgrade, 1969 (rpt. 1976), provides the most reliable text of oral poems which Karadžić published in his lifetime. This edition will henceforth be referred to as *Karadžić*. For Karadžić's work as a collector and publisher of oral poetry and the later editions of his material see Appendix I.

former and advising the German students of Slavonic languages to learn Serbo-Croat for the sake of these 'excellent songs'.[12] He also persuaded Therese Albertine Luise von Jakob, a young lady who knew some Russian and was devoted to Goethe and poetry, to translate some of these songs into German. The German translation—*Folksongs of the Serbs* (*Volkslieder der Serben*, 1825; second volume 1826)—was for years a minor literary classic: Engels had it, for instance, on his short reading list for Marx's daughter.[13] As early as 1827 *Servian Popular Poetry* —John Bowring's translation of the German translation— appeared in English.[14] Mérimée was also inspired by the vogue to produce his Ossianic fraud *La Guzla* (1827)[15] and the subject had, for a time, both a scholarly and an exotic international reputation.

In the later nineteenth century the exotic aspects achieved political significance. The Serbo-Croat oral epics appeared to be such a trustworthy embodiment of national character that they came to be widely discussed in British journalism in the political and military contexts of the Near Eastern Question, particularly at the time of the Balkan crisis.[16] The political interest in this subject was also lively, and better informed, at

---

[12] 'Narodne Srpske Piesme . . .', *Kleinere Schriften*, iv, pp. 197, 199, 204. This review was originally published in *Göttingische gelehrte Anzeigen*, No. 177–8 (1823), pp. 1761–73.

[13] See Ch. Tsuzuki, *The Life of Eleanor Marx 1855–1898*, Oxford, 1967, p. 24.

[14] John Bowring, *Narodne srpske pjesme—Servian Popular Poetry*, London, 1827. This is obviously a translation of the well-known German translation by Therese Albertine Luise von Jakob—even if Bowring also had the Serbo-Croat original in his hands (see D. Subotić, *Yugoslav Popular Ballads*, pp. 230–7). Bowring refers to this German lady as 'an amiable woman' ('Introduction', p. xlvi), but claims that his translation aimed above all at preserving 'most faithfully the character of the original '(ibid., p. xlviii).

[15] See Anon. [P. Mérimée], *La Guzla; ou Choix de poésies illyriques, recueillies dans la Dalmatie, la Bosnie, la Croatie et l'Herzegovine*, Paris, 1827.

[16] See, for instance, the unsigned articles 'Servia. An Historical Sketch', *All the Year Round*, N.S., xv, pt. i (20 Nov. 1875), pp. 174–80; pt. ii (27 Nov. 1875), pp. 198–202; 'Servia and the Slavs', *Dublin University Magazine*, lxxxviii, pt. i (Oct. 1876), pp. 385–96; pt. ii (Nov. 1876), pp. 513–22; pt. iii (Dec. 1876), pp. 773–9; lxxxix, pt. iv (Jan. 1877), pp. 140–6; 'Marko Kralievitch: The Mythical Hero of Servia', *Macmillan's Magazine*, xxxv (Jan. 1877), pp. 222–9; 'The Literature of the Servians and the Croats', *The Westminster and Foreign Quarterly Review*, N.S. liii (April 1878), pp. 303–27.

the time of World War I.[17] But it was above all on account of its comparative interest and Homeric relevance that Serbo-Croat oral epic singing became an important topic in international scholarship.

There is sufficient evidence that Vuk Stefanović Karadžić was aware of the Homeric aspects of his material even before the first of his collections was published.[18] But there is no doubt that the question whether Homer was many people or just one man haunts many of the nineteenth-century reviews and studies of Karadžić's materials, together with several other Delphic riddles of Homeric scholarship.[19] However, it was only in the twentieth century, in the field-work of M. Murko, in the Chadwicks' and in C. M. Bowra's theories and discussions of the poetry of the heroic age, in M. Parry's and A. B. Lord's field-work and their theory of formulaic composition, that Serbo-Croat oral epic poetry was established as an important area in the modern studies of oral expressive forms.[20] But after A. B. Lord has done so much to explain Homer by the material he found in a twentieth-century oasis of Serbo-Croat oral epic singing, after M. McLuhan has claimed that this study is particularly 'appropriate to our electric age' and that his own *Gutenberg Galaxy* is 'in many respects complementary to *The Singer of Tales* of Albert B. Lord',[21] it may also be useful to examine the main body of the oral epic material in Serbo-

[17] This is reflected in the republication of O. Meredith, *Serbski pesme or National Songs of Serbia*, London, 1917, as well as in several other books and booklets (R. W. Seton-Watson, *Serbian Ballads*, London, 1916; M. A. Mügge, *Serbian Folk Songs, Fairy Tales and Proverbs*, London, 1916; J. W. Wiles, *Serbian Songs and Poems—Chords of the Yugoslav Harp*, London, 1917).

[18] See N. Banašević, 'Ranija i novija nauka i Vukovi pogledi na narodnu epiku', *Prilozi za književnost, jezik, istoriju i folklor*, xxx (1964), pp. 171–2. This article has been reprinted in V. Nedić, ed., *Narodna književnost*, Belgrade, 1966, pp. 392–416.

[19] See Appendix II.

[20] See in particular M. Murko, *Tragom srpskohrvatske narodne epike*, i–ii, Zagreb, 1951; H. M. and N. K. Chadwick, 'Yugoslav Oral Poetry', *The Growth of Literature*, ii, Cambridge, 1936, pp. 297–456; C. M. Bowra, *Heroic Poetry*, London, 1952; M. Parry, A. B. Lord, *Srpskohrvatske junačke pesme*, Belgrade–Cambridge, Mass., 1953; M. Parry, A. B. Lord, *Serbo-Croatian Heroic Songs*, Cambridge, Mass.–Belgrade, 1954; A. B. Lord, *The Singer of Tales*, Cambridge, Mass., 1960; M. Braun, *Das Serbo-croatische Heldenlied*, Göttingen, 1961.

[21] M. McLuhan, *The Gutenberg Galaxy*, London, 1971, p. 1.

Croat, recorded from the fifteenth to the nineteenth century, in its immediately relevant historical, social, and cultural setting. This is the primary purpose of this book and, one hopes, some justification for offering an English version of a work which was originally written for a Yugoslav audience.[22]

[22] S. Koljević, *Naš junački ep*, Belgrade, 1974.

PART ONE

The Growth of the Song

1. The Roots

A Byzantine chronicle, dating from the first half of the seventh century, describes, among other things, three Slav spies who were captured in the vicinity of Constantinople, carrying some sort of cither instead of arms and claiming that their people preferred singing to fighting.[1] If cithers could be used as disguise for espionage by the seventh-century Slavs in the Balkans, or even if such a story could be made up by the enemy, it suggests that the Balkan Slavs of this time had, or thought they had, a reputation for singing. The reports of the Arab travellers contain similar evidence suggesting that the *gusle* were used by Slavs in the tenth century.[2] And it might be also significant that the Slav word *igrici* was used in Hungarian to describe professional singers until the twelfth century.[3] However, as there are no extensive descriptions of the setting and the subjects of the earliest Slav songs in the Balkans, this evidence is interesting only in so far as it confirms what could have been taken for granted—that the Slav tribes in the Balkans cultivated singing for a long time before any of their songs were described or written down.

When literacy came in the wake of Christianity in the ninth century, the enmity of the Church to pagan oral traditions was hardly a stimulus for their recording. However, as Christianity spread and absorbed many of the earlier pagan customs, this enmity became more discriminate. There is, for instance, some evidence both of collective and individual epic singing in two Serbian medieval biographies—that of Stefan Nemanja, the twelfth-century founder of the Serbian medieval state, and that of his son Sava, the great pioneer of its flourishing monastic culture. In the biography of Stefan Nemanja, Domentijan, a Serbian monk writing about 1264, describes the events which

---

[1] See V. Latković, 'O pevačima srpskohrvatskih narodnih pesama do kraja xviii veka', *Prilozi za književnost, jezik, istoriju i folklor*, xx (1954), p. 188. Reprinted in V. Nedić, ed., *Narodna književnost*, pp. 292–313.

[2] See ibid.

[3] See ibid.

happened (and probably some which should have happened) in 1192. Of course, he could not have been their eyewitness, but they did not belong to a mythic past and his imagination must have been working within certain limitations of reality. The focus of his interest was, among other things, Sava's—or Rastko's, as he was then called—departure for Mount Athos, a historical fact which has inspired for centuries some of the finest tales and poems in the language. (See also Pl. 1.) With somewhat stylized clerical naïvety Domentijan describes the parents' tears for this early loss of their dearest son and the sense of 'horror', as he puts it, which spread all over the country. In short, Rastko's gesture—the decision of a young prince, the country's darling, to renounce worldly life—had a touch of personal daring of public significance: it was epic in character. The consternation and the grief which struck the country were expressed, according to Domentijan, in song: 'some people, taught by the Holy Spirit, thought up poems and sang sadly about the departure of this God-enlightened youth'.[4] Domentijan might have been recording what actually happened or what should have happened, but it is clear that he was addressing an audience capable of appreciating this kind of story. It must have been an audience living within the tradition which made it possible to 'think up' poems and sing immediately about events of public importance and epic character. Moreover, the context of Domentijan's story rules out the possibility that this might have been, as some have thought, a form of ecclesiastical singing. For why should monks, of all people, sing 'sadly' and join the grief of the parents on such an occasion? This evidence of early lay epic singing in what was probably a collective performance has never been questioned even by those historians who were not so patriotic as to be easily duped in such matters.[5]

Teodosije, the biographer of St Sava, writing at the end of the thirteenth century, probably before 1292, in the monastery of Chilandarion in Mount Athos, offers more colourful evidence of medieval songs in Serbia—probably because he was far more sophisticated than Domentijan in his didactic and hagio-

---

[4] Domentian, 'Život svetoga Simeona', *Životi svetoga Save i svetoga Simeona, Stare srpske biografije*, iv, tr. L. Mirković, Belgrade, 1938, p. 244.

[5] See, for instance, S. Stanojević, 'Gregoras o našim junačkim pesmama'. *Stražilovo*, v (1892), p. 413.

graphical assumptions. Teodosije was a widely travelled man, perhaps the most learned Serbian monk in the reign of King Milutin (1282–1321), an exceptionally enterprising Serbian ruler even by medieval standards. Apart from conquests of new lands, Milutin married four times, blinded his own son for disobedience and erected or renewed some thirty churches and monasteries in which several thousand paintings and objects of precious metal were made.[6] This implied, of course, a social setting different from the one which Domentijan was addressing; and Teodosije was in fact instructing this new monastic and court audience in many things, among others in the great moral examples offered by the ancient epic heritage—such as the romances about Alexander the Great and the story of Troy. It is in this new spirit of his times that he refers to what can be found in 'the pagan writings about the manhood of some heroes in ancient wars', in the stories which can teach their readers 'to be eager, skilled and dauntless in battle'.[7]

Similarly, there are interesting shades in his attitudes to popular oral compositions. On the one hand, for instance, he praises his future saint as a young man who avoided from his earliest days 'empty prattle and improper laughter'[8] and, appropriately enough, 'hated indecent and harmful songs of youthful desires which weaken the soul in the extreme'.[9] These must have been the songs which not only weaken the soul but also excite the body—the jovial, usually lascivious songs, sometimes connected with revelling or just youthful merry-making, popular in the oldest as in more recent times.[10] They are interesting perhaps only in so far as they illustrate the range of collective singing in medieval Serbia—a range which is always important in the genesis of such an eclectic folk form as oral epic poetry has to be. But it is also important to note that Teodosije was condemning only a particular kind of folk song as lascivious. As an outstandingly well educated and perceptive man, a monk with a taste for the classical epic heritage, he did

---

[6] See M. Kašanin, *Srpska književnost u srednjem veku*, Belgrade, 1975, p. 178.

[7] See ibid., p. 179.

[8] Teodosije, 'Život svetoga Save', *Stare srpske biografije*, i, ed. M. Bašić, Belgrade, 1930, p. 89.

[9] Ibid.

[10] See for instance M. Leskovac, *Bećarac*, Novi Sad, 1958.

not share the general prejudice of many of his less enlightened colleagues against lay epic singing—the prejudice at work, for instance, in medieval Hungary where the art of court singers was classed among twenty-four major sins.[11] That such a prejudice was also cultivated in the Slav lands in the Balkans can hardly be doubted: the fifteenth-century *Statute of Poljica* entitled parents to disinherit their sons if they became professional singers.[12]

The position of this sinful craft in medieval Serbia is vividly mirrored in what Teodosije has to tell us about medieval pious fervour in warfare, which he paints in such lively colours. He describes, for instance, with some zest the cruel pranks of Dobrimir Strez, a powerful feudal lord who demonstrated the independence of his mind by devising strange ways of killing people. Even for a minor offence he would have a man thrown from his high walls to the River Vardar, merrily exclaiming: 'Mind your sheepskin does not get wet!'[13] King Stefan the First-Crowned, who had been Strez's patron, condemns 'himself in his conscience for having saved from death such a cruel-minded steer, for having fed him and turned him into a lord'.[14] But Stefan's pricks of conscience and remonstrances arouse only anger and hatred in Strez and in this situation St Sava decides to go to see Strez, to teach him the wisdom of God and make him give up his intentions of warfare and bloodshed. As his instruction is of no avail, St Sava kills Strez by prayer: God sends 'an angry angel to stab him in the middle of his angry heart'.[15] So King Stefan is not forced 'to do his human duty'[16] and stain his hands with blood. This kind of providential moral interference in historical situations will become very important in later oral epic poems, but almost exclusively in the poems which are deeply rooted in the Middle Ages. Thus we find it in the poems about ancient legends which reached the singer by medieval literary transmission ('Simeun the Foundling',

[11] See S. Stefanović, 'Nekoji podaci iz mađarske literature za datiranje naše narodne poezije', *Prilozi proučavanju narodne poezije*, iv (1937), p. 29.

[12] See V. Latković, op. cit., p. 190; also M. Pavić, *Istorija srpske književnosti baroknog doba*, pp. 427–8.

[13] Teodosije, op. cit., p. 177.

[14] Ibid., pp. 177–8.

[15] Ibid., p. 182.

[16] Ibid., p. 179.

'Momir the Foundling' and others[17]) and in the poems in which medieval feudal lords and rulers figure as heroes ('Uroš and the Mrljavčevići', 'The Building of Skadar', 'The Downfall of the Serbian Empire' and others[18]).

Finally, it is also in the spirit of this crusading fervour, so characteristic of some of the later oral epics, that Teodosije in the next chapter describes Stefan the First-Crowned keeping vigil all the night in the church at the grave of his father Stefan Nemanja. His piety is magnificently joined to a warrior's virtues: Stefan, says Teodosije, 'found himself closer and closer to God and men in everything praised by God, experienced in military matters and appreciative of courage; for when he sat at the head of the table he delighted the noble-born by drums and *gusle*, as is the custom of autocrats'.[19] This description of epic singing and *gusle* at the Serbian medieval court can be fully understood only within the wider picture of Teodosije's assessment of the moral interference of Providence in human affairs and the imaginative intertwining of the ways of God and men—so prominent in later oral epics.

This clear evidence of the *gusle* and the epic spirit makes irrelevant the patriotic game of wild or strained speculation about the 'hidden' decasyllabic lines in older hagiographical, administrative and autobiographical prose[20]—as well as some of the other highly questionable historical references to epic

[17] See below pp. 115–20.

[18] See below pp. 138–41, 147–50, 161–2.

[19] Teodosije, op. cit., pp. 190–1.

[20] So for instance Đ. Živanović finds that Konstantin of Ostrovica was writing Polish prose with Serbian decasyllabic rhythm in his ear in the fifteenth century. Apparently, when Konstantin describes Turkish horsemen with two horses (leading one and riding the other—'*jeden wiedzie, a na drugiem jedzie*'), he breaks the rules of Polish grammar to obtain a decasyllabic line with a caesura after the fourth syllable (see Đ. Živanović, 'Predgovor' in Konstantin Mihailović iz Ostrovice, *Janičarove uspomene*, Belgrade, 1966, p. 66). However, if it is true that in modern Polish Konstantin would have to say '*jednego wiedzie*', there is no breaking of Polish fifteenth-century grammar in the form which Konstantin uses (according to Dr A. E. Pennington)—apart from the fact that we are not faced with Konstantin's manuscript which has not been preserved, but with a copy of a Polish manuscript which might be a translation! D. Kostić is even less convincing when he removes 'unnecessary' conjunctions and gets decasyllabic lines in Serbian early fifteenth-century prose (see id., *Starost narodnog pesništva našeg*, Belgrade, 1933, p. 21).

singing on Serbian medieval soil.[21] But Teodosije's evidence
only hints at the rich oral epic traditions of the Slavs in the
Balkans; they are reflected at much greater depth and in more
detail in Father Dukljanin's *Chronicle*, which contains a confused
and often fictitious genealogy of medieval Slav rulers, and an
account, for the most part legendary, of their exploits from the
middle of the fifth to the middle of the twelfth century. At the
time when he wrote his *Chronicle*—and historians at least agree
that it must have been between the twelfth and the fifteenth
centuries[22]—Father Dukljanin was an old Catholic cleric who

[21] The most notorious among those is Nicephorous Gregoras's description
of his journey to Serbia in 1326. This refined Byzantine diplomat was most
appropriately bewildered by the primitive conditions of life in the area near
the river Strumica. He had to spend a night in a forest there and he must
have been much more frightened than his soldiers: 'there were some in our
entourage who sang tragic songs, because they little feared the present
danger; they sang about famous men of whose famous deeds we have heard'
(quoted from S. Stanojević, op. cit., p. 413). It used to be thought that
Gregoras's words hid 'very important evidence of ancient Serbian-
Bulgarian epic poetry' (V. Jagić, 'Građa za slovinsku narodnu poeziju',
Rad JAZU, xxxvii [1876], p. 112). However, Gregoras does not say a word
about the nationality of the warriors in his entourage; had they been
Serbs or Bulgarians, he would not have understood what they sang about
and it is hardly likely that they would have had any difficulties in communi-
cating with other natives in this area—difficulties which Gregoras explicitly
mentions (see S. Stanojević, loc. cit.).

[22] See S. Mijušković, 'Uvod', *Ljetopis popa Dukljanina*, Titograd, 1967. The
earliest Latin copy of the manuscript of this Chronicle dates from the middle
of the seventeenth century (Vatican Library, photostat in Mijušković's
edition). The earliest copy of a Serbo-Croat translation of this Chronicle
dates from 1546 (Vatican Library). It is a copy of an earlier manuscript
which was lost but exists in the Latin translation by M. Marulić (1510).
Several copies of this translation have been preserved. Modern editions are:
F. Šišić, *Letopis popa Dukljanina*, Belgrade–Zagreb, 1928; V. Mošin, *Ljetopis
popa Dukljanina*, Zagreb, 1950 (based on Šišić). However, Mijušković has
shown many inaccuracies in these texts and translations, so that they have
proved to be far less reliable than is generally assumed in modern historical
scholarship. Mijušković argues that the glaringly inaccurate account of
twelfth-century history in this Chronicle shows that it must have been
written much later, probably between the middle of the fourteenth and the
middle of the fifteenth century. This was the time of the dissolution of
medieval Serbia and the rising ambitions of the Montenegrin feudal lords,
particularly the Balšići. It is in this context that Father Dukljanin's
Chronicle, in Mijušković's opinion, 'with its evocation of the glory and the
power of the destroyed "Kingdom of the Slavs" might have had a political
justification' (op. cit., p. 107).

lived in the fortified patrician city of Bar, a few miles inland in southern Montenegro. However, whether Father Dukljanin was writing in a small Montenegrin patrician city at the watershed of the twelfth-century Byzantine and Roman worlds, or, which is more probable, at the later fifteenth-century watershed of Christendom and the rising Ottoman Empire, it was a setting in which the legendary interpretations of ancient times had an immediate political and moral significance.

This comes out quite clearly in Father Dukljanin's introductory address to his reader in which he explains why he has undertaken to translate into Latin the Chronicle which, apparently, he wrote initially in Slavonic. What he has to say about this illustrates that from the beginning of time to the present day—from *Gilgamesh*, *Mahabharata* and *The Iliad* to *War and Peace* and more recent war films—nothing has been quite so enthralling for the human heart as warfare and the cult of its memories. For Father Dukljanin begins by telling us how many different people cultivated this kind of love for history and begged him to translate his chronicle into Latin. There were, first of all, his 'beloved brothers in Christ and the honourable clergy of the holy episcopal seat of Duklja's church as well as many patricians, and particularly the young men of the city of Bar, who take delight not only in listening to or reading accounts of wars, but also in participating in them—as the custom is with young people'.[23] In short, when there is no heroic, if gory, reality at hand, a story will do, and in order to meet such spiritual needs Father Dukljanin had 'forced his old age' to undertake the task.[24]

However, he could hardly have performed what he set himself to do if he had had an eye on satisfying the standards of accuracy and veracity of twentieth-century scholarship. If that had been his purpose, he would probably have written nothing at all; but as he was aiming at creating a lively and instructive image of the past which would move his contemporaries to patriotic action, he turned above all to the oral traditions and legendary material. If historians read this as a kind of historical document and found it unreliable, this was bound to lead to controversy, but if read as a patriotic recording of current oral

[23] S. Mijušković, ed., *Ljetopis popa Dukljanina*, pp. 173–4.
[24] Ibid., p. 174.

traditions, the *Chronicle* offers what one would expect to find in it. To begin with, Father Dukljanin imagines—or pretends to imagine—that it contains the whole truth and nothing but the truth: 'And yet let no reader think that I have written anything except the relations of our [clerical] predecessors and ancient patricians, relations which reached me by trustworthy narration'.[25]

This is why there is so much colour in many of the dramatic scenes in this *Chronicle*. Such is, for instance, the description of the deserved punishment of a feudal lord who failed in his loyalty to his sovereign: pursued by the sovereign's army, he is cut down by his own men while crossing a bridge and thrown into the river in which 'he disappears' for ever.[26] In another story we are faced with Providential punishment of fratricide: 'God who loves every good and hates every evil and sin, soon sent the plague and death on the father, sick in body and mind, and on his sons, so that they all disappeared, like their brothers and cousins, whom they themselves had killed'.[27] Another example of magnificent Providential interference is found in the story of Prince Gojislav who, at the height of the battle, runs into his father in a wood. It is dark and both fighters are covered in dust and blood. So Gojislav fails to recognize his father, he rushes at him and throws him off his horse. But when the father cries for mercy, Gojislav recognizes his voice and so the place where this happens gets its name: 'The Mercy of God'.[28] In the same way the place where Lazar falls off his horse in the later famous epic poem 'The Building of Ravanica' comes to be called 'The Tumbling of the Tsar'.[29] There are, of course, many place-names of such origin, but the point is that an existing linguistic feature is used in the same imaginative way in Father Dukljanin's story and the later epic song.

But it is perhaps more interesting to note that Father Dukljanin's *Chronicle* also contains a beautiful medieval hagiography with distinct folk epic touches, the story of Vladimir and Kosara. King Vladimir grows up 'adorned with every knowledge and holiness', but he is attacked by a vicious Bulgarian

[25] *Ljetopis popa Dukljanina*, p. 174.   [26] Ibid., p. 220.
[27] Ibid., p. 230.   [28] 'Božija milost', ibid., p. 251.
[29] 'Carevo Bupilo', 'Zidanje Ravanice', *Karadžić*, ii, No. 36, l. 246. See below p. 146.

emperor and has to retreat to a mountain.[30] There are 'fiercely
poisonous snakes' in this mountain and 'whoever is bitten by
them dies instantly'.[31] After King Vladimir's prayer none of his
people are bitten by snakes and 'to this day if a man or a beast
is bitten by a snake in this mountain, both the man and the
beast remain alive and without any injury'.[32] But a 'treacherous
Judas' betrays King Vladimir and so the Bulgarian emperor
captures him and puts him into prison.[33] An angel comes to
console him; he prays and fasts. One day the emperor's
daughter Kosara, 'inspired by the Holy Spirit', begs her father
to let her 'wash the head and the feet of the chained and the
imprisoned'.[34] This provides the beginning of a love romance
and Vladimir's return to his throne. However, the emperor is
eventually replaced by one of his bad sons, a fratricide, who
invites King Vladimir to visit him and sends him a gold cross as
a token of his faith. But Vladimir asks for the pledge of a
wooden, not of a gold or silver cross, for he trusts 'with the faith
and the power of our Lord Jesus Christ, the life-giving cross and
the precious wood'.[35] The wicked king sends such a cross which
protects Vladimir on his journey. But Vladimir is eventually
killed by fraud, and before he dies he invokes 'the honourable
cross' to witness his innocence to the 'Day of the Last Judgement'.[36]

This might be a distant echo of various legends about the
return of the true cross to Jerusalem after its recovery by
Heraclius from the Persians in AD 628; several variants of such
legends were recorded in medieval Serbian monastic literature.[37] But more specifically 'the honourable cross' as a pledge
of good faith is a standard medieval legal concept in the
Balkans: the inhabitants of Dubrovnik swore their loyalty to
King Vladislav (1234–40) 'by the honourable and life-giving
cross' and the same phrase was used as a guarantee of rights
granted by the charter which King Milutin issued to the

[30] Op. cit., p. 232.   [31] Ibid., pp. 232–3.   [32] Ibid.
[33] Ibid., p. 233.   [34] Ibid., p. 235.
[35] Ibid., p. 238.   [36] Ibid., p. 239.
[37] See S. Matić, 'Beleške i objašnjenja' in V. S. Karadžić, *Srpske
narodne pjesme*, ii, Belgrade, 1958, p. 653. Matić's 'Beleške i objašnjenja'
('Notes and Explanations') in this edition will henceforth be referred to as
Matić.

monastery of Banjska and on many other analogous occasions.[38] And there is no doubt that this is the wider background of 'the honourable cross' as a standard formula in the later decasyllabic heroic songs; for the 'shedding of blood' or 'fighting' for 'the honourable cross' are formulaic patterns, particularly prominent in the songs describing the defeat in the Battle of Kosovo.[39] Together with Prince Lazar's dilemma between 'the heavenly' and 'the earthly Kingdom', also of monastic literary origin, they are central to the whole epic landscape.[40] But does not the phrase 'the honourable cross' itself imply a distinction from the older pagan crosses—idols which were in use among the Serbian people in pre-Christian times and survived in some later village customs?[41] And does not this association come to the surface in the instances in which the singer refers to the 'honourable crosses' in the plural form? For this is the case in 'Tsar Lazar and Tsaritsa Milica', one of the greatest of Kosovo poems, as well as in 'The Honourable Crosses', the much

[38] In his charter (*c.* 1316) King Milutin curses the man who questions the rights granted to the monastery of Banjska: 'May the power of the honourable and life-giving cross kill him.' Queen Jelena (1273–1314) curses in similar wording the man who takes away by violence the cross which she presents to the monastery of Sopoćani: 'May God and the honourable cross kill him.' An 'honourable and life-giving cross' was carried—some time between 1391 and 1425—when the boundaries of the lands of the monastery of Vatopedi in Mount Athos were marked. See Š. Kulišić, P. Ž. Petrović, N. Pantelić, *Srpski mitološki rečnik*, Belgrade, 1970, p. 180.

[39] The duty 'to spill blood for the honourable cross' ('za krst časni krvcu proljevati') is invoked twice in 'Tsar Lazar and Tsaritsa Milica' ('Car Lazar i carica Milica', *Karadžić*, ii, No. 45, ll. 66, 92). This concept is obviously connected with 'the flag with the crosses' ('krstaš barjak' or simply 'krstaš') which occurs (each time in a different position in the line) four times in this poem (ll. 29, 41, 61, 185). Another variant of this phrase—'krstat . . . barjak' in which 'cross' is adjectival—is also found in 'Musić Stefan' (*Karadžić*, ii, No. 47, l. 44). S. Matić claims that the lines 'to spill blood for the honourable cross / and die for the faith' ('Za krst ćasni krvcu proljevati / I za svoju vjeru umrijeti') 'show ecclesiastical influence' and 'cannot be found outside Kosovo poems' (*Matić*, p. 710). However, the first of these lines is also used in 'The Beginning of the Revolt Against the Dahijas' ('Početak bune protiv dahija', *Karadžić*, iv, No. 24, l. 13). On the other hand, M. Popović insists on the 'pagan' nature of the 'honourable crosses' mistaking their ultimate origin for their epic significance (see *Vidovdan i časni krsti*, Belgrade, 1976, pp. 97–116.)

[40] See below pp. 161–4.

[41] See V. Čajkanović, *Mit i religija u Srba*, pp. 52ff.

poorer poem which tells, in a crude and cruel way, the story of the recovery of the true Christian 'crosses', made of gold, but stronger than stone.[42] Of course, the singer could have found the general idea for this story in the 'prologue' to the service for Holy Cross Day, celebrating 'the elevation of the honourable and life-giving Cross'.[43] But there is no reason why this formula should not have come from more than one source, combining pagan loyalites, legal obligations, and Christian sanctities, and creating an imaginative epic world in which it stands for the honourable fighting of lost battles to their bitter end. In short, as many of the epic stories exploit the dramatic tension of the diverse sources of their anachronistic material, so a single formula can live in the wide range of its etymological and semantic starting-points and associations.

And how could one possibly pin down the origin and the meaning of the central moral concepts of loyalty and treason, of *vjera* and *nevjera* ('faith' and 'unfaithfulness'), which dominate the whole epic landscape and appear in some of its most dramatic moments?[44] For there is no doubt that the concept of *vjera* ('faith') is rooted as much in common language as in common need, that its religious associations give it a dramatic colouring which it could hardly possess without them, even if it is also important to note that it was a medieval legal concept, 'used in treaties, to assert the intention of the party or parties that the terms of the treaty will be performed "in good faith", and as a pledge'.[45]

This kind of semantic transformation and growth—in which ancient associations sometimes come to the surface soon to be submerged again—is also reflected in the shift of meaning of 'the good horse', one of the commonest formulas in Serbo-Croat epic singing.[46] A 'good horse'—there are also good horses in *The Iliad*—may seem to be only an indispensable part of the epic paraphernalia which comes from the nature of the subject-matter. And, indeed, in most instances, this is all there is to it. However, in some poems, usually at their beginning, we

---

[42] 'Časni krsti', *Karadžić*, ii, No. 18.   [43] *Matić*, p. 653.
[44] See below pp. 47–8, 164–5.
[45] J. Brkić, *Moral Concepts in Traditional Serbian Epic Poetry*, The Hague, 1961, p. 111.
[46] See note 31, p. 40.

find the fairly standard epic ultimatum requesting the surrender of 'the good horse', sometimes together with the surrender of the weapons and the 'love' (wife),[47] the ultimatum which is an echo of the medieval legal concept which defined 'the good horse'—the one which could carry a warrior in full armour—as a symbol of feudal power. Thus Article 48 of Emperor Stefan Dušan's *Code of Laws*, written in the middle of the fourteenth century, was quite explicit on this point: 'When a nobleman dies, the good horse and the weapons are to be given to the emperor.'[48] In short, the fact that the nobleman's family could not inherit his horse and arms after his death, because they were symbols of feudal power and as such belonged to the suzerain, is clearly what lies behind the epic requests for the surrender of horse and weapons. This is not to say, of course, that in such instances the singer and his audience inevitably remembered Article 48 of Emperor Stefan Dušan's *Code*. But even for them a vague association with something more grand and important than the immediate reality of the epic statement must have been at work as a part of the mysterious significance attached to a horse. There are, moreover, even more complex instances in which 'the good horse' seems to hover in no-man's land between a major feudal symbol and a standard epic formula, but they will have to be discussed in their specific contexts.[49] And so will the epic transformation of the meaning of the choice between 'the heavenly' and 'the earthly kingdom', a commonplace in medieval historiography, which will later achieve a distinctly heroic significance associated with concept of an honour that has to be defended in the battle which must be fought even if it cannot be won.

This shift of meaning, which always breathes new life into the dying pattern which inspires it, can be also traced in the existing early evidence of the growth of the epic story and the change of character which it brings about. In this sense an early sixteenth-century travel book—B. Kuripešić's *Journey through Bosnia, Serbia, Bulgaria, Rumelia, 1530*—is of considerable interest. Kuripešić was a learned Slovene cleric who led a

---

[47] See below pp. 89–91.

[48] N. Radojčić, ed., *Zakonik Cara Stefana Dušana 1349 i 1354*, Belgrade, 1960, p. 102.

[49] See below pp. 53–4, 110–11.

diplomatic mission through the Slav lands which had come under Turkish rule in the course of the fifteenth century. He noted that heroic poems glorifying Miloš Obilić, who killed Sultan Murad in the Battle of Kosovo, were sung all over the large area stretching from Kosovo to Croatia,[50] the area which is usually considered the heart of Dinaric epic singing.[51] However, in Kuripešić's account Miloš Obilić, or Miloš Kobilović as he calls him, figures above all as a loyal defender of an uncertain frontier—a hero much more in the historical setting of Kuripešić's times than those of the Battle of Kosovo when Serbia still stood its ground as a fairly strong and independent state. For Kuripešić sees Miloš not only as a man who, slandered and unjustly suspected, remains true to his master and sacrifices his own life to kill the Sultan, but also, even primarily, as 'a famous and glorious knight who performed great deeds every day along the border, the deeds which are sung so much today among Croatians and in those regions'.[52] Of course, borderland military performance became an everyday feature of Balkan history only much later when the Turks, as in Kuripešić's times, became fully established in the Balkans. But in this way an old legend is transformed to meet the needs of the later times—and the process is analogous to the shift of meaning of oral epic formulas of medieval literary origin.

Kuripešić also gives an interesting account of Prince Lazar's feast on the eve of the battle, which will later become the subject of one of the greatest Kosovo poems.[53] 'At this time', says Kuripešić, 'the Prince gave a feast at his camp. He had many young noblemen and courtiers sit at his table and showed them marks of honour, while letting him, the old knight [Miloš], stand by the table.'[54] When Miloš sees that he has lost the favour of his master, he becomes 'sad' and, innocent as he is, with 'a heavy heart' he addresses Prince Lazar after the feast to remind him of his previous merits which have not been properly honoured.[55] He is, in short, conceived as a humble loyal

[50] See B. Kuripešić, *Putopis kroz Bosnu, Srbiju, Bugarsku i Rumeliju 1530*, Sarajevo, 1950, p. 133.

[51] See below pp. 301–2.

[52] B. Kuripešić, op. cit., p. 33.

[53] 'Pieces from Various Kosovo Poems, iii' ('Komadi od različnijeh kosovskijeh pjesama, iii', *Karadžić*, ii, No. 50). See below pp. 164–6.

[54] B. Kuripešić, op. cit., p. 34.   [55] Ibid.

knight within the framework of medieval chivalric etiquette. The epic story of the feast—which may have actually taken place, because it is also mentioned in the Turkish sources[56]— has just begun to feel the pressure of oral transmission which gives it the imprint of Kuripešić's times, of the moral lessons which they need. These are above all the moral lessons of civilized obedience and humility, the major virtues along the frontiers of discordant Christendom exposed to Turkish pressure. But this didactic feudal legend will later receive the imprint of a different spirit. It will come to be associated with the biblical story of the Last Supper—vivid in the popular imagination, among other reasons, because it was often represented on medieval and later fresco paintings. Thus the ominous feast, including a motif of treachery, will be raised in epic and moral stature.[57] Besides, Miloš Obilić will no more be seen as an old medieval knight, humbly devoted to his sovereign, but as an independent, defiant rebel of Karadžić's times. The rebel will still remain in a medieval court setting, he will be as loyal and as brave as his medieval ancestor, but he will not fully trust the courage of his own sovereign and will send him a false report underestimating the enemy's strength lest the Prince should avoid engaging in battle![58] In short, oral epic singing at its best is often an art of blending anachronisms, of successfully exploiting their historical, moral and dramatic tensions and possibilities, within a highly stylized convention which creates the illusion of a unified reality.

Kuripešić's testimony is significant for two more reasons. First, it is early evidence that oral epics about the Battle of Kosovo spread to the west and north-west of Kosovo in the areas under Turkish rule where they could not have been written down for obvious political reasons, even had the standards of literacy among the Christian population not fallen as low as they had. And this, of course, includes the area of the central Dinaric belt which is usually taken as the cradle of the

[56] Mehmed Neshri, an early sixteenth-century Turkish historian, describes the feast in the Serbian army on the eve of the battle. He says that Serbian soldiers had a good time 'feasting and drinking wine' and that they were all drunk and boasted that they would be selling Turks as slaves. See J. Ređep, 'Razvoj kosovske legende', *Priča o boju kosovskom*, Zrenjanin, 1976, p. 190.

[57] See below pp. 164–6.

[58] See below pp. 166–7.

epic songs. Secondly, Kuripešić bears witness to the spreading of the art among the whole population—he mentions no foreign *jongleurs*, native professionals, and other types of wandering Bohemians which figure in the earlier medieval references to the court performers and public entertainers.[59] It might have become more difficult for them to go on making a living from their art in the regions under Turkish rule.

However, there is plenty of evidence of their retreat to some other Christian lands in the north. Thus special edicts were issued against them in the course of the fifteenth century in Poland,[60] which suggests, of course, that they were not just 'common' people, keeping up their heroic spirit by their own fireside. They must have been worthy of the edicts—either as professional competitors or because they inspired moral indignation among the clergy. But even the edicts could not exterminate them completely: the Polish poet Caspar Mias-kowski (1549–1629) describes much later a Serbian *guslar* who 'sadly turned his head to one side pulling the long bow across his fiddle, singing an old heroic song about the battles with the Turks'.[61] The posture unmistakably suggests the standard later representations of *guslars*; the theme and sadness seem to associate him with the singers of the feudal *bugarštice* recorded along the Adriatic coast, some of them at approximately the same time.

But the clearest and most extensive evidence of the Serbian feudal epic singing and its professional performers retreating to the north is to be found in Hungary, where it must have been quite widespread in the first half of the sixteenth century. The famous Hungarian singer Tinodi—who, in stone, still stands holding his lute in front of the National Theatre in Budapest—describes them quite clearly:

> We have many singers in Hungary,
> Best in Serbian manner Dimitrije Karaman,

[59] See V. Latković, 'O pevačima srpskohrvatskih narodnih epskih pesama do kraja xviii veka', *Prilozi za književnost, jezik, istoriju i folklor*, xx (1954), pp. 191–2.
[60] See V. M. Jovanović, 'O srpskom narodnom pesništvu', *Srpske narodne pesme—antologija*, Belgrade, 1937, p. xv. Partly reprinted in V. Nedić, ed., *Narodna književnost*, pp. 16–20.
[61] V. M. Jovanović, loc. cit.

He bows his head, he strikes his violin—*egede*
To Uluman all this is good fun,
He gave him gifts many and various,
But this service beggared Dimitrije Karaman.[62]

This suggests that professional Serbian performers sang in
Hungary in sufficient numbers for their performance to be
recognized as a distinct 'manner'.[63] It also tells us something
about one of such singers which may perhaps have been
imagined, but is not insignificant. His absorption in his art is
reflected in his head bowed over his fiddle, his social status in
the gifts he received from his feudal patrons and his subsequent
poverty. This picture has some unmistakable associations with
the later singers as described by Karadžić—particularly
Višnjić's wanderings and changing luck.[64] This kinship of fate
and of the way of life between the earlier feudal and the later
village singers underlies the continuity and the merging of the
two epic cultures in the same language. For the performers
themselves were not divided by the same gap which is so easy
to imagine as dividing their respective historical audiences.
After all, the earlier professional singers were not feudal lords;
and neither were the later *guslars* ordinary peasants—at least
not the best among them, even if they could master their art at
home. The outstanding representatives of both groups had
great if sometimes undesired mobility—social as well as
geographical; and their major historical and social routes

[62] 'Ima mnogo guslača ovde u Mađarskoj, / Ali od Dimitrija Karamana
nema boljeg u rackom načinu, / . . . On svoje egede (gusle) kida pognute
glave, / Uluman to prima kao razonodu, / Obasipa ga bogatim poklonima,- /
Ova služba ga je dovela do prosjačkog štapa.' Magdalena Veselinović
Šulc's unpublished Serbo-Croat translation from D. S. Vujicsics, 'Egy
Szerb Guszlár a xvi. Szāzadi Magyarorszāgon', *A Hungarológiai Intézet
Tudományos Közleményei*, iii (1971), p. 135. See also S. Stefanović, 'Nekoji
podaci iz mađarske literature za datiranje naše narodne poezije', *Prilozi
proučavanju narodne poezije*, iv (1937), pp. 27–35. Note that the last of the
quoted lines is mistranslated in Stefanović as 'But gambling brought him
to drink' ('Ali ga kocka dovede do pijanstva', p. 32).

[63] A later seventeenth-century reference to 'the Serbian manner' ('modi
et styli Sarbiaci')—made in Slavonia by the learned cleric Juraj Križanić—
is further corroborative evidence of the movement of Serbian singing to the
north and the west. See E. Fermendžin, 'Prinos za životopis Gjurgja
Križanića', *Starine*, xviii (1886), p. 229.

[64] See 'Predgovor', *Karadžić*, iv, pp. 365–6.

followed the main highways of the Serbian migrations from the fifteenth to the nineteenth century. (See Map 4.)

These routes led not only to the north and the west, but also to the Adriatic coast and it is perhaps significant that the first recorded fragment of a Serbo-Croat epic song was written down in southern Italy, in the small town of Gioia del Colle, at the end of the fifteenth century.[65] For it was in this little town that Isabella del Balzo, the Queen of Naples, arrived on 31 May 1497 and was met and entertained on the following day with great pomp. Strangely enough, among other real and fictitious distinctions, the Queen held the title of 'Dispota di Servia' and, appropriately enough, the entertainment for her was provided by some Slavs, who must have lived in one of the many Slav colonies in Italy, established by people who could afford to retreat so far under the pressure of the Turkish conquests of the Balkans. What happened on this occasion is described in considerable detail by the Queen's conscientious court poet Rogeri de Pacientia (Ruggero Pazienza) in the fifth of the eight books of his courtly epic poem *Lo Balzino*, which glorifies various illustrious aspects of the Queen's life in about eight thousand lines written in *ottava rima*.[66] The Queen's Slav entertainers (Scavoni), according to Pacientia's meticulous report, shouted, drank, danced, and 'jumping like goats, turned round and round and sang together the following words':[67]

An eagle hovered over the city of Smederevo,
No one wanted to speak to the eagle,
But Janko the Duke spoke from the gaol:

[65] I owe this information in all its pertinent details to Professor M. Pantić who kindly gave me a manuscript copy of his article 'Nepoznata bugarštica o despotu Đurđu i Sibinjanin Janku iz xv veka' ('An Unknown *Bugarštica* about Despot Đurađ and John Hunyadi from the XVth Century'), meanwhile published in *Zbornik Matice srpske za književnost i jezik*, xxv (1977), pp. 421-39.

[66] A manuscript copy of this work is in City Library 'Augusta', Perugia, Antico Fondo, F. 27. B. Croce drew some attention to it by his essay 'Isabella del Balzo regina di Napoli in un inedito poema sincrono', *Archivio storico per le provincie napoletane*, xxii (1897), pp. 632-701. But Pacientia's work was not published until 1977 (Rogeri di Pacienza di Nardo, *Opere*, ed. M. Marti, Lecce, 1977). As M. Pantić points out, his text owes a great deal to this edition, but Pantić was the first scholar who succeeded in reading the *bugarštica* in Pacientia's work.

[67] M. Pantić, 'Nepoznata bugarštica . . .', p. 427.

'Eagle, come down a little, I beg you,
I want to speak to you; brother-in-God,
Go to the [lords] of Smederevo, let them beg
The glorious Despot to free me from Smederevo gaol;
And if God helps me, if the glorious Despot frees me
From Smederevo gaol, then I will feed you
On red blood of Turks and white bodies of knights'.[68]

Written down as a collective song of many singers, whom
Pacientia lists under characteristic medieval Slav names,[69]
these lines are indubitably a fragment of an epic poem set in
mid-fifteenth-century Serbian history. Janko the Duke is—as
in some other *bugarštice*—John Hunyadi, who plundered the
lands of the Serbian Despot Đurađ Branković after the Despot
refused to join him in his badly organized warfare against the
Turks. Hunyadi was severely defeated in the second Battle of
Kosovo (1448), imprisoned by the Serbian Despot and kept as
a hostage until the Despot recouped his losses. It can be argued,
of course, that the Despot was a wise judge of the situation or
that he was a prevaricating scoundrel—as he came to be seen
against the wider background of the struggle between the Cross
and the Crescent not only in English historiography but also in
later Serbo-Croat epic poetry.[70] But it is perhaps more perti-

---

[68] In M. Pantić's reconstruction this text reads as follows: 'Orao se vijaše
nad gradom Smederevom. / Nitkore ne ćaše s njime govoriti, / nego Janko
vojvoda govoraše iz tamnice: / 'Molim ti se, orle, sidi malo niže / da s tobome
progovoru: Bogom te brata jimaju / pođi do smederevske [gospode] da s'
mole / slavnome despotu da m' otpusti iz tamnice smederevske; / i ako mi
Bog pomože i slavni despot pusti / iz smederevske tamnice, ja te ću napitati /
črvene krvce turečke, beloga tela viteškoga' (op. cit., p. 429). Pacientia's
text reads as follows: 'Orauias natgradum smereuo nit core / nichiasce snime
gouorithi nego Jamco / goiuoda gouorasce istmize molimti se / orle sidi
maolonisce dastobogme / progouoru bigomte bratta zimaju / pogi dosmeder-
esche dasmole slauono / mo despostu damosposti istamice / smederesche
Jacome bogomposte / Islaui dispot pusti Ismederesche / tamice Jatechui
napitati seruene / creucze turesche bellocatela vitesco / cha:' (M. Pantić,
op. cit., pp. 427–8).

[69] e.g. Vuico (Vujko), Raschio (Raško), Buciza (Vučica), Ruscia (Ruža),
Radognio (Radonja), Miliza (Milica), Bucetta (Vučeta), Radoslauce
(Radoslavče), Buca (Vuka), Busicchio (Vučić), Bucascino (Vukašin),
Buciza (Vučica) etc. Pantić points out that many of these names are
confirmed by medieval Serbian charters and other writings.

[70] See note 6, p. 4.

nent to note that the first recorded lines of a Serbo-Croat epic
song deal with a historical occasion which lived so vividly in the
popular memory that a Serbian proverb about Janko's—John
Hunyadi's—defeat at Kosovo defines to this day the ultimate
in disaster.[71]

Fortunately, Pacientia's pedantry matched his ignorance of
Serbo-Croat so perfectly that it was possible for a distinguished
Slavonic paleographer to read his text. But once properly read,
these lines foreshadow, and mirror, several characteristic
features of Serbo-Croat oral epic conventions. To begin with,
the description of the eagle 'hovering' over the city of Smederevo
is closely parallel in its specific wording, as Professor M. Pantić
has noted, to the description of a 'hovering' hawk in another
bugarštica in which John Hunyadi also figures as a hero.[72]
Besides, a swallow seems to 'hover'—in a slightly diffeient
verbal form of the same semantic root—'over the city of Blagaj'
in a decasyllabic poem recorded in Dalmatia in the eighteenth
century.[73] And is not a 'hovering' or 'flying' bird—usually a
hawk, a raven, a pair of ravens or, sometimes, a whining
swallow—in the opening line or lines of an epic poem a standard
feature of the convention?[74] The phrase 'Janko the Duke spoke'
is also found in another *bugarštica* recorded at the beginning of
the eighteenth century in the Bay of Kotor (Bocche di Cattaro)
—again in wording which is more characteristic of epic singing
than of common speech.[75] 'Glorious' is not only a fixed epithet
with princes, kings or their Christian names,[76] but Đurađ

---

[71] 'Prošao kao Janko na Kosovu' ('He fared like Janko on Kosovo'),
V. S. Karadžić, *Srpske narodne poslovice*, ed. M. Pantić, *Sabrana dela*, ix,
Belgrade, 1965, p. 246.

[72] 'Soko se vijaše po jajeru vedra neba' ('A hawk hovered in the air of the
clear sky'), *Bogišić*, No. 19, l. 18.

[73] 'Izvila se ptica lastovica, / Izvila se nad Blagajom gradom' ('A swallow
hovered in the air, / It hovered over the city of Blagaj'), *Bogišić*, No. 119, ll. 1–2.

[74] See, for instance, *Bogišić*, No. 36, l. 1; No. 50, l. 1; No. 51, ll. 1–16;
G. Gezeman (Gesemann), *Erlangenski rukopis starih srpskohrvatskih narodnih
pesama*, Sremski Karlovci, 1925, No. 179, l. 1 (this collection will henceforth
be referred to as *Gesemann*); *Karadžić*, ii. No. 45, l. 1; *Karadžić*, iii, No. 86, l. 1;
Karadžić, iv, No. 26, l. 1; No. 30, l. 1.

[75] 'A Janko ti vojvoda banoviću govoraše' ('And Janko the Duke spoke to
the ban'), *Bogišić*, No. 19, l. 4.

[76] 'Slavni kralj' ('glorious king'), *Bogišić*, No. 29, l. 39; 'slavni kralj
Vladisav' ('glorious King Vladisav'), ibid., l. 54; 'slavni Lazar' ('glorious

Branković—who will come to be seen usually as a 'faithless' and sometimes as a 'graceless' man—is also referred to as the 'glorious Despot' in a *bugarštica* recorded at the beginning of the eighteenth century in the Bay of Kotor.[77] Of course, this might be merely a matter of standard epic conventions, but it could also be a remnant of Đurađ Branković's earlier epic stature— of his epic stature in his lifetime or among those who were in his or his heirs' political orbit. Finally, the lines recorded at Gioia del Colle describe a hero in trouble addressing a friendly bird. This is a common motif of Byzantine legends and hagiographical works which inspired, as we shall see, some later heroic songs about Marko Kraljević.[78]

As regards the collective manner of the performance in Gioia del Colle—the shouting in the vernacular and the goat-like prancing—it seems to suggest two possibilities. Either the Queen of Naples witnessed—which is most unlikely—the performance of a professional troupe of Slav feudal entertainers in exile; or—which is much more likely—she was faced with a stage in the slow social downgrading of medieval Serbian feudal epic tradition in which some members of the once grand audience were merged in exile with their earlier entertainers, sharing a patriotic attachment to their common past. But be this as it may, it is beyond doubt that epic songs were cultivated at medieval Serbian courts, that they followed the major routes of Serbian migrations and that their earliest recordings illustrate a deep linguistic, formulaic and cultural kinship with later epic conventions. This will be seen in much clearer and richer detail only a few decades later—when Petar Hektorović, a distinguished Croatian Renaissance poet, wrote down the first two complete oral epics which were sung to him by his two simple fishermen—and sung, characteristically enough, 'in Serbian manner'.[79]

Lazar'), *Bogišić*, No. 1, ll. 80, 248 [250], 249 [251]; *Karadžić*, ii, No. 44, ll. 98, 123; 'slavni knez Lazare' ('glorious Prince Lazar'), ibid., ll. 125, 176, 178.

[77] 'Ovako ti poruči slavnome despotu Đurđu' ('Send the following message to glorious Despot Đurađ'), *Bogišić*, No. 11, l. 69.

[78] See below pp. 182–4.

[79] See below pp. 31–2.

2. The Grand Stammer

When Petar Hektorović, a grand literary nobleman, went for a short trip in a boat, probably in 1555, with the best two fishermen he could find on his island of Hvar, he was an old and tired man looking only for a few days' outing. Apart from the excitement of fishing the two fishermen entertained their master by telling stories, singing songs, solving riddles, discussing all sorts of questions. The old poet enjoyed the trip and what he heard so much that he decided to describe it in the spirit of his pastoral literary tastes, in the form of popular Italian eclogues in which fishermen, instead of shepherds, were often the speakers. This is how he came to write, probably in the same year, in doubly rhymed twelve-syllable lines his long poem *Fishing and Fishermen's Conversations* which was published in Venice in 1568.

Apparently, on the second day of the trip the toil of rowing began to tell, and as the party was approaching the island of Šolta the younger of the two fishermen addressed his older friend and suggested that in order to cheer themselves up, they should each sing an epic song:

'To while away time let us each tell
a fine *bugaršćina*, not to feel the toil,
in Serbian manner, my dear comrade,
as we have always done among our friends.'[1]

This invocation in the rhymed twelve-syllable lines—the standard form of Hektorović's versification—is obviously given in the poet's own wording, but there is no reason to doubt that the reference to the 'Serbian manner' is correct and authentic. Some of the names of the heroes as well as the geographical references in the recorded songs suggest the Serbian, Bulgarian, and Romanian lands, the Balkan Christian frontier on the eve

---

[1] 'Recimo po jednu, za vrime minuti, / Bugaršćinu srednu i za trud ne čuti, / Da sarbskim načinom, moj druže primili, / Kako meu družinom vazda smo činili'. P. Hektorović, *Ribanye i ribarscho prigovaranye*, Venice, 1568, f. 12ʳ (photographic edn. Zagreb, 1953).

of its collapse at the end of the fourteenth century, under the pressure of the Turkish invasion.[2] Sporadic linguistic features, as we shall see later, also point in the same direction. And as the Hungarian singer Tinodi referred almost at the same time to the 'Serbian manner' of epic singing in Hungary, the assumption that this 'manner' followed the main routes of Serbian migrations seems beyond reasonable doubt. However, whereas the Hungarian singer referred to a skilled professional colleague who cultivated an alien oral epic form in a feudal social setting, the words of Hektorović's fisherman suggest a popular form of entertainment among illiterate townsmen in an urban Adriatic milieu. For at this time Hvar was the richest Venetian commune in Dalmatia, with a long monastic tradition, with patrician political life, a good school, a theatre, and flourishing humanistic literature. As a winter resort of the Venetian fleet, it was also a target of Turkish military attacks, devastated in 1539, only sixteen years before the first two complete *bugarštice* were recorded, so that Petar Hektorović, the head of one of the two most distinguished families, had to leave the island and spend a year in Italy.

Many other *bugarštice*—mostly lamenting fifteenth-century Turkish conquests and describing in the same moanful, often hoarse poetic voice the later battles and skirmishes with the Turks—were also written down a little later, in the seventeenth and the eighteenth centuries, in the urban Adriatic areas exposed to the threat of Turkish invasion, particularly in the

[2] Two *bugarštice* were recorded on this occasion: 'Marko Kraljević and His Brother Andrijaš' ('Marko Kraljević i brat mu Andrijaš') and 'Duke Radosav of Severin and Vlatko of Vidin' ('Vojvoda Radosav Siverinski i Vlatko Udinski'). Marko Kraljević is the epic name of King Marko who ruled his lands from the city of Prilep as a Turkish vassal after the defeat of the Serbian army in the Battle on the Marica (1371) until his death in 1395. 'Kraljević' is a common patronymic in Serbo-Croat, but when it precedes the Christian name it denotes the title of a Prince. In heroic poetry Kraljević Marko and not Marko Kraljević is the rule even when there are no particular metrical reasons for the inversion. But in all the titles of heroic poems, given by their collectors (including V. S. Karadžić) this hero is called Marko Kraljević. His brother Andrijaš is also a historical figure. The names of the two heroes in the second *bugarštica* suggest the Bulgarian and the Romanian lands which also lay on one of the main directions of the Turkish invasions in the fourteenth century: Turnu Severin on the River Danube and Vidin, the Bulgarian capital, also on the Danube.

immediate vicinity of Dubrovnik and Kotor. It is also significant, perhaps, that both these cities had been closely linked with medieval Serbia. Dubrovnik was the principal exporter of Serbian silver to the west, and in the Middle Ages it was often visited by Serbian feudal dignitaries, including such important epic figures as Prince Lazar and, possibly, Marko Kraljević.[3] Emperor Stefan Dušan, the greatest medieval Serbian ruler and legislator, paid several visits to this city—one at the height of his power, when the whole peninsula of Pelješac had to be taxed to provide an appropriate welcome for this most important customer who was as interested in the commercial facilities of Dubrovnik and its navy as Dubrovnik was interested in his political and military power, and particularly in the export of his silver.[4] Dubrovnik also gave refuge to Serbian despots and feudal lords—some of whom were to become the heroes of *bugarštice*—during the fifteenth century, in the last stage of dissolution of their authority over their provinces. The Brankovići were many times in Dubrovnik and Despot Đurađ Branković was treated here as a sovereign even after the fall of Novo Brdo (1455),[5] the richest Serbian silver mine and one of the strongest fortresses which defended the last vestiges of feudal independence in Turkish vassalage.

So it is not surprising that we find a *bugarštica* about the death of the fifteenth-century Serbian Despot Vuk Branković in a manuscript which the Dubrovnik merchant Nikola Ohmućević (?–1666) copied in his own hand probably in patriotic moments of leisure during his journeys to Prague, Vienna, and Biscay. Another *bugarštica*—describing the death of the Hungarian King Vladislav, another Christian fighter against the Turks—also fills some of the pages of this manuscript.[6] But most are taken up with *Osman*, the long literary epic written by Ohmućević's famous fellow citizen Ivan Gundulić, celebrating the contemporary Polish military victories and discerning in the janissaries' insurrection great hopes for

[3] See J. Tadić, *Promet putnika u starom Dubrovniku*, Dubrovnik, 1939, pp. 49–50.
[4] See ibid., p. 44.   [5] See ibid., p. 94.
[6] See MS Biblioteka Male braće, Dubrovnik, B. 262, ff. 175ᵛ–176, 178ᵛ–181; and *Pantić*, pp. 59–60, 266. Both these *bugarštice* are published in A. Pavić, 'Dvije hrvatske pjesme', *Rad JAZU*, xlvii (1879), pp. 93–128; the first of them is also in *Pantić*, pp. 61–4.

Christianity. It might be also worth noting that Gundulić included four literary compositions in the manner of *bugarštice* in the eighth canto of his epic, which was soon to live also in oral 'transliteration' in the neighbouring area of Kotor.[7] The political climate of this poetry is also reflected in a note in one of the existing manuscripts of *Osman* suggesting that the missing cantos had to be destroyed on the order of the Senate of Dubrovnik which feared that excessive Christian zeal might irritate the Turks beyond the point where the Republic was reasonably safe.[8] In a similar spirit of patriotic zeal Juraj Baraković, a cleric in Zadar, wrote his literary *bugarštica* 'Mother Margarita'—one of the most famous poems in Serbo-Croat, still often treated as a genuine oral composition—and included it into his *Slav Fairy*.[9]

However, it is only at the end of the seventeenth century that we find the first substantial collection of *bugarštice*. It was then that Đuro Matijašević, a patriotic Dubrovnik cleric, made the wise decision to give up writing his own poetry for a time and, almost in the spirit of an antiquarian, wrote down fifteen *bugarštice* which were sung in Dubrovnik and perhaps in some neighbouring villages 'where urban speech prevailed'.[10] His

[7] See M. Pavić, *Istorija srpske književnosti baroknog doba*, p. 426.

[8] See *Enciklopedija Jugoslavije*, iii, Zagreb, 1958, p. 636.

[9] J. Baraković, *Vila Slovinka*, ed. F. Švelec, Zagreb, 1964, pp. 333–7. See also *Pantić*, pp. 53–8. M. Pantić believes that Baraković adapted a genuine *bugarštica* to the circumstances of his own family and improved it 'here and there' (*Pantić*, pp. 51–2). He does not rule out the possibility that Baraković may have written this poem in the manner of *bugarštice*. However, the stylistic evidence puts this beyond reasonable doubt, because the manner itself is severely modified and stylized. No other *bugarštica* was sung in unrhymed couplets of comparable regularity: not only do the refrains recur constantly, but the second line of each couplet of long lines provides, after the refrain, the first long line of the couplet which follows. This cannot be seen in Bogišić's edition because all the repeated lines have been left out (see *Bogišić*, No. 82).

[10] Fourteen of these *bugarštice*—together with many other *bugarštice*, decasyllabic heroic poems, lyrical folk songs, proverbs and other matters—are in PS (Nos. 1–14; published in *Bogišić*, Nos. 34, 2, 38, 80, 32, 57, 53, 79, 3, 37, 41, 45, 76, 55). In a manuscript completed by 1691 (Biblioteka Male braće, Dubrovnik, B. 95) there is one more *bugarštica* in Đ. Matijašević's handwriting (published in *Pantić*, pp. 77–9; see also Pantić's note, pp. 268–269). It is a variant of PS, No. 80. For a description of PS see 'Predgovor', *Bogišić*, pp. 126–33; on linguistic features of *bugarštice* see ibid., pp. 36–9.

work was continued in the eighteenth century by Jozo Betondić (1709–64), an educated layman who was also well-advised to relinquish, if only temporarily, his attempts at satire and translations from Latin and Italian, and write down eighteen *bugarštice* which were also sung in the vicinity of Dubrovnik.[11]

Many more of the existing *bugarštice* were written down in the area of the Bay of Kotor[12] which was strongly connected with medieval Serbia and immediately exposed to border fighting in the Turco-Venetian wars. As both these features were richly reflected in many *bugarštice*, it should be remembered that Stefan Nemanja, the twelfth-century founder of the Serbain state, built one of his palaces in Kotor and that this city provided for a long time many diplomats and highest officials for

[11] All these *bugarštice* are in PS (Nos. 15–32; with the exception of No. 24 they are all published in *Bogišić*, Nos. 33, 78, 23, 20, 30, 4, 9, 1, 10, [PS No. 24 missing], 14, 15, 47, 40, 35, 13, 16, 39).

[12] Twenty-four of these *bugarštice* are in a manuscript written by two hands at the beginning of the eighteenth century in the Bay of Kotor (Jugoslavenska akademija znanosti i umjetnosti, Zagreb, IV. a. 30, previous No. 638). This manuscript also contains a variant of 'Mother Margarita' and a poem which is not of oral or folk origin. All its *bugarštice* are published in *Bogišić*, Nos. 77, 29, 27, 22, 51, 43, 83, 8, 7, 50, 25, 12, 84, 17, 18, 21 (in the manuscript copy *Bogišić*, No. 28 is inserted in this poem), 36, 56, 19, 31, 11, 81, 58. For a description of this manuscript see 'Predgovor', *Bogišić*, pp. 135–6 and *Pantić*, p. 270. Three more of these *bugarštice* are in another manuscript, containing pious songs, decasyllabic poems, and poems which are not of oral or folk origin. It was also written, in the first half of the eighteenth century, in the Bay of Kotor (Jugoslavenska akademija znanosti i umjetnosti, I. b. 80, previous No. 641). Two of these *bugarštice* are published in *Bogišić*, Nos. 5, 52 and the third one is a variant of *Bogišić*, No. 83. For a description of this manuscript see 'Predgovor', *Bogišić*, p. 136; M. Rešetar, *Stari pisci hrvatski*, Zagreb, 1917, pp. xix–xxi; *Pantić*, p. 270. Nine more of these *bugarštice*—together with fifteen decasyllabic poems, two of which are variants of the *bugarštice* in the same manuscript—are in the Balović manuscript, prepared for publication by Professor M. Pantić. All these *bugarštice* are published in *Bogišić*, Nos. 59, 61, 63, 65, 67, 69, 71, 73, 75. Eight of them have their decasyllabic variants (*Bogišić*, Nos. 60, 62, 64, 66, 68, 70, 72, 74— all published from the Mazarović manuscript. Nos. 66, 74, copied in Mazarović from Balović, are in Balović-Pantić, *not* in Mazarović-Pantić). In Bogišić's opinion the Balović manuscript dates from the end of the seventeenth or the beginning of the eighteenth century and the Mazarović manuscript is dated on its cover 1775. The latter contains mostly decasyllabic poems and some poems which are not of oral or folk origin. For a description of the Balović and the Mazarović manuscripts see 'Predgovor', *Bogišić*, pp. 133–5.

the medieval Serbian court. During the Turkish period Herceg-Novi which commands the entrance to the Bay was ruled by the Turks from 1481 to 1687, with only a brief interruption, and Kotor was an important stronghold of the Venetian presence in the Adriatic—second only to Hvar until the eighteenth century when the winter resort of the Venetian fleet was moved from Hvar to Kotor. This area supplied the soldiers and gave many captains for the Venetian regular military units and the fighting of these units in the immediate Turkish borderland provided many subjects for *bugarštice* as well as for decasyllabic village songs. The two epic traditions— often using the same formulas and formulaic patterns in two different but basically trochaic metric systems and sometimes even telling the same stories—can be observed in close contact here.

Generally speaking, the earlier recorded *bugarštice* are clearer in narrative and more inspired in their imagery than the later ones, but with one major exception ('Marko Kraljević and His Brother Andrijaš', written down about 1555 in the vicinity of Hvar) and several grand fragments, they mirror the social and artistic downgrading and degeneration of an older, feudal form of epic singing. Their grand heroic diction had been uprooted from its feudal medieval setting; it survived this original historical setting in the form of popular entertainment among the illiterate sections of some of the principal Adriatic cities and their environs—that is, in a highly developed urban milieu. So this epic debris is primarily interesting in what it had to offer the rising tradition of popular decasyllabic village singing. This was the bequest of some important historical themes, many sporadic motifs, dozens of narrative and stylistic devices, hundreds of stock phrases, phrasal patterns, formulaic expressions and formulas which came to their full epic life in the decasyllabic village singing.

To begin with, some of the best-known themes of the later decasyllabic songs about the Serbian disaster in the Battle of Kosovo, the heart of the national mythology, are to be found in *bugarštice*: Prince Lazar's feast on the eve of the battle, Vuk Branković's treason, Miloš Obilić's assassination of the Turkish Sultan Murad, the story of the hero who came too late for the battle but not too late to die, a girl's grief for her betrothed who was killed in the battle.[13] Some of the best-known decasyllabic tales about Marko Kraljević are also to be found in *bugarštice* —in particular the story of his revenge on Mina of Kostur (Castoria) which is parallel in many details to several later decasyllabic versions.[14] The evidence of direct contact, as we shall see later, is also glaringly obvious in the *bugarštice* and decasyllabic poems dealing with the same contemporary subjects, written down in the same area and often in strikingly parallel wording.[15]

Moreover, *bugarštice* contain several characteristic recurring motifs which are also found not only in Serbo-Croat poems but in the heroic songs of many different nations: banquets and toasts which promise loyalty and threaten treason, the last utterances of dying heroes, grief for those who have been killed in battle. But the point is that these motifs will later be embedded in closely parallel wording in many of the later decasyllabic songs.[16] Besides, *bugarštice* provide many of the

---

[13] *Pantić*, pp. 118–24 (*Bogišić*, No. 1); *Bogišić*, No. 2. See below pp. 59–60.

[14] See below pp. 77, 195–6.   [15] See below pp. 68–77.

[16] Thus, for instance, we find the following toast in a *bugarštica*: 'A health to you Damijan, this cup of cool wine / Drink the wine and the cup is your gift!' ('Zdrav ti budi, Damijane, ovi pehar hladna vina, / Vino da mi popiješ, pehar da ti na dar bude!'—*Bogišic*, No. 11, ll. 33–4). In a famous decasyllabic poem Prince Lazar proposes his toast to Miloš in closely parallel wording: 'Health to you, drink this toast, / Drink this wine and this cup is yours!' ('Zdrav mi budi! i zdravicu popij: / Vino popij, a na čast ti pehar!'— *Karadžić*, ii, No. 50 (iii), ll. 35–6). The two scenes are also thematically parallel: both toasts contain insinuations about the prospective treason and both heroes accept the offered gifts (cups) and refuse the insinuations. It is also significant that the wording of these toasts closely follows that in a prose version of the Kosovo legend which was recorded much earlier (see note 23, p. 164). The epic etiquette of dying in the *bugarštice* and the decasyllabic poems is also often similar, both because it mirrors similar customs and because it expresses them in the formulaic language of oral epic poetry. Thus when Dragon Despot Vuk (Zmaj despot Vuk) is about to die in a *bugarštica*, he sends a message to his 'blood-brother' ('pobratim') telling him that 'heavy wounds have befallen' him ('teške rane dopadnule'), that he will not recover ('priboljeti') and asking him to come quickly to his 'white palaces' ('bijele dvore')—see *Bogišić*, No. 16, ll. 36–8. In the decasyllabic poem which describes the death of Ilija Smiljanić the dying hero is also visited by his 'blood-brother' ('pobratim') who asks him if he will recover from his wounds ('rane preboljeti'). The hero replies that he wants to be taken to his 'white palaces' ('bijele dvore') and nursed by his mother, wife, and sister (*Karadžić*, iii, No. 32, ll. 19–23). And when a hero dies, either in a *bugarštica* or in a

later decasyllabic stylistic and narrative devices, such as the standard beginnings and endings, including several examples of Slavonic antithesis. In this figure of speech a statement is usually made at the beginning of a poem to be immediately denied and followed by an explanation: the two screaming swallows in the first line of 'Mustafa's Combat with Karajovan' turn out not to be two screaming swallows but Mustafa's two 'loves'—and such examples of denied statements which have the function of significant comparisons can be found both in *bugarštice* and the later decasyllabic poems.[17] But above all the

decasyllabic poem, 'tears' ('suze') stream 'on the faces' of those who grieve for him (*Bogišić*, No. 78, l. 64; *Karadžić*, ii, No. 51, l. 131). There is also an instance of this formula in *Gesemann*, No. 151. In this poem 'tears stream' on a queen's 'face' ('proli suze niz bijelo lice', l. 51) when she sets her own brother free after having kept him, unawares, in her prison for a very long time.—For details about this collection see below pp. 81–2.

[17] See 'Mustafa's Combat with Karajovan' ('Megdan Mustafe s Karajovanom', *Bogišić*, No. 50, ll. 1–8). Another example can be found at the beginning of the famous 'Mother Margarita' ('Majka Margarita', *Pantić*, p. 53; *Bogišić*, No. 82 is unreliable—see note 9, p. 34): in this poem a screaming swallow turns out to be a grieved 'old mother' ('stara majka'). Even if in all probability this is not a genuine oral poem (see note 9, p. 34), the Slavonic antithesis in its opening lines is obviously an imitation of an oral epic device. An instance of a 'broken' Slavonic antithesis—in which the statement and its denial with explanation are separated by several interpolated lines—can be found in 'Marko Kraljević and His Brother Andrijaš' (see below pp. 53–4). Similar examples of latent comparisons in the form of denied statements can also be found in some of the earliest decasyllabic songs (see *Gesemann*, No. 29, ll. 1–5; No. 131, ll. 1–4), but the greatest classic example is to be found at the beginning of 'God Leaves No Debt Unpaid' in which the imagery establishes a significant relationship between the human, the natural, and the supernatural ('Bog nikom dužan ne ostaje', *Karadžić*, ii, No. 5, ll. 1–7; see below pp. 113–15). However, there is also another type of Slavonic antithesis: a series of questions followed by negative answers and a positive statement at the end. This type of Slavonic antithesis can be found only in the decasyllabic poems (see *Bogišić*, No. 114, ll. 1–8; *Gesemann*, No. 80, ll. 1–6; No. 123, ll. 1–6; No. 163, ll. 1–5; No. 177, ll. 1–8; No. 211, ll. 1–7; *Karadžić*, ii, No. 52, ll. 1–4; iii, No. 80, ll. 1–7; iv, No. 1, ll. 1–8). These are only two basic types of Slavonic antithesis; M. Maticki, for instance, lists the following categories of Slavonic antithesis: 'negative comparison, metaphorical Slavic antithesis (Slavic antithesis of colour, sound, movement, and symbols), complex metaphorical Slavic antithesis (Slavic antithesis of images and dreams) and non-metaphorical Slavic antithesis of dialogue' ('Poetika epskog narodnog pesništva—slovenska antiteza', *Književna istorija*, iii (1970), p. 152).

evidence of close and immediate links—between the dying feudal *bugarštice* and the decasyllabic village epic singing vigorously groping for a new epic voice—is mirrored in the stock phrases, formulaic expressions and formulas which provide the warp and woof of oral epic composition. Of course, the peasant decasyllabic singing may or may not be ultimately older in origin, but that it had much in common with *bugarštice* and took over some of the feudal elements and concepts from them is beyond doubt.

Admittedly, *bugarštice* contain some stylistic devices, stock phrases, formulaic expressions, and formulas which are peculiar only to themselves. Thus—owing to their feudal customs and 'high' social setting—the 'fine-dressed hero'[18] or the 'good knight'[19] turns up only in *bugarštice*. Even the 'fine-dressed girl'[20]—a common feature of *bugarštice*—survives only in one or two instances in some of the earliest decasyllabic poems.[21] And whereas in the decasyllabic poems the friendly heroes usually 'spread their arms and kiss one another's face',[22] in *bugarštice* they 'bow finely',[23] or 'bow' to everyone in their 'proper order'[24] —eight times, for instance, in the first thirty odd lines of a

[18] 'Gizdav junak', *Bogišić*, No. 37, l. 1; No. 52, l. 35; No. 83, l. 7. These are not three instances of the same formula, but three formulaic variations of the same basic pattern: 'gizdav junak', 'gizdavi junak' (the long-form adjective functions also as a definite article). Such and similar distinctions (cases, inversions of word order, diminutive forms of nouns, etc.) are disregarded in the examples which follow, for it makes much more sense to concentrate on the common heritage of traditional formulaic expressions rather than strictly on formulas, particularly as there is considerable variety of metrical systems in Serbo-Croat oral epic tradition.

[19] 'Dobar vitez' (in fact, invariably in plural form), *Bogišić*, No. 63, l. 12; No. 65, ll. 17, 32, 68, 80, 83, 125, 128; No. 67, ll. 65, 83.

[20] 'Gizdava devojka' ('djevojka', etc.), *Bogišić*, No. 6, ll. 48, 54 (in fact ll. 49, 55 as l. 40 is missing in *Bogišić*—cf. *Pantić*, p. 45); No. 8, ll. 38, 41, 52, 77, 83, 87, 89; No. 11, ll. 5, 47, 50; No. 28, ll. 11, 20, 23, 26, 33.

[21] See *Gesemann*, No. 69, l. 4; No. 150, l. 27; No. 215, l. 20.

[22] 'Ruke šire, u lica se ljube' ('ruke šire, te s' u lica ljube', etc.), *Karadžić*, ii, No. 40, ll. 101, 172, 232; No. 89, l. 44; *Karadžić*, iii, No. 22, ll. 367, 381; No. 54, l. 105.

[23] 'L'jepo se je . . . poklonio', *Bogišić*, No. 1, l. 57; No. 10, ll. 45, 74 (in fact, l. 75 as l. 66 is missing in *Bogišić*—cf. PS, No. 23); No. 30, ll. 19, 31, 36, 37.

[24] 'Svakome se po redu . . . poklonite', *Bogišić*, No. 30, ll. 15, 26.

single poem.[25] When a decasyllabic hero—in exceptional circumstances—makes his 'bow', he tends to overdo it in a way which clearly shows that he is an outsider to this etiquette: he bows 'all the way down to the black earth'![26]

On the other hand, some long-winded formulaic expressions, like the ones with double epithets, are almost exclusively characteristic of *bugarštice* for purely metrical reasons. The 'heroic good horses'[27] and the 'red and white face'[28] have in Serbo-Croat at least seven syllables in their shortest possible forms, so they can fit into a line usually varying from fourteen to sixteen syllables, but can never be squeezed into the decasyllabic line which is always divided into two parts by the caesura after the fourth syllable. However, the 'white faces' tend to add a picturesque touch to many descriptions (not least when the heroes weep[29] or kiss each other in greeting[30]), the 'good horses' are as indispensable in Serbo-Croat epics as they used to be in Homer, and this is why the single-epithet variants of these formulas are found both in *bugarštice* and in the decasyllabic poems.[31]

Of course, not all the double-epithet formulas are acceptable to the decasyllabic singer in single-epithet variants which might easily fit into the decasyllabic line. 'The uncounted small coins', for instance, together with their single-epithet variants, can be

---

[25] See *Bogišić*, No. 30, ll. 15–37.

[26] 'Pokloni se do zemljice crne' ('pak se klanja do zemljice crne', 'ud'ri licem o zemljicu čarnu', etc.), *Karadžić*, ii, No. 14, l. 164; No. 30, l. 332; No. 50 (iii), l. 38.

[27] 'Junački konji dobri', *Bogišić*, No. 1, l. 147 ('junaške' instead of 'junačke' in *Pantić*, p. 122, which is a feature of the Dubrovnik dialect); No. 24, l. 10; No. 49, ll. 14, 36.

[28] 'Rumeno bijelo lišce', *Bogišić*, No. 1, l. 69; No. 15, l. 44; No. 23, l. 43.

[29] 'Grozne suze proljeva niz svoje niz b'jelo lišce', *Bogišić*, No. 1, l. 98 ('lice' corrected to 'lišce' as in PS, No. 22); 'Suze su ga polile niz njegovo b'jelo lišce', *Bogišić*, No. 1, l. 239 [241]; 'Proli suze niz bijela lica', *Gesemann*, No. 76, l. 18; No. 78, l. 128; *Karadžić*, ii, No. 14, l. 153; No. 45, l. 111; No. 51, l. 131.

[30] 'U b'jela se lica izljubiše', *Karadžić*, ii, No. 29, l. 163.

[31] 'Dobri konji' ('konj dobri', 'konjic dobar', etc.), *Bogišić*, No. 1, ll. 112, 151, 189 [190], 194 [195], 215 [216]; No. 17, ll. 7, 10, 12, 27, 36, 37, 43; No. 18, ll. 37, 55, 94; *Gesemann*, No. 81, ll. 21, 24, 37; No. 83, ll. 25, 36; No. 110, ll. 44, 64, 72, 87, 104, 124; *Karadžić*, ii, No. 16, ll. 37, 41, 81: No. 48, ll. 19, 21, 26, 34; No. 51, l. 124.

found almost exclusively in *bugarštice*,[32] even if 'the small coins' and 'uncounted coins' survive in one or two instances in the earliest recorded octosyllabic and decasyllabic poems.[33] This formula disappeared probably not only because the word 'spenza' (coins, money) was not intelligible outside Dalmatia, but also because the concept of riches in separate coins which should be counted was much more characteristic of the mentality in commercialized urban settings along the Adriatic coast than of the more primitive inland village life. When the village singer manifests his interest in riches, in money or booty, he usually refers to 'two'[34] or 'three loads of treasure'[35] or 'two'[36] or 'three boots full of treasure'[37] and, on occasion, to 'uncounted treasure'.[38] If he descends to refer to actual pieces of money, we are usually faced with 'three hundred ducats',[39] if not with 'seven towers of groschen and ducats'.[40]

But the decasyllabic singer is not opposed in principle to double-epithet formulas: 'hawk the grey bird',[41] for instance, had better luck both because its six syllables could easily fit into the second part of a decasyllabic line and also perhaps because the peasant found it easy to share his interest in hunting with his feudal lord. Sometimes the village singer adds his own second epithet to a formula which he inherits from his feudal predecessors: such are the instances of his 'grey green hawk'[42],

[32] 'Nebrojena drobna spenca', *Bogišić*, No. 51, l. 13. 'Drobna spenca', *Bogišić*, No. 5, ll. 10 [6], 14 [10]; No. 25, ll. 28, 29; No. 47, l. 23; No. 63, l. 83 [84].

[33] 'Drobna spensa', *Gesemann*, No. 214, l. 25. 'Spensa nebrojena', *Gesemann*, No. 24, l. 103.

[34] 'Dva tovara blaga', *Gesemann*, No. 98, ll. 25, 31.

[35] 'Tri tovara blaga', *Gesemann*, No. 83, l. 15; No. 123, ll. 72, 83, 89, 113; No. 127, l. 50. *Karadžić*, ii, No. 56, ll. 56, 83; No. 61, ll. 143, 149; No. 73, ll. 19, 28.   [36] 'Dvije čizme blaga', *Karadžić*, ii, No. 56, l. 167.

[37] 'Tri čizme blaga', *Karadžić*, ii, No. 56, l. 254.

[38] 'Blago nebrojeno', *Gesemann*, No. 161, l. 81; *Karadžić*, ii, No. 29, l. 451; No. 67, l. 36; *Karadžić*, iv, No. 4, ll. 29, 52.

[39] 'Tri stotin' dukata', *Gesemann*, No. 71, l. 22; No. 77, l. 56; No. 83, l. 34; *Karadžić*, ii, No. 57, ll. 38, 52.

[40] 'Sedam kula groša i dukata', *Karadžić*, ii, No. 23, l. 5.

[41] 'Soko siva ptica', *Bogišić*, No. 36, ll. 2, 5; No. 51, ll. 17, 23; *Karadžić*, ii, No. 46, ll. 1, 4; No. 54, ll. 9, 15.

[42] 'Siv zelen sokole', *Gesemann*, No. 55, l. 49; No. 138, l. 71. 'Sivi soko', *Gesemann*, No. 109, l. 12; No. 112, l. 20; No. 166, ll. 5, 14, 23; *Karadžić*, ii, No. 5, ll. 39, 43; No. 46, ll. 49, 57; No. 47, l. 62.

his 'big dapple horse',[43] his 'great and strong army'.[44] But, of course, the question of metrical adjustment of formulas and formulaic patterns is a much more complex issue in Serbo-Croat epic singing than these considerations can suggest. Not only because there are seven cases in singular and plural forms, or because an adjective can figure in its definite or indefinite aspect,[45] because a noun or an adjective can be easily expanded by a syllable,[46] because a vowel in almost any word can be

[43] 'Šaren konj veliki', *Karadžić*, ii, No. 62, ll. 123, 137, 151, 166. 'Konj veliki', *Bogišić*, No. 42, l. 20; No. 53, l. 23; No. 57, l. 70 (owing to different arrangement of lines this is l. 53 in PS, No. 14); *Gesemann*, No. 31, ll. 5, 12, 19, 31; No. 50, ll. 83, 86; No. 120, l. 12; *Karadžić*, ii, No. 10, ll. 106, 156, 164; No. 50 (v), l. 11.

[44] 'Mloga silna vojska', *Karadžić*, ii, No. 25, l. 60. 'Vojska silna', *Bogišić*, No. 36, l. 15; *Gesemann*, No. 116, ll. 20, 24, 32; *Karadžić*, ii, No. 44, ll. 121, 126; No. 46, l. 72; No. 50 (iv), l. 9.

[45] The long-form adjective is standard, for instance, in 'sivi soko' ('grey hawk'), but when another epithet is added, the indefinite aspect is used for metrical reasons: 'siv zelen sokole' ('grey-green hawk'). See note 42, p. 41. In one of these instances we find a very common example of the longer vocative form ('sokole') used in the function of the nominative ('soko'): 'Da je Nuko siv zelen sokole' ('If Nuko were a grey-green hawk'), *Gesemann*, No. 138, l. 71. Obviously, the singer needed only one extra syllable and the vocative form as a standard device was perhaps more convenient than using the longer, definitive form of only one of the two adjectives. However, in another instance—'kod mojega siv zelen sokola' ('near my grey-green hawk'), *Gesemann*, No. 55, l. 49—we find only the noun and the possessive pronoun in the genitive form, whereas both adjectives have the indefinite aspect and are used in the nominative form even if their function is genitive. Of course, the singer could have easily made a grammatically correct line ('kod mog sivog zelenog sokola'), but in his poetic language certain formulaic patterns and their unity within a part of the line are sometimes stronger than grammatical habits.

[46] An extra syllable can always easily be added in a poem to a noun by using the vocative form in the nominative function: 'Razbolje se Kraljeviću Marko' ('Marko Kraljević fell ill'), *Karadžić*, ii, No. 54, l. 1. Another standard device is the diminutive ending: instead of the standard 'dobri konj', or 'konj dobri', or 'dobri konji' ('a good horse', 'good horses', *Gesemann*, No. 81, ll. 21, 24, 37) we also find 'dobar konjic' (*Gesemann*, No. 97, l. 31; No. 98, ll. 49, 63); instead of the standard 'vjerna ljuba' ('a faithful love', *Bogišić*, No. 12, l. 16; *Gesemann*, No. 71, ll. 2, 21; *Karadžić*, ii, No. 25, ll. 89, 105, 137) we also find 'vjerna ljubovca' (*Bogišić*, No. 5, l. 23; *Karadžić*, ii, No. 25, l. 25; No. 51, l. 116). Less commonly the adjective itself is turned into a noun: 'ljuba vijernica' (*Karadžić*, ii, No. 26, ll. 154, 164). The word 'vijernica' is not used in this sense in common language (when used it denotes 'a pious woman'); is this form the result of the singer's urge to vary

easily left out,[47] or because 'ekavic', 'ikavic' or 'ijekavic' forms appear as the need arises or chance determines;[48] but also because the inflections of Serbo-Croat make it very easy to invert the standard word order[49] and still keep the semantic unity of a formulaic expression even when its elements are separated and placed in two different lines.[50]

However, the interplay of *bugarštice* and the decasyllabic singing is most clearly reflected in the stock phrases and formulaic expressions which are common to both traditions. Many of them are at the same time the basic springs of the narrative mechanism. In both traditions, for instance, heroes live in their 'white palaces',[51] even if in the decasyllabic songs

a standard formula, and to vary it by analogy with the sounds of another existing variant: 'vjerna ljubovca'—'ljuba vijernica'? An extra syllable can be added to an adjective either by using its hypocoristic form: 'zlaćeni' instead of 'zlatni noži' ('gilt knives', *Karadžić*, ii, No. 5, ll. 65, 66); or by using the longer form of a case ending: 'groznijem' instead of 'groznim suzama' ('terrible tears', *Karadžic*, iv, No. 28, l. 38).

[47] See, for instance, *Karadžić*, ii, No. 5, l. 4—'međ'' (for 'među'); l. 12—'vid'la' (for 'vidjela'); ll. 18, 64, 82, 105—'al'' (for 'ali'); ll. 25, 80, 85, 112, 116—'konjma' (for 'konjima'); l. 74—'zašt'' (for 'zašto'); l. 106—'id'' (for 'idi').

[48] Depending on the development of the old Slavonic 'jat' ('ѣ') three types of pronunciation are differentiated: 'ekavic' ('e'), 'ijekavic' ('ije', 'je') and 'ikavic' ('i').—*Karadžić*, ii, No. 44 is in 'ijekavic' standard; but instead of the standard formulaic form 'bijela ruka' ('white hand' or 'arm'), which could be easily shortened into 'b'jela ruka', the singer uses the 'ikavic' form 'bila ruka' (ll. 69, 709). *Karadžić*, ii, No. 47 is almost completely in the 'ekavic' standard, but the 'ijekavic' forms are used for 'bijele čalme' ('white turbans') and 'bijele klobuke' ('white hats') ll. 130–1. This may be only a matter of metrical convenience, but it might also be noted that the two nouns were more widespread in the 'ijekavic' than in the 'ekavic' areas, i.e. in Bosnia and in Croatia than in Serbia.

[49] For instance, the standard form 'bojno koplje' ('battle lance', *Bogišić*, No. 1, ll. 108, 197; *Gesemann*, No. 96, ll. 13, 24; *Karadžić*, ii, No. 44, ll. 602, 617) also figures as 'koplje bojno' (*Bogišić*, No. 68, l. 51 (in fact l. 52 as l. 14 is missing in *Bogišić*; cf. Mazarovic-Pantić, No. 485); *Gesemann*, No. 89, l. 7; *Karadžić*, ii, No. 25, l. 243; No. 44, l. 627.

[50] For instance, 'sitna knjiga' ('small-lettered book') is a standard formulaic expression, but there are examples when the noun appears in the first part of one line and the epithet in the second part of the line which follows: 'Gledi knjigu vojvoda Prijezda, / Onu gledi, drugu sitnu piše', *Karadžić*, ii, No. 84, ll. 16–17. What happens, of course, is that the same noun is assumed, but not actually repeated.

[51] 'Bijeli dvori', *Bogišić*, No. 67, ll. 16, 30, 61, 67, 97; No. 69, ll. 6, 46, 49;

'the palaces' often denote ordinary peasant houses.[52] This is where they 'drink wine',[53] or 'hold a council',[54] write or receive messages—usually in the form of letters called 'thin'[55] or 'small-lettered books'[56]—perhaps because long letters were difficult to write and even the short ones seemed like books when it came to reading. The messages usually lead to journeys —for which 'the good horses',[57] the 'white tents'[58] and some-

No. 78, ll. 2, 59; *Gesemann*, No. 92, ll. 47, 57; No. 98, ll. 39, 76; No. 109, ll. 4, 11, 37, 52; *Karadžić*, ii, No. 26, ll. 98, 225, 230; No. 45, ll. 18, 109; No. 56, ll. 38, 137, 243; No. 57, ll. 29, 36, 46, 59, 65.

[52] Such are, for instance, 'the white palaces' of the Montenegrin warrior Tašo Nikolić, where the outlaws get together before they proceed on their mission of vengeance in *Karadžić*, iii, No. 69, ll. 45, 66.

[53] 'Vino piju' or 'vino . . . pijahu', *Bogišić*, No. 55, l. 1; *Gesemann*, No. 6, l. 1; No. 15, l. 1; No. 63, l. 1; *Karadžić*, ii, No. 59, l. 1; No. 67, l. 1; No. 73, l. 1.

[54] 'Zbor zborahu', *Bogišić*, No. 8, l. 1. In the third line the same idea is repeated in a different wording :'v'jeće v'jećahu'. In this wording it is also found in *Bogišić*, No. 31, l. 1; No. 80, l. 1. 'Zbor zborila' is also found in *Karadžić*, ii, No. 23, l. 1; No. 24, l. 1.

[55] 'Tanka knjiga', *Bogišić*, No. 15, l. 1 ('Tanku knjigu napisa od Budima sv'jetli kralju'—'The bright king of Budim wrote a thin book'); No. 67, ll. 10, 13; No. 71, l. 1 ('Tanka knjiga dopade od Novoga grada b'jela'—'A thin book came from the white city of Novi'); *Gesemann*, No. 120, ll. 22 ('knjigu tanjenu'); No. 120, l. 32 ('gleda knjigu, drugu tanku piše'—'he looks at the book, he writes another thin one'); No. 123, l. 76 ('gleda knjigu, drugu tanku piše'). In the opening lines of the decasyllabic poems the epithet 'thin' is usually omitted because the name of the hero who writes the book has to be mentioned and economy has to be exercised: *Gesemann*, No. 17, l. 1 ('Knjigu piše Mandušiću Vuče'—'Vuk Mandušić writes a book'); No. 47, l. 1 ('Iše knjigu baša smeterevski'—'The pasha of Smederevo writes a book'); *Karadžić*, ii, No. 25, l. 1; *Karadžić*, iii, No. 34, l. 1. 'Books often' (go, come) is another variant of this opening formulaic pattern: *Karadžić*, ii, No. 31, l. 1 ('često knjige'); No. 84, l. 1 ('česte knjige'—'frequent books').

[56] 'Sitna knjiga', *Gesemann*, No. 143, l. 3; No. 210, ll. 14, 42; *Karadžić*, ii, No. 50 (i), ll. 2, 16; No. 56, l. 95; No. 59, ll. 25, 38. It might be noted that 'small-lettered', not 'thin', books are the rule in Karadžić's collections— perhaps because the difficulty of reading them and/or their size struck the peasant eye. See R. Samardžić, 'Hajdučka pisma', *Usmena narodna hronika*, Novi Sad, 1978, pp. 79–81.

[57] See note 31, p. 40.

[58] 'Bijeli šator', *Bogišić*, No. 19, ll. 12, 19, 43; No. 35, l. 30; No. 55, ll. 26, 34, 54 (l. 53 in PS, No. 14 because Bogišić prints l. 39 as two lines); *Gesemann*, No. 59, ll. 69, 91; No. 87, ll. 5, 8; No. 110, ll. 2, 108, 109; *Karadžić*, ii, No. 29, l. 388; No. 44, l. 472; No. 56, ll. 221, 228.

times even 'silk tents'[59] are required, and where thirst has to be quenched by 'cold water'[60] or, preferably, just as at home, by 'cool'[61] or 'red wine'[62] (even if some scholars suggest that what everyone imagines to be 'red wine' in Serbo-Croat epics is, in fact, what everyone, equally mistakenly, calls 'white' wine[63]). The journey is often interrupted by a sudden ambush or it ends in a battle or in single combat. But whatever turn the story takes the hero has, in the songs about the good old days, to trust his 'battle lance',[64] his 'naked sword',[65] his 'sharp'[66] or

[59] 'Svilen šator' or 'svioni šator', *Bogišić*, No. 1, l. 159; No. 4, ll. 1, 29, 31, 45, 53; No. 35, ll. 4, 19, 23; in *Gesemann* we usually find 'šator od zelene svile' ('a tent of green silk'), No. 114, l. 65; No. 157, l. 31; No. 59, ll. 92–3, 110–11; in *Karadžić* we find 'svilni' or 'svilen šator', iii, No. 7, ll. 123, 235, 260, 263.

[60] 'Hladna voda', *Bogišić*, No. 4, ll. 4, 38, 39, 46, 51; No. 35, ll. 41, 42, 44, 47, 49, 51, 58, 59, 66; No. 59, ll. 44 [43], 46 [45], 84 [83], 85 [84]; *Gesemann*, No. 110, ll. 29, 41; No. 126, l. 51; No. 176, ll. 4, 28; *Karadžić*, ii, No. 51, ll. 8, 15, 27; No. 55, ll. 8, 15; iv, No. 33, l. 449.

[61] 'Hladno vino', *Bogišić*, No. 12, ll. 49, 57, 69; No. 18, ll. 28, 33, 45, 70, 87; No. 19, ll. 22, 57, 64; *Gesemann*, No. 63, ll. 5, 18, 33; No. 78, ll. 81, 145; No. 117, ll. 51, 127; *Karadžić*, ii, No. 50 (iii), l. 49; iii, No. 7, l. 286.

[62] 'Rujno vino', *Bogišić*, No. 14, l. 38; No. 20, ll. 76, 78; No. 26, l. 61; *Gesemann*, No. 59, l. 73; No. 117, l. 101; No. 216, l. 32; *Karadžić*, ii, No. 25, l. 52; No. 47, ll. 27, 80, 94; No. 59, ll. 87, 93, 129.

[63] See T. Maretić, *Naša narodna epika*, Belgrade, 1966, pp. 73–4. Maretić's argument is partly etymological: 'rujno' is derived from 'ruj' ('sumach', German *Gelbholtz*) which has yellow flowers. Most people, however, would immediately think of 'ruj' in connection with its reddish autumn colours. But it might be also worth noting that Karadžić defines 'rujno vino' as *'gelblicher Wein'* ('yellowish wine') in his *Serbian Dictionary* (*Srpski rječnik*, ed. P. P. Đordević and Lj. Stojanović, Belgrade, 1935, p. 676—based on second revised ed., Vienna, 1852; first ed., Vienna, 1818). S. Vulović points out that 'rujno' sometimes denotes 'new' ('this year's') and that 'new', lighter wine might be particularly suitable for fighters ('Rujno—Prilog ispitivanju epiteta u narodnoj [usmenoj] srpskoj poeziji', *Godišnjica Nikole Čupića*, vi [1884], pp. 263–70.) These arguments seem to be far-fetched and there is no doubt that an ordinary native speaker would think of 'rujno vino' only as rosé or red wine.

[64] 'Bojno koplje', *Bogišić*, No. 1, ll. 108, 197 [198]; No. 15, ll. 12, 14; No. 47, ll. 37, 46; *Gesemann*, No. 89, ll. 7, 10; No. 96, ll. 13, 24; No. 134, ll. 2, 8; *Karadžić*, ii, No. 44, ll. 602, 617, 627; No. 49, ll. 46, 47; No. 51, l. 121.

[65] 'Gola sablja', *Bogišić*, No. 46, ll. 40, 52; No. 26, l. 33 ('gola korda'); No. 53, l. 31 ('gola korda'); *Karadžić*, iii, No. 50, l. 61; iv, No. 26, ll. 167, 192.

[66] 'Ostra sablja', *Bogišić*, No. 27, l. 22; No. 24, ll. 16, 21 ('oštra korda'); No. 40, l. 86 ('oštra korda'); *Gesemann*, No. 70, l. 106; No. 87, ll. 19, 117, 120, 121; No. 89, ll. 9, 14.

'razor-sharp sword'.[67] In the songs about the more recent but hardly less heroic times the hero usually fires 'a small gun':[68] it starts 'a living flame'[69] which sows death and saves life. There is, further, a vivid perception of what battles and arms bring: wounds which can, or cannot, be healed,[70] or the final utterance followed by 'the parting from the sinful soul'.[71] Those who are left behind or left out drop 'terrible tears'[72] which, we are told, are etymologically not 'terrible' but only as large as 'grapes'.[73] And finally 'black' is the colour both of

[67] 'Britka sablja', *Bogišić*, No. 65, l. 154; No. 67, l. 48; No. 78, l. 24; *Gesemann*, No. 110, ll. 24, 75, 78, 90; No. 114, l. 53; No. 161, ll. 59, 68; *Karadžić*, ii, No. 25, ll. 71, 182; No. 44, ll. 478, 564, 583, 646; No. 50 (v), ll. 2, 3.

[68] 'Mala puška', *Bogišić*, No. 63, ll. 59 [60], 60 [61]; *Gesemann*, No. 135, l. 52; *Karadžić*, iv, No. 32, ll. 211, 279.

[69] 'Oganj živi', *Bogišić*, No. 60, l. 68; No. 62, l. 60; No. 65, l. 162; No. 73, l. 51; *Gesemann*, No. 94, l. 35; No. 128, l. 24; *Karadžić*, iv, No. 32, ll. 281, 300 ('živa vatra'); No. 34, l. 280 ('živa vatra').

[70] The usual phrase, sometimes split into two lines, is 'rane . . . preboliti' or 'priboljeti' ('to recover from the wounds'), *Bogišić*, No. 16, ll. 36–7; *Gesemann*, No. 89, l. 20; No. 96, l. 17; *Karadžić*, ii, No. 16, ll. 173, 180; iii, No. 32, l. 13.

[71] 'S grešnom dušom razd'jelio', *Bogišić*, No. 16, l. 85; No. 35, l. 93; No. 52, ll. 30, 33; No. 78, ll. 54, 57; *Gesemann*, No. 108, l. 46 ('s dušom delijaše'—'parting from his soul'); No. 108, l. 54 ('dušicu pusti'—'breathed out his soul'); *Karadžić*, iii, No. 1, l. 69 ('dok sam njega s dušom rastavio'—'before I separated him from his soul').

[72] 'Grozne suze', *Bogišić*, No. 1, l. 98; No. 16, ll. 43, 45; No. 82, ll. 23, 63, 113 (in fact ll. 34, 100, 182—see *Pantić*, pp. 53–8 and note 9, p. 34); *Gesemann*, No. 49, l. 32; No. 213, l. 95; *Karadžić*, ii, No. 30, l. 213; iii, No. 78, l. 181; iv, No. 28, ll. 38, 120.

[73] It is in this sense that the meaning of 'grozne suze' is defined in *Rečnik srpskohrvatskog književnog i narodnog jezika*, iii, ed. M. Stevanović *et al.*, Belgrade, 1965, p. 661 and also in *Rečnik srpskohrvatskoga kniiiževnog jezika*, i, ed. M. Stevanović, Lj. Jonke *et al.*, Novi Sad–Zagreb, 1967, p. 574. Both possibilities of meaning (the older 'terrible' or 'bitter' or 'sad tears' and the more recent poetic usage in the sense of 'tears as large' or as 'plentiful' as 'grapes') are listed in *Rječnik hrvatskoga ili srpskoga jezika*, iii, ed. P. Budmani, Zagreb, 1887–91, p. 464. It is true that 'grozan' is used in oral epic poetry as an adjective of 'grožđe' (grapes): 'grozni vinograd', *Karadžić*, ii, No. 39, l. 12; but we are probably faced here with another word different in origin and pronunciation ('grôzan' as distinguished from 'grôzan'). However, even if the question of etymology may be doubtful, the explanation that 'grozne suze' denote 'tears as large as grapes' takes every native speaker by surprise—hardly an essential feature of a good definition.

'blood'[74] and of 'the earth'[75] which is always there ready to receive those whom luck has left. And 'black ravens', usually in pairs,[76] provide an ominous setting for the news about the tragedy which has taken place.

But if death, sometimes foreshadowed by a 'strange dream'[77] or brought about by 'bad luck',[78] preys from all sides, the darkness of this epic landscape is often illuminated in *bugarštice* by the 'bright crowns'[79] and usually dispelled, particularly in the decasyllabic songs, by the 'bright arms'[80] and the colourful appearance of the hero, who sometimes turns up decorated with 'white feathers',[81] as a rule in his cap or hat, and is often seen as a 'hawk'.[82] In fact, the 'grey hawks'[83] inhabit the same

[74] 'Crna krvca', *Bogišić*, No. 23, l. 3; *Gesemann*, No. 86, l. 15; No. 117, ll. 76, 78, 83; No. 120, l. 24; *Karadžić*, iii, No. 7, l. 211.

[75] 'Crna zemlja', *Bogišić*, No. 48, l. 9 (owing to different arrangement of lines this is l. 6 in PS, No. 47); No. 50, l. 79; No. 63, l. 63 [64]; *Gesemann*, No. 18, l. 46; No. 58, l. 77; No. 131, l. 54; *Karadžić*, ii, No. 78, l. 242; iii, No. 2, l. 180; No. 78, ll. 162, 174.

[76] 'Crni vran', *Bogišić*, No. 32, ll. 57, 59, 72, 74 (owing to different arrangement of lines these are ll. 52, 57, 63, 64 in PS, No. 5). 'Dva vrana gavrana' ('two black ravens'), *Gesemann*, No. 179, l. 1; *Karadžić*, ii, No. 45, ll. 120, 130, 131, 137; No. 48, l. 58; iv, No. 26, l. 1; No. 30, l. 1.

[77] 'Čudan san (sanak)', *Bogišić*, No. 28, ll. 10, 17; No. 50, l. 10; *Gesemann*, No. 80, ll. 22, 25; No. 109, l. 10; No. 163, ll. 20, 24; *Karadžić*, ii, No. 25, l. 138; No. 62, ll. 64, 65; iii, No. 14, l. 28.

[78] 'Huda sreća', *Bogišić*, No. 1, ll. 118, 183 [184], 186 [187]; No. 43, ll. 12, 39; No. 78, ll. 25, 31, 49; *Gesemann*, No. 108, l. 39; No. 67, l. 32 ('zla sreća'); *Karadžić*, ii, No. 51, l. 134; No. 25, l. 183 ('loša sreća'); iv, No. 31, l. 294 ('loša sreća').

[79] 'Svijetla kruna' ('the illustrious crowned head'), *Bogišić*, No. 15, l. 73; No. 25, l. 11; No. 54, ll. 56, 58, 60, 62, 64.

[80] 'Svijetlo oružje', *Bogišić*, No. 18, l. 91; *Gesemann*, No. 83, l. 45; No. 163, l. 5; No. 188, l.75; *Karadžić*, ii, No. 30, l. 84; iv, No. 24, l. 555; No. 30, l. 116.

[81] 'B'jelo perje', *Bogišić*, No. 32, l. 35 (owing to different arrangement of lines this is l. 30 in PS, No. 5); No. 45, l. 20; No. 50, l. 13; *Gesemann*, No. 64, l. 52; No. 80, l. 12; No. 100, l. 17; *Karadžić*, ii, No. 47, l. 110 ('bela kita perja').

[82] 'Soko', *Bogišić*, No. 30, l. 6; No. 57, l. 66 (owing to different arrangement of lines this is l. 49 in PS, No. 5); No. 58, ll. 6, 7, 8, 18, 19, 22; *Gesemann*, No. 83, l. 62; No. 87, l. 10; No. 92, ll. 42, 43; *Karadžić*, ii, No. 44, ll. 4, 26, 456, 507; iii, No. 50, ll. 21, 27; iv, No. 28, l. 7.

[83] 'Sivi soko' ('soko siva ptica' or 'dva siva sokola'), *Bogišić*, No. 36, ll. 1, 2, 5; No. 51, ll. 16, 17, 23; No. 58, l. 20; *Gesemann*, No. 109, l. 12; No. 112, l. 20; No. 166, ll. 5, 14, 23; *Karadžić*, ii, No. 5, l. 124; No. 46, ll. 49, 57; iii, No. 3, l. 52; No. 78, l. 34.

world in which the heroes move, a world of struggle and
uncertainty, a world in which a knight, a wife, a friend or a
servant can be either 'faithful'[84] or 'unfaithful',[85] but in which
'firm faith'[86] or 'God's faith'[87] has to be kept and the 'faithless
brood'[88] has to be tied to the horses' tails.[89] This moral clarity
is both a reflection of religious faith and of the pagan light which
comes from the 'hot sun'[90] in the 'clear sky'[91] and shines on man

---

[84] 'Vjera' (literally 'faith') sometimes denotes fidelity or the honouring of
a pledge, *Bogišić*, No. 61, l. 15; No. 65, l. 237; *Karadžić*, iv, No. 6, l. 24;
No. 24, l. 434. It also often denotes a faithful knight or friend, a person who
keeps faith, *Bogišić*, No. 14, ll. 58, 61, 138; *Karadžić*, ii, No. 50 (iii), ll. 31,
32, 53. But the 'faithfulness' of wives and servants is denoted by specific
formulaic patterns: 'vjerna ljuba' ('faithful love'), *Bogišić*, No. 5, l. 23; No.
12, l. 16; No. 59, l. 53 [52]; *Gesemann*, No. 70, l. 103; No. 109, l. 15; No. 112
l. 10; *Karadžić*, ii, No. 25, ll. 25, 89, 105, 137; No. 26, ll. 70, 85, 104, 110
154, 164; No. 44, l. 147; 'vjerna sluga' ('faithful servant'), *Bogišić*, No. 8
ll. 55, 59; No. 20, l. 77; No. 22, ll. 19, 25; *Gesemann*, No. 21, l. 50; No. 59,
ll. 56, 57; No. 98, ll. 20, 21; *Karadžić*, ii, No. 25, l. 293; No. 26, l. 28; No. 44,
ll. 36, 144. Finally, the epic concept of 'vjera' is also derived from the usage,
of this term in medieval law (see above p. 21).

[85] 'Nevjera' (literally 'unfaithfulness') sometimes denotes infidelity or the
dishonouring of a pledge, *Bogišić*, No. 36, l. 46; No. 65, l. 237; No. 73, l. 66;
Gesemann, No. 83, l. 55; *Karadžić*, ii, No. 47, ll. 71, 84, 121. It also often
denotes an unfaithful person, particularly a treacherous knight in battle,
Bogišić, No. 14, ll. 58, 61, 138; No. 61, l. 20; *Karadžić*, ii, No. 50 (iii), ll. 31,
32, 44, 48, 53.

[86] 'Tvrda vjera', *Bogišić*, No. 65, ll. 228, 240, 246; *Karadžić*, ii, No. 29,
l. 92; No. 67, l. 9; iv, No. 4, l. 8.

[87] 'Božja vjera'. In *bugarštice* this formulaic pattern figures as 'vjera Boga
velikoga' ('the faith of great God'), *Bogišić*, No. 17, ll. 21, 25; No. 40, l. 103;
No. 61, l. 15; in the decasyllabic poems it usually figures as 'božja vjera
tvrda' ('God's firm faith'), *Karadžić*, ii, No. 26, l. 91; No. 44, l. 404.

[88] 'Nevjerno koljeno', *Bogišić*, No. 14, l. 122; *Gesemann*, No. 6, l. 24;
Karadžić, iii, No. 7, l. 256.

[89] See *Karadžić*, ii, No. 5, ll. 80, 85; No. 25, l. 294.

[90] 'Žarko sunce', *Bogišić*, No. 18, ll. 39, 51; No. 20, l. 19; No. 23, l. 15;
No. 37, l. 9 (owing to different arrangement of lines this is l. 6 in PS, No.
10); *Gesemann*, No. 67, l. 55; No. 71, l. 43; No. 75, ll. 3, 9, 41; *Karadžić*, ii,
No. 10, l. 28. But 'jarko sunce' is a much more common form in Karadžić's
collections; see *Karadžić*, ii, No. 29, l. 565; No. 44, l. 321; iii, No. 78, ll. 161,
173; iv, No. 24, l. 446.

[91] 'Vedro nebo', *Bogišić*, No. 1, ll. 74, 81; No. 28, ll. 12, 25; No. 30, ll. 67,
70, 76, 90; *Gesemann*, No. 10, l. 2; No. 47, l. 86; No. 75, l. 39; No. 109, l. 18 ;
Karadžić, ii, No. 10, l. 79; No. 55, l. 34; iii, No. 31, ll. 3, 21; iv, No. 24,
l. 95.

and beast and the 'supple fir-tree'[92] alike. Moreover, in the decasyllabic poems the hero knows the animal tongue; he talks to an eagle, his horse or his hawk,[93] and his birthplace is sometimes seen as a 'hawks' nest'.[94] He moves 'like a star across the clear sky',[95] his sword 'flashes like the hot sun',[96] a 'supple fir-tree' can protect him from his enemy[97] and can be the ultimate witness of truth at the end of the epic story.[98] In short, historical, natural, and spiritual morality are not only meta-phorically analogous: they appear identical in essence—the light of the world which man inhabits, the light he lives and dies by.

A glimpse into the merging of the historical, the natural, and the spiritual imagery is offered in the first recorded oral epic poem in Serbo-Croat, 'Marko Kraljević and His Brother Andrijaš', which was published together with the much poorer *bugarštica* 'Duke Radosav of Severin and Vlatko of Vidin' in Hektorović's *Fishing and Fishermen's Conversations*.[99] The first of the two poems was recited by Paskoje Debelja, the older of Hektorović's two fishermen, whom the poet describes as 'a good and upright husband', whereas the poorer one was recited by the 'young and fine-dressed' Nikola Zet.[100] The first poem

---

[92] 'Vita jela', *Bogišić*, No. 83, ll. 13, 19; *Gesemann*, No. 17, l. 70; No. 174, ll. 1, 20; *Karadžić*, ii, No. 74, ll. 46, 58 ('tanka jela'); iii, No. 7, ll. 66, 75, 77; No. 78, l. 205.

[93] The hero talks to an eagle in the fragment of the first recorded *bugarštica* in Serbo-Croat (see above pp. 27–9). The hero and his horse talk to each other in *Karadžić*, ii, No. 25, ll. 197–209; Marko Kraljević also talks to his horse before he dies, *Karadžić*, ii, No. 74, ll. 9–17; he talks to a hawk in *Karadžić*, ii, No. 54, ll. 15–18 and the hawk replies to him (ll. 20–30). In another variant of this poem an eagle talks to a *vila* (*Karadžić*, ii, No. 55, 18–63). For *vila*, see Appendix III.

[94] 'Gn'jezdo sokolova', *Karadžić*, iv, No. 28, l. 7; No. 32, l. 335.

[95] 'Kako zvizda priko vedra neba', *Gesemann*, No. 47, l. 86; No. 143, l. 104; *Karadžić*, iv, No. 39, l. 153.

[96] 'Sja (mu) korda (na bedri), k'o (na gori) žarko sunce', *Bogišić*, No. 23, l. 15; 'Sinu sablja kako žarko sunce', *Gesemann*, No. 67, l. 55.

[97] *Karadžić*, iii, No. 7, ll. 66–70.

[98] *Gesemann*, No. 17, l. 70.

[99] *Pantić*, pp. 44–9. See also P. Hektorović, *Ribanye i ribarscho prigovaranye*, ff. 12ʳ–15ᵛ; *Ribanje i ribarsko prigovaranje i razlike stvari ine*, ed. M. Franičević, Zagreb, 1968, ll. 524–92, 595–685.

[100] *Ribanye i ribarscho prigovaranye*, f. 3ʳ; *Ribanje i ribarsko prigovaranje i razlike stvari ine*, ll. 45–6.

deals with the traditional epic subject of fratricide and opens
with a formulaic line which will often be found at the beginning
of the later decasyllabic poems about this subject.[101] This line
is a starting point for a 'broken' Slavonic antithesis—a stylistic
device characteristic both of *bugarštice* and the decasyllabic
poems.[102] It contains a number of traditional formulaic
expressions, some of them peculiar to *bugarštice* and some
characteristic both of *bugarštice* and the later decasyllabic songs.
Thus we find in it the 'heroic good horses', a characteristic
example of the double epithets in *bugarštice*, which will recur in
the decasyllabic poetry in the single-epithet form of 'good'
horses.[103] There is also a 'bright sword' which will be 'torn'
from its sheath;[104] the 'hero mother'[105] and the 'fine-dressed
girl'[106] recur several times in the poem and there are also
several highly formulaic expressions,[107] including the ending in

[101] 'Dva mi sta siromaha dugo vrime drugovala' ('Two poor men were
good friends for a long time'), *Pantić*, p. 44 (*Bogišić*, No. 6, l. 1). Bogišić's
text is not reliable—among other things line 40 is missing in it. Several
variants of this opening formulaic pattern can be found in later decasyllabic
poems: 'Tri su druge drugovale' ('Three girls were good friends'), *Gesemann*,
No. 52, l. 1; 'Dva su bratca u milosti rasla' ('Two brothers grew up in love'),
Gesemann, No. 121, l. 1; 'Tri su bratca u milosti rasla' ('Three brothers grew
up in love'), *Gesemann*, No. 149, l. 1; 'Dva se brata vrlo milovala' ('Two
brothers lived in great love'), *Karadžić*, ii, No. 10, l. 1; 'Dva su brata divno
živovali' ('Two brothers lived wonderfully'), *Karadžić*, ii, No. 11, l. 1.

[102] See above p. 38.

[103] 'Junačke dobre konje', *Pantić*, p. 44 (*Bogišić*, No. 6, l. 5). See notes 27,
31, p. 40.

[104] 'Potrže svitlu sablju', *Pantić*, p. 44 (*Bogišić*, No. 6, l. 14). For 'svitla
sabljica' see also *Bogišić*, No. 49, l. 47; *Karadžić*, iv, No. 33, l. 29. But 'svijetlo
oružje' ('bright arms') is a much more common formula, see note 80,
p. 47.

[105] 'Junačka majka', *Pantić*, pp. 44–5 (*Bogišić*, No. 6, ll. 23, 31, 34).

[106] 'Gizdava devojka', *Pantić*, p. 45 (*Bogišić*, No. 6, ll. 48 [49], 54 [55]).
See note 20, p. 39.

[107] For instance, there is the formulaic pattern of a noble lie: 'Nemoj to
joj, mili brate, sve istinu kazovati' ('Do not tell her, dear brother, the whole
of the truth'), *Pantić*, p. 45 (*Bogišić*, No. 6, l. 29). The word 'sve' (whole) is
missing in Bogišić. A variant of this formulaic pattern can be found in
Karadžić, ii, No. 50 (iv), l. 47: 'Nemoj tako knezu kazivati' ('Do not tell the
Prince so'); *Karadžić*, ii, No. 29, 123: 'Ne piš'te mu što je i kako je' ('Do not
write to him what the matter is').

There is also the formulaic pattern of the address in low voice at a crucial
moment: 'Tere knezu Marku potihora besijaše' ('and spoke to Marko the

which the singer wishes mirth to his master and his company.
The second of the two poems contains such universal formulas as
the 'white city',[108] the 'good horse',[109] the 'black wood' (or
'mountain'),[110] the 'white hands' (or 'arms'),[111] the 'faithful
servants',[112] and the major moral concept of 'faith' and its

Prince quietly'), *Pantić*, p. 44; *Bogišić*, No. 6, l. 17). Several variants of this
formulaic pattern can be found in later decasyllabic poems: *Gesemann*, No.
25, l. 31 ('Porjen ljubi po tiho govori'—'Porjen spoke to his love quietly');
No. 49, l. 1 ('Grujo majki po tiho govori'—'Grujo spoke to his mother
quietly'); No. 143, l. 90, ('I konju potiho govorio'—'He spoke to his horse
quietly'); No. 213, l. 7 ('Ivo Ani po tiho govori'—'Ivo spoke to Ana quietly'),
l. 12 ('Ivi Ana po tiho govori'—'Ana spoke to Ivo quietly'). The classic
example of the use of this formulaic pattern is to be found in 'The Death of
the Mother of the Jugovići' ('Smrt majke Jugovića'), *Karadžić*, ii, No. 48,
l. 76 ('Pak je ruci tijo besjedila'—'And she spoke to the hand quietly').

The ending of the poem on a note of merriment or with wishes of mirth
and/or good health is also fairly common: *Pantić*, p. 46, *Bogišić*, No. 6, ll.
67–9 (68–70 because l. 40 is missing in *Bogišić*); No. 7, l. 160; No. 9, ll. 110–
111; No. 11, l. 87; No. 33, l. 99; No. 38, l. 87 (l. 73 in PS, No. 3); No. 45,
ll. 100–1, (owing to different arrangement of a line these are ll. 99–100 in
PS, No. 12); No. 49, ll. 89–91; No. 50, l. 90; No. 52, ll. 37–9; No. 53, ll. 46–
47; *Gesemann*, No. 17, l. 71; No. 67, l. 72–3; No. 172, l. 68; *Karadžić*, ii, No.
12, l. 271; No. 31, ll. 389–90; No. 52, l. 123; No. 57, l. 291; No. 77, l. 170;
iii, No. 15, l. 154; No. 24, l. 649; No. 28, ll. 347–8; No. 31, l. 81; No. 35,
l. 232; No. 38, ll. 252–3; No. 44, l. 105; No. 46, ll. 139–40; No. 47, l. 296;
No. 49, ll. 197–8; No. 52, l. 191; No. 58, ll. 310–11; No. 63, l. 55; No. 71,
l. 132; No. 72, l. 303; No. 81, l. 280; iv, No. 1, l. 140; No. 2, l. 177; No. 3,
l. 170; No. 6, l. 154; No. 9, l. 180; No. 10, l. 293; No. 13, ll. 112–13; No.
19, ll. 64–5; No. 33, l. 634; No. 34, l. 389; No. 43, l. 164; No. 47, l. 144,
No. 62, l. 128.

[108] 'Beli grad', *Pantić*, p. 47 (*Bogišić*, No. 49, ll. 4, 5). See also *Bogišić*, No.
36, ll. 28, 52, 59, 72; No. 58, l. 111; No. 65, ll. 23, 106, 252; *Gesemann*, No.
80, l. 80; No. 87, ll. 39–40; No. 92, ll. 4, 13, 46; *Karadžić*, ii, No. 25, l. 4;
No. 49, l. 2; No. 78, ll. 2, 194.

[109] 'Dobri konj', *Pantić*, pp. 47, 48 (*Bogišić*, No. 49, ll. 14, 36, 50). See
notes 27 and 31, p. 40.

[110] 'Crna gora', *Pantić*, pp. 45, 47 (*Bogišić*, No. 49, ll. 15, 16). See also
Bogišić, No. 6, l. 56 (in fact l. 57 as l. 40 is missing, cf. *Pantić*, p. 45); *Gesemann*,
No. 150, ll. 3, 7, 8; No. 167, l. 4; No. 176, ll. 3, 9; *Karadžić*, ii, No. 50 (iv),
l. 23; iv, No. 33, l. 123.

[111] 'Bele ruke', *Pantić*, p. 49 (*Bogišić*, No. 49, l. 68). See also Bogišić, No.
15, l. 68; No. 20, l. 42; No. 26, l. 41; *Gesemann*, No. 6, l. 72; No. 47, ll. 23,
26, 40, 43, 78, 80; No. 123, l. 12; *Karadžić*, ii, No. 5, ll. 70, 83; No. 29, ll.
164, 512; No. 45, ll. 105, 113.

[112] 'Verne sluge', *Pantić*, p. 49 (*Bogišić*, No. 49, l. 86). See note 84,
p. 48.

betrayal.[113] It also ends with the traditional wishes of happiness, health and mirth.

As regards the origin of the oral epic language in which the two poems were sung, the linguistic evidence corroborates what the names of the heroes and the geographical references suggest. The 'Serbian manner' in the mouths of the Croatian singers, which the younger of the two singers specifically referred to in his invocation, is reflected above all in the 'ekavic' elements which intrude in the 'ikavic' standard of the songs. Significantly enough, the 'ekavic' elements survive in formulas: 'bele ruke' ('white hands' or 'arms'),[114] 'verne sluge' ('faithful servants'),[115] 'gizdava devojka' ('fine-dressed girl').[116] It may also be worth adding that some of these 'ekavic' features ('beli', 'devojka') are not to be found in Hektorović's own poetry and prose.[117] Besides, it is also significant that in Nikola Zet's invocation Hektorović uses the younger form 'meu' (amongst), whereas in the actual recital there are also examples of the older 'meju', indicating the beginning of the fifteenth century.[118] Similarly, as A. Mladenović points out in his analysis, the first line of 'Marko Kraljević and his brother Andrijaš' contains an example of an older, fifteenth-century dual enclitic verb form ('sta').[119] Finally, it is also significant that we find both 'l' and 'o' endings in the past participles ('pošal', 'obljubio'), because the former feature had disappeared from the relevant dialect after the middle of the fifteenth century.[120] This 'mixing', in A. Mladenović's opinion, could have most probably occured 'at the time when the older feature "l" had not yet been suppressed by the innovation "o" ', i.e. 'at the end of the fourteenth or the beginning of the fifteenth century'.[121]

The 'anachronistic' linguistic features are above all interesting as symptoms of much wider issues in the genesis of oral epic

[113] 'Vera' ('faithfulness', 'faith'), *Pantić*, pp. 48, 49 (*Bogišić*, No. 49, ll. 61, 78). See notes 84–8, p. 48.

[114] See note 111, p. 51 and note 48, p. 43. In spite of the complexity of the Serbo-Croat dialect map in this context 'ekavic' is certainly a Serbian and 'ikavic' a Dalmatian feature.

[115] See note 84, p. 48.

[116] See note 20, p. 39.

[117] See A. Mladenović, *Jezik Petra Hektorovića*, Novi Sad, 1968, p. 155.

[118] See ibid., p. 164.   [119] See ibid., p. 173.

[120] See ibid., pp. 161–2.   [121] Ibid., p. 186.

diction, particularly of diachronic social and historical realities embedded in its poetic language. For not only some sporadic linguistic features, but also the tale and the underlying social and moral drama, 'remember' much more than the singer does. This can be particularly well observed in 'Marko Kraljević and His Brother Andrijaš', and this fact seems to be significantly connected with the nature of the poetic achievement of this song. For it lives, undoubtedly, on the interplay of the ancient pagan, the younger feudal and the more recent, contemporary social and historical realities connected with outlawry and brigandage in a universal story of fratricide which unites them with great dramatic power.

The link with feudal history is reflected in the name of Marko Kraljević who lived in Prilep as a Turkish vassal, keeping his Christian faith, after his father King Vukašin had been killed in the Battle on the Marica (1371). In the opening lines Marko and his brother Andrijaš (also a historical figure) quarrel about the division of booty—and this is a universal motif which plays such an important part, for instance, in the plot of *The Iliad*. But from the beginning Marko and his brother Andrijaš are represented in at least two specific historical contexts. At first we are misled to believe that they are two poor outlaws—who have always lived in love and shared their loot equally. This illustrates the central patriarchal ideal of loyalty and brotherly love, which can be found in similar wording in the opening lines of later decasyllabic songs about fratricide.[122] However, Marko and Andrijaš are soon at daggers drawn, because they cannot agree how to divide the third of the horses which they have captured. They 'swear' at each other, in proper and dramatic outlaw fashion, but the quarrel about a 'good horse' is a standard epic motif which takes us back to feudal times. The 'good horse', as we have seen, was defined in Stefan Dušan's *Code of Laws* as a symbol of feudal power and the vassal's bond to the suzerain: after a nobleman's death it had to be returned to the emperor.[123] And indeed, after the bitter quarrel of two apparent 'outlaws' we are told explicitly that in fact Marko and his brother were not poor outlaws:

[122] See note 101, p. 50.
[123] See above pp. 21–2.

But one of them was Sir Marko Kraljević,
Sir Marko Kraljević and his brother Andrijaš,
                                The young knights.[124]

This is, of course, a characteristic *volte-face* of a broken Slavonic antithesis,[125] but it gives to what had appeared as a dramatic personal quarrel of two poor outlaws a higher social standing, an aura which becomes important in the grand development of the poem. For it centres on the nobility of feeling embodied in what Andrijaš has to say while dying, with his brother's sword in his heart, and clutching at Marko's 'right hand':

'Brother, my dear, I beg one thing of you,
Do not pull your sword out of my heart,
                                O brother, O my dear,
Until I say two or three words to you.
When you come to our hero mother, Marko, Prince,
Do not give our mother a crooked share,
Give her my share too, Marko, Prince,
To our mother, my brother,
For she will get no more sharing from me.
And if our mother should ask you,
                                Sir Marko:
"My son, why is your sword running with blood?"
Do not tell her the whole of the truth,
O my brother, O my dear,
Do not let our mother be distressed,
Say these words to our hero mother:
"My mother, my darling, a quiet deer
Would not step out of my road,
                                Hero mother,
Neither he from me, my mother, my darling,
Nor I from him.
I stood my ground and drew my hero sword,
And struck into the quiet deer's heart.
And when I looked and saw that quiet deer
While his soul parted from him on the road,

[124] 'Da jedno mi biše vitez Marko Kraljeviću, / Vitez Marko Kraljeviću i brajen mu Andrijašu, / Mladi vitezi', *Pantić*, p. 44 (*Bogišić*, No. 6, ll. 11–13).
[125] See note 17, p. 38.

I loved the quiet deer like my brother,
                              The quiet deer,
If he came back I would not murder him."
And when our mother presses you and asks:
"Where is your brother Andrijaš, my Prince?"
Then do not tell the truth to our mother,
Say: "The hero stayed in a foreign land,
My mother, my darling.
For love he cannot leave that land,
                              Andrijaš.
In that land he has kissed a fine-dressed girl.
And ever since he kissed that fine-dressed girl,
He comes no longer to the wars with me,
And he has never shared the loot with me.
She has given him herbs I do not know,
And the wine of forgetting to the hero,
                              That fine-dressed girl.
Do not expect him soon, mother, my dear."
When pirates drop on you in black forest,
Do not fear them, my brother, my dear,
Cry out to Andrijaš to your brother,
Though you will call in vain to me, brother,
When they hear you call my name,
                              The cursed pirates,
Heroes will scatter from before your face,
As they have always scattered, my brother,
Whenever they have heard you call my name.
And may your beloved companions see
That you murdered your brother without cause.'[126]

---

[126] 'Jeda mi te mogu, mili brate, umoliti, / Nemoj to mi vaditi sabljice iz srdašca, / Mili brajene, / Dokle ti ne naručam do dvi i do tri beside. / Kada dojdeš, kneže Marko, k našoj majci junačkoj, / Nemoj to joj, ja te molim, kriva dila učiniti, / I moj dil ćeš podati, kneže Marko, našoj majci, / Zašto si ga nigdar veće od mene ne dočeka. / Ako li te bude mila majka uprašati, / Viteže Marko: / " 'Što mi ti je, sinko, sabljica sva krvava?' " / Nemoj to joj, mili brate, sve istinu kazovati, / Ni naju majku nikako zlovoljiti, / Da reci to ovako našoj majci junačkoj: / " 'Susrite me, mila majko, jedan tihi jelenčac, / Koji mi se ne hti sa drumka ukloniti, / Junačka majko, / Ni on meni, mila majko, ni ja njemu, / I tuj stavši potrgoh moju sablju junacku, / I udarih tihoga jelenka u srdašce. / I kada ja pogledah onoga tiha jelenka, / Gdi se htiše na drumku s dušicom razdiliti, / Vide mi ga milo biše kako

This drama of the sound of a dead brother's name coming to
rescue the brother who had killed him can be 'explained' in
many of its details by customs and beliefs belonging to different
centuries and places. When Andrijaš pleads that his share of the
loot, together with what she herself is entitled to, be given to
their mother, the singer takes his fourteenth-century feudal
princes into a much more homely, relevant and dramatic
context of sixteenth-century life under the Turkish rule, the
life of the destitute Christian patriarchal communities for whom
plunder was a major branch of national economy and outlawry
often the only means of physical survival. The actual historical
social norms of these communities included the obligation to
share the loot with one's own family as well as with the family
of the outlaw who had been killed in action. Another, more
personal aspect of the patriarchal moral image of the world is
embodied in Andrijaš's concern that their mother must be
spared the knowledge that one of her sons had killed the other.
Andrijaš advises Marko to explain the blood on his sword by
telling their mother that he had killed a deer—the most
generous sacred animal which, in ancient pagan belief preserved
in much later customs,[127] was prepared to sacrifice its own life

mojega brajena, / Tihoga jelenka, / I da bi mi na povrate, ne bih ti ga
zagubio.' " / I kada te jošće bude naju majka uprašati: / " 'Da gdi ti je,
kneže Marko, tvoj brajen Andrijašu?' " / Ne reci mi našoj majci istine po
ništore: / " 'Ostao je,—reci,—junak, mila majko, u tujoj zemlji, / Iz koje se
ne može od milin-ja odiliti, / Andrijašu. / Onde mi je obljubio jednu
gizdavu devojku. / I odkle je junak tuj devojku obljubio, / Nikad veće nije
pošal sa mnome vojevati / I sa mnome nije veće ni plinka razdilio. / Ona
t' mu je dala mnoga bil-ja nepoznana / I onoga vinca junaku od zabitja, /
Gizdava devojka. / Li uskori mu se hoćeš, mila majko, nadijati.' " / A kad
na te napadu gusari u crnoj gori / Nemoj to se prid njimi, mili brate pripad-
nuti / Da iz glasa poklikni brajena Andrijaša, / Bud' da me ćeš zaman, brate,
pri potrebi klikovati. / Kada mi te začuju moje ime klikujući, / Kleti gusari,
/ Taj čas će od tebe junaci razbignuti, / Kako su se vazdakrat, brajene,
razbigovali / Kada su te začuli moje ime klikovati. / A neka da ti vidi tvoja
ljubima družina, / Koji me si, tvoga brata, bez krivine zagubio!' *Pantić*,
pp. 44–6 (*Bogišić*, No. 6, ll. 18–66—in fact l. 67 as l. 40 is missing). Cf. P.
Hektorović, *Ribanye i ribarscho prigovaranye*, ff. 12r–13v.

[127] The deer was deemed a sacred animal among many nations—in Asia
Minor from the second half of the third millennium BC. In a Serbian legend
the deer is represented as a sacred animal devoted even to the people who
fail to observe its sanctity. This is the significance of the story about a
sacrificial stone in Jablanica near Petrova Gora which had to be sprinkled

for the sake of the people who failed to offer it due sacrifice. This association provides a magnificent background for two dramatic aspects of Andrijaš's monologue: the generosity of his forgiveness as well as the enormity of Marko's crime. And when Andrijaš demands that his absence be explained to the mother by the fact that he had fallen in love with 'a fine-dressed girl' in 'a foreign land' we are faced again with a paradox in which personal feelings seem to triumph over the actual moral norm in a way in which the patriarchal sense of love and its obligations is not denied but enriched and strengthened. For the assumption is that the mother might be consoled by the personal happiness of her son, even if this happiness involves a moral and economic betrayal of his basic obligations to his native community; a great epic hero has certainly no business to chase 'fine-dressed girls' in 'foreign lands'.

Finally, the pirates in the black wood—in the scene in which the patriarchal outlaw ideal of brotherly love finds its simplest and most moving expression—also come from history which must have been very near to the singer's eyes and heart. For if it is true that pirates had never been seen before, or since, in Marko Kraljević's homeland (see Map 1), they were the scourge of the Adriatic in the sixteenth century. It was in this century that the African Berbers and the Turkish pirates from Albania became operative in the Adriatic;[128] moreover, the border raiders from Senj, controlled by Austrians, were engaged in plundering Venetian and Turkish lands,[129] and the regular Venetian and Turkish naval units were also engaged in legalized piracy, particularly in times of food shortage.[130] And, more particularly, the Turkish devastation of Hvar in 1539—which inspired Hektorović to write his most moving lines in a

---

every year by a sheep's blood in the recognition of the holiness of the great deer with golden horns—the deer who came in order to be sacrificed himself when people failed to observe this custom. The deer's sacrifice was probably a pledge of good harvest. See Š. Kulišić, P. Ž. Petrović, N. Pantelić, *Srpski mitološki rečnik*, p. 160.

[128] See B. Hrabak, 'Dubrovnik i rodski pirati', *Istoriski glasnik*, Belgrade, No. 2 (1956), p. 1.

[129] See G. Stanojević, *Senjski uskoci*, Belgrade, 1973, pp. 95–141.

[130] See B. Hrabak, 'Gusarstvo i presretanje pri plovidbi u Jadranskom i Jonskom moru u drugoj polovini xv veka', *Vesnik vojnog muzeja*, Belgrade, iv (1957), p. 97.

description of his escape in a ship on a dark night[131] may have also been even more immediately appreciated in the social setting of singers like Paskoje Debelja, among people who were hardly in a position to leave the island for a long time or to use the occasion to cultivate their literary tastes in Renaissance Italy.

The diverse social, historical, and moral settings, customs and beliefs in this, the greatest of all *bugarštice*, illustrate the possibilities of achievement when the singer works in anachronistic and 'anatopistic' material, exploiting the dramatic possibilities of a rich and conflicting historical heritage. For it is the outlaw customs and gestures in this poem which instil blood into a high feudal drama of the struggle for seniority; and this is how the great patriarchal ideal of brotherly love comes to imaginative life beyond the frontiers of historical needs and realities. Moreover, the tragic climax of the story demands that the pirates appear where they have never been seen before or since, but the singer's sense of the nature of what he has to say is so strong that all his 'mistakes', all the anachronisms and anatopisms in his story, work for him, providing the warp and woof of a great imaginative pattern in a moving song about the possibilities and frustrations of brotherly love. For if Paskoje Debelja, Hektorović's 'good and upright husband', might have been, and must have been, unaware of many aspects of the background of his story—of Article 48 of Emperor Stefan Dušan's *Code*, of the distance of the coast from Marko Kraljević's homeland, of the ancient belief in the holiness of the deer—he knew at least how to make them speak with a hundred tongues, expressing what he must have felt as the ultimate in human love.

The 'anachronistic' nature of his achievement is not surprising: it worked itself out in the language of oral conventions which took a long time to develop in a migratory culture. (See Map 4.) But the tragic structure of the story and the overwhelmingly moaning voice of all *bugarštice* seem to mirror as much the history of the disasters of medieval Christian lands in the Balkans as the actual position of the feudal oral epics which were uprooted from their 'high' social setting and dying in a

---

[131] Hektorović describes this escape in his epistle to Nikola Nalješković in 1541. See P. Hektorović, 'Odgovor Nikoli Nalješkoviću', *Ribanje i ribarsko prigovaranje i razlike stvari ine*, pp. 243–5.

much 'lower' alien environment. For it is certainly true that all
the other sporadic achievements in the tradition of *bugarštice*—
and this is what makes them so different from the decasyllabic
oral epics—are to be found exclusively in desperate narrative
contexts. To begin with there are only two more examples of
bugarštice which hold together as epic wholes, with a certain
degree of narrative and tonal coherence, and they bewail the
Serbian and the Hungarian defeats respectively in two
important battles on the field of Kosovo. The first of these two
poems 'The Song of the Battle of Kosovo'—recorded by the
Dubrovnik poet Jozo Betondić (1709–64) either in the peninsula
of Pelješac where he lived for a time or on the island of Šipan
which he sometimes visited—tells the story of Prince Lazar's
disaster in 1389.[132] Admittedly, Prince Lazar seems to lead a
Hungarian army in this poem, which suggests, of course, that
the singer has simply confused two historical occasions—the
two battles of Kosovo fought in 1389 and 1448 respectively.
Besides, most of the motifs of this song will grow later into
separate and superior decasyllabic songs.[133] And yet, this
bugarštica, unlike so many others, tells its tale with a moving if
simple coherence. It opens in highly formulaic language with a
scene in a Serbian 'white palace',[134] with its view of 'a bright
dawn'[135] and 'the clear sky',[136] soon to be blurred by an
ominous dream, also a standard narrative device. Then there
are tears streaming down the 'red white face'[137] of Prince
Lazar's wife, his appearance on a 'good horse'[138] and the
readiness of the Jugovići to use their 'battle lances',[139] 'the
black earth'[140] waiting impatiently to receive the victims. And,

[132] 'Popijevka o kosovskom boju', *Pantić*, pp. 118–24 (*Bogišić*, No. 1).

[133] The pleading of Prince Lazar's wife to have one of her brothers stay
with her, the supper with the exchange of toasts and accusations of treason,
the spying on the Turkish army, Miloš's assassination of the Turkish Sultan
Murad, the treason of Vuk Branković, the defeat of the Serbian army—all
these are subjects of the later decasyllabic songs. See below pp. 159–70.

[134] 'Bijeli dvor', *Pantić*, p. 118 (*Bogišić*, No. 1, l. 3). See note 51, pp. 43–4.

[135] 'Svijetla zorica', *Pantić*, p. 118 (*Bogišić*, No. 1, l. 4).

[136] 'Vedro nebo' *Pantić*, p. 118 (*Bogišić*, No. 1, l. 5). See note 91, p. 48.

[137] 'Rumeno bijelo lišce', *Pantić*, p. 120 (*Bogišić*, No. 1, l. 69). See note 28,
p. 40.

[138] 'Konj dobri', *Pantić*, p. 121 (*Bogišić*, No. 1, l. 112). See note 31, p. 40.

[139] 'Bojna kopja', *Pantić*, p. 121 (*Bogišić*, No. 1, l. 108). See note 64, p. 45.

[140] 'Crna zemlja', *Pantić*, p. 121 (*Bogišić*, No. 1, l. 107). See note 75, p. 47.

finally, there is treason and 'the living heart' of Prince Lazar's wife 'breaks'[141] when she learns the sad news about the national catastrophe. The second of these two *bugarštice* 'Duke Janko Flees Before the Turks'[142]—recorded in the area of the Bay of Kotor about the middle of the eighteenth century—describes the Hungarian defeat which has given rise to a still current Serbian proverb defining the ultimate in disaster.[143] There are no striking ineptitudes or absurdities in the story: it opens with the vision of 'a clear dawn'[144] and a wounded soldier who comes to tell Duke Janko (John Hunyadi) about the defeat of his army and the advancing Turks. The despair of Duke Janko's flight is conjured up in his moving prayer:

> 'Give me, my God, silent dew in the plain,
> > All-seeing God!
> Silent dew in the plain, grey fog in the mountain.'[145]

In the same moving formula God grants the prayer:

> And God gave silent dew in the plain,
> > To the hero in his trouble,
> Silent dew in the plain, grey fog in the mountain.[146]

What could express the victims' sense of history better than the prayer for the dew and the fog?

In a similar way a miraculous element is the only grain of poetry in the chaff of the much poorer song about two brothers Stjepan and Mitar Jakšić. While the two brothers are happily riding through a green wood, Mitar suddenly threatens to kill Stjepan, accusing him of having raped his wife. Stjepan swears to his innocence which is miraculously confirmed by water

---

[141] '(Bješe jom se od žalosti) živo srce raspuknulo', *Pantić*, p. 124 (*Bogišić*, No. 1, l. 253 [255]).

[142] 'Vojvoda Janko bježi pred Turcima', *Bogišić*, No. 25.

[143] See note 71, p. 29.

[144] 'Jasna zora', No. 25, ll. 1, 2.

[145] 'Dopust′ meni, moj Bože, tihu rosu u ravnini, / Moj vidovni Bože! / Tihu rosu u ravnini, sinju maglu u planini.' *Bogišić*, No. 25, ll. 37–9 ('ravnici' corrected to 'ravnini 'as in the manuscript iv a. 30 in Yugoslav Academy of Sciences and Arts [Jugoslovenska akademija znanosti i umjetnosti], Zagreb).

[146] 'Bog mu bješe dopustio tihu rosu u ravnini, / Nevoljnu junaku, / Tihu rosu u ravnini, sinju maglu u planini.' Ibid., ll. 43–5.

rushing forth from 'the cold marble'[147] and yellow blossom blooming on 'a dry maple tree'.[148] And it is this which, in spite of the slightly absurd initial setting, makes us grasp the enormity and the perversity of the slander in a dramatically meaningful way. For it is not, of course, coincidental that water in the mountain, which had always been a means of survival for those who had to take to the woods, and the maple tree, embodying the cult of the ancestors and supplying wood for the *gusle*,[149] save a human life in a miraculous way in such extremity.

And it is also significant that this miraculous element often lives as great poetry in the dirges and utterances of personal grief in some of the *bugarštice*. The greatest of these examples and one of the finest gems in Bogišić's collection is to be found in a poem about a girl's prayer to 'all-seeing God', which is only formally in the epic tradition:

> 'God, do not kill me by living desire,
>   All-seeing God,
> By living desire do not kill me.'[150]

This voice of unhappy love reaches hope through despair when the girl goes on praying to be changed into 'a supple fir-tree',[151] to have her hair turned into 'clover'[152] and her eyes into springs of 'clear water',[153] so that she could offer her lover a shade for his rest, food for his horse, water for his thirst. As the sentiment is so selfless, is it surprising that the prayer is granted?

But it would be difficult to quote many more examples of a spark of poetic genius in *bugarštice*, particularly outside the miraculous context. Perhaps nothing short of miracles could bring to life the feudal epic voice which had been uprooted from its natural setting and developed such a narrative and

---

[147] 'Mramor studen', *Bogišić*, No. 41, l. 36. The same formulaic expression (including the variant 'mramor studen kami') is also found in ll. 17, 21, 23, 28, 31.

[148] 'Javor suhi', ibid., l. 37. The same formulaic expression including the variant 'suho drvo javorovo' is also found in ll. 18, 22, 24, 29.

[149] See above p. 1.

[150] 'Nemoj mene, moj Bože, živom željom umoriti, / Moj vidovni Bože, / Živom željom umoriti . . .', *Bogišić*, No. 83, ll. 4–7.

[151] 'Vita jela', ll. 13, 19. See above p. 49.

[152] 'Trava djetelina', ll. 15, 21.   [153] 'Bistra voda', ll. 16, 22.

tonal stammer in its new urban and commercial environment, so alien to its basic spirit. The first symptoms of this progressive paralysis of *bugarštice* can be traced from the first recorded songs. It is in this respect, perhaps, that 'Duke Radosav of Severin and Vlatko of Vidin', the song which Hektorović wrote down from Nikola Zet, his 'young and fine-dressed' fisherman, is of some historical interest. The general setting of the poem seems to suggest the rivalries of Christian feudal lords on the eve of the Turkish invasion of the Balkans. For both Turnu Severin and Vidin were important fortresses on the Danube; Vidin was in fact the old Bulgarian capital which was captured after the Turkish victory over the Hungarian armies in the Battle of Nikopolje in 1396. But the interpolation of the later and 'lower' outlaw elements in this high feudal story is completely unlike the dramatic interplay of anachronisms in 'Marko Kraljević and His Brother Andrijaš'. And it is, in fact, as an illustration of the 'anachronistic' flaw, more frequently characteristic of oral epics than the dramatic interplay of diverse elements belonging to different times and places, that this poem is particularly interesting.

It opens with Duke Radosav's farewell to his 'white city'[154] of Turnu Severin; troubled with a vague foreboding, the great duke wonders whether he will ever come to see his city again. But in the ensuing scene the duke sits down to drink wine with his company in the outlaw setting of a 'black wood'.[155] In the same 'outlaw' key he instructs his entourage not to rob the approaching Turkish merchants but only to buy some wine from them. At this moment, however, the singer lets down the narrative expectations roused by the story and the appearance of the Turkish merchants and introduces what is in fact a different tale in which Duke Radosav of Severin comes to fight his opponent, the much more powerful feudal Duke Vlatko of Vidin. Their fight is seen in terms of single combat in a feudal tournament: Duke Vlatko places his 'slender lance'[156] between the ears of his 'swift horse',[157] Radosav makes the appropriate move, deftly evades the blow and cuts the lance with his sword.

---

[154] 'Beli grad', *Pantić*, p. 47 (*Bogišić*, No. 49, ll. 4, 5).
[155] 'Crna gora', *Pantić*, p. 47 (*Bogišić*, No. 49, ll. 15–16).
[156] 'Vito kopje', *Pantić*, p. 48 (*Bogišić*, No. 49, l. 53).
[157] 'Brzi konj', *Pantić*, p. 48 (*Bogišić*, No. 49, l. 53).

Vlatko is so impressed by Radosav's chivalric skill and the courage he has displayed that he offers to take him into his service. Radosav, taking up the offer, disarms, but the grand epic ambitions of this moment are immediately dispelled as Vlatko, quite unexpectedly, orders his hands tied! Less unexpectedly, perhaps, Radosav comments on Vlatko's treachery and makes broad hints about the sexual habits of his 'love'. Is this meant to explain why Vlatko has Radosav executed? If so, it goes against the grain of the whole narrative in which we saw Radosav in a completely different light.

In short, what begins as a dignified feudal farewell suddenly dissolves into an outlaw scene, to be followed by another story in which a chivalric duel ends in a trick, an insult, and a murder. The two grand scenes—Radosav's farewell to his city and the duel which promises to turn enemies into friends—are lost in the stammer of moral, social, and narrative confusion. This reflects the singer's ineptitude, his lack of experience and/or gift, his inability to blend the diverse social customs and settings of his story in a humanly and dramatically significant way. But it also mirrors a highly characteristic social and historical dislocation of an earlier form of feudal epic singing which struggles for survival in an urban Adriatic setting, distant from its roots and hardly congenial to its spirit. In most *bugarštice* we are faced with similar remnants of a 'higher' epic diction which fails to adapt itself to its social and historical 'downgrading'. This is what makes most of these poems such confused and heavy reading in comparison with the narrative ease and clarity of the later decasyllabic songs.

The confusion of the historical settings, facts, and customs in many *bugarštice* is significant, not because an epic singer could not be 'pardoned' a factual error, but because his 'mistakes' blur the moral and narrative outlines of the story and result in a confused and meaningless image of history. Instead of an imaginative interpretation of history, of a creative interplay of the present with all that is embedded in the language of an oral tradition, we get an absurd collage. The flourish of factual errors is significant, in short, as a symptom of a wider historical, moral, and imaginative confusion. It is in this sense that it may be worth noting that in one *bugarštica* the Serbian Despot Stefan Lazarević (*c.* 1370–1427), who had no children, is represented as the father of the great Hungarian hero John Hunyadi (1378–1456), a man only about eight years younger than himself![158] In another *bugarštica* the Hungarian King Matijaš comes to ask the Ban of Bosnia to visit him on the day of his family patronal festival ('slava')—denoting a custom which has never been observed in Hungarian families.[159] The Hungarian King Vladislav—who was killed at the Battle of Varna in 1444—comes to die in a battle of Kosovo,[160] perhaps in the one fought before he was born, but, more probably, in the other one, which was fought after he had been dead for some time. And it is easy to imagine what happens when the singer steps into the wider international scene and different times, manners, and customs of a vast area stretching from the Levant and the Black Sea to Russia, Poland, and Austria: the basic logical and factual expectations of singing about history are mocked, particularly in the songs which masquerade as chronicles, by an absurd correlation of historical facts, social idiom and costume.[161]

However, the grand epic diction of the *bugarštice*, equally ill-adjusted for major topics of Balkan and international feudal history, runs into even greater trouble when the singer applies it to contemporary local events which he sees in absurd international proportions. Thus the inhabitants of the small town of Perast appear to wage the major seventeenth-century European wars against the Ottoman Empire not quite alone. The Knights of Malta, the Croats, the Venetians, the Italians, and the Spaniards are also there to help them liberate Herceg-Novi from the Turks. The Christian side—in what was in fact a major episode in these wars—is also supported by the forces of the neighbouring city of Kotor; and, as one would expect, the malicious Kotorans—who were 'cowardly' and easily 'frightened',[162] who 'cheated' [163] and 'betrayed'[164] their friends—

[158] See *Bogišić*, No. 8.
[159] *Bogišić*, No. 12, l. 36. On family patronal festival see Appendix IV.
[160] *Bogišić*, No. 29.
[161] See, for instance, the *bugarštice* on the Battle of Levant (1571) and the siege of Vienna (1683), *Bogišić*, Nos. 57, 58.
[162] 'Plašivi', *Bogišić*, No. 73, l. 62. Bogišić reads tentatively 'u boju (?) plašivi'; Pantić's reading 'u barzo plašivi' suggests 'quickly frightened'—see Balović-Pantić, No. 153.
[163] 'Prijevaru učiniše', ibid., l. 64.   [164] 'Nevjeru učiniše', ibid., l. 66.

provide an important centre of moral interest. It is not, perhaps, insignificant that this poem was written down in the Balović Manuscript at the end of the seventeenth century in the neighbouring town of Perast.[165]

This dislocation of historical perspective in which the anachronistic and 'anatopistic' elements are not a source of dramatic tension but of absurd epic distortions of historical fact is also marked by the inconsistency of moral and imaginative sympathies which is most clearly reflected in the narrative stammer, making such stories difficult to follow and their sporadic sparks of epic life hard to spot and enjoy. Such discrepancies were as inevitable in *bugarštice* as they are in the more recent twentieth-century decasyllabic poems in which we are faced, for instance, with Professor Milman Parry drinking 'cool wine' in the 'Hotel Imperial' in Dubrovnik.[166] Similar poetic catastrophe is inevitable when a twentieth-century *vila* addresses Lazar the headmaster instead of Lazar the Prince.[167] In short, the downgrading of a grand heroic diction seems to make it suitable only for mock-heroic purposes.

But it is perhaps more to the point to remember that the great debris of the feudal epic diction of *bugarštice* also left its bequest of a heap of historical themes and motifs, dozens of narrative and stylistic devices, hundreds of formulaic phrasal patterns and formulas which came to their second epic innocence in the later decasyllabic village singing. For Bogišić— who wrote about *bugarštice* with more insight and wisdom than anyone before or since—was fundamentally right in his judgement of the two oral epic traditions in the Serbo-Croat language:

[165] See 'Predgovor', *Bogišić*, p. 133.

[166] 'Milman Parry set off from the harbour, / To the 'Hotel Imperial' he came, / Here he sat to take his ease, / And drank enough cool wine.' ('Milman Parry s pristaništa pođe, / Pa u hotel Imperial dođe. / Tu je sjeo pa se odmorijo, / I ladna se vina napojio', A. B. Lord, *The Singer of Tales*, p. 273).

[167] '*Vila* calls headmaster of the school: / "O, Professor, O you young headmaster, / Can't you see what will happen now?" / . . . Lazar wanted to obey the *vila*, / Shut the roll book, put it in the archives.' ('Vila zove direktora škole: "Profesore, direktore mladi, / Zar ne vidiš o čemu se radi?" / . . . Htjede Lazar da posluša vilu, / Sklopi dnevnik, stavi u arhivu.' Lazo-Car Kujundžić, 'Kragujevački Oktobar', *Narodne pjesme*, pp. 3, 4 [no indication of publisher, place or date of publication, a copy of this book can be found in the National Library in Sarajevo]). For *vila*, see Appendix III.

What most strikes the eye is that they [*bugarštice*] have withered, become somehow flaccid, as compared to the living vigour and vitality of the decasyllables; what then we notice is the lack of genuine beauty, the lack of any plan and of any artistic and logical interweaving of particular elements as well as the lack of natural and logical denouement of the narration.[168]

But what plan, vigour, and denouement could one expect in the tales of an older form of feudal epic singing, uprooted from its natural environment and fumbling for survival in the backwaters of the Adriatic urban settings which had far more vigorous literary expressive forms of their own?

---

[168] 'Predgovor', *Bogišić*, p. 61. This judgement has been challenged with more vehemence than insight by N. Ljubinković (see 'Narodne pesme dugog stiha', *Književna istorija*, iv (1972), pp. 573–601; v (1972), pp. 18–41; v (1973), pp. 453–79).

3. The New Voice: in Dalmatia

At the end of the seventeenth century, or just a little later, an unknown hand wrote down nine *bugarštice* and fifteen decasyllabic songs in the small town of Perast in the Bay of Kotor. Two of the decasyllabic songs in this, the so-called Balović manuscript are variants of two *bugarštice* and all of them deal with local historical subjects. In a later, the so-called Mazarović manuscript, dated 1775 and also written in this area, there are both oral and literary compositions; it contains no *bugarštice*, but several of its decasyllabic songs deal with the same local historical subjects which were treated in the *bugarštice* of the earlier Perast manuscript.[1] Both these manuscripts were preserved in the houses of distinguished and educated families —the first one in the patrician family of the Balovići, whose members published books in Italian on local Perast architecture and history.

For Perast was at this time, on the one hand, a Venetian patrician commune ruled by Slav families, with a Franciscan school and a few hundred sailors and fishermen, some well-off merchants, and distinguished Venetian naval officers. On the other hand, however, Perast was also the seat of Slav border fighters and outlaws, often recruited into regular Venetian military units, particularly when heavy fighting was going on along the Dalmatian borders: during the Candian War (1645–1669) in which Turks captured Candia, the capital of Crete and the last Venetian stronghold in the Levant, and, a little later, during the Morean War (1684–99) in which the Venetian Republic gained control of all the Peloponnese (Morea). It was at this time that the Montenegrin outlaws in the Bay of Kotor took part in the fighting of the Venetian military units which in 1687 liberated Herceg-Novi, the fortified town which commands the entrance into the Bay. But as the local fighters had no source of income during the time of peace, they often lived on private enterprise by raiding the neighbouring Turkish territories.

[1] See note 12, p. 35.

So there was no shortage of material for epic singing; and the double—patrician and outlaw—social setting of the town of Perast provided the soil on which the feudal *bugarštice* and the village decasyllabic songs lived together in close contact. It is in this sense that the comparison of the Perast *bugarštice* with their decasyllabic variants is particularly interesting. For we are not faced here only with the unity of a number of formulas, formulaic patterns, narrative and stylistic devices, or the repetition or elaboration of a sporadic theme, but with very similar stories sometimes told in closely parallel phrasing.

So for instance one of these *bugarštice* tells the story of how the honourable young men of Perast punished a nasty Spanish duke who dishonoured two orphan girls: they raped his wife before his eyes and 'tore off'[2] his mouth to keep the memory of his lust alive and make him the target of ridicule of his countrymen. This crude incrustation of local detail into a degenerating feudal epic form is as characteristic as the way in which the story is told; from the very beginning it reads like a word-for-word translation from a dead language:

When the Spanish abode in the strong city of Novi,
For a short time,
To dishonest deeds of evil those Spanish accustomed,
One day Don Carlos the Duke went off,
The horse duke,
To go off with horsemen, to visit all his land,
That day two orphan girls of Perast came along,
Two maid-servants
Came about their business where their master had sent them.[3]

The poetic stammer of this utterance, the sluggish and uncertain movement of the line, the obscure turns of phrase searching for each other, contrast with the clarity of a decasyllabic version of this story which was found in the later Perast manuscript:

[2] 'Otkinuše (ta sramotna svoja justa)', *Bogišić*, No. 59, l. 74 [73].
[3] 'Kad Španjoli ulodžahu u tvrdome Novome gradu / Za kratko vrijeme. / U zulume nepoštene ti Španjoli obiknuti, / Jedan danak otide ta Don Karlo vojevoda, / Konjska vojevoda, / S konjicima otiti, da pohodi svu državu, / Ta' se danak namjeriše dvije Peraške orfane, / Dvije službenice, / Koje bijahu poslom došle, đe ih gospodar poslao.' *Bogišić*, No. 59, ll. 1–9 ('konjcima' corrected to 'konjicima' and 'taj' to 'ta'' as in Balović-Pantić, No. 155).

When the Spanish took the city of Novi,
They took and held that city a short time,
And they did shameful evil deeds in it.
One day the Duke, Don Carlos the Duke,
Who was horse duke, went to visit his land,
With horsemen of his company, his knights,
On that day two orphaned maid-servants
Of Perast, without father or mother,
Came by, being sent by their masters.[4]

This may not be great poetry; and, indeed, all the barbarous
elements—including the dishonouring of the Duke's wife and
the 'cutting off'[5] of his mouth—will be also found here. But this
is much clearer speech: 'they did shameful evils there' instead
of 'to dishonest deeds of evil those Spanish accustomed'. The
fluency of a more natural word order reflects the ease and
vigour of the new folk epic idiom.

Besides, the decasyllabic version substitutes the homely
sirota ('poor', 'without parents') for the foreign *orfana* ('orphan')
which sounds very artificial in a Serbo-Croatian epic line. And
when we are told next that the two girls were 'without father
or mother',[6] we may well ask if there is anything more obvious
to be said about two orphans. But this is not only one of the
commonest phrases in the language, it is also the beginning of
the natural growth of what will often be used later as a great
epic formula. For the phrase—'without father or mother'—is
a tragic echo of the patriarchal cult of one of the basic family
relationships, as characteristic of the Balkan village civilization
during the Turkish rule as of its epic singing. And, indeed, this
phrase provides a formulaic pattern of a description of a hero
in another decasyllabic poem written down in the vicinity of

[4] 'Kad Španjuli Novi grad uzeše, / Uzeše ga za malo vrijeme, / I zulume
sramotne činjahu. / Jedan danak vojvoda Don Karlo, / Koji bješe konjski
vojevoda, / I on pođe pohodit državu, / S konjicima svojijem vitezovom; /
Ta se danak bjehu namjerile, / Dvije sirote brez oca i majke, / Službenice
to bjehu peraške, / Koje poslaše svoji gospodari'. *Bogišić*, No. 60, ll. 1–12
('države' corrected to 'državu', 'dv'je' to 'dvije' as in Mazarović–Pantić,
No. 486)

[5] '(I sramotna justa) osijecaju', *Bogišić*, No. 60, l. 85 (owing to a mistake
in counting this line is correctly marked even if l. 71 is missing—cf.
Mazarović–Pantić, No. 486).

[6] 'Brez oca i majke', *Bogišić*, No. 60, l. 9.

in the eighteenth century; the fighter is no more
usually was in *bugarštice*, as one of the 'young noble-
a 'fine-dressed hero',[8] but as a lonely man:

> Who has no mother, knows no faithful love,
> Whose mountain-cloak is the house that he lives in,
> His sword and gun—his father and mother.[9]

The whole of this formulaic pattern—used here to describe a
vizier's muster of his army—originates from and will be soon
attached to the predicament of Christian border fighters and
outlaws.[10] It mirrors a different historical situation and conjures
up a new decasyllabic epic landscape of desperate heroic zest—
even if it will come to full flower only in the early nineteenth-
century poems where it will be interwoven with the imagery of
hawks among the clouds living in the freedom of the skies.[11]

In this growth of a formulaic pattern—which comes to mirror
several centuries of national history in the personal predicament
of the hero—its basic constituent elements are deeply affected.
Thus the traditional 'faithful love'—as common in *bugarštice* as
in the decasyllabic poems[12]—is no more a grand feudal lady
waiting for her lord in one of 'the white palaces';[13] her absence
and the fact that the hero has no mother, father, or home define
the human destitution of an outlaw who has nothing to lose,
no one to love or to be loved by. And it will not be very long
before we shall come to see a queen-mother as a wise old
peasant woman claiming to be tired of washing the blood-
stained clothes of her heroic son Marko Kraljević and instructing
him to earn his living by ploughing instead of by highway
robbery.[14] We cannot tell whether the mother is really tired,
worried for the life of her son, or moved by a sense of justice.
But the shift of an older layer of social history into the living
environment of later outlawry and the village patriarchal
feeling makes the historical 'blunder' irrelevant—for after all

---

[7] 'Mladi gospodičići', *Bogišić*, No. 32, ll. 6, 43 (owing to different
arrangement of lines these are ll. 4, 37 in PS, No. 5).

[8] 'Gizdav junak', *Bogišić*, No. 37, l. 1; No. 52, l. 35; No. 83, l. 7.

[9] 'Koji svoje ne imade majke, / A za vjerne ljubi i ne znade; / Komu no
je kuća kabanica, / Mač i puška i otac i majka.' *Bogišić*, No. 102, ll. 11–14.

[10] See below p. 83. [11] See below pp. 238–9.

[12] See note 84, p. 48. [13] See note 51, pp. 43–4.

[14] See *Gesemann*, No. 102; *Karadžić*, ii, No. 73.

the ultimate aim of epic poetry is not to root a moral vision in the so-called 'facts' of a particular period of social and political history.

In a long tradition of epic singing which involves social changes the epic language grows into a kind of memory of history which plays upon the singer's sense of his historical present. As we have seen, many of the formulas and formulaic patterns of the feudal *bugarštice* were easily absorbed into the later decasyllabic village singing. Apart from those which describe the appearance of the heroes, their arms and their horses, their journeys and their battles, their triumphs and their disasters,[15] there were also those describing persistent social customs: the wine-drinking or the holding of a council at the beginning of many poems, the wishes of mirth and health at the end.[16] Finally, there are such stylistic devices as Slavonic antithesis which do not depend strictly either on metrical conditions or on social setting and which can be found both in *bugarštice* and in the decasyllabic poems.[17] But sometimes, as we have seen, there were also difficulties: some double-epithet phrases had to be broken up to fit as single-epithet phrases into the shorter lines. Sometimes the basic rules of grammar were sacrificed so that a double-epithet phrase could be used and, occasionally, a double-epithet phrase was discarded, not for metrical but for social reasons: the imagination of the village singers saw the loot not in terms of 'uncounted small coins' but in terms of 'loads of treasure' or 'towers of groschen and ducats'.[18] Of course, this process of persistence and adaptation of the epic language was not as rational as it appears in an analysis which has the advantage of hindsight. While learning the technique of shortening phrases for decasyllabic purposes instead of lengthening them as he often had to do in *bugarštice*, the singer himself often did not know what he was really after and it is not surprising if we sometimes find him groping his way towards an uncertain aim. In this sense the song 'Ivo Senjanin Liberates Mihailo Desančić from Asan-aga's Prison', written down in the vicinity of Dubrovnik in the eighteenth century, is

[15] See above pp. 43–9.
[16] See note 107, pp. 50–1.
[17] See note 17, p. 38.
[18] See above pp. 40–2.

particularly interesting. It contains sixty-six decasyllabic lines and eighty-eight lines ranging from nine to fourteen syllables. The number of decasyllabics suggests only the general direction in which the singer was going; his uncertainty of his way and his fumbling are perhaps best illustrated not only by the great number of lines of differing lengths, but also by his double use of a preposition with a noun and its epithet—for instance in the line literally rendered:

Quickly they jump on [their] feet on heroic.[19]

This old stylistic habit of the *bugarštice*, which also recurs in later decasyllabic poems,[20] serves no metrical purpose here: it defeats the singer's basic aim of achieving decasyllabics because the line acquires a superfluous syllable.

But considering that so many of the formulaic and stock phrases of feudal *bugarštice* persist unchanged, that so few of them undergo any extensive social and semantic adjustment to the village setting, why is it that the voice of the Dalmatian decasyllabic songs strikes such a totally different poetic note? Much of this difference can be explained in terms of a more natural word order, of the new folk epic idiom which tells its story with the greater clarity and quicker movement of the short line—but it is also a matter of a different quality of folk epic imagination. For the decasyllabic imagination is also distinguished by its greater sense of mystery and its stronger emotional response to whatever it happens to be describing. One of the Dalmatian decasyllabic poems contains a line in which the singer invokes God or his audience to witness 'the great wonder' of his story,[21] a line which will become a standard formulaic opening in the decasyllabic songs.[22] They also abound

---

[19] 'Plaho skaču na noge na junačke', 'Ivo Senjanin oslobađa Mihaila Desančića iz tamnice Asan-agine', *Bogišić*, No. 108, l. 51.

[20] Bogišić points out that this feature of *bugarštice* is also characteristic of the Russian *byliny* (see 'Predgovor', *Bogišić*, pp. 20–1), but in old Russian it is also found in prose. For the discussion of examples from decasyllabic poems see T. Maretić, 'Metrika narodnih naših pjesama', *RAD JAZU*, clxx (1907), pp. 93–5.

[21] 'Mili bože, čuda velikoga' ('Kind God—a great wonder'), *Bogišić*, No. 100, l. 61.

[22] *Karadžić*, ii, No. 1, l. 1; No. 22, l. 1; No. 27, l. 1.

in 'great' or 'enormous troubles'[23] and 'terrible tears'[24] are much more lavishly shed in them. The 'banners' of the enemy's army are seen as 'clouds' which will also soon become for-mulaic.[25]

But the flights of the Dalmatian decasyllabic songs into the fantastic—reflecting a passionate, magic sense of natural environment and history—can be perhaps best appreciated if we compare the *bugarštica* and the decasyllabic poem telling the story of the liberation of Herceg-Novi in 1687. The long-winded *bugarštica*, recorded in Perast, begins its story by a characteristic flat statement:

When the general prepared to attack the city Novi . . .[26]

It sustains this key of prosaic information stuttering through two hundred and seventy-eight lines without a single imagin-ative spark, to tell us, eventually, that 'the stink of Mohammed' was driven from the Bay of Kotor.[27] However, the decasyllabic version of this poem, also recorded in Perast, tells the same story in a much more exciting way in only one hundred and thirteen much shorter lines. If this brevity is perhaps atypical—some of the decasyllabic songs are much longer than any *bugarštice*—the dramatic and imaginative compression of the opening lines is highly characteristic. Instead of being faced with a foreign-sounding general ('zenerao'), we witness an ominous dream of an innocent Turkish girl stitching her needlework on the threshold of this historical turmoil:

> Stitching her needlework a girl in Novi,
> In Novi, under a yellow orange-tree,
> Stitching her needlework she fell asleep,
> And in that sleep she saw a strange dream:
> The heavens breaking open above Novi,

[23] 'Velika' or 'golema nevolja', *Bogišić*, No. 100, l. 35; *Gesemann*, No. 83, l. 68; No. 124, l. 89; No. 134, ll. 6, 12; *Karadžić*, ii, No. 9, l. 70; No. 25, l. 90; No. 51, l. 33.

[24] 'Grozne suze', see notes 72 and 73, p. 46.

[25] 'A barjaci kako i oblaci', *Bogišić*, No. 116, l. 171 [172]; cf. *Karadžić*, ii, No. 50 (iv), l. 24; iv, No. 40, l. 31.

[26] 'Kad pripravi zerenao postupit' Novoga grada', *Bogišić*, No. 65, l. 1 ('žerenao' corrected to 'zerenao' as in Balović–Pantić, No. 158).

[27] '(Da) Muhamed (već) ne smrdi (u ove strane od svijeta)', ibid., l. 267.

The stars dropping down out of the sky,
Above the city fierce snakes flying.[28]

The imagery of the breaking skies, falling stars, and flying snakes foreshadows the approaching turmoil and expresses a magic relationship between the natural and the historical as much as the drama of an innocent girl caught in a historical whirlwind. In this sense it provides some of the great patterns which are characteristic of the later decasyllabic singing, even if the narrative device of a dream can also be found in some *bugarštice*.[29]

The same imaginative quality of the decasyllabic singing is also reflected in 'The German Ban and Duke Momčilo's Wife', inferior as this version is to the famous later 'Wedding of King Vukašin.' In this Dalmatian decasyllabic poem, recorded in the eighteenth century near Dubrovnik, we are again faced, though not at the beginning, with an ominous dream of helplessness—the dream which takes the form of a 'grey mist'[30] coiling, like a 'fierce snake',[31] around the hero's heart. The dream foreshadows the treachery of the hero's 'wretched love'[32] who burns the wings of the hero's horse so that he is left, at the critical moment of the battle, 'like a snake on a dry tree'.[33] And when the hero, finally, comes, fleeing for his life, to the gates of his city to find them closed by his treacherous wife, his sister will try in vain to help him by throwing a length of linen down the

[28] 'Vezak vezla Novkinja đevojka / U Novome pod žutom narančom; / Vezak vezla, mlada zadremala, / U sanku je čudan san vidjela: / Pod Novijem se nebo prelomilo, / A iz neba zvijezde padahu, / Ljute zmije nad grad letijahu', *Bogišić*, No. 66, ll. 1–7 ('devojka' corrected to 'đevojka' as in Balović-Pantić, No. 169).

[29] See note 77, p. 47.

[30] 'Sinja magla', *Bogišić*, No. 97, l. 39. This is a formulaic expression both in *bugarštice* and in the decasyllabic poems. See *Bogišić*, No. 25, ll. 39, 45; No. 35, ll. 32, 35; *Gesemann*, No. 131, ll. 1, 2.

[31] 'Ljuta zmija', *Bogišić*, No. 97, l. 41. This is a common formulaic expression in all of the epic tradition. See *Bogišić*, No. 58, ll. 5, 9, 10, 16; No. 66, l. 7. In the decasyllabic poetry it occurs very frequently in the description of a hero, 'shrieking like a fierce snake' ('ciknu . . . kako smija ljuta'), either ready to attack or in bitter woe. See *Gesemann*, No. 87, ll. 35, 132; No. 124, l. 122; *Karadžić*, ii, No. 25, l. 229; iii, No. 7, l. 212; iv, No. 33, l. 223.

[32] 'Nesrećna ljubovca', *Bogišić*, No. 97, ll. 82, 88.

[33] 'Kano zmija na drvetu suhu', ibid., l. 68.

walls, the linen which his wife cuts as he is trying to climb up the walls. This length of linen will become later a length of 'linen rag'—a traditional formula used in several poems to express the helplessness of a man trying to catch at a straw.[34]

Many of these dramatic narrative details will be found later in the famous 'Wedding of King Vukašin'; some of them—like the Ban's discovery that he had killed a better hero than himself, that Momčilo has 'two heroic hearts', one 'tired' and the other 'just beginning to dance'—will be found in other well-known poems.[35] But as regards the formulaic pattern of 'the grey mist' and 'the fierce snake', it is much more characteristic of the imaginative drama of decasyllabic singing, even if each of these expressions can be found separately in *bugarštice*.[36] For never in a *bugarštica* has a 'grey mist' appeared in a hero's dream and coiled, like 'a fierce snake', around his heart, to make such a fantastic starting-point for such a clear narrative. The dream will eventually come true in the story when the hero is killed, but what immediately follows it is the tragic irony of his brothers' consolation that 'dreams delude, God Himself is truth'.[37] For the line does not only tell us how much his brothers wish him well, it also provides a highly misleading narrative excitement which is peculiar only to the decasyllabic village singing. In short, this Dalmatian decasyllabic song suggests some of the imaginative quality and narrative excitement of the poetic voice of the decasyllabic village singing—far as it is from the ultimate epic achievements of 'The Wedding of King Vukašin'.

However, apart from reflecting the narrative ease of the new folk idiom, its formulaic and imaginative growth, the

[34] 'Krpa platna', *Karadžić*, ii, No. 25, ll. 219, 223, 235,; No. 57, l. 15; No. 78, l. 170. See below pp. 88–9, 130, 187.

[35] '(Al' u njemu) dva srca junačka, / (Jedno mu se srce) umorilo, / (A drugo se) ištom razigralo.' *Bogišić*, No. 97, ll. 99–101. Cf. *Karadžić*, ii, No. 67, ll. 254–8: 'Al' u Musi tri srca junačka, / Troja rebra jedna pod drugijem; / Jedno mu se srce umorilo, / A drugo se jako razigralo, / Na trećemu ljuta guja spava' ('There were three heroic hearts in Musa, / Three pairs of ribs one under the other; / One of his hearts was tired, / The second was dancing wildly, / And in the third a fierce snake was sleeping').

[36] See notes 30, 31, p. 74.

[37] 'San je klapnja, sam je Bog istina', *Bogišić*, No. 97, l. 47. The same proverb is repeated in slightly different wording in the much richer context of dramatic irony in *Karadžić*, ii, No. 25, l. 152. See below p. 129.

eighteenth-century Dalmatian decasyllabic songs also illustrate new interests and skills in handling a growing bulk of more and more lively epic material. Admittedly, some of them—like many of the luckless *bugarštice*—tell the stories of Russian, Austrian, and Venetian wars with Turkey; and as these wars take place in distant lands, little known to the village singer, one should not be surprised if occasionally the seas run red with Turkish blood all round the walls of Vienna.[38] But several of them bring in stories of outlaws and border raiders; even if fairly crude, these stories suggest the names of some important later epic heroes—such as Ivo of Senj, Novak and Radivoje.[39] Thus they reflect an interest in the epic material which was probably at the heart of the making of new folk epic idiom and which can be much more fully examined in the decasyllabic poems recorded in Slavonia at the beginning of the eighteenth century.[40] However, the new thematic interest and approaches of the village decasyllabic singing to its historical material are most richly reflected in the Dalmatian decasyllabic songs about Marko Kraljević.

The most popular epic hero among the Southern Slavs is no more, as in the first recorded *bugarštica*, just a casual peg for a great story about fratricide. One of these poems, in fact, seems to try to dispute the awkward epic tale of the *bugarštica* in which Marko was seen as such a rascal that he killed his brother because of a horse. But if in this poem—'Marko Kraljević Takes Revenge For the Death of His Brother Andrijaš Killed by the Turks'[41]—our hero only kills nine Turks and 'digs out' the black eyes of the girl who gave his brother wine to drink, in some of these poems he begins to emerge in the light which will make him such a fascinating epic figure in later times. The singer begins to come to grips with the historical fact that his greatest national hero was a Turkish vassal; and a sense of humour, so hopelessly lacking in *bugarštice*, is obviously needed for major epic discoveries in this direction. And indeed Marko

[38] See *Bogišić*, No. 114, ll. 27–30.

[39] See *Bogišić*, Nos. 106–11.

[40] See below, pp. 82–6.

[41] 'Marko Kraljević osveti brata Andrijaša koga mu Turci pogubiše', *Bogišić*, No. 89. Another variant of this poem was published from Karadžić's manuscripts in Ž. Mladenović, V. Nedić, eds., *Srpske narodne pjesme iz neobjavljenih rukopisa Vuka Stef. Karadžića*, Belgrade, 1974, ii, No. 47.

Kraljević begins to be seen in close contact with the Turks: l
defies them by dancing with Turkish girls and indulging in
wine-drinking, his favourite pastime, at the time of the Ramadan fast. When the sultan sends two constables to arrest him,
Marko proves that he is stronger than they are, but he still
obeys the summons. And when he appears before the sultan, the
sultan is so frightened that he gives him some money for wine—
and Marko seems to be appeased by his triumph.[42]

The zest of this new spirit of epic singing is perhaps more
significantly, if less obviously, reflected in the difference between
a *bugarštica* and the livelier of the two decasyllabic versions
which tell the story of Marko Kraljević's duel with Mina of
Kostur (Castoria).[43] In both these songs Marko Kraljević
enters Mina's house disguised as a monk, kills Mina and
releases his 'faithful love'. But the *bugarštica* makes no attempt
to exploit the comic resources of disguise and fraud. It is only in
the decasyllabic version that we see Marko Kraljević on Mount
Athos as a hero who 'has cut strange clothes for himself';[44] and
indeed the monks' black robes must look odd on this irascible
man of enormous stature. And when he turns up in this disguise
at Mina's house, his drinking and dancing bring out his
cunning:

> He began to dance a light monkish dance,
> But the windows shifted in their frames.[45]

He is no more a faded medieval knight as he was in the
bugarštica; he comes to life as a cunning club-wielding hero who
mirrors a peasant sense of humour and who will later provide
such fascinating possibilities of epic identification and growth
for the nineteenth-century Serbian rebels. And these possibilities
will be much more vigorously exploited in a nineteenth-century
version of his duel with Mina of Kostur which Karadžić will
write down from an anonymous singer.[46] In the Dalmatian
decasyllabic song they are still in the offing.

---

[42] See *Bogišić*, No. 90, ll. 36–42. See also below pp. 189–90.

[43] See *Bogišić*, Nos. 7, 86, 87.

[44] 'Čudnu ti je dolamu skrojio', *Bogišić*, No. 86, l. 110.

[45] 'Poče igrat' lako kaluđerski, / Al' pendžeri iz temelja kreću!' Ibid.,
ll. 165–6.

[46] *Karadžić*, ii, No. 62. See below, pp. 195–6.

And so in fact is everything else—with one major exception which tells the story of a great domestic drama. For it is only in 'The Wedding of Duke Pavle' that a major imaginative endeavour is fully sustained throughout a Dalmatian decasyllabic poem as a whole. The poem tells the story of a tragic wedding journey, promising happiness and ending in bloodshed. It opens with an image of fully-grown clover which must be immediately cut to provide food for the horses which have to travel through six forests—'three of firs and three of maples'.[47] In the patriarchal decasyllabic village singing evergreen firs are the trees of life, but sometimes tragically connected with youth and, more particularly, with young girls;[48] the maples—traditionally used for coffins and *gusle*—provide an equally ambiguous suggestion.[49] This ambiguity is sustained in the dance which the bride's mother leads with one hand, wiping her tears with the other. For the moment, of course, this may be taken as only the mixture of the mother's joy and sorrow at the prospect of her daughter's marriage. But when the daughter, longing for love, yet begs to be left at home, the ominous suggestions become more disturbing. They are resolved in the climax of the story when the girl dies in one of the six forests, her farewell words echoing her desperate desire:

'O Pavle, you were not my destiny!'[50]

At this moment the whole pattern of the story and its imagery falls together: the cut clover, the journey among the trees of life and death, the mother's tears in her dancing, the bride's reluctance to follow the beguiling promise of happiness. And the uncertainties come to rest in the closing lines which mirror the realities of traditional customs and their emblematic significance:

She was buried in her grave,
Round the grave a church was built,
Round the church a rose was planted,
Round the rose water was channelled,

[47] 'Tri jelove a tri javorove', *Bogišić*, No. 95, l. 11.
[48] For instance in *Karadžić*, ii, No. 5, ll. 1–9. See below pp. 113–15, 117.
[49] See above p. 1.
[50] 'O ti Pavle, moje nesuđenje!', *Bogišić*, No. 95, l. 108.

Who is pious, let him pray to God,
And who is fine, let him pluck the rose,
Who is thirsty, let him drink the water.[51]

On the one hand, these lines reflect some ancient rites and customs; fruit-trees, vines, and roses are among the most frequent plants on pagan graves: they embody the very old belief that they will offer rest to the human soul.[52] But in their more immediate poetic context these lines embody the rhythms of life and death and bring the story to its inevitable end.

This end, however, is also an imaginative beginning. Each of the phrases and each of the lines, themselves echoes of earlier customs and songs, will be repeated on similar occasions in later decasyllabic singing.[53] Moreover, some of the elements of these formulaic patterns will also be repeated and used as models for new variations, differing in meaning and syntactic

[51] 'Oni su je u grob ukopali, / Oko groba crkvu sagradili, / Oko crkve ružu nasadili, / Oko ruže vodu navratili; / Ko je devot, neka Boga moli, / Ko je gizdav, neka ružu bere, / Ko je žedan neka vodu pije.' Ibid., ll. 112–18.

[52] See V. Čajkanović, *Mit i religija u Srba*, pp. 6, 9.

[53] An earlier variant of two of these lines—summing up the tragedy of unfulfilled love in the images of a rose and water on a grave—was written down at the beginning of the eighteenth century in Slavonia: 'Tko e žedan neka vodu pie / Tkomu milo nek se ružom kiti' ('Who is thirsty, let him drink the water, / Who desires it, let him deck himself with roses'), *Gesemann*, No. 56, ll. 104–5. The grief of Duke Janko for his nephew Sekula—the frail, beautiful young man whom his sisters wanted to keep at home—is described in the lines which follow a similar formulaic pattern: 'I lepo ga Janko ukopao / I kod groba posadio glube / I kod glube izveo vodicu / Tko tie trudan neka počiva / Tko e žedan nek pie vodicu' ('And Janko buried him fine and well, / He put a bench beside the grave, / And channelled water beside the bench, / He that is weary, let him have rest, / And who is thirsty, let him drink the water'), *Gesemann*, No. 157, ll. 45–9. The 'bench' mirrors an ancient custom —the duty of the traveller to sit for a while, *paulisper assidere* as the Roman norm has it, when passing by a holy place (see V. Čajkanović, op. cit., p. 9). In fact, Čajkanović makes this point in connection with the analogous lines in 'The Wedding of Milić the Ensign' ('Ženidba Milića bajraktara', *Karadžić*, iii, No. 78): 'Saraniše lijepu đevojku . . . / Čelo glave vodu izvedoše, / Oko vode klupe pogradiše, / Posadiše ružu s obje strane: / Ko j' umoran, neka se odmara; / Ko je mlađan nek se kiti cv'jećem; / Ko je žedan neka vodu pije' ('And they buried the beautiful girl . . . / Above her head water was channelled, / Beside the water benches were set up, / They planted roses this side and that: / He that is weary, let him have rest; / Who is young, let him deck himself with flowers; / Who is thirsty, let him drink the water'), op. cit., ll. 192, 195–200.

structure.[54] But is it not also significant that in the eighteenth century—at the time of the recording of the Dalmatian decasyllabic songs—history seems to provide only a background for a great personal drama which only makes use of the form of an epic song? The voice of this drama and this song will be essential, however, when history comes to the epic foreground in the early nineteenth-century decasyllabic tales.

[54] Such a model—illustrating some semantic similarities, but also semantic and syntactic differences—is followed by the singer who describes the fears of two brothers that their prospective wives, 'foreign women' ('tuđe seje'), might spoil the harmony of their brotherly love: 'Baška će nam dvore pograditie, / Između njih trnje posaditi, / I kroz trnje vodu navratiti, / Neka trnje u visinu raste, / Da se nikad sastat ne moremo' ('They will separate the courtyards of our houses, / They will plant hedges of thorns in between them, / And they will channel water through the thorns, / So that the thorns will grow up high, / and we shall never be able to meet'), *Karadžić*, ii, No. 10, ll. 12–16. However, in 'The Building of Ravanica' we find an example in which the singer follows the same basic syntactic pattern in a completely different semantic field, when he quotes Prince Lazar's order that his rapacious vassal Jug-Bogdan must be hanged. See below p. 146. Of course, the whole set of these examples is interesting primarily in so far as it illustrates a common feature in oral epic composition: the endless substitution of elements in a basic syntactic or semantic pattern.

4. The New Voice: in Slavonia

About 1720 an unknown German gentleman wrote down two hundred and seventeen diverse folk lyrics and epics, probably sung by Slav soldiery in Austrian frontier military camps in Slavonia, on the left bank of the river Save. The gentleman was well-versed in south-German baroque calligraphy, in 'the manner of writing of the Habsburg administration';[1] and he exercised his considerable accomplishments and talents in this field in beautiful Cyrillic handwriting with highly ornamented initials, taking down oral poems in a language which he could sometimes understand and often even hear properly. His manuscript—which was buried in archives for over two hundred years and discovered only in 1913 in the Erlangen University Library—is a baroque monument to his interests, perseverance, and faith. Nothing, apparently, could stop him, not even hundreds of curious semantic jokes lurking under the voiced consonants which he heard as voiceless, and *vice versa*. But the grotesqueness of the calligraphy and 'phonetics' of *The Erlangen Manuscript* makes it in a sense more reliable; it is hardly likely that there was any chance or temptation of conscious editing.

Though set in German calligraphy and phonetics, the 'linguistic basis' of these poems is *štokavic*.[2] This is to say that their dialectal features—as well as the Cyrillic script—suggest a predominantly Serbian setting. As many Serbs at this time filled the Austrian battalions along the military frontier in Slavonia and as most of them came from the central range of the Dinaric mountains, the cradle of decasyllabic epic singing, the basic epic geography seems to be fairly clear. It confirms what has been suggested by the dialectal features and the

---

[1] G. Gezeman (Gesemann), 'Uvod', *Erlangenski rukopis*, p. xii.

[2] Ibid., p. xxviii. There are three basic dialects of Serbo-Croat, classified according to the word for 'what': 'štokavic' ('što'), 'kajkavic' ('kaj') and 'čakavic' ('ča'). 'Štokavic'—which is the basis of modern standard Serbo-Croat—predominates in Serbia and the central Dinaric area (Montenegro, Bosnia and Herzegovina, Croatia). Broadly speaking 'kajkavic' is the dialect of the area of Zagreb and 'čakavic' of Dalmatia.

themes of the first two complete *bugarštice*, that epic singing in Serbo-Croat was deeply rooted in the Serbian migrations.[3] (See Map 4.) However, many of the poems mirror recent history and customs; some of them, particularly those with urban and suburban motifs, contain distinctly *kajkavic* features.[4] This shows that the Croat population in Slavonia, particularly in urban settings, also cultivated and contributed to the convention of this singing. And, finally, some sporadic linguistic features point in the direction of Dubrovnik, the Adriatic coast, and Herzegovina; these 'must have come with this poetic diction to the northern areas'.[5]

Moreover, many of the decasyllabic epics in *The Erlangen Manuscript* describe wars and raids not only along the Slavonian, but also along the Dalmatian frontiers. Their heroes are military captains and soldiers, often seen as outlaws or as the leaders of outlaws; not only because wars were not easy to distinguish from raids in these areas, but also because regular soldiers, border raiders and outlaws were often the same people. At times of peace, particularly in Dalmatia, raids were the only means of subsistence for the soldiers who were only paid while on military duty during times of war.[6] The historical picture was further complicated by the actual conflicts among the border raiders themselves, because the booty was not always easy to divide, particularly when they were in conflict with their military superiors who sometimes wanted to encourage and sometimes to bridle their actions, but were always eager to avail themselves of their raids and plunder. This historical setting gave rise to a typical destitute epic hero, distinguished by desperate courage and unperturbed mockery of whatever may stand in his way. It is in this light, for instance, that we see the Dalmatian captain Ivan Šandić and his border raiders, or outlaws, when they refuse the request of the great Ban of Zadar to raid the Turkish lands for him and bring him rich booty. Ivan Šandić explains that it is easier to drink 'cool wine'[7] at the fortified gate of 'white Zadar'[8] than to fight with the Turks, and

---

[3] See above pp. 52–8, 62–3, and below pp. 301–4.
[4] See G. Gezeman (Gesemann), 'Uvod', op. cit., pp. xxxviii–liv.
[5] Ibid., p. xxviii.   [6] See below pp. 220–3.
[7] 'Ladno vino', *Gesemann*, No. 63, l. 18.
[8] '(Na kapiji) satru bijelome', ibid., l. 2.

addresses the great Ban in a rich epic voice of challenge, mockery and the courage of those who have nothing to lose and little to fear:

> 'Why not keep your mouth shut a bit, my Ban,
> Just keep it shut and do not talk too much,
> For there are certain self-willed children here,
> Who have no father and have no mother,
> But gun and sword are father and mother.'[9]

But this pungent epic voice is a lonely outburst of imaginative achievement in a crude story of confused and conflicting motivation in which Ivan Šandić will prove his courage by refusing the order to fight the Turks and killing his great Christian Ban. Too many things are too obviously wrong with the story; the great formulaic pattern ('gun and sword are father and mother')—which will later sum up the predicament of the fighters against the Turks—is still floating, in more than one sense. It turns up in several eighteenth-century decasyllabic poems, but it does not always find its 'proper' place in the general epic landscape which purports to represent the struggle of Cross and Crescent. In a Dalmatian poem, as we have seen, it was used to describe the mustering of the Turkish army;[10] in another, Slavonian, poem about the Dalmatian border raiders in the vicinity of Šibenik it comes nearer its epic mark when used in a message which one outlaw captain sends to another describing the ideal fighters who should be recruited for their common exploit:

> 'O my brother, gather sixty outlaws,
> Homeless outlaws that have not got a home,
> Such as do not know any old mother,
> Such as do not know any faithful love,
> Such as care nothing for their hero heads.'[11]

The last line illuminates the heroic meaning of the whole

[9] 'Lijepo tie pomučati Pane / Pomučati ne govorit Mnogo / Er ovdi ima detcah samovolnih / Koi nemaju ni otca ni maike / Puška i sablja otac i maika', ibid., ll. 55–9.

[10] See above p. 70.

[11] 'Kupi bratco šest deset aidukah / Brez domaca koi doma neima / A za staru i ne znadu maiku / A za vjerne i ne znadu ljube / Za junačke i ne haju glave', *Gesemann*, No. 136, ll. 6–10.

formulaic pattern, but its full epic ring fails to find a corresponding story and gets lost in the mutual treacheries and
frauds of the heroes who have been outlined at first with
moving historical dignity. As if a fragmentary insight into the
human drama of history were mirrored in a magnificent
formulaic pattern; but if it is true that it glimmers with the
epic excitements to come, its language is still in search of a
coherent epic vision.

The search is also interesting to follow when at least a thread
of this formulaic pattern seems to be more successfully interwoven into an epic story. This is what happens in one of the
Slavonian decasyllabic poems about a Dalmatian border
raider from the famous, or notorious, northern Adriatic
fortress of Senj, who selects his company among those who have
'no old mother or faithful love'.[12] The basic suggestions of this
formula grow as the the story develops and the captain takes
his company in disguise to a Turkish town where they join a
ring-dance and make off with the Turkish girls. The spirit of
the formula—its playful challenging of fate—is justified in the
story which also expresses a grand foolhardy gesture which
almost equals the perils of life as the heroes of the poem had
come to know them. This is, of course, not so much the question
of a patriotic use of a formulaic pattern as the question of its
suitability to and growth in the story; and this example—
significant as it is in its playfulness—is still far away from the
immensely enriched usage of this formulaic pattern in the
early nineteenth-century decasyllabic poems where it will come
to sum up the daring of the outlaws on their historical razor-
edge.[13]

And in fact the Slavonian decasyllabic poems are interesting
above all in that they offer some historical glimpses into the
formulaic and thematic growth of the poems about border
raiders and outlaws, the poems which will later colour so much
of the whole epic landscape of Karadžić's singers. In this sense
it is highly significant that in one of the Slavonian decasyllabic
poems an outlaw is seen as a historical martyr of his mission and
his faith, in the formulaic pattern which will be richly echoed
about a hundred years later in one of the greatest decasyllabic

[12] 'Stare maike i vijerne ljube', *Gesemann*, No. 113, l. 16.
[13] See below pp. 238–9.

poems. This Slavonian poem is also set in Livno, an important Turkish military outpost in southern Bosnia, which was exposed to severe border fighting and raiding from the end of the seventeenth century, after the Dalmatian military frontier had been pushed back to its vicinity. Against this historical background of a fortress which was often adorned by the heads of the outlaws and border raiders, a captured hero addresses his brother on the threshold of torture and death:

'But I beg of you, my brother, my dear,
Whenever they begin to torture us,
They will torture us with all kinds of tortures,
They will break our legs, they will break our arms;
And if their tortures kill us in the end,
Do not betray, my brother, any friend
Or any storeplace where we left our things
Or any houses where we spent our nights
Or any places where we sat to eat.'[14]

These lines—embedded as they are in a stark story—mirror the historical and also the epic no-man's land, in which real and imaginary figures of outlaws and border raiders merge. They provide a clear insight into the moral core of the best later singing in which the outlaws and the border raiders will be seen as martyrs. They also contain many traditional formulas, a major pattern in which they will keep coming together and they also suggest, if in embryo, the tale of the later 'Old Vujadin' in which they will come to full flower.[15]

But it is not very often that the poems in *The Erlangen Manuscript* mirror such major aspects of the growth of the decasyllabic epic tradition. For the most part we find in them only numerous traditional formulas, motifs, stylistic and narrative devices which are also common to the *bugarštice*, to the Dalmatian decasyllabic songs and to the great material recorded by Karadžić.[16] They reflect, in short, an early, crude stage of an epic tradition in its growth—the stage in which the

[14] 'Već molim te moi mili braine / Kada nas stanu moriti mukam / Mučiće nas mukom svakojakim / Pribitiće nam noge i ruke / Aкoће nas umoriti muke / Ne izdai brate druga niednoga / Ni ostava gdismo ostavljali / Ni konaka gdismo noćivali / Ni večera gdi smo večerali', *Gesemann*, No. 168, ll. 13–21.

[15] See below pp. 243–6.   [16] See above pp. 43–9.

language seldom rises above the level of the neutral tone of scanned chronicles and often betrays the failure of the epic imagination to come to full moral and dramatic grips with the cruelty of its historical material. In this sense the poem which tells the story of an outlaw's triumph at the moment when he burns his treacherous wife alive is not completely atypical, at least in so far as it shows no trace of moral awareness of what is actually being described—the helplessness of the victim and the pity of her son which will be magnificently interwoven in one of the later versions of the same story.[17]

The same crude and cruel spirit prevails in most of the Slavonian decasyllabic poems about Marko Kraljević. In one of them—in which a jocular touch is obviously intended—he kills a mountain nymph (a *vila*) to avoid paying the water-tax;[18] in another he discovers, by crude stratagem, that his wife is unfaithful to him, kills her lover and digs out her eyes.[19] He is also prepared to bet with a Turkish officer on the honour of his wife; the wife makes her slave go to bed with the officer and misleads him into imagining that he had won the bet.[20] But apart from such material which illustrates a military sense of humour and largely remains outside the mainstream of the Serbo-Croatian epic tradition, some of the Slavonian decasyllabic poems about Marko are interesting because we see him in the same light in which he appears in some of the eighteenth-century Dalmatian and many other, later, poems about him: as a Turkish vassal, the Sultan's adoptive son,[21] unruly but prone to be appeased when given an adequate tip for wine.[22] Some of his other tricks and gimmicks are also significant because they will persist in the tradition—in the later poems he will also give his horse wine to drink[23] and he will also be often described as 'strange-tempered'.[24] But on the whole such

---

[17] See below pp. 231–4.   [18] *Gesemann*, No. 176. For *vila* see Appendix III.
[19] *Gesemann*, No. 139.   [20] *Gesemann*, No. 151.
[21] See *Gesemann*, No. 87, l. 103. Cf. *Bogišić*, No. 92, l. 43; *Karadžić*, ii, No. 71, l. 68.
[22] See *Gesemann*, No. 140, ll. 49–60. Cf. *Bogišić*, No. 90, ll. 36–42; *Karadžić*, ii, No. 71, ll. 93–8. See above p. 77 and below pp. 189–90.
[23] See *Gesemann*, No. 124, l. 178; cf. *Karadžić* ii, No. 66, l. 315.
[24] 'Čudnovate ćudi', *Gesemann*, No. 124, l. 215. Marko Kraljević's hot temper is also a standard feature in many of the later songs about him (see *Karadžić*, ii, No. 67, ll. 151ff; No. 70, l. 113; No. 74, ll. 137–40).

instances of the perseverance of some of Marko's features suggest that these poems contain many of the motifs, personal characteristics, and narrative elements of what will only later grow into a great epic comedy.

The difference between anecdotes about a successful rogue and the later songs about a historically significant comic hero comes out most clearly in the two existing versions of the story about Marko Kraljević's ploughing. In the *Erlangen* version Marko follows his mother's advice, decides to mend his blood-thirsty ways, buys a horse and a plough, but 'does not feel like ploughing'.[25] Instead he offers his services as guide to an innocent Arab, leads him through a mountain, kills him by fraud, brings back home his 'treasure'[26] and tells his mother that that is what he 'has ploughed out'.[27] The later version—which Karadžić recorded from one of his anonymous singers—opens in a similar spirit of the hero's decision to apply himself to honest agricultural activities. But the defiant note in his character comes out immediately because he applies himself to the ploughing of 'the Emperor's great roads'[28] which brings him into a dramatic conflict with the Turks who come his way:

'Hey Marko, don't plough on the great road!'
'Hey, you Turks! Don't walk on my ploughland!'[29]

Not only does the conflict of the story begin to make much clearer epic and historical sense; it establishes a pattern of dauntless, if limited defiance, the pattern of a slightly comic hero—and thus Marko Kraljević becomes the prototype of other similar characters in completely different settings, such as Miloš Voinović in 'Dušan's Wedding'[30] or the early nineteenth-century rebel Ilija Birčanin in 'The Beginning of the Revolt against the Dahijas'.[31]

This difference between a loose tale and an epic insight into the human drama of history is also clearly reflected in the

[25] '(Ali muse) orati ne dade', *Gesemann*, No. 105, l. 10.

[26] 'Blago', *Gesemann*, No. 105, l. 31.

[27] 'Izorao', ibid., l. 33.

[28] 'Careve drumove', *Karadžić*, ii, No. 73, l. 17.

[29] 'More, Marko, ne ori drumova!' / 'More, Turci, ne gaz'te oranja!', ibid., ll. 21–2.

[30] 'Ženidba Dušanova', *Karadžić*, ii, No. 29; see below pp. 121–2.

[31] 'Početak bune protiv dahija', *Karadžić*, iv, No. 24; see below p. 293.

respective versions of some other poems about subjects from earlier feudal history. Thus the poem about Ivo Karlović in *The Erlangen Manuscript*[32] presents only a narrative series of vague, stammering hints at the drama which will grow in Karadžić's time into the poetic world of 'Sick Dojčin'.[33] The two respective stories seem to be sufficiently parallel: a sick hero dominates the scene, an Arab threatens the honour of his sister, the hero's horse cannot be shod before the duel because a blacksmith also wants the sister to pay with her honour (in the version recorded by Karadžić the sister's role is taken here by the wife), the sick hero dies after his victory. But whereas in the earlier version, for instance, the brother appeals to his sister:

> 'Elica, my dear sister,
> Belt me up with a silk belt
> From my waist up to my throat,
> And his sister belted on his belt',[34]

the later version brings out the human drama of this moment in the wording which makes both a more physical and a more suggestive impact:

> 'O Jelica, my sister, my dear,
> Bring me a length of linen rag,
> Wrap me tightly, sister, up from my thighs,
> Tied from my thighs up to my supple ribs,
> So that my bones shall not be separated,
> Shall not be separated, bone from bone.'[35]

The difference between an elegant 'silk belt' and a homely 'linen rag', between the 'waist' and the 'white throat' on the one hand, and 'thighs' and 'supple ribs' on the other, the introduction of the image of the bones coming apart—all these illustrate the difference between a statement and a drama. The 'length of linen rag'—charged in Serbo-Croat with the association of the last resort of a heroic striving—is particularly

[32] *Gesemann*, No. 110.

[33] 'Bolani Dojčin', *Karadžić*, ii, No. 78.

[34] 'Elice draga sestrice moja / Opaši me svilenim pojasom / Od svitnjaka do bijela grla / I njega je sestra opazala', *Gesemann*, No. 110, ll. 68–71.

[35] 'O Jelice, moja mila sejo! / Donesi mi jednu krpu platna, / Utegni me, sele, od bedara, / Od bedara do vitih rebara, / Da se moje kosti ne razminu, / Ne razminu kosti mimo kosti', *Karadžić*, ii, No. 78, ll. 169–74.

characteristic as a traditional formula; it will also be used in other poems—by a sister to help her brother escape his enemies by climbing his city wall,[36] by a Turkish girl to help her Serbian brother-in-God, wounded and drowning, to pull himself out of a wild river.[37]

A much more drastic example of an enormous difference in epic impact between two versions of the 'same' story is to be found in the poems about Duke Prijezda's defence of Stalać. The two poems are rooted in history in so far as the commander of Stalać indeed refused to surrender his fortress to the Turks and was burned in it in 1413; and Prijezda was the name of the commander of Novo Brdo, the richest medieval mine of Serbia and its last stronghold of resistance to the Turks. However, the *Erlangen* version is only a chronicle of the heroic defence of the besieged city; it mirrors the indifference and the stupidity of an 'objective' attitude, and is told occasionally even from the point of view of the Turkish enemy which the singer neither understands nor controls, if indeed he is aware of it. But Karadžić's version which was recorded from Jeca who lived in Zemun—one of those strangely gifted blind women singers[38]— is focused from its opening to its closing line on the fate of Duke Prijezda and his wife, on the discovery of the horror and the greatness of their tragedy. In the first line of Jeca's poem we are not told that 'the tsar of Mostar writes a book';[39] the story does not open with a glaring factual mistake and from the Turkish end, but begins as a threat, as a series of 'books' following each other, implacably, as omens of what is coming:

Books chase books, one after the other.[40]

Among the many variants of a standard formulaic opening which can be found in many other early and later poems[41] Jeca picks up the one which is highly appropriate to her story. In a similar sense it is significant that in both versions Duke Prijezda is asked to surrender his sword, his horse and his wife, the

[36] *Karadžić*, ii, No. 25; see below p. 130.
[37] *Karadžić*, ii, No. 57, l. 15; see below p. 187.
[38] See below pp. 319–20.
[39] 'Knjigu piše c're iz mostara', *Gesemann*, No. 70, l. 1.
[40] 'Česte knjige idu za knjigama', *Karadžić*, ii, No. 84, l. 1.
[41] See note 55, p. 44.

feudal symbols of his power and honour, recognized as such in the medieval Serbian legal procedures of heritage.[42] But whereas the 'Erlangen', formulaic horse has no immediate connection with the defence of Stalać—he can only 'catch up a *vila* in the mountain',[43] Jeca's horse can

> Fly through the air
> And overleap two fortress walls in one single leap.[44]

Similarly, whereas the 'Erlangen' sword cuts only 'heroes in armour',[45] Jeca's sword

> 'Cuts through trees and through rocks,
> Through the wood, through the stone, through cold iron';[46]

—it is in immediate and magnetic connection with the ramparts and the defence of Stalać. Finally, at the tragic moment of the choice of death in the *Erlangen* version Duke Prijezda will stutter:

> 'Come on, love, to the Morava water.'[47]

In Jeca's version it will be the wife who, realizing the despair of the situation, will find ultimate mercy for her husband:

> 'The Morava water has bred us up,
> Let the Morava water bury us!'[48]

This dramatic placing is as important as the invocation of the great river of life which has so often flowed beyond its banks to many songs which express, in their nostalgic tone, a sense of national identity; almost as important as the proverbial utterance which perseveres in language and mirrors the obstinacy of the tragic course of things. This wording does not

---

[42] See above pp. 21–2.

[43] 'Koi stigne u gorici vilu', *Gesemann*, No. 70, l. 14. On *vila* see Appendix III.

[44] '(Koji konjic može) preletiti / Zasobice i po dva bedena', *Karadžić*, ii, No. 84, ll. 12–13.

[45] '(Koja seče) oklope junake', *Gesemann*, No. 70, l. 10.

[46] '(Koja) seče drvlje i kamenje, / Drvo, kamen i studeno gvožđe', *Karadžić*, ii, No. 84, ll. 9–10.

[47] 'Aidi ljubo u moravu vodu', *Gesemann*, No. 70, l. 118.

[48] 'Morava nas voda odranila, / Nek Morava voda i sarani!', *Karadžić*, ii, No. 84, ll. 104–5.

only tell us what happened; it also brings out the intensity of a personal and historical fate.

In short, Karadžić's singers inherited many of their tales, dozens of their motifs, of their narrative and stylistic devices, hundreds of their formulas from their epic predecessors—from the unknown medieval feudal bards whose voices remained unrecorded, from the Dalmatian and, perhaps, Slavonian singers of *bugarštice*,[49] from the Dalmatian and Slavonian decasyllabic village singers. This can be easily established by the internal evidence of recorded songs. Their debts to the epic singers in the central Dinaric belt, particularly in Herzegovina and Montenegro, must have been at least as great if not much greater; but so far as we know until the nineteenth century not a single one of the epic songs was written down in these largely illiterate areas under the Turkish rule. And yet this enormous ☞ oral epic heritage—undoubtedly feeding also on more or less distant literary sources—came fully to life only at the time of the great national movements at the beginning of the nineteenth century. No one includes in an anthology an earlier or a later epic poem if there is an existing version in Karadžić's collections —for the simple reason that it was at this time that the fragmentary epic heritage came together and was illuminated by a new light. This resulted in much clearer narratives which themselves present a great unified epic poem in one of the last stages of its making. The unity of this narrative springs from the shared awareness of Karadžić's singers of the whole epic landscape of Serbian history. For they largely tell a fairly coherent story about the grandeur and the corruption of medieval Serbia facing its doom, about the Doomsday in the

---

[49] The only trace of the singing of *bugarštice* in Slavonia are the three lines which Juraj Križanić recorded in his grammar in 1666; two of these lines describe the conversation between Marko Kraljević and Radosav of Severin —the heroes who are mentioned in the two sixteenth-century *bugarštice* which P. Hektorović wrote down from his fishermen (see 'Predgovor', *Bogišić*, p. 76). J. Križanić also refers to 'the Serbian manner' of singing in Slavonia (see note 63, p. 26) and, finally, he mentions that Serbian and Croatian soldiers used to stand behind their masters during their feasts and sing about the exploits of their famous ancestors (see M. Pavić, *Istorija srpske književnosti baroknog doba*, p. 421). Considering the comparatively favourable conditions of literacy in Slavonia at this time this is indeed slim but perhaps convincing evidence of the existence of *bugarštice* in this area.

Legend:

- KRUŠEVAC — Pre-Turkish Times
- PRILEP — Marko Kraljević
- LIVNO — Outlaws and Border Fighters
- MIŠAR — Serbian and Montenegrin Wars of Independence

Map labels: VENICE, SENJ, BIHAĆ, UDBINA, RAVNI KOTARI, ŠIBENIK, LIVNO, SARAJ, THE DALMATIAN LITTORAL, NEVES, TREB, BUDA (BUDAPEST), AZAK (AZOV), HADRIANOPOLIS, CARIGRAD (CONSTANTINOPLE), Chilendarion, Mt. Athos, KARAMANIA

1. Topography of Major Epic Themes.

KARLOVAC
(SREMSKI KARLOVCI)
RAŠNICA SALAŠ
ŠABAC
ŽNICA MIŠAR
ČOKEŠINA
JANJA
VALJEVO
BELGRADE
Sava
TOPOLA
Morava
RUDNIK
IVANKOVAC •Ravanica
STALAĆ
DELIGRAD
Drina KRUŠEVAC
MT ČEGAR
GOLEŠ NIŠ
Studenica MOUNT
Tara Mileševa SUHA
MT PIRLITOR PAZAR
DURMITOR Lab
Morača Banjska VUČITRN
KOLAŠIN ZVEČAN Sitnica Samodreža
ŠIĆ ROVCI THE FIELD Gračanica
AN OF KOSOVO
KOTOR
PODGORICA
NOVI
SKADAR PRIZREN
(SCUTARI)
Bojana
ALBANIA Vardar

MOUNT URVINA
(THE VILLAGE
OF ROVINE)
Danube

BULGARIA

Marica

PRILEP

KOSTUR (CASTORIA)

Battle of Kosovo, about the vassalage and limited defiance of Marko Kraljević, about the lonely and desperate fighting of the outlaws and border raiders. To these stories which the singers have for the most part inherited, they added the final canto on the fight for freedom in their own times. (See Map 1.) For they lived at a time when the epic voice was vigorous enough to produce major songs about contemporary historical events. Even though the epic convention has survived to the present day, this historical moment was soon to disappear. But while it lasted it meant that the singers could see the present with the eyes of the past and express the past with the intensity of the immediate involvement in the burning issues of history. This explains the dramatic nature of their achievement—the vision of the major issues of history intensely mirrored in personal fates.

PART TWO

On the Eve of Kosovo

1. Medieval Serbia and Its Epic Image

In the great migrations in the fifth century the Slavs reached the northern banks of the Danube in present-day Romania where they were stopped by the Byzantine military fortifications. However, after the assassination of the Byzantine Emperor Mauricius in 602 the military commander of the Byzantine frontier rushed to Constantinople to secure the throne for himself. The Slavs crossed the unprotected frontier and in a few years reached the Adriatic Sea, Thessaloniki, and the southern parts of the Peloponnese and permanently settled in the Balkans. In the ninth century they were cut off from the rest of the European Slav population by the Hungarians who, retreating from the lower regions of the Danube in the vicinity of the Black Sea, populated the Pannonian plains and laid the foundations of one of the most powerful central European states in the centuries to come.

The organization of the early medieval Slav states in Bulgaria, Macedonia, Serbia, Bosnia, Croatia, and Slovenia was shaped by the spreading of Christianity and the international conflicts in the Balkans. The seventh and eighth centuries were the age of the Byzantine reconquest of the eastern parts of the peninsula, but the rise of the Venetian power soon threatened Byzantine control of the cities along the Dalmatian coast and in Greece. The Slovene political communities in the west were exposed to the domination of the Franks and the Germans; the Croatian states to that of the Franks, the Germans and the Hungarians. The split between Roman and Orthodox Christianity in 1054, and the Crusades complicated further the political map of the Balkans and gave their strong imprint to local feudal factions and struggles for supremacy—often among rulers belonging to the same families.

During the major wars between Hungary and Byzantium in the twelfth century the rulers of Raška, the eastern part of the so-called 'Baptized Serbia', succeeded both in organizing their country on the Byzantine military, administrative, and ecclesiastical models and in edging their way out of the Byzantine political orbit. Stefan Nemanja, the Great Zupan of Raška and founder of the dynasty which was to reign in medieval Serbia for almost two centuries, came to power by defeating his elder brother, who was supported by the Byzantine forces. He conquered the neighbouring territories of Kosovo, Metohija, and the area between the West and the Great Morava, annexed some littoral regions, including Duklja (later Zeta, Montenegro) to his state, and built one of his palaces in Kotor. It was from this area that many of the later great builders and high officials in the Serbian administration were recruited; it may have also mediated in supplying the builders for Studenica, the first of the great fortified Serbian monasteries which remained for a long time the mausoleum of the Nemanjići. It was here that Nemanja entered the monastic order when he had to abdicate under Byzantine pressure in 1196. However, he soon left for Mount Athos where he joined his youngest son Sava, renewed the monastery of Chilandarion and secured it for Serbian monks. Sava organized the monastic life in Chilandarion on Byzantine models and this monastery soon became the nursery of Serbian medieval monastic culture. All the greatest Serbian medieval writers—Domentijan, Teodosije, Danilo, and others—were educated in Chilandarion, and so were in touch with other great monasteries on Mount Athos, which contained several thousand monks, among them some of the most learned men of their time.

When Nemanja abdicated he was still powerful enough to nominate his younger son Stefan instead of the elder, Vukan, for his successor. But Stefan had to fight for his questionable right of succession against Vukan, who had already established his authority in Duklja—and this kind of family distribution of power and the ensuing enmities established a recurring pattern in Serbian feudal history and epic poetry. When Stefan assumed authority, he was already sufficiently strong to have been considered worthy of the hand of a Byzantine princess, but he was also sufficiently weak to have to recognize Byzantine sovereignty. But he exploited the Byzantine defeats in the conflicts with the West and after the Crusaders under Venetian command had taken Constantinople in 1204, Stefan extended his territories from the Morava to the Adriatic Sea and received his crown from the Pope's legate in 1217.

Stefan the First-Crowned was greatly helped in establishing the Serbian medieval state and its cultural identity by his brother Sava who, after Nemanja's death in 1208, brought his father's body to Serbia and buried it in the monastery of Studenica. Nemanja was canonized as the first Serbian Orthodox saint (St Simeon) and Sava's biography of his father and the hymns he composed for the service in his father's honour established the cult of Nemanja as the founder of the Serbian medieval state and its national identity. Sava himself spent a number of years as the Archimandrite of Studenica, helping his brother Stefan in diplomatic and political missions. After his brother was crowned, Sava made it possible for the Serbian Orthodox church to attain autocephalous status. In 1219 Sava was made its first archbishop; owing to his work on the organization of religious life in Serbia, he is considered the father of Serbian medieval monastic culture. His translations and adaptations of the rules for monastic life and his *Nomocanon* supplied the basis for ecclesiastical and civil law in medieval Serbia. He was also canonized after his death and one of the greatest tributes to his spiritual and historical importance for the Serbian people was paid by the Turks when they took his relics away from the monastery of Mileševa and burnt them on the mount of Vračar near Belgrade in 1594, more than three and a half centuries after his death.

In the course of the thirteenth century the expansion of the Serbian state continued and reached its climax in the middle of the fourteenth century under the rule of Stefan Dušan the Mighty. At this time the territories under Serbian control extended from the Danube to the Adriatic, the Ionian and the Aegean Seas. (See Map 2.) Emperor Stefan Dušan ruled Macedonia and most of Greece from Skopje and his son Uroš governed Serbia as its king. The legal basis for the government of such heterogeneous political communities was supplied by Stefan Dušan's *Code of Laws* proclaimed at the state council in Skopje in 1349. The articles added in 1354 show that 'the feudal lords and the Emperor's officials often abused their rights at the expense of the imperial authority and the established feudal order'.[1] In this sense they suggest the beginning of the

[1] I. Božić, S. Ćirković, M. Ekmečić, V. Dedijer, *Istorija Jugoslavije*, Belgrade, 1972, p. 74.

deep political crisis which became apparent soon after Stefan
Dušan's sudden death in 1355. His son Uroš found it more and
more difficult to control his powerful feudal lords who took over
the administrative, financial, and military authority in their
areas. This led to the dissolution of the Serbian Empire on the

2. Stefan Dušan's Empire

eve of the Turkish invasions. (See Map 3.) The southern regions
in Macedonia, ruled by King Vukašin and his brother Uglješa
Mrnjavčević, were the first to be conquered by the Turks. In the
Battle on the Marica in 1371 both Vukašin and Uglješa were

killed, Vukašin's son Marko—the famous Marko Kraljević of
the epic songs—kept the royal title but ruled as a Turkish
vassal. The next in order were the lands of Prince Lazar
Hrebeljanović and his son-in-law Vuk Branković; they were
conquered after the Serbian defeat in the Battle of Kosovo in
1389, which came to live in popular imagination as the ultimate
national calamity. Lazar and Vuk Branković were respectively
turned into the greatest martyr and the greatest traitor in later
heroic songs.

The military conquests and political and cultural achievement of medieval Serbia were based on a prosperous and
versatile economy. The mountains, the plains, the rivers and the
seas stimulated commerce and also agriculture and cattle
breeding. As Serbia lay on the main commercial routes between
East and West, the movement and the exchange of people,
goods, and ideas was intense. Foreign miners, mostly Saxons,
were a common feature in some Serbian towns: the amount of
silver which was exported from Serbia and Bosnia only through
Dubrovnik to the West 'in 1422 amounted to more than one
fifth' of the total European production[2]—which means that
during the first half of the fifteenth century Serbia and Bosnia
were if not the biggest certainly one of the biggest producers of
silver in Europe.[3] That crafts flourished in towns is indicated
by the quality of the very few remnants of the material culture
which survived the Turkish conquest. Life in the court, the
castle and the army was modelled on the Byzantine pattern;
the use of forks, for instance, was common before they were
accepted in the west. In the monastic literature, Greek and
Byzantine in origin, the Church Slavonic language soon
predominated over Greek and the lives of Serbian rulers and
saints and the accounts of Serbian history in chronicles soon
became standard topics. And both the eastern Oriental stories

[2] S. Ćirković, 'Dubrovačka kovnica i proizvodnja srebra u Srbiji i Bosni',
Istorijski glasnik, Belgrade, No. 1–2 (1976), p. 94.

[3] See ibid., p. 97. There are several specific references to this historical
fact in epic songs: Stevan Musić, one of the Kosovo heroes, is described as a
man who comes from the area of a mine of 'pure silver' ('od maidana čista
srebr'noga', *Gesemann*, No. 92, l. 37; 'U Majdanu čisto srebrnome', *Karadžić*,
ii, No. 47, l. 2.); Prince Lazar, intent on building in silver and gold, refers
to his great mines of Rudnik and Kopaonik in 'The Building of Ravanica'
(see below pp. 144–5).

and the western romances and hagiographies found their way into it. But the greatest achievement of medieval Serbia were its romanesque churches and monasteries crowned with Byzantine cupolas. This architecture—of the so-called Ras School—involved not only technical problems, but also what we would call today a unique creative challenge. Some of these churches and monasteries—like Studenica, Mileševa, and Sopoćani—were decorated by fresco paintings which are among the greatest European achievements before Giotto. Many of them are distinguished by the characteristic medieval sense of the local and the particular within a universal spiritual composition.

Many of the aspects of medieval Serbia and its culture live in the so-called 'oldest' heroic poems of Karadžić's singers, with one exception the first thirty-seven poems of the second volume of the Viennese edition (1845).[4] Some of these songs tell hagiographical and apocryphal medieval tales, basing them on the later moral norms and family relations of Serbian patriarchal village life under the Turkish rule. Sometimes a folk tale, an Oriental or a Byzantine legend is told in a similar manner, but the best among them are simply patriarchal dramas in a tragic natural setting, taking place in a never-never land, with or without an occasional medieval reference. But apart from this cluster of poems about tragic family relations, there are also the 'historically' more specific ones: those about the factions of Serbian medieval feudal lords, princes and kings and those about the building of the medieval castles and monasteries (for their topography, see Map 1).

However, what gives imaginative unity to this epic landscape of mythic and pre-Turkish times is the singers' awareness of the approaching Turkish conquest. For the singers see both the patriarchal never-never land of tragic family relations and the historical medieval Serbia, with its feudal lords, princes and kings, and its builders of the great monasteries, as the world of

---

[4] See *Karadžić*, ii, Nos. 1–6, 8–37. No. 7('Zaručnica Laza Radanovića'— 'The Betrothed of Laza Radanović') is a wedding story. In its imaginative setting it belongs to much later times, and Karadžić left instructions, followed by many later editors, to have it moved to volume iii (No. 79). See R. Aleksić, 'Pogovor' in V. S. Karadžić, *Srpske narodne pjesme*, ii, ed. S. Matić, Belgrade, 1953, p. 828.

'the last times'. The phrase—derived from the concept of the Last Judgement—occurs in 'The Building of Ravanica'.[5] Prince Lazar—the last independent Serbian ruler who was killed in the Battle of Kosovo—wants to build his church in silver, gold, pearls, and jewels, but Miloš Obilić persuades him to build in stone because 'the last times' are approaching. The story is of mixed historical and legendary origin[6] and it is significant perhaps that its governing concept ('the last times') recurs in another poem in which Prince Lazar figures prominently. This poem tells the story of the mad pride of the Serbian medieval nobleman Jug-Bogdan, who refuses Emperor Stefan Dušan's request to let his daughter marry Prince Lazar until he reads in ancient prophetic books that this marriage is inevitable and that 'the last times' are coming.[7] But whereas in 'The Building of Ravanica' 'the last times' are seen explicitly in terms of the approaching Turkish conquest, in 'The Wedding of Prince Lazar' they are seen as a natural catastrophe which follows on the transgressions of the patriarchal norms of family life.[8] Thus the idea of 'the last times' connects the failures in family life with natural catastrophes and the decisive moments of Serbian medieval history; in fact, it governs the singers' awareness of history in this part of their epic landscape.

And sometimes, indeed, this idea of Hubris and Nemesis provides the main interest in the poems which take their stories from apocryphal religious literature and give them a distinctly apocalyptic significance.[9] In such poems the transgressions of patriarchal moral norms are always seen as the root of the evil; and this suggests an interplay of the biblical ideas as popularly understood with the historical social concepts of later Serbian history under the Turkish rule. However, in such poems the Nemesis of the Flood is usually seen in the much more immediately relevant terms of a drought—as in the poems about medieval Serbia the Day of the Last Judgement is largely understood in terms of the approaching Turkish conquest. And

[5] 'Pošljednje vrijeme', 'Zidanje Ravanice', *Karadžić*, ii, No. 35, l. 89; No. 36, l. 73. See also below pp. 144–6.

[6] See below pp. 143–4.

[7] 'Ženidba kneza Lazara', *Karadžić*, ii, No. 32, ll. 67, 107.

[8] See below pp. 125–6.

[9] See below pp. 107–9.

of course it was as natural as it was inevitable that the singer should look to medieval Christian concepts as the key for the interpretation of his sense of history: after all, from his point of view Prince Lazar, Nemanja, and Sava were not merely great historical figures, but also the greatest national saints.

Besides, in the Serbian villages under the Turkish rule religion was a family way of life: the day of the family patronal festival ('slava') was respected as much as Easter and Christmas.[10] Moreover, Serbian Orthodox Christianity was deeply immersed in many folk customs;[11] and, last but not least, under the pressure of the Turkish terror, the Serbian semi-literate and sometimes illiterate priesthood shared the way of life and the culture of its villagers, often providing political leadership for Serbian migrations and ammunition for resistance to the Turks.[12] How can one draw the line dividing the literary from the oral culture in this situation? But perhaps one can illustrate the situation itself by Njegoš's great figure of Father Mićo who stutters while he tries to read a letter but is able to sing the holy service like an epic song.[13]

[10] See I. Božić et al., *Istorija Jugoslavije*, p. 146. For *slava* see Appendix IV.

[11] The 'folk' character of many customs in Serbian Orthodox Christianity can be partly explained by the fact that the first Serbian archbishop, Sava (1174–1235) instructed the clergy not to try to abolish by violence 'old folk beliefs and customs but to give them a Christian imprint' (Š. Kulišić et al., *Srpski mitološki rečnik*, p. 175). On the other hand the 'folk' imprint on Serbian Orthodox Christianity is also due to the conditions of social and religious life under the Turkish rule which brought clergy and people closer together than they could ever be in an independent national state. Diverse aspects of this phenomenon are richly reflected in all the standard works in this area, such as S. Stanojević, ed., *Narodna enciklopedija srpsko-hrvatsko-slovenačka*, 4 vols., 'Zagreb, 1925–9, Š. Kulišić et al., *Srpski mitološki rečnik*, V. Čajkanović, *Mit i religija u Srba*.

[12] This is again a major feature of Serbian history (see I. Božić et al., *Istorija Jugoslavije*, pp. 145–7, 164–5, 174–5). Perhaps the most interesting single document is the *Memoirs* of Matija Nenadović, one of the great religious, national, and political leaders of the First Serbian Uprising against the Turks (*The Memoirs of Prota Matija Nenadović*, ed. and tr. by L. F. Edwards, Oxford, 1969).

[13] When teased for his poor reading performance by the grand and illiterate Montenegrin military captains and asked how he can read the liturgy, Father Mićo answers that he does not read it and has never any need to open a book in his church: whatever he needs, he knows by heart and 'sings it like a song' (see P. P. Njegoš, *Gorski vijenac*, ed. R. Bošković and V. Latković, Belgrade, 1952, ll. 2060–90).

Finally, medieval facts and fantasies lived vividly for the later epic singers because they could see them on the fresco paintings of the Serbian churches and monasteries, together with some of their epic heroes—the medieval Serbian rulers and saints.[14] (See Pls. 1–3). This interplay of fact and fiction, of 'high' and 'low' culture, involving occasional details from the singer's own biography and experience, suggests that the singer could be successful only in so far as he could shape a coherent dramatic and moral interest in the diversity of his fundamentally anachronistic material. For his response to his own historical reality had to be expressed in material and concepts belonging to different historical times and traditions. It is in this sense that his concept of 'the last times'—which governs the epic landscape of a mythic and pre-Turkish era—was rooted in the biblical idea of the Last Judgement, in its representations on fresco paintings, in the peasant experience of drought, in the urge to give moral significance to personal misery and to the sense of national catastrophe. To sum up, motley seems to be the only possible wear in this kind of creative interplay between diverse elements of the epic tradition and an individual talent.

[14] See below pp. 131, 138, 140.

2. Nature and Family

With one exception the first twenty-three poems among the 'oldest' heroic songs of Karadžić's second volume have a medieval aura about them. Their subjects are sometimes of medieval literary origin and their heroes bear the names of saints, angels, apostles, occasionally of a historical medieval figure, even if they sometimes have the names of a hero of a folk tale, or just any of the common Serbian names, on one or two occasions semantically connected with what the story is about.[1] They usually tell the tales of tragic disregard of sacred family obligations which create an epic world of betrayed kinship, but the social and moral norms of this world do not mirror so much the historical Middle Ages as the later times of Serbian patriarchal village life and outlawry under the Turkish rule. One or two of the heroes—Mujo, Alija, Milan-bey, Dragutin-bey—even have names which clearly suggest a later Turkish origin. But in these poems, as Karadžić noted, guns never shoot.[2] This mirrors the singers' 'historical' assumptions and it is in this sense that they are usually referred to as the 'oldest' among the 'old' songs.

In this mythic and miraculous world of medieval grandeur and later patriarchal life the transgressions of any of the obligations of blood-kinship, or of any of its extensions, lead to natural catastrophes. In short, the ancient pagan animistic beliefs, so conspicuous in all Serbian folk culture, their later Christian modifications, and, above all, the sense of doomed medieval Serbia (of course, from a much later point of view) give these patriarchal dramas of the Turkish times their full epic scope. Many of the elements in this landscape are inevitably 'anachronistic' and sometimes they are not sufficiently merged

---

[1] So for instance the names of the heroes in 'Predrag and Nenad' ('Predrag i Nenad', *Karadžić*, ii, No. 16) are connected with the story of great brotherly love which ends in sudden and unexpected death. See below p. 249.

[2] See B. Marinković, ed., V. S. Karadžić, *O srpskoj narodnoj poeziji*, Belgrade, 1964, p. 279 (letter to Miloš Obrenović dated 9 Nov. 1823).

1. St. Sava in the Monastery of Mileševa.

into a unified epic picture. But when the singer is successful, his drama of patriarchal village life and outlawry attains not only a feudal social grandeur, but is also illuminated by animistic and Christian moral concepts which give it a powerful spiritual and human relevance.

The two versions of 'The Saints Divide the Treasure'—the introductory poems in Karadžić's collection—are characteristic both of the nature of the singer's difficulties and of the possibilities of his achievement. Both poems are based on medieval apocryphal stories about God's punishment of mankind for their sins. One of them is explicitly placed in India, 'India the cursed land'—perhaps because the Apostle Thomas's suffering in India was known in Serbian medieval literature,[3] unless the connection is purely acoustic and linked with the name of a small town in Srem (Inđija) where the poem was written down. In the second version, written down in Montenegro, the name of St Sava is explicitly invoked,[4] perhaps because he was an obvious choice for a saint with power over the snow, as his day falls on 27 January. But as this is the only specific 'historical' reference, it also suggests that the singer connects in some way his story with medieval Serbia. For he would be most unlikely to make a 'mistake' about such a universally known saint, the most popular medieval figure, who was often represented in fresco paintings—in the monastery of Mileševa drawn from life. (See Pl. 1.)

The singer's difficulties and failures in bringing his diverse epic material together are reflected in the basic allegorical framework of both versions. For in spite of the grand didactic intentions it seems in fact that some outlaws, keen on vengeance, in a typical situation of dividing their booty, are masquerading as Christian saints who address each other like Serbian peasants. The version which Karadžić wrote down in Srem from blind Stepanija—born in Serbia in his own native area—begins with a Slavonic antithesis which is hardly an appropriate opening for a meeting of the holy saints with Blessed Mary:

> Kind God! a great wonder!
> Is this thunder, is this the earth quaking,

[3] '(Iz) Inđije iz zemlje proklete', 'Sveci blago dijele' ('The Saints Divide the Treasure'), *Karadžić*, ii, No. 1, l. 20. See *Matić*, p. 625.

[4] See *Karadžić*, ii, No. 2, ll. 30, 51.

> Is it the ocean beating on the cliffs?
> It is not thunder, not the earth quaking,
> The ocean is not beating on the cliffs,
> But holy saints are taking their treasure.[5]

And when the Blessed Mary tells the holy saints how far things have gone in India where the young do not respect their elders, the children do not obey their parents, and even the sacred Serbian obligations of a godfather are trodden upon, Elijah the Thunderer, the loudest among his warlike brethren, threatens punishment. But the wording of this punishment mirrors the peasant's fear of drought and of the human misery it brings. It is not surprising perhaps that the singer's epic voice becomes suddenly much more moving and sure of itself; Elijah the Thunderer says that he will ask God for the keys of the skies and seal up the clouds so that

> No rain will fall from the clouds,
> No streaming rain, no quiet dew,
> And no bright shining of the moon,
> No rain will fall for three years of seasons,
> No wheat will grow, no vine will flourish.[6]

The lines will be repeated a little later when the threat becomes reality and some of their formulas are undoubtedly as old as man's sense of his dependence on earth and rain. But the way in which the betrayal of kinship and the destruction of the natural order of things come together in a fragment of this poem suggests what is at the heart of Serbian epic singing—the animistic sense of broken family norms, of a broken unity of human life which leads to a natural catastrophe, to the drying up and the disappearance of all that one lives by and lives for—fruit and beauty, the rain and the dew, the moonlight, the wheat, the wine.

In the anonymous Montenegrin version of this poem the difficulties of telling a saintly story in the language which has

[5] 'Mili Bože! čuda velikoga! / Ili grmi, il' se zemlja trese! / Il' udara more u bregove? / Niti grmi, nit' se zemlja trese, / Nit' udara more u bregove, / Već dijele blago svetitelji', *Karadžić*, ii, No. 1, ll. 1–6.

[6] 'Da ne padne dažda iz oblaka, / Plaha dažda, niti rosa tiha, / Niti noću sjajna mjesečina, / Da ne padne za tri godinice; / Da ne rodi vino ni šenica', ibid., ll. 44–8.

emerged from outlaws' history are again left behind as soon as
the singer touches on the great theme of 'the last times', the
theme so near to his heart and mind, to his sense of his personal
misery and historical fate:

> And the sun of heaven burned them with fire,
> Burned them with fire for three years of seasons,
> Until the brains of the heroes were broiled,
> And the rocks cracked open in the woods,
> And forest withered away on the mountains,
> And the black earth cracked,
> The black earth itself cracked open three fathoms deep,
> And heroes and their horses broke therein.[7]

This drought is more frightening, visually and dramatically,
because it is intensified by the quality of the soil, by the
Montenegrin karst burning in the Mediterranean sun, by
the Montenegrin experience of history. This is what makes the
brains broil, the rocks crack open, the forests wither and the
earth crack to swallow up the heroes and their horses. This epic
moment is earthed in the typical Montenegrin imagery which
enables the singer to refract his sense of 'the last times' with
such intensity and colour. In short, the biblical inevitability of
deserved punishment lives here in the peasant's 'feel' of the
unity of nature and man, of its moral character and historical
significance.

This sense of doomed humanity in a distant mythic land is
far more richly sustained in the poems which focus on some
more specific and particular dramas of Serbian family life.
Sometimes the ideal of brotherly love provides an ominous,
dream-like quality in the opening lines of the poems about
fratricide. Thus 'Milan-bey and Dragutin-bey' echoes the
formulaic opening of several poems about fratricide which were
recorded before it, including 'Marko Kraljević and His
Brother Andrijaš',[8] but adds to it the second line which is an
unmistakable touch of the singer's personal genius:

[7] 'Pa ih Bože sunce izgorelo, / Gorelo ih tri godine danah, / Dok uzavre
mozak u junaka, / Dokle puče kami u lugove, / A osanu gora proz planine; /
Dokle crna zemlja ispucala, / Puče crna zemlja po tri lakta, / Te se lome
konji i junaci', *Karadžić*, ii, No. 2, ll. 43–50.

[8] See note 101, p. 50.

> The brothers lived in so great love
> That their horses were kissing under them.[9]

However, as soon as the idyllic point is made, an ominous note is immediately struck: Milan-bey begins to suspect that the wives will 'plant thorns'[10] between him and his brother:

> And they will channel water through the thorns,
> So that the thorns will grow up high,
> And we shall never be able to meet.[11]

At the end, however, after Milan kills his brother, he recognizes the nature of his crime and the ideal moral order is re-established in his punishment:

> He left his own houses and his own lands
> And went to wander over the world.[12]

Driven from his own, his only possible world, Milan-bey incurs the punishment which is in the patriarchal order of things almost commensurate with his crime.

'Mujo and Alija' tells the same story, illuminating the imaginative vitality of the patriarchal epic tradition which could shape such diverse patterns of language from the warp and woof of one and the same theme. The opening image of brotherly love—characteristic of most of these poems—seems to be almost the same:

> How wonderfully they lived together,
> They would exchange their horses for each other's,
> They would exchange their bright weapons of war.[13]

Of course, the singer does not know that this line echoes the medieval legal status of horses and arms as the vassal's symbols of power given to him by his suzerain.[14] But why should he

---

[9] 'Koliko se braća milovala, / Pod njima se dobri konji ljube', 'Milan-beg i Dragutin-beg', *Karadžić*, ii, No. 10, ll. 3–4.

[10] 'Trnje posaditi', ibid., l. 13.

[11] 'I kroz trnje vodu navratiti, / Neka trnje u visinu raste, / Da se nikad sastat' ne moremo', ibid., ll. 14–16.

[12] 'On ostavi dvore i timare, / Pa otide glavom po svijetu', ibid., ll. 165–6.

[13] 'Koliko su divno živovali, / Ispod sebe konje mijenjali / I sa sebe svijetlo oruže', 'Mujo i Alija', *Karadžić*, ii, No. 11, ll. 3–5.

[14] See above pp. 21–2.

know this—his imagery works in its own right. And he achieves
the same effect—unique because it is so deeply immersed into
a traditional pattern of the story and its language—when Mujo,
having killed his brother, comes to recognize what he has done,
again far away from home, 'in the midst of a road':[15]

> He met a raven lacking its right wing,
> This is the word he said to the raven:
> 'Tell me, raven, tell me, black bird,
> How you feel without your right wing?'
> The raven replied to him in a croak:
> 'Lacking my right wing I feel
> As a brother feels lacking a brother.'[16]

And the same rich links between the natural and the human
world are also reflected in several other poems about fratricide,
particularly in the better version of 'The Division of the Jakšići'
in which this theme is connected with the names of the fifteenth-
century Serbian feudal lords. In this song, which Karadžić
wrote down from his memory of his father's singing, the perilous
desire of two mighty brothers to divide their estate is set from
the beginning in the framework of cosmic imagery. In the
opening lines the moon reproaches the morning star for having
been absent and wasted 'three white days'[17] and she replies that
she had been watching 'brothers dividing their inheritance'[18].
The sanctity of the norm that patrimony should not be divided,
that joint family estate is a sacred patriarchal and economic
institution, underlies the question and the answer—as well as
their scope suggested by cosmic imagery. The two brothers
cannot agree about the division of a horse and a hawk; the
legal significance of a horse as a symbol of feudal power in
medieval Serbia is again only a distant historical association of
which the singer is not aware. On the morning after the quarrel
Dmitar takes the horse and the hawk and before he goes
hunting he instructs his wife to kill his brother. The wife

[15] 'Nasred druma puta', op. cit., l. 55.
[16] 'Srete vrana bez desnoga krila, / Pa je tici riječ govorio: / "A tako ti,
crna tice vrane! / Kako ti je bez desnoga krila?" / No mu tica piskom
odgovara: / "Mene jeste bez krila mojega, / Kako bratu, koji brata nema" ',
ibid., ll. 56–62.
[17] 'Tri bijela dana', 'Dijoba Jakšića', *Karadžić*, ii, No. 98, l. 4.
[18] 'De dijele braća očevinu', ibid., l. 9.

disobeys her husband and makes a magnificent present to his brother for which she asks and receives the gift of his horse and his hawk. In the meantime the hawk has its right wing broken off by a gold-winged wild duck and falls into a lake. Dmitar takes the hawk out of the lake and the hawk tells him:

> 'Lacking my right wing,
> I feel as a brother feels lacking a brother.'[19]

It is the voice of the hawk which opens Dmitar's eyes; he hurries back to save his brother and his horse breaks both its legs on the way, but brotherly feelings triumph owing to feminine love which had already eroded the male hatred and ambition. Thus the framework of cosmic and natural imagery is reaffirmed in the story which establishes the basic moral norms beyond their immediate historical realities.[20]

Sometimes, however, this patriarchal tragic sense of life grows into epic tales of much greater complexity—easily understood perhaps in their own times, but much more difficult to grasp today when many of the assumptions and customs behind them have been blurred or have completely disappeared. In the gloomiest, and in its crude way perhaps the most moving of these poems—'The Brothers and Their Sister'—almost everyone seems to be victimized in the end. A great authority on the subject had the misfortune to sum up its story by finding that God 'killed off nine brothers here . . . without any reason and then took pity, raised the youngest brother from his grave and sent him to visit his sister'.[21] It seems, however, that the singer had far too sophisticated a sense of God's actions for a modern scholar to grasp. For what happens, in fact, in the story is that the brothers disregard the mother's advice to marry their sister

---

[19] 'Meni jeste bez krila mojega, / Kao bratu jednom bez drugoga.' *Karadžić*, ii, No. 98, ll. 82–3.

[20] It is also significant perhaps that in the second, much poorer version of this poem (*Karadžić*, ii, No. 99) there is no cosmic imagery in the opening section and the story is enslaved in cruel historical realities in which the wife is seen as the culprit for the brothers' hatred of each other so that she has both her eyes dug out in the end. This illustrates the inability of the singer to come to ultimate terms with the moral and human significance of his historical material.

[21] V. Đurić, 'Srpskohrvatska narodna epika', *Antologija narodnih junačkih pesama*, Belgrade, 1973, p. 25.

to 'a neighbour in the village'[22] and give her instead to 'a Ban from overseas'.[23] This means that the brothers have not only disregarded their mother's wise advice, but also sinned against a time-honoured patriarchal moral norm by marrying their sister into an alien world. The sister is obviously innocent: her duty was to obey the males who always have and should have the last word in such matters. This is why God punishes the brothers by death, but when the innocent sister claims her patriarchal right to be visited by one of them, when she comes to 'shriek bitterly'[24] in an alien world, God is moved by her undeserved fate and he says to His angels:

'Go down, my two angels,
To the white tomb of Jovan,
Jovan—the youngest brother.
Breathe into him your spirit,
Make a horse for him from his tomb,
Make cakes of earth for him,
Cut his shroud into gifts:
And prepare him to visit his sister.'[25]

The lines mirror patriarchal customs—the strictly observed obligation to visit and bring presents to a married sister or daughter—but their compelling cruelties express, above all, the sister's yearning for her brother, her right to see for a moment a part of her own world which she was in duty bound to leave. But when the brother returns to his grave, the sister and the mother also die—innocent but tied by their blood and fate to their men.

The same courage in facing the cruel realities of actual life and the same moral significance is also to be found in 'God Leaves No Debt Unpaid', by general consent the greatest among the poems about the betrayal of kinship. The Slavonic antithesis in the opening lines evokes a patriarchal ideal of

---

[22] 'U selo komšiji' ,'Braća i sestra', *Karadžić*, ii, No. 9, l. 9.
[23] 'S preko mora banu', ibid., l. 10.
[24] 'Ljuto pišti', ibid., l. 32.
[25] 'Id'te dolje, dva moja anđela, / Do bijela groba Jovanova, / Jovanova brata najmlađega, / Vašijem ga duhom zadanite, / Od groba mu konja načinite, / Od zemljice mijes'te kolače, / Od pokrova režite darove; / Spremite ga sestri u pohode.' Ibid., ll. 36–43.

human love in the form of an image of natural harmony:

> Two pines grew side by side,
> Between them a slim-topped fir;
> They were not two green pines,
> Nor a slim-topped fir between them;
> They were two brothers, born of one blood,
> One was Pavle, the other Radule,
> And Jelica their sister between them,
> The brothers dearly cherished their sister,
> And they brought every sign of love to her,
> Last of all two inlaid daggers,
> Silver-inlaid and gilded daggers.[26]

Of course, the image of the two pines with 'a slim-topped fir between them' is denied as an actual proposition—but it illuminates the illusion which it embodies, it sheds its light on what comes to replace it, the patriarchal ideal of the brothers' love for their sister. However, at the heart of this illusion lurk the daggers as tokens of love—the daggers which foreshadow what is actually coming. Pavle's absolute love for his sister will inspire an equally absolute hatred for her in his wife: she will kill their child with Jelica's daggers and Jelica will be unable to prove her innocence. Her brother will not believe her true story even when she comes to swear by his life, not just her own. So the innocent sister, slandered by her sister-in-law, will be killed by her brother and a whole pattern of moral and natural order will be broken. It will be re-established at the end of the poem—in reality by the just punishment of the culprit, beyond reality in the natural and supernatural justice of the basil which grows on the innocent sister's tomb and the thorns and the nettles which grow on the tomb of her evil sister-in-law. This moral illumination by natural imagery in a world of total destruction is deeply analogous to the *fata morgana* of the Slavonic antithesis at the beginning of the poem, and this stylistic illumination of the patriarchal sense of cosmic harmony

[26] 'Dva su bora naporedo rasla, / Među njima tankovrha jela; / To ne bila dva bora zelena, / Ni međ' njima tankovrha jela, / Već to bila dva brata rođena: / Jedno Pavle, a drugo Radule, / Među njima sestrica Jelica. / Braća seju vrlo milovala, / Svaku su joj milost donosila, / Najposlije nože okovane, / Okovane srebrom, pozlaćene.' 'Bog nikom dužan ne ostaje', *Karadžić*, ii, No. 5, ll. 1–11. Recorded from one Rovo ('pock-marked').

lies at the heart of many of the greatest Serbo-Croat decasyllabic songs.

It is also found in the poems which—like 'Momir the
Foundling', 'Simeun the Foundling', and 'Dušan's Wedding'—
echo ancient legends, re-shape them on the patterns of Serbian
patriarchal village life during the Turkish times and sometimes
pin them down to the names of medieval Serbian historical
figures. Similarities have been noted between foundling Momir
and foundling Mimir in the *Nibelungenlied*;[27] more obviously,
however, the poem tells the tale which comes ultimately from
'The Story of the Ten Viziers' in *1001 Nights*.[28] In the Oriental
legend a king brings up a gifted boy unaware that the boy is
his son; in the poem which Karadžić wrote down from blind
Živana in Srem the greatest Serbian medieval ruler Stefan
Dušan the Mighty—called Tsar Stepan in the poem as he was
always officially called in his own time[29]—adopts the child he
finds while returning from unsuccessful hunting. Adoption—
like blood-brotherhood, blood-sisterhood, *kumstvo*[30]—was one
of the sacred links of Serbian patriarchal village life, often the
pledge of economic, social, and historical survival under the
Turkish rule. In such links the relationship established by free
choice was expected to partake of the nature of a blood tie;
this is what makes these extensions of blood ties particularly
dramatic in the patriarchal Serbian village civilization and in

[27] See *Matić*, p. 676.
[28] See T. Maretić, *Naša narodna epika*, Belgrade, 1966, p. 283.
[29] See note 52, p. 121.
[30] *Kum* is a godfather, or the best man officiating at the wedding ceremony, or any member of either family. The institution of *kumstvo* was the
strongest extension of family ties and it was honoured as much as the closest
family relations. It was more important than brotherhood in blood, because
it did not only link two men but whole families for many generations.
Kumstvo was sanctioned by the church; it was a pledge of reconciliation in
blood feuds; in some areas the earth was kissed before the *kum*'s feet. There
were also folk beliefs that *kumstvo* could bind a snake not to bite, a wolf not
to kill cattle and so on (see Š. Kulišić *et al.*, *Srpski mitološki rečnik*, 'kumstvo',
pp. 187–90). Among many references to the institution of *kumstvo* in epic
poetry perhaps the most telling one is the warning of a bride to her best man
when he tries to seduce her that the earth would tremble to bits and the
heaven would crack open over their heads if such a crime were committed
('The Wedding of Marko Kraljević', 'Ženidba Marka Kraljevića', *Karadžić*,
ii, No. 56, ll. 189–90; see below pp. 206–7).

its epic poetry. In this poem adoption is dramatically seen as a substitute for the link of a natural parent from the moment when Tsar Stepan finds a helpless child in 'the green wood':

> Wrapped around in the foliage of the vine,
> And tied with bands in tendrils of the vine
> And his face covered by a leaf of vine.[31]

The intertwining of vines, leaves, and human affection—often found in the decasyllabic singing both in idyllic and tragic connections[32]—is the last trace of the mother's care and love for her little boy whom she had thrown away.

In the next major step in the Oriental story ten viziers are jealous of the noble and wise young man and they scheme to destroy him by making the king believe that the boy has dishonoured the queen. In the decasyllabic poem the nine viziers (as they are called, though the term was not used in the Serbian medieval court and suggests later Turkish times) are also jealous; a similar plan is made for Momir's destruction, but the part of the king's wife is taken here by Tsar Stepan's daughter Grozdana. Moreover, the wicked scheme is devised by vizier Todor—related to the Tsar by the sacred link of a *kum* (godfather, or the best man at the wedding). This is also an important part of the patriarchal drama:

> 'The unfaithful *kum*, may his faith strike him dead!'[33]

And finally, whereas the Oriental tale has a happy ending in which the king discovers that the boy is his son before he is executed, the ending of the decasyllabic poem mirrors the singer's vision of medieval Serbia as the country of 'the last times' and this is why it has a distinctly tragic imprint. The *kum*, who should be the most trustworthy friend in the world, makes a devilish design; its success depends on the ideal, innocent sisterly love which Grozdana feels for Momir:

> 'I will make Momir the Foundling drunk,
> And take him to the palace of the Tsar
> To the upper rooms where Grozdana sleeps,

---

[31] 'U gori zelenoj / U vinovo lišće zavijeno, / A vinovom lozom povijeno, / A po licu listom pokriveno', *Karadžić*, ii, No. 30, ll. 13–16.

[32] See, for instance, above pp. 38 (note 17), 47–9, 78–9.

[33] 'Kum neverni, vera ga ubila!', *Karadžić*, ii, No. 30, l. 103.

And I will put him in his sister's arms,
This is a kindness in any sister,
A sister has pity for a brother,
And she will hold him closer to herself.'[34]

When the sisterly embrace leads to Momir's execution and
Grozdana hangs herself, the story returns to its initial imagery
which suggests a tragic triumph of love over death and life:

Above Momir's grave a green pine has grown,
Above Grozdana's—the vines;
The vines have grown around the trunk of a pine
As a sister's arm round her brother.[35]

The significance of this animistic growth of the natural
imagery and patriarchal relations can also be grasped by a
comparison with a feudal *bugarštica*, written down at the
beginning of the eighteenth century in the Bay of Kotor, which
reduces the same story to a love affair in a rose garden between
a Christian knight and a Turkish Sultana.[36] For most of the
passionate *bugarštica* verges on the absurd: the knight is brow-
beaten into sensuality and when his 'heroic heart' warms up to
the occasion, the affair is discovered by the janissaries and he is
hanged on a maple tree. It is only in the last few lines—when
the Sultan's daughter cuts her hair in grief and puts it on her
lover's face to protect him from the sun before hanging herself
on the same maple—that the poem strikes a moving note.

But, of course, the success or failure in merging diverse epic
material into a poem depends not only on the vitality of the
tradition, but also on the gift of a particular singer. In this
respect the differences between the two decasyllabic versions of
'Simeun the Foundling' are of some interest. Both poems follow
in some detail the Serbian medieval hagiography about Pavle
of Kesarija, ultimately rooted in the Oedipus story. But whereas
the version which Karadžić recorded from his best poet

---

[34] 'Opojiću Naoda Momira, / Odneću ga u careve dvore / Na čardake gdi
Grozdana spava, / Metnuću ga sestrici na ruke, / A sestra je svaka milostiva /
I na brata svoga žalostiva, / Ona će ga lepše prigrliti', ibid., ll. 117–23.

[35] 'Na Momiru zelen bor nikao, / Na Grozdani vinova lozica, / Savila se
loza oko bora, / Ko sestrina oko brata ruka', ibid., ll. 391–4.

[36] 'Sultana Grozdana and Young Vlach Mlađen' ('Sultana Grozdana i
vlašić Mlađen', *Bogišić*, No. 56).

Tešan Podrugović shows a vivid sense of physical and spiritual reality in every detail, the anonymous version seldom misses a chance of deviating into an absurdity or a platitude. In Podrugović's poem Simeun is found as an abandoned baby by an 'old monk'[37] who rises up early and goes

> To the Danube, to the cold water,
> To scoop up water out of the Danube,
> To wash his face in water and to pray.[38]

But in the anonymous version instead of the old monk the greatest Serbian saint, Patriarch Sava, appears as a fast runner and a keen hunter, features not exactly compatible with his status either as a saint or as a wise foster father. Besides, before the patriarch-hunter puts in his appearance, there is a story about a tsar who adopted a girl, brought her up and raped her! Admittedly, this explains the appearance of the baby; but the mother's crime is explained by the need to wipe out such an injustice from the face of the earth! As if this were not enough, the poor girl exclaims that 'a foster father is like a real one'![39] This proverb which sums up the obligations and respect due to a foster father is hardly appropriate in what has to be considered as an incestuous context.

In Podrugović's poem the old monk's love for the helpless child—the core of this epic drama—is evoked in simple and straightforward details which are not found in the anonymous version:

> He will not give the child up to a nurse,
> He feeds the child in his monastery,
> He feeds him with honey and with sugar.[40]

And whereas in the anonymous version we are only told that 'the child learned his books beautifully',[41] in Podrugović's

---

[37] 'Starac kaluđere', 'Nahod Simeun', *Karadžić*, ii, No. 14, l. 1.

[38] 'Na Dunavo na vodu studenu, / Da zavati vode na Dunavu, / Da s' umije i Bogu se moli', ibid., ll. 2–5.

[39] 'Ranitelj je kako i roditelj', *Karadžić*, ii, No. 15, l. 17. Also quoted as an actual proverb in V. S. Karadžić, *Srpske narodne poslovice*, p. 305 (under 'hranitelj').

[40] 'Ne šće davat' čedo na dojilje, / Već ga rani u svom namastiru, / Rani njega medom i šećerom', *Karadžić*, ii, No. 14, ll. 18–20.

[41] 'Lepo dete knjigu izučilo', op. cit., l. 36.

poem the process of learning lives in its mystery and excitement:

> Simo learned his book marvellously,
> He has no fear of any other boy,
> Nor no fear of his abbot the old man.[42]

In both versions the hero goes into the world in search of his parents; but only in Podrugović's poem is his incestuous relationship with his mother partly explained by the fact that he was 'deceived by wine'.[43] There is no attempt at this interplay of situation and character in the anonymous version; and Simeun's confession of his sin, twice as long as Podrugović's rendering, tells us nothing that we had not already learned—that Simeun 'sinned greatly against God'.[44] Instead of the narrator's generalized moral indignation Podrugović's poem offers the hero's confession which lives as a drama of speech, feeling, and action. Words seem to fail Simeun's sense of the enormity of his sin; he almost shrinks from his urge to confess and he finally comes to see his sin both as accident and fate:

> 'Do not ask me, abbot my father!
> In a bad hour I went to seek my kin,
> And in a worse one I came to Budim!'[45]

The old monk has no comment to make; without a word he shuts the door of 'the cursed gaol'[46] and throws its keys into the river:

> 'When the keys come out of the Danube,
> Let Simeun's sin be pardoned!'[47]

And the poem ends on a miraculous hagiographical note: nine years later the keys are found in a fish and Simeun is discovered with the aura of a saint in the gaol, sitting at a gold table and holding the Gospels in his hands. In short, the poem holds together as a unique mosaic of the patriarchal and the miraculous

---

[42] 'Čudno Simo knjigu izučio, / Ne boji se đaka nijednoga, / Ni svojega starca igumana', op. cit., ll. 29–31.

[43] 'Vino prevarilo', op. cit., l. 119.

[44] 'Bogu vrlo sagrešio', op. cit., l. 96.

[45] 'Ne pitaj me, oče igumane! / U z'o čas sam roda potražio, / A u gori doš'o do Budima!', op. cit., ll. 170–2.

[46] 'Tavnicu prokletu', ibid., l. 176.

[47] 'Kad izišli ključi iz Dunava, / Simeun se grija oprostio!' Ibid., ll. 183–4.

elements; whereas the anonymous version which ends in a
similar way, abounds in absurd overtones such as the patriarch's
comment on the enormity of Simeun's sin:

'It's no joke—one's old mother!'[48]

The ability of a bard of Podrugović's calibre to absorb such
diverse material from different oral and literary sources into a
single Serbian patriarchal drama is also reflected in 'Dušan's
Wedding'. It is one of the many variants of the wedding story
with obstacles; the girl has to be brought from a distant land,
the wedding deal has to be made with crafty, treacherous
foreigners who demand that the wedding guests should disarm,
several difficult tasks have to be performed before the girl is
given and they are not performed by the bridegroom but by
one of the heroes in his party. These details suggest a common
if distant oral background with the adventures of Gunther's
courting of Brünhild in the *Nibelungenlied*.[49] More specifically,
the heroic tasks which have to be performed before the bride
can be led away—the shooting of a golden apple, the leaping
over horses, the recognition of the bride among the girls who
look exactly like her—are not only wandering motifs of epic
singing, but are also found in a closely parallel form in the
bugarštica 'When Duke Janko Beat Despot Đurađ with his
Mace', which was recorded in the eighteenth century near
Dubrovnik.[50] Finally, not only did Stefan Dušan not actually
marry a Venetian wife, but as far as we know he never had
anything to do with any Roksanda, least of all with Alexander's
wife, the daughter of the Persian Emperor Darius, the well-
known character of a romance which was also popular in
Serbian medieval literature. As regards the general references
to 'the treacherous Latins' in the poem,[51] they are very much in
the standard repertory of Serbian history and epic singing and
need not be understood specifically as summing up Stefan
Dušan's relations with the Venetian Republic which preferred

[48] 'Nije šala svoja stara majka!' Op. cit., l. 103.
[49] See T. Maretić, *Naša narodna epika*, pp. 261–2.
[50] See 'Kad je Janko vojvoda udarao Đurđa despota buzdohanom',
Bogišić, No. 9.
[51] 'Latini su stare varalice', 'Ženidba Dušanova', *Karadžić*, ii, No. 29, l.
112.

the existence of a weak Byzantium to conquering it with such a formidable ally as Stefan Dušan.

The only historical 'references' are the names of Stefan Dušan himself[52] and of the main hero Miloš Voinović who was in fact one of Dušan's military captains.[53] But they are seen in a dramatic patriarchal relationship, reflecting perhaps some earlier assumptions about feudal loyalties, and this gives a unique imaginative imprint to the whole story. A sly peasant wit dominates their relationship; and the largely comic story of dauntless courage mirrors the temper of Podrugović himself who extemporized with the same craft and zeal with which he fought at the time when his outlawry was raised to the pedestal of a national and historical ideal during the Serbian Uprisings against the Turks.[54] The Voinovići are seen as Stefan Dušan's cousins—partly as shepherds, partly as well-to-do cattle raisers. They remain loyal to their sovereign even after he is misled into snubbing them by leaving them out of his wedding party; they only worry what will happen to him in a foreign land full of trickery without a single hero 'of his own kin'.[55] Miloš—the youngest brother and the greatest hero—has to be brought by fraud from the mountain where he looks after the shepherds and their sheep; the message says that his mother is dying and so he cannot ignore it. When he learns the truth, he decides to join the wedding party in disguise; for whom would he help—as he puts it—if not his uncle in need? His magnificent horse is disguised in a bear's skin, but the horse attracts the attention of the wedding party and treacherous merchants offer him a 'better horse'[56] and a hundred ducats to buy himself a plough and so earn his bread. In the tradition of the pride of

---

[52] In the title of the poem Karadžić uses the name Dušan, but throughout the poem Dušan is referred to as Serbian tsar 'Stjepan'. In fact Stefan Dušan used his first name (Stefan) in all his official documents, because Dušan was his patronymic. But Dušan is a common Serbian first name, and this is perhaps why this ruler came to be referred to in later sources and Serbian historiography as Tsar Dušan. See T. Maretić, *Naša narodna epika*, p. 214.

[53] Miloš Vojinović represented Stefan Dušan in his dealings with Dubrovnik and he is referred to in the charter of Ston, dated 1333. See *Matić*, p. 673.

[54] See below pp. 311–14.

[55] 'Od roda svojega', *Karadžić*, ii, No. 29, l. 109.

[56] 'Konja još boljega', ibid., l. 279.

the cattle raisers, he tells them that his father earned his living without a plough and that he would not know what to do with their ducats as he would be unable even to count them. After the tricksters are tricked and duly punished, Miloš Voinović cheers himself up with a little wine in another comic scene in a tavern. These scenes owe some of their formulas to the poems about Marko Kraljević—not surprisingly, perhaps, as Podrugović himself made up many poems about the most popular and often comic Serbian hero. [57] Finally, the clumsy and sly peasant hero fights a duel for his sovereign and threatens his elegant opponent—following the outlaws' custom—that he will wear his clothes after the victory. When it comes to leaping over three horses with sword-shaped flames above them, the sovereign curses Miloš's tailor who made him such a long mountain-cloak and advises him to take it off, but Miloš answers in his—or Podrugović's—unmistakable accent of defiance and sly mockery:

> 'Sit down, my Tsar, and drink red wine,
> Do not worry about my mountain-cloak;
> If there is a heart in the hero,
> Mountain-cloak will not be in his way;
> When a sheep is fretting over its own fleece,
> There will be no sheep, there will be no fleece. [58]

The same triumph of tonal deflation—or uplifting—rings in the scene in which Miloš is faced with the task of recognizing the grand foreign princess. He tells his sovereign that there is nothing to worry about: as he could tell, by the mother sheep, each of the three hundred lambs which were born in a single night in the mountain, why should he have any difficulty in recognizing a mere princess? When the tale—tonally sustained in Podrugović's great art—comes to its end, Miloš Voinović reveals himself to his uncle, and the uncle is again worried at having snubbed him and shown him so little consideration. Even the last reflective line—the proverb expressing the idea

[57] See below pp. 181, 187–8, 191, 195–8, 204–8.

[58] 'Sjedi, care, pak pij rujno vino, / Ne brini se mojom kabanicom; / Ako bude srce u junaku, / Kabanica ne će ništa smesti: / Kojoj ovci svoje runo smeta,/ Onđe nije ni ovce ni runa.' *Karadžić*, ii, No. 29, ll. 479–84.

that man is bound to come to woe wherever he has no next-of-kin—seems to partake some of Podrugović's lightness of touch, the lightness of a brave outlaw whose sense of humour was equal to his instinctive trust in the sacred patriarchal ideal of loyalty. In short, Podrugović's greatness—and he was undoubtedly the greatest of all the poets in the tradition—springs from his ability to bring to life the norms of his time in a story set in the political world of medieval Serbia, but told with the full richness of his own comic epic voice. 'Dušan's Wedding' shows an imaginative range capable of coming to grips with the diversity of its material—basically in the same way in which Podrugović's 'Simeun the Foundling' mirrors a partiarchal sense of life in an ancient legend, summing up its ultimate significance in the tragic flowering of natural imagery expressing the ancient animistic beliefs so prominent in Serbian folk culture.

3. The Lords

The tonal scope of the Serbo-Croatian folk epic singing—ranging from a blunt view of history to its hagiographical understanding—is richly exploited in the poems about Serbian medieval feudal lords. Historical and fictitious heroes, actual details and legends, major Christian moral concepts, and the norms of Serbian patriarchal village life under the Turkish rule live here in a language in which a blurred feudal epic idiom has merged with the speech of the later border raiders, outlaws, and rebels. And seldom have such diverse elements been so successfully harnessed to such conflicting imaginative purposes. For apart from the rebels' need to see medieval Serbia as a lost national paradise of grandeur and freedom, soon to be regained, there was also the urge to account for its downfall. And in this account the biblical concept of the Last Judgement looms large from an epic landscape of social crime and punishment, a landscape which comes to life primarily in terms of the experience of the later history of the Turkish rule of the Balkans.

Sometimes the singer pins his faith in the grandeur of medieval Serbia to a magnificent fictitious hero like Strahinić Ban. Usually he links it with an 'actual' figure like Duke Momčilo, most often in a story in which the hero is historical only in name. But sometimes a grand tragic figure, like that of Prince Lazar, shows that considerable knowledge of factual history has been sifted down to the songs through oral and literary transmission. Most frequently, however, a historical fact is twisted in a way which yet mirrors a general social fact behind it: Prince Lazar, Stefan Dušan's favourite, but not a man of the highest birth, is represented as a servant pouring wine at the Emperor's table. Similarly, the rivalries and factions of many grand feudal lords are mirrored in the actions of only a few major historical villains, like King Vukašin and his brother Despot Uglješa. A fictitious third brother (Gojko) is added to take part in their wicked scheming, but on other occasions he is seen as their innocent victim. More significantly, perhaps, the singer's sense of innocent victimization in medieval Serbia is linked with Tsar Uroš—probably because the singer knows that he presided over the dissolution of the Serbian lands, that he was ten when he came to rule the old part of Serbia and still under age when he succeeded his father Stefan Dušan the Mighty in 1355. The latter is remembered in several ways, but mostly, like the great Jugovići, as a symbol of unbridled power and considerable corruption. In one of the poems he marries his sister and burns the youngest monks, the lowest in their order, because, unlike the grand bishops, they fail to pay lip service to incest. And last but not least, the whole epic landscape is filled out with many figures who are usually considered fictitious—Rade the Mason who has built all the monasteries, tricky foreigners usually called Mihailo, treacherous women sometimes called Vidosava or Ikonija and faithful loves who are often called Jelica. Strictly speaking, however, they are hardly less historical than the medieval rulers and knights; they all live in the same epic landscape which mirrors an awareness of history, hardly less significant perhaps than many of its official and scholarly versions.

These heroes inhabit a world in which even the winged horses cannot escape their destiny, a world ominously threatened by the approaching disaster of Kosovo. This sense of coming doom is most clearly reflected in the poem about 'The Wedding of Prince Lazar' which Karadžić wrote down from Old Raško who had left Kolašin in Herzegovina (later Montenegro), and come to live in liberated Serbia.[1] In this poem Prince Lazar is seen as a very humble attendant reproaching Stefan Dušan for not having married him off before —'in the days of my youth and beauty'.[2] The possibility of full-hearted happiness seems to have been already forgone even if a wife were to be produced immediately. Moreover, the arrogance of one of the most powerful feudal families has to be faced before a marriage can be arranged. Stefan Dušan the Mighty himself is frightened at the thought of having to ask old Jug-Bogdan, proud but not quite senile, to give his daughter to Lazar:

[1] See 'Predgovor', *Karadžić*, iv, p. 368.
[2] 'Za mladosti i ljepote moje', 'Ženidba kneza Lazara', *Karadžić*, ii, No. 32, l. 29.

'It's not easy to approach him,
For Bogdan is of noble birth,
He will not give his daughter to a servant'.[3]

And when Dušan plucks up his courage and brings out Lazar's proposal, the nine sons of old Jug-Bogdan draw out their swords 'to kill the tsar in his chair'.[4] What despair will be needed to make the Jugovići accept such a proposal?

They lay by their swords when their father tells them in a spasm of humiliation—'he reads the book, he drops terrible tears'[5]—that 'Milica is destined to be Lazar's wife'.[6] Modern research tells us that the singer got Milica's name right and her father's name wrong; moreover old Jug-Bogdan has only a slim chance of being 'historical': the names of Juga and Južić have been recorded among noble families, but not Jugović.[7] This, however, is hardly the point; the helplessness of the most arrogant among the mighty of feudal Serbia is complete because they have already learned that the end of the world is looming large on the historical horizon:

'And the last times shall come,
And the sheep and the wheat shall vanish away,
And the bee and the field flower shall vanish;
Brother-in-God shall take brother to court,
Brother shall call out brother to duel'.[8]

The wording echoes some of the greatest lines from the poems about patriarchal family life, particularly those with apocryphal and hagiographical elements;[9] but it is of some interest that it provides a setting for the marriage of the central figure in the epic landscape of Serbian medieval history.

[3] 'Nije lasno njemu pomenuti, / Jer je Bogdan roda gospodskoga, / Ne će dati za slugu đevojku', *Karadžić*, ii, No. 32, ll. 45–7.

[4] 'Da pogube cara u stolici', ibid., l. 144.

[5] 'Knjige uči, grozne suze roni', ibid., l. 153.

[6] 'Milica je Lazu suđenica', ibid., l. 5.   [7] See *Matić*, p. 682.

[8] 'Nastanuće pošljednje vrijeme, / Nestanuće ovce i všenice / I u polju čele i cvijeta; / Kum će kuma po sudu ćerati, / A brat brata zvati po megdanu', ibid., ll. 107–11. *Kum*—translated here as 'brother-in-God'— usually denotes a godfather or the best man at the wedding ceremony, but also any member of the family (see note 30, p. 115). In broader usage *kum* also denotes a blood-brother and in colloquial Serbo-Croat it is also used as a non-specific form of address ('chap', 'fellow').

[9] See above pp. 108–9 and below p. 160.

This landscape is—not surprisingly perhaps—far more dramatically and vividly evoked in 'The Wedding of King Vukašin', which Karadžić wrote down in 1820 from Stojan the Outlaw who was serving his sentence in a Serbian prison for having killed a woman, a witch who, he was sure, had eaten his child.[10] The poem is a very great achievement as an epic hotch-potch of facts, fantasies, legends, and history. Historically, King Vukašin started factions which led to the Serbian defeat in the Battle on the Marica in 1371; but he figures historically in the poem only in so far as he is seen as the father of Marko Kraljević and a man of very small stature.[11] (See Pl. 2.) The tale tells the story of how he won, by treachery and fraud, the wife of Duke Momčilo, a far better man than himself. So King Vukašin is a historical villain in a fictitious story; and the historical status of Duke Momčilo is equally ambiguous. For there was, in fact, a Duke Momčilo—a kind of a grand outlaw, a *Raubritter*, who lived in his own fortress in Rodopa and was killed in 1361 in a battle against the Turks near the littoral town Peritheorion. The old chronicles record his death and call him a 'brave', 'strong knight', but misled by the location where he was killed, they refer to him as the Duke of Peritheorion. In the oral epic tradition Peritheorion was reduced to the much more natural and nicer sounding Pirlitor and moved from the coast to the vicinity of the mountain of Durmitor— not only for acoustic reasons but also because the glorious mountain provided a much more appropriate historical and epic setting for the grand heroic drama which takes place in the poem. Finally, the great hero Duke Momčilo was given, as he deserved, a magic sword and a winged horse. Both are, of course, of ancient legendary origin, but they appear in the poem in a fairly specific manner. The horse's wings are eventually burnt and what is left of them is tarred; the sword is dipped into salty blood so that it sticks to its sheath. These details link the poem with *Buovo d'Antona*, the chivalric romance which was available in a Serbo-Croat translation from the sixteenth

---

[10] See 'Predgovor', *Karadžić*, iv, p. 368. In popular belief a witch can by a miraculous wand open the breast of a man or a child who is asleep, take the heart out and eat it. The victim either dies instantly or lives for a time and dies the death which has been decided by the witch. See Š. Kulišić *et al.*, *Srpski mitološki rečnik*, p. 64.

[11] See below pp. 131–2.

century—in the Adriatic littoral region, not far away from the singer's home and the place where his hero and his winged horse lived.[12]

The story is fictitious: Duke Momčilo was not betrayed by his wife but by his subjects, he was not killed by King Vukašin but died in a battle with the Turks, King Vukašin did not end up by marrying Duke Momčilo's sister, having been moved by moral considerations to give up the idea of marrying Duke Momčilo's wife, after the two of them succeeded in assassinating her husband by fraud. And yet the poem mirrors richly a great medieval social and human drama of its soil: the clash of the central Serbian rulers with the local tribal lords in Montenegro. For Duke Momčilo appears in the poem surrounded by the love of his brothers and cousins. He is, as a Montenegrin poet put it, 'a local feudal lord who still lives on tribal ties', 'fed and protected by the strength and love of his tribe, tempered by the cruel mountain of Durmitor'; whereas King Vukašin is seen as one of the crafty, alienated 'magnates of the state'.[13] For diverse specific and general historical reasons the dramatic appeal of such a story to the spirit of the Serbian rebels fighting their wars of national liberation must have been enormous. And this is reflected in the picture of Duke Momčilo's heroic grandeur, of his courage equalled by his innocence and generosity, in the portrait of King Vukašin's cunning and cruelty, in the magnificent evocation of the patriarchal drama of perfidious wives and loyal sisters. This is what makes this poem speak with the thousand voices of the past and present. For it is its dramatic and historical intensity, the rich economy of its suggestive language, that makes it so superior to 'The German Ban and Duke Momčilo's Wife', the earlier decasyllabic version of the same story which was recorded in the eighteenth century in the vicinity of Dubrovnik, much nearer to the historical area of the poem and its singer.

In both versions the hero is seen with the moral aura of a tragic gloom, so characteristic of many of the greatest medieval knights who live in the epic landscape lit by the approaching doom of Kosovo. And in both versions this tragic aura takes the

[12] See *Matić*, pp. 662–3. See also T. Maretić, *Naša narodna epika*, pp. 193–5.
[13] R. Zogović, 'Predgovor', *Crnogorske epske pjesme raznih vremena*, Titograd, 1970, p. 21.

form of a dream which foreshadows the wife's treachery and the hero's death.

In the earlier version Duke Momčilo tells his brothers that in his dream 'grey mist'[14] spread from Germany, 'a fierce snake'[15] coiled round his heart and he called in vain his love to help him. However, in the version which Karadžić wrote down Duke Momčilo does not tell his dream to his brothers, but to his 'faithful love' who had already burnt the wings of his horse and dipped his sword into salty blood:

> 'Vidosava, my faithful love,
> I dreamed a strange dream in the night:
> A fleece of mist wound itself along
> From the Vasojevići, their bad country,
> It wound itself round Durmitor,
> And I struck through that raw wool of mist,
> With my nine loving brothers,
> And twelve close cousins of my father's blood
> And forty soldiers of the Emperor.
> My love, we separated in the mist,
> We separated not to meet again,
> God knows this will not end well.'[16]

This brings out not only the hero's tribal ties but also an innocence which equals his heroic spirit; besides, the 'fleece of mist' is a more vivid perception than the more clichetic 'grey mist' and it is part of the tragic irony which comes out even more fully in what Vidosava has to say about this dream:

> 'Do not be afraid, my kind Lord,
> A good hero has dreamed a good dream,
> The dream deceives, God is truth.'[17]

[14] 'Sinja magla', 'Od Nijemaca ban i žena Momčila vojvode', *Bogišić*, No. 97, l. 39.

[15] 'Ljuta zmija', ibid., l. 41.

[16] 'Vidosava, moja vjerna ljubo! / Ja sam noćas čudan san usnio / Đe se povi jedan pramen magle / Od proklete zemlje Vasojeve, / Pak se savi oko Durmitora; / Ja udarih kroz taj pramen magle / Sa mojijeh devet mile braće / I s dvanaest prvo bratučeda / I četr'est od grada levera, / U magli se, ljubo, rastadosmo, / Rastadosmo, pak se ne sastasmo; / Neka Bog zna dobra biti ne će', 'Ženidba kralja Vukašina', *Karadžić*, ii, No. 25, ll. 137–48.

[17] 'Ne boj mi se, mili gospodaru! / Dobar junak dobar san usnio; / San je laža, a Bog je istina', ibid., ll. 150–3.

The ironic tenderness of this response to dreams, truth and deceit is not to be found in the answer of Duke Momčilo's brothers in the earlier version—even if both quote the same proverb in slightly different wording.[18] And it is only in the later version that Duke Momčilo finds at the critical moment that he cannot draw out his sword: 'as if it had been grafted into the sheath'![19] Finally, the two respective versions of the great scene when Momčilo comes to the closed gates of his city illustrate the same basic difference. In the earlier version the hero's sister throws a 'length of linen' down the city walls,[20] the wife cuts the linen while her husband tries to climb up and, as his enemies are already waiting for him, he is killed immediately. But in the later version the sister's hair has been tied to the roof-beams by the treacherous wife; when she sees her helpless brother, she shrieks 'like a serpent in fury', tugs 'with her head and her strength',[21] pulls her hair out of her head and throws a length of 'linen rag' down the city walls, the last thread of hope for Momčilo.[22] Even the phrasal difference—between a 'length of linen' and a length of 'linen rag'—is significant. The latter suggests the despair of Momčilo's predicament; the despair which links him with 'the linen rag' which a sister used as a bandage to keep together the bones of her sick brother before his duel ('Sick Dojčin'),[23] or with the predicament of another wounded Serbian hero whom a good Turkish girl pulls out of the river before her brother comes to kill him to get his sword.[24] Moreover, when the legth of 'linen rag' is cut in the later version, Momčilo does not fall merely on the ground, but 'into the swords and the battle lances'.[25] And it is only in this version that he comes to address his assassin before he dies:

> 'King Vukašin, these are my dying words,
> Do not take Vidosava,

[18] See above p. 75, and note 27, p. 328.

[19] 'Kao da je za kore prirasla', *Karadžić*, ii, No. 25, l. 166.

[20] '(Pruži) platno (dvoru niz prozore)', *Bogišić*, No. 97, l. 85.

[21] '(Ona ciknu,) kako ljuta guja, / (Manu) glavom i ostalom snagom', *Karadžić*, ii, No. 25, ll. 229–30.

[22] 'Krpa platna', ibid., ll. 233, 235.   [23] See above pp. 88–9.

[24] See 'Marko Kraljević Knows His Father's Sword'—'Marko Kraljević poznaje očinu sablju', *Karadžić*, ii, No. 57, l. 15, and below p. 187.

[25] 'Na mačeve i na koplja bojna', *Karadžić*, ii, No. 25, l. 243.

2. Tsar Uroš and King Vukašin in the Monastery of Psača.

Vidosava, my unfaithful love,
She will have your head as she had mine,
Today she has betrayed me for your sake,
Tomorrow she will also betray you,
But take my loving sister,
Jevrosima, my loving sister,
She will be true to you forever,
She will bear you a hero as I was.'[26]

This tragic summit of the tale, this vision of the hero's generosity, pushes beyond the boundaries of social custom and history; there is no 'reason', no norm in any actual moral code, which would explain why the hero behaves as he does. And the question of how the singer uses history and creates a 'myth' is less interesting than how the myth uses the singer, how he becomes the medium of an art far more fascinating than his own historical attitudes could ever hope to be.

Last but not least, in the earlier version King Vukašin kills off Duke Momčilo and his wife and marries his sister in the last sixteen lines. In the later version, however, the singer returns from the tragic summit of his story to historical realities in a comic way which serves brilliantly his poetic purposes: Duke Momčilo's calpac hangs all round the shoulders of the dwarfish Vukašin, his boot holds Vukašin's both feet, his gold ring can take Vukašin's three fingers, his gown and sword drag on the ground when Vukašin takes them. There are several kinds of 'history' behind this scene: King Vukašin was in fact very short in stature—he is represented, for instance, as a dwarfish old man on a fresco painting in Psača.[27] (See Pl. 2.) The way he steps immediately into his victim's clothes mirrors some outlaw customs of the later times. But this is hardly the point; the comic dispersal of a heroic story in the end illustrates the central epic awareness that grand tragic gestures take place in a

---

[26] 'Amanet ti, Vukašine kralju: / Ti ne uzmi moju Vidosavu, / Vidosavu, moju nevjernicu, / Jer ć' i tvoju izgubiti glavu, / Danas mene u tebe izdala,/ A sjutra će tebe u drugoga; / Već ti uzmi moju milu seju, / Seju moju milu, Jevrosimu, / Ona će ti svagda vjerna biti, / Rodiće ti, k'o i ja, junaka', ibid., ll. 249–58.

[27] See S. Radojčić, 'O nekim zajedničkim motivima naše narodne pesme i našeg starog slikarstva', *Zbornik radova SAN*—Vizantološki institut SAN, ii, (1953), p. 167.

petty world of history and its comic intrigues, in the world of the Vukašins and the Vidosavas. In this respect the poem answers some questions which one should perhaps try to learn to ask. But if King Vukašin provides the social décor and the dense historical specification for Momčilo's tragic greatness, yet Momčilo is represented as possessed of an inner freedom which makes him a complete master of his spiritual fate. His generosity and breadth of vision are not enmeshed in personal reactions to the horrors which break his life; he remains inspired by something greater than a mere reaction to his historical setting.

This kind of epic vision and this range of epic tone are also achieved in the fantastic interplay of the realistic and apocalyptic detail in 'Banović Strahinja', one of the longest and perhaps the greatest single epic poem in Serbo-Croat.[28] It has been suggested that Strahinić Ban—for the hero is called Banović Strahinja only in the title of the poem—might be Đurađ Stracimirović Balšić and that the Jugovići, his in-laws, might be conceivably connected with the Jugas—a fairly common name in medieval Serbian feudal history. This may or may not be so, but it belongs to the field of speculation of how widespread were certain names.[29] In a similar spirit, it has sometimes been asked why Karadžić entitled his greatest poem 'Banović Strahinja' when the hero is called in the poem itself Strahinić Ban. Is it because there is a perfectly straightforward and very poor version of the same story in a *bugarštica* in which the hero is called Banović Strahinja?[30] Or did Old Milija, who could not sing without sipping slivovits, make this mistake? And was it due to alcohol or, as a more recent critic puts it, to 'the fermentation of thought'?[31]

But the poem is both more serious and much lighter in touch than such questions suggest. At the very beginning Strahinić Ban appears in all the epic glory of the Serbian world before the Turkish days: dressed in 'brocade and velvet',[32] he figures

[28] 'Banović Strahinja', *Karadžić*, ii, No. 44.   [29] See above, p. 126.

[30] See 'Banović Strahinja' in *Pantić*, pp. 128–31. This is one of the eighteen *bugarštice* which Jozo Betondić (1709–64) wrote down in the vicinity of Dubrovnik (first published in *Bogišić*, No. 40).

[31] P. Bakotić, 'Starac Milija,' *Školski vjesnik*, xii (1962), No. 8, p. 26. Reprinted in V. Nedić, ed., *Narodna književnost*, pp. 339–43.

[32] 'Dibu i kadifu', 'Banović Strahinja', *Karadžić*, ii, No. 44, l. 22.

like a 'Serbian hawk',[33] the pride of his country. But he does not ride on a winged horse surrounded by his brothers and cousins and for the moment he could be taken for any of the grand feudal lords. His in-laws, the great and powerful Jugovići, entertain him with the same zest with which he 'prides himself on his in-laws home'.[34] This is why it is mistaken to analyse his later conflict with his in-laws in terms of a social clash between a local feudal lord and the great magnates of the state.[35]

The clash opens with the news that a Turk has ravaged Ban's palaces and taken his wife away: Ban expects that the Jugovići will come with him to the field of Kosovo and rescue their sister and daughter. But even when they refuse to do so, they cast their eyes down with a sense of shame—which suggests that they still share his values. However, whereas they propose to find him a better wife, he is struck with grief, 'ready to weep':[36]

> He was in pain and in sorrow,
> And his face was melancholy sad,
> The ends of his dark moustache hung down,
> His dark moustaches drooped on his shoulders.[37]

The image of 'the drooping moustaches' is not perhaps uncommon, but it is usually linked with the feeling of bitterness rather than of sorrow, and no other epic hero has ever been

[33] 'Srpski soko', ibid., l. 26.
[34] 'Ponosi se bane u tazbini', ibid., l. 63.
[35] This was argued by H. Barić (see 'Netko bješe Strahiniću bane' *Srpski književni glasnik*, N.S. xlix (1936), pp. 595–6, 601–2, rpt. in V. Nedić, ed., *Narodna književnost*, pp. 196–206) and R. Zogović, (see 'Predgovor', *Crnogorske epske pjesme raznih vremena*, p. 28). The argument seems to boil down to the fact that Strahinić Ban is described as coming from '*small* Banjska' ('malena Banjska', *Karadžić*, ii, No. 44, ll. 2–3). It is true that 'small' is not a fixed epithet in this connection, but the poem as a whole does not so much deny as transcend socio-historical interpretations. Strahinić Ban is socially as acceptable to the Jugovići as he is proud of them; he is not their victim; they are aware that they should—even if they cannot—help him and it is clear to the end that they inhabit the same social world of values, even if the Jugovići fail to rise up to them.
[36] 'Gotove mu suze udariti', ibid., l. 159.
[37] 'Muka mu je i žao je bilo, / U obraz je sjetno neveselo, / Mrke brke nisko objesio, / Mrki brci pali na ramena', ibid., ll. 154–7.

described as 'melancholy sad'. And it is this personal, 'psychological' trait which governs Ban's response to misfortune that contrasts him with his father-in-law, old Jug-Bogdan. The old man does not respond emotionally to the misfortune; he tries to manipulate it. He has the experience and the ability for a realistic assessment of every situation; after all he knows so much about so-called life. As his moral senility is worthy both of his years and his high political position, he keeps his head cool and minds his own, not his daughter's, business. Hence his sharp retort to Ban's request to let his children come with him to Kosovo:

> 'My sons shall not go to Kosovo
> Though I never see my daughter again.'[38]

And hence, once the decision has been announced in the form which rules out further argument, the need of the old fox—or is it only his interest or perhaps just his manner?—to ingratiate himself with his worthy son-in-law in words which scintillate with love, understanding, and a spontaneously cynical wisdom:

> 'Brave Strahinj-ban, my dear son,
> O why are you so deeply sorrowing?'[39]

For after all, it is only a daughter that has been raped by a Turk —and who can tell if she may not enjoy it:

> 'By God, it is a curse sent by Heaven,
> She likes him better than you, my son;
> Let her go, and may the devil take her!'[40]

And to leave no chord untouched, there is also a kind of man-to-man honesty which is convincing in so far as it conveys a note of genuine indifference to his own child:

> 'If she has spent one whole night with him,
> One whole night with him under the tent,
> She can never be dear to you again.'[41]

[38] 'Ne dam đece vodit' u Kosovo, / Makar šćeri nigda ne vidio', *Karadžić*, ii, No. 44, ll. 247–8.

[39] 'Mio zete, deli Strahinj-bane! / Rašta si se tako razdertio?' Ibid., ll. 249–50.

[40] 'Bog j' ubio, pa je to prokleto, / Voli njemu, nego tebe, sine; / Neka ide, vrag je odnesao!' Ibid., ll. 255–7.

[41] 'Al' ako je jednu noć noćila, / Jednu noćcu šnjime pod čadorom, / Ne može ti više mila biti', ibid., ll. 252–4.

There is, among other things, some wisdom in this judgement: it will be proved right in the end. Meanwhile, suffice it to note that Jug-Bogdan's selfish calculation of personal safety and family interest is in perfect accord with patriarchal assessment of the worth of a woman and his own philosophy of sex. In short, it is a highly convincing if somewhat cynical dramatization of a psychology and a social point of view, the judgement of someone who has a lot to lose and who knows how things 'stand' and 'go'. And he would not stand where he does if he did not also know how to ingratiate himself with other people while frustrating them.

Strahinić Ban is not a man of different class but a man of different mettle. There is nothing foolhardy about his journey to Kosovo; he will disguise himself and take all possible precautions in what only appears to be the venture of an honourable madman. In order to recapture his wife from the midst of the Turkish army, he will fall back upon all his personal resources—no others have been left him—and trust even his knowledge of foreign languages, such as it is. But he does not delude himself even as a linguist:

> 'I can speak Turkish and Mânic Turkish,
> And I can understand Arabian,
> And I can gurgitate Albanian.'[42]

It is such measures of precaution and disguise, with their realistic and slightly comic colouring, that make the great epic hero appear almost like a character in a novel. And yet, his assessment of reality, of what can and must be done, is different from that of Jug-Bogdan. It is subservient to his personal feeling and his personal sense of honour, to what he feels must be done to save the life of his innocent and beloved wife. The fact that his wife is not as innocent as he imagines helps us to appreciate the tragic and the ironic interplay between the two codes of behaviour—his and Jug-Bogdan's. In order to act Ban has both to respond to reality and to overestimate its possibilities; this is how he avoids the limitations of the historical morality and vision of his social group—as the development of his conflict with old Jug-Bogdan will show. And, ultimately, he

---

[42] 'Mogu Turski, i mogu Manovski, / I Arapski jezik razumijem, / I na krpat sitno Arnautski', ibid., ll. 226-8.

finds himself on the creative side of history—on the side which changes the world for the better or, if defeated, suggests that it might be worth changing for the better.

But there is little doubt that the theme of ravaged home and Ban's emotional response to it touches the singer to the quick—having had to leave his own home near Kolašin, Old Milija sings about abandoned homes with devastating nostalgia. Admittedly, the theme is almost as standard in epic poetry as it was in Serbian history, but Old Milija, as we shall see, exploits its dramatic possibilities as no other singer has ever done before or since. Ban, who failed to find a common language with his in-laws, achieves a deep understanding with a homeless old Turkish dervish, a solo-drinker into the bargain, as Old Milija himself was.[43] For our first glimpse of the old dervish—'he pours alone, he drinks his glass alone'[44]—leads to his warm recollection of the days when he was Ban's prisoner:

> 'You gave me wine enough to be my drink,
> You gave me white bread enough to be my eat,
> You let me often warm up myself in the sun'.[45]

He recalls, moreover, how Ban took pity on him, how he let him go home and send his ransom afterwards, taking only his word for it. And when he describes his return to his home ravaged by plague, 'with elder trees sprouting out of walls',[46] he touches a chord which will obviously move Strahinić Ban and which was so close to the singer's own heart.

The dervish's description of the blessings of his imprisonment and the curse of his return to freedom explains perhaps why he refrains from betraying his helpless enemy—or friend?—in the middle of the Turkish army. But there is no personal sharing of someone else's fate and experience in Ban's generosity in the end, when he sets free his wife after she has sided with his enemy. There is no doubt that she should have been tied to the horses' tails according to the social moral code—so why does he let her go unpunished? Perhaps because he has no abstract

---

[43] See below p. 315.

[44] 'No sam lije, no sam čašu pije', *Karadžić*, ii, No. 44, l. 339.

[45] 'Dosta si me vinom napojio, / Bijelijem ljebom naranio, / A često se sunca ogrijao', ibid., ll. 463–5.

[46] 'Iz duvara zovke proniknule', ibid., l. 417.

sense of justice; he did not risk his life only to cultivate a moral concept but also to save a living woman and, as he thought, her sense of honour. When it turns out that the Jugovići's cynical assessment of the situation was after all right, they are ready to execute their daughter and sister even though they were not prepared to risk anything to save her life when she appeared only a helpless victim. But Ban has no need to prove that he is an honourable man; after the betrayal of his wife is revealed, his task is completed and he has nothing else to do. Or is his generosity, his refusal to let the Jugovići execute their sister and daughter, his revenge on his in-laws in their own terms? Does he need to demonstrate that, with all his in-laws hale and hearty, he has 'no one to drink the cool wine with'?[47] Be that as it may, the ending defines Ban's ultimate loneliness; he finds himself in a world in which he has lost his *raison d'être*.

However, as the dwarfish monstrosities of King Vukašin remained in the shadow of Momčilo's farewell to his murderer, so the crafty selfishness of the Jugovići is above all the light which illuminates and brings into full contrast the moral character of Ban's personality. This is why the sociological explanations of the greatest epic poems in terms of class conflict are fundamentally mistaken. For in such explanations the concepts of greed, treachery, cowardice, hatred, and arrogance are self-evident; and they undoubtedly throw some light on an important part of the story. But what can they tell us about Duke Momčilo who advises his murderer to marry his sister or Strahinić Ban who spares the life of his treacherous wife? For if it were true, as such critics insist, that Jug-Bogdan's character expresses the serfs' hatred of the feudal magnates, we would yet have to conclude that, terrible as that hatred was, more penetrating than any hatred can possibly be, it was outshone by the serfs' love and admiration for the small feudal lord, for all that Ban—in the eyes of such critics—stands for.[48] But, it is

---

[47] 'Nemam s kime ladno piti vino', ibid., l. 807.

[48] See R. Zogović, 'Predgovor', *Crnogorske epske pjesme raznih vremena*, p. 28; H. Barić, 'Netko bješe Strahiniću bane', *Srpski književni glasnik*, N.S. xlix (1936), pp. 601–2. J. Deretić makes a much more pertinent point suggesting that the unexpected moral denouement in 'Banović Strahinja' 'follows the logic of the poem and the moral habits of its singer Old Milija' ('Banović Strahinja—struktura i značenje', *Književna istorija*, iv (1972), p. 423).

perhaps more pertinent to note that both Duke Momčilo and Strahinić Ban create and inhabit a tragic epic landscape, a landscape in which ideals survive the physical destruction of the hero or the devastation of a whole heroic world. For if Duke Momčilo's death means that the world is inherited by scoundrels, if Ban's triumph deprives him of his own *raison d'être*, this is certainly not a didactic message but a tragic vision of the historical destiny of medieval Serbia, of 'the last times' of its grandeur.

The same kind of interplay between the ultimately idealistic and the lucidly realistic elements, leading to a tragic denouement, is also to be found in 'Uroš and the Mrljavčevići', one of the greatest poems about feudal factions during the twilight of medieval Serbia. (See Map 3.) The poem turns the historical drama of Emperor Stefan Dušan's succession, which marked 'the last times' of medieval Serbia, into an epic narration which feeds on the conflicts of characters and moral attitudes. Its historical background is the fact that two brothers, King Vukašin and Despot Uglješa, refused to recognize the sovereign power of Stefan Dušan's son Tsar Uroš, who was very young at the time and a weak ruler. The popular tradition—which turned King Vukašin and Despot Uglješa into the villains of many fictitious stories, and Tsar Uroš into their helpless and innocent victim—was very strong and widespread. It explains perhaps why Uroš, who had been represented as a tall vigorous young man in the older fresco paintings in the church of St Nicholas in Ohrid and in the monasteries of Dečani and Psača, lost so much in his stature that from the sixteenth century onwards he came to be painted as an ever-diminishing and finally dwarfish figure.[49] (See Pls. 2, 3.) But the most important part of this historical picture is the fact that the feudal factions led to the Serbian disaster at the Battle on the Marica in 1371.

So history provides, in a way, the basic pattern of conflict in this poem, but the poem adds to the list of scoundrels a fictitious third brother called Gojko and ascribes to King Vukašin's son Marko Kraljević the tragic role of denying his father's and his uncles' false claim to the succession. Thus the

[49] See S. Radojčić, 'O nekim zajedničkim motivima naše narodne pesme i našeg starog slikarstva', *Zbornik radova SAN*—Vizantološki institut SAN, ii (1953), p. 171.

conflict between father and son comes to lie at the core of the epic tale which sees history above all as a family drama. On the other hand the tale is also a moral fable of unbridled greed and cruelty opposed by simple and dauntless courage in defending legality and truth. All the four contestants are in the field of Kosovo; Uroš is silent and helpless, and the three brothers are ready to murder each other with their gold daggers. They send their 'fiery heralds'[50] to bring Father Nedeljko to settle their dispute. The messengers, raging in their arrogance, drive their horses into the church and whip the humble, helpless father who weeps but is not to be hurried with his holy service. Finally he tells them that he asked Tsar Dušan only about his sins, not about worldly matters, and directs them to King Vukašin's son Marko Kraljević:

> 'Marko will tell the truth,
> He fears no man,
> Only the one true God.'[51]

Before Marko leaves his home, his old mother—the standard epic figure of patriarchal love, honesty, and wisdom—gives him advice in a moving scene which suggests that she knows that there may be more important things in the world than the life of her only son:

> 'Marko, the only son of your mother,
> That my milk is not a curse to you,
> Do not, my son, speak dishonest words,
> Not for your father's sake or your uncles',
> But speak the justice of the God of truth!
> Do not suffer your soul's loss, my son,
> Because it is better to lose your life
> Than sin against your soul!'[52]

The mother's advice mirrors the landscape of 'the last times' in suggesting that Marko has to face the task in which he must

[50] 'Ognjeni čauši', *Karadžić*, ii, No. 34, l. 45.

[51] 'Hoće Marko pravo kazivati, / Jer se Marko ne boji nikoga, / Razma jednog Boga istinoga', ibid., ll. 80–3.

[52] 'Marko sine, jedini u majke! / Ne bila ti moja rana kleta, / Nemoj, sine, govoriti krivo, / Ni po babu, ni po stričevima, / Već po pravdi Boga istinoga; / Nemoj, sine, izgubiti duše; / Bolje ti je izgubiti glavu / Nego svoju ogr'ješiti dušu.' Ibid.. ll. 126–33.

risk his life to save his honour. The sense of doom is akin to the
destruction of 'the bee' and 'the flower', 'the wheat' and 'the
vine' in 'The Wedding of Prince Lazar'. The generosity and
self-sacrifice, the courage and simplicity with which they are
undertaken, are analogous to the great moment of Duke
Momčilo's death. And the commitment to honour and martyrdom is parallel to Strahinić Ban's decision to go alone into the
midst of the Turkish army to save his wife. All these elements,
however, will flourish in the myth and legends of the poems
about the disaster in the field of Kosovo. In 'Uroš and the
Mrljavčevići' the full tragedy is only scented and, as in the
other poems about medieval feudal lords, embedded in a
realistic sense of dislocated history. This is why the poem turns
from its tragic summit in the direction of dramatic ironies:
King Vukašin welcomes his son and is sure of his judgement
because it is clear that the son will inherit what his father gets.
Uncle Uglješa offers to start a dual monarchy at once. Uncle
Gojko reminds Marko of his love for him when he was a small
child and promises that he will be the second-in-command.
Uroš welcomes Marko as his godfather and only says that
Marko will decide the issue. And after Marko speaks up and
tells his father and his uncles what he thinks of their lust for
power, King Vukašin draws his dagger and, as a son cannot
fight against his father, what can the greatest hero of Serbo-
Croat epic singing do but take to his heels? The chase is seen as
a ring-dance repeated three times round the church; until
Marko escapes into the church and leaves his father by the
bleeding doorpost. However, Marko survives—as usual; only
an angel has been killed—one of those angels who, in fact, from
the middle of the fourteenth century, stand on fresco paintings
'on the left and the right side of the entrance' to Serbian
churches and like their 'guardians and sharp censors write down
in their books all the sins of those who enter'.[53] And it is of
course significant that King Vukašin—the villain in the epic
story about feudal factions which lead to the destruction of
Serbian medieval empire—is left cursing his noble-minded son
on this imaginative threshold of the Last Judgement:

[53] S. Radojčić, 'O nekim zajedničkim motivima naše narodne pesme i
našeg starog slikarstva', *Zbornik radova SAN*—Vizantološki institut SAN,
ii (1953), pp. 166–7.

'Before you are separated from your soul
May you see service under a Turkish tsar!'[54]

But at the same time Uroš blesses his *kum*:

'Godfather Marko, God be good to you!
May your face shine in the council!
May your sword cut in duels!
May no hero be better than you!
May your name be remembered everywhere,
As long as the sun and the moon shine!'
And as they said then, it happened.[55]

The full ambiguity of this ending—in which a historical and a family drama have become an issue of magic—can be appreciated only in the light of the epic poems about Marko in which he will come to be seen as the greatest hero, patching up what has been left of Serbian honour and glory after the Turkish conquest.

[54] 'I da bi ti duša ne ispala, / Dok turskoga cara ne dvorio!' *Karadži ć*, ii No. 34, ll. 248–9.
[55] 'Kume Marko, Bog ti pomogao! / Tvoje lice sv'jetlo na divanu! / Tvoja sablja sjekla na mejdanu! / Nada te se ne našlo junaka! / Ime ti se svuda spominjalo, / Dok je sunca i dok je mjeseca!' / Što su rekli, tako mu se steklo.' Ibid., ll. 251–7. For *kum*, see note 30, p. 115.

4. The Builders

Several poems about the building of the medieval monasteries and the fortress of Skadar (Scutari) are interesting, among other reasons, because they mirror the singer's imaginative awareness of the medieval spiritual grandeur of Serbia, its wealth and the nature of its worldly power. Of course, the singer does not know that medieval Serbia was a major European exporter of gold and silver[1]—but he is not perhaps as wide of the mark as it might be thought when he makes the great feudal Christian lords ask St Sava where his father's, 'Tsar' Nemanja's, treasure has gone—'the seven towers of groschen. and ducats'.[2] A mixture of historical fact and fiction also lurks in St Sava's answer, in blind Stepanija's version of this poem:

> 'Do not speak stupidly, Christian lords!
> My father did not waste his treasured wealth
> On battle-axes and on battle maces,
> Or on rich equipment for good horses;
> My father spent his treasury of wealth
> Building many foundations of the soul.'[3]

For it is true that Nemanja, the twelfth-century founder of the Serbian medieval state, built the monastery of Studenica in Serbia and restored from ruins Chilendarion in Mount Athos, even if the singer adds some other churches which were not built by Nemanja. But the spiritual purpose of the building of the houses of God, the worldly abodes of the infinite, comes out more clearly in the version which Karadžić recorded from Filip Višnjić, one of his best singers. This version is superior not only because it contains, as some editors point out, a longer list

---

[1] See above p. 101.

[2] 'Sedam kula groša i dukata', 'Sveti Savo', *Karadžić*, ii, No. 23, l. 5; No. 24, l. 5. This phrase occurs in both versions of 'Saint Sava' which Karadžić wrote down from blind Stepanija and Filip Višnjić respectively.

[3] 'Ne ludujte, gospodo rišćanska! / Nije babo raskovao blago / Na nadžake ni na buzdovane, / Ni dobrijem konjma na ratove, / Već je babo poharčio blago / Sve gradeći mloge zadužbine.' *Karadžić*, ii, No. 24, ll. 11–16.

of monasteries and shows a better knowledge of history and geography.[4] Apart from coming from a more widely travelled singer it shows a greater imaginative range. It also begins by contrasting the building of monasteries with the spending of material goods for the destructive purposes of war, but it adds in an afterthought some details which are not to be found in Stepanija's version:

> 'The rest of the treasure that was left,
> The rest of the treasure he spent
> Making stone pavements where there had been mud,
> And building bridges over the waters,
> Giving alms to the crippled and to the blind,
> Till he had seized a place for his soul.'[5]

The urge to build is earthed here in a way which makes the poem more than a list of medieval foundations; and this worldly extension of a religious impulse will always be important in the best epic songs about the building of monasteries.

The difference between the two versions of the epic story of Prince Lazar's 'Building of Ravanica' is in this respect illuminating. Both versions tell the story of mixed legendary and historical origin which can be fairly accurately traced: Prince Lazar wants to build his foundation in silver, gold, pearls, and jewels, but in the end he obeys Miloš Obilić's advice to build in stone because 'the last times' are approaching. The story and the phrase must have reached the singers ultimately from the Byzantine *Narration of Saint Sophia*, a plebeian urban miscellany of anecdotes, facts and legends connected with the building of Saint Sophia. This work originated in the eighth or the ninth century in Constantinople, in an urban social setting which forgot the names of the great builders and architects, but remembered that one of the earlier 'owners of the later building site of Saint Sophia had the nick-name "Duck".'[6] Whether the story and the phrase reached the singer via the Greek original or a twelfth-century Russian translation which was used as a kind

---

[4] See for instance *Matić*, p. 661.

[5] 'Ostaloga što preteče blaga, / Ostalo je blago poharčio / Zidajući po kalu kaldrme / I gradeći po vodam' ćuprije, / Dijeleći kljastu i slijepu, / Dok je duši mjesto uvatio', *Karadžić*, ii, No. 24, ll. 38–43.

[6] S. Radojčić, 'Zidanje Ravanice', *Uzori i dela starih srpskih umetnika*, Belgrade, 1975, p. 246.

of tourist guide for pilgrims, it is impossible to say.[7] But suffice it
to note that the singers' performance often took place after the
liturgy on the monastery grounds—an ideal setting for the meeting of the 'high' and the 'low', the monastic and the folk culture.

On the other hand, it has also been shown that both versions
reflect the historical background of Serbian realities in which
the old Byzantine legend came to new epic life: probably the
early sixteenth century, 'the days when, after the Turkish
plundering, the monks and their flock realized clearly that all
the precious ornaments in churches, particularly the metal ones,
were constantly exposed to destruction and that stone was the
only thing which remained'.[8] In fact, Ravanica itself 'was
devastated so many times that it would be useless to try to pin
down the origin of the poem to a particular occasion'.[9] And, of
course, both versions assume—the anonymous one, as we shall
see, in a specific reference—the fact that medieval Serbia was
rich in precious metals.

Above all, however, it is worth noting that the inferior of the
two versions—written down from Old Raško, one of Karadžić's
outstanding singers—is a much shorter, 'purer', 'more religious'
poem in which Lazar's intention to build is described as a
debate in a church. In the far superior anonymous version the
setting of the debate is a worldly occasion, a royal feast, and
the poem tells a much more lively and intricate story of what
happens to a grand religious purpose in the course of its
realization which involves much more human 'psychology' and
diverse worldly matters. In short, we find in it social colour and
human drama which are inconceivable within Old Raško's
framework. While the debate about Prince Lazar's holy design
to build a church worthy of his ancestry and of his idea of himself goes on, a servant has to taste the wine to make sure that his
master should not drink poison. And it is only in this version
that the master refers explicitly to his great mines:

> 'the two gold mines:
> One mine which is in Mount Kopaonik,
> The other is the mountain of Rudnik'.[10]

[7] See S. Radojčić, 'Zidanje Ravanice', op. cit., p. 246.
[8] Ibid., pp. 250–1.   [9] Ibid., p. 251.
[10] 'Dva majdana zlatna: / Jedan majdan u Kopaoniku, / Drugi majdan
Rudnička planina', *Karadžić*, ii, No. 36, ll. 56–8.

Rudnik and Kopaonik—as their names suggest—were actually the great mining centres of medieval Serbia, even if the mining of silver there was incomparably more important than that of gold. Besides, it is only in the anonymous version that Prince Lazar's intention to build is described in glaring terms as a social ambition. He wants to build, above all, *ad majorem sui gloria*—for the reasons which, when he insists on building in gold and silver, he himself makes, inadvertently, apparent:

'Let it shine, let the world know who I am!'[11]

And whereas in Raško's version the grand feudal lords support their master's royal folly in a perfectly straightforward manner:

'Build, Prince, build it for your soul's health',[12]

the anonymous version shows a much more dramatic sense of the psychology involved in the relationship between power and wisdom in a political debate:

No one says: 'You're right, Tsar!'
No one says: 'You're wrong, Tsar!'[13]

And it is only in the anonymous version that Miloš begins his firm opposition to Prince Lazar's intent to build in gold and precious stone by making a sly bow to his power:

'You can do it, Tsar, it is in your power'.[14]

This suggests—among other things—what a different sense of humour has to be cultivated by an honest man who is on the weaker side. The only kind of irony he can afford is that at the expense of the uselessness of his own argument and wisdom in matters in which worldly power has the final word.

The two versions are closely parallel in their warning to Prince Lazar that 'the last times' are coming and that he should build in stone because this would be the only chance for the church to survive the Turkish conquest. This suggests that both singers saw their subject in terms of the approaching disaster of Kosovo, obviously the next chapter in the general epic story.

[11] 'Nek se sjaje, nek se moje znaje'. Ibid., l. 65.
[12] 'Gradi, kneže, biće ti za dušu', *Karadžić*, ii, No. 35, l. 67.
[13] 'Ni ko veli: "Jeste tako care!" / Ni ko veli: "Nije tako care!" ' *Karadžić*, ii, No. 36, ll. 66–7.
[14] 'Možeš, care, i u ruci ti je', ibid., l. 70.

And, finally, the story of the actual building of the church follows only in the anonymous version. Prince Lazar soon finds out that gold matters even if one builds in stone: the great lord Jug-Bogdan has kept for himself the money which should have gone to the builders and the master mason. And when Rade the Mason—who has built all that was worth building in epic medieval Serbia—comes to complain to Prince Lazar and tells him that his men have not been working on a house of God but on their own gaol, Lazar asks Miloš Obilić to 'cut up' old Jug-Bogdan and hang him 'on four boughs':[15]

> 'Who is curious, let him wonder,
> Who is timid, let him not pass by'.[16]

The lines not only echo a basic formulaic pattern of several other decasyllabic songs,[17] but also show that Lazar still needs a spectacular gesture. When he decided to build in stone, he only changed his mind—not his nature. And the moral drama of his conflict with Miloš is further developed when Miloš disobeys this order—his punishment of old Jug-Bogdan goes no further than is necessary to pay the builders and have the building completed. And finally, when the grand purpose is achieved, the singer finds a way of avoiding a pompous touch in the expression of his admiration:

> When the tsar approached the church,
> The church shone like the burning sun,
> A ray struck the horse's eye,
> The horse reared up under the tsar,
> And threw the tsar on the ground.[18]

The impact of beauty is vividly conveyed: it is equally significant that a horse should respond to it and that Prince Lazar should finally get a proper perspective for admiring his grand achievement.

This mastery of realistic touches bordering on broad comedy

[15] 'Ras'jeci ga (na četiri strane /, Objesi ga) o četiri grane', *Karadžić*, ii, No. 36, ll. 162–3.
[16] 'Ko je čudan, nek se čudu čudi, / Ko je strašiv, da ne smije proći.' Ibid., ll. 164–5.
[17] See above p. 79.
[18] 'Kad je care bio prema crkvi, / Sinu crkva, kao jarko sunce, / Konju ždraka u oči udari, / Pod carem je konjic poskočio, / I sa sebe cara obalio', ibid., ll. 241–5.

in the development of the theme which has for the singer and his audience grand religious and metaphysical status mirrors an awareness that the greatest spiritual dramas are shaped in the discrepancies of their historical and human context. And this is an important source of imaginative interest in Serbo-Croat epic poetry; but it is only a part of the singer's total awareness of the human predicament. There are also poems about building endeavours which converge much more radically towards a tragic understanding of the human position in history; and among these 'The Building of Skadar' has for a long time been the most controversial. Ever since Goethe—missing all the tragic overtones in this moving story about a terrible human sacrifice in a grand building endeavour—referred to 'the super-stitious and barbaric attitudes' in this poem,[19] it has been a target for the moral indignation of semi-enlightened optimists. It is, of course, true that this poem is based on the ancient belief that a human being has to be walled up alive into the founda-tions of a great edifice if it is to prosper—a belief which can be found not only in Albanian, Macedonian, Bulgarian and Greek variants of this poem,[20] but is also reflected in the Old Testament.[21] This belief is voiced in the poem by a *vila*—a most ambiguous mountain nymph who figures sometimes as a good fairy and sometimes as an evil spirit in South Slav pagan mythology and Serbo-Croat epic poetry.[22] In this poem it is

[19] J. W. Goethe, 'Serbische Lieder', *Schriften zur Literatur*, ii, Berlin, 1972, p. 278. First published in *Über Kunst und Altertum*, xv, ii (1825).

[20] See S. Stefanović, *Legenda o zidanju Skadra*, Belgrade, 1928.

[21] 'In his days did Hiel the Beth-elite build Jericho: he laid the foundation thereof in Abraham his first-born, and set up the gates thereof in his youngest *son* Segub, according to the word of the Lord, which he spake by Joshua, the son of Nun', I Kgs. 16: 34. J. A. Montgomery points out that this translation is inaccurate and that the correct rendering is not 'he laid the foundation thereof in Abraham', but 'at the cost of' Abraham. The sacrificial interpretation of this passage has also been questioned and the archaeological finds of bodies immured in building foundations throughout the ancient world have been explained as fatalities which were later interpreted as sacrifices (see J. A. Montgomery, *A Critical and Exegetical Commentary on The Book of Kings*, ed. H. S. Geheman [*The International Critical Commentary*, vol. 10], Edinburgh, 1951, pp. 287–8). But whatever turn this argument takes, it illustrates how widespread was the belief in human sacrifice.

[22] See Appendix III.

certainly not the voice of Divine Justice; moreover, the story is shaped in the mutual treacheries of the Mrljavčevići—the medieval Serbian feudal lords whom we have already seen as villains in the epic presentation of the factions which led to the Serbian catastrophe after the death of Stefan Dušan the Mighty. Historically, the Mrnjavčevići had nothing to do with Skadar; but as Skadar was an important crossroads for the Adriatic routes and inland Montenegro, as Stefan Dušan lived there for a time and had a palace in the vicinity and as it was involved in bitter struggles of late medieval Serbia against the Turkish invasion, the singer came to see the building of its fortress as important in his general epic medieval landscape. However, the story is shaped, as usual, in terms of family conflicts and the patriarchal dramas which mirror the customs and social norms of Serbian village life during the Turkish times.

The diverse elements of ancient legend, pagan Slav mythology, medieval history and the later Serbian patriarchal world are merged in the poem into a great tragic narrative. For three years three hundred masons try in vain to build the foundations of the fortress for the three brothers Mrljavčevići: whatever they build by day, a *vila* pulls down by night. Finally she tells them that they must find a brother and a sister, Stoja (Constance) and Stojan (Constantine), and wall them up alive to make the foundations firm (*postojani*). So it is not just any human sacrifice that is required; only the ideal form of human love, that of a brother and a sister, the most lasting and firm kind of love (hence the names: Stoja, Stojan), can enable the builders to accomplish their grand design. Is this a sign of the perversity of the singer's imagination or of his response to the tragic pathos of a grand human endeavour? Anyway, as no brother and sister can be found, the *vila* is helpful again—she offers the three brothers to have only one of their wives walled up, whichever one comes to the river next day to bring the workers food.

The brothers—with their grand feudal sense of reality, after all *noblesse oblige*—agree to the proposal. The two elder, 'historical' brothers Vukašin and Uglješa tell their wives about agreement and warn them in time. The youngest, 'unhistorical' brother Gojko plays fair. He and his wife are repeatedly described as 'young',[23] his wife also as 'green';[24] and the way the tale is told from this point is worthy of Shakespeare's dramatic sense. We follow, step by step, the casual innocence of Gojko's wife as she tries to explain to her sisters-in-law that she cannot go to the river and take food to the workers because her little son must have a bath, because her linen has not been washed. The humble tasks as well as the sly relationships of the sisters-in-law derive obviously from later patriarchal village life, but they bring out the full human drama of the story. Finally, Gojko's 'young' and 'green' wife will come to tread the path of death with equal innocence at the moment when the walling up begins: she laughs, she still hopes it is a joke. When the truth dawns on her, to whom should she plead but her brothers-in-law not to let her be walled up alive? Of course, the irony of a great patriarchal ideal lurks in this plea: for if a husband can be so cruel to his wife, for whatever reason of human or inhuman intolerance, how could a brother-in-law let his sister-in-law perish like this? The strange apotheosis of tragic innocence leads ultimately to an insane moral hope; divested of her sense of 'shame and all offence',[25] she begs her brothers-in-law to send a message to her mother to buy a slave who could be walled up 'into the tower's foundations'.[26] Is this a moral breakdown? Or a tragic vision of the inevitable madness of the heroine? And why is she doomed to such a death? Because a grand design demands a terrible sacrifice? Or because the late medieval Serbian feudal lords, Vukašin and Uglješa, are cruel and treacherous? Or because her loving husband—he is aware, his head averted in distress and woe, that he has lost his 'golden apple'[27]—is so honest and so true to his word?

Once innocence has been driven mad, the poem moves towards the regions of appeased passions. Gojko's wife pleads with Rade the Mason, whom she appeals to as her 'brother in God', to leave 'a window at her breasts' so that she could suckle her little son.[28] The mason responds to her plea and, long after 'her

---

[23] 'Young Gojko did not trample on his faith' ('Mladi Gojko vjeru ne pogazi', *Karadžić*, ii, No. 26, l. 116); his wife is described as 'young' ('mlada') in ll. 135, 149, 176, 203.

[24] 'Zelena', ibid., l. 197. [25] '(Tad se prođe) srama i zazora', ibid., l. 200.

[26] 'Kuli u temelja', ibid., l. 207. [27] 'Od zlata jabuku', ibid., l. 165.

[28] 'Bogom brate, (Rade neimare)! / (Ostavi mi) prozor na dojkama', ibid., ll. 212–13.

voice had gone',[29] the milk comes out of the stone not only for
her son but for all the mothers and children who need it.
Exceptional as this tragic miraculous note is in Serbo-Croat
epic singing, it is perhaps less strange than Goethe's shock at
'the superstitious and barbaric attitudes' in this poem, at its
'human sacrifice of the most repulsive kind'.[30] Strangest of all,
some modern scholars still find it possible to refer to 'The
Building of Skadar' as 'an example of savagery' in epic poetry.[31]
Of course, it would be most comforting to think that the tragic
cruelties of this poem are only concoctions of notoriously
perverse artistic imagination, or that they are the exclusive
monopoly of the barbaric, distant times, of the pre-historical
stage in the grand moral growth of the human animal. But even
if the need for such fantasies can be readily shared, it is no
reason for the misreading of the tragic pathos of the milk and
the stone, of the drama of Gojko's honesty and his wife's
maddening suffering, of the grand irony of human goodness
displayed in the little window which Rade the Mason leaves to
the victim as he walls her up alive. In short, the poem should be
read precisely and, above all, in its own tragic and dramatic
context which makes it clear that it is no more a 'barbarous'
or 'atrocious' proposition than *Macbeth*, and that there is as
little likelihood that anyone might be misled by a bad example.
But the context of 'The Building of Skadar' is, admittedly,
difficult to grasp, and the difficulties begin with the appearance
of the *vila* who is, as we have seen, morally the most ambiguous
mythic figure in all Serbo-Croat epic singing. Moreover, the
poem is rooted in many of its details in specific assumptions about
particular family relationships in Serbian patriarchal village life.
But even a cursory glimpse at it as a whole reveals that the
singer is fully aware of the cruelties and treacheries which led to
the destruction of medieval Serbia, and which the singer could
not conceivably have condoned. At the same time, however, the
figures of Gojko, his wife and her destiny as well as the magic
imagery of its ending embody the same morality of martyrdom
which was mirrored in some of the poems about tragic family
relationships and which will flourish in the Kosovo poems.

[29] 'Izgubila glasa', *Karadžić*, ii, No. 26, l. 236.
[30] J. W. Goethe, 'Serbische Lieder', *Schriften zur Literatur*, ii, p. 278.
[31] *Matić*, p. 665.

PART THREE

Triumph in Disaster

1. Between Fact and Fiction

The image of disaster of the Battle of Kosovo has lived for centuries in Serbian literary and oral traditions with the elusive vividness of a hallucination. For there is perhaps no other major event in Serbian history about which so little is known and so much has been assumed. What is known is that the Battle took place on St Vitus' Day, on 15 or, according to the old Orthodox calendar, 28 June 1389. Prince Lazar was the commander of the Serbian armies and he applied, successfully, for help from many feudal lords and rulers in the neighbouring areas which were already torn asunder by the factions which had begun after Stefan Dušan's death. (See Map 3.) Miloš Obilić, one of Lazar's knights, killed the Turkish Sultan Murad and Lazar was also killed in the battle. The Turkish victory used to be a simple historical fact, but in the light of modern research it has turned into a source of sophisticated bewilderment.[1]

There is little doubt, however, that the aftermath was as colourful as the battle itself. The succession to the Turkish throne was so uncertain that the Venetian messenger sent in July to the Grand Porte had two letters of congratulation in his pocket: one addressed to Bajazid and the other to his brother Jacub. Besides, he was not instructed to congratulate the new sultan on his victory but to assure him that it was impossible to believe the rumours about his father's battle with Prince Lazar.[2] On the other hand, Prince Lazar's wife Milica and their son Stefan followed the advice of the Serbian clergy and

---

[1] Thus S. Ćirković claims that 'our knowledge' about the Battle of Kosovo 'is so uncertain that we cannot be sure what its actual outcome was' ('Kosovska bitka', 'Dopune i objašnjenja' in S. Novaković, *Srbi i Turci xiv i xv veka*, Belgrade, 1960, p. 453). R. Samardžić points out how consistently the contemporary evidence contradicts the Serbian defeat in this battle. In his opinion the heavy losses of the Serbian army, which could not be restored, and the economic and military impetus of the Ottoman Empire created the illusion of a Turkish victory which soon became also a historical reality. See R. Samardžić, 'Oko istorijskog i legendarnog u kosovskom predanju', *Usmena narodna hronika*, pp. 28–30.

[2] See S. Ćirković, op. cit., p. 455.

nobility and went as far as Sivas (Senastija) to negotiate some sort of settlement with the Turks.[3] Lazar's daughter Olivera was soon to be rendered the honour of being accepted in Sultan Bajazid's harem.[4] And for several decades Serbia was to

3. Prince Lazar's Lands and the Neighbouring Territories

undergo the agonies of recuperation in vassalage, the agonies of faction, treacheries and defeats which would turn it before long into largely depopulated and illiterate land.[5] There was no human drama or historical impetus lacking for the Battle of

[3] See I. Božić, 'Neverstvo Vuka Brankovića', *O knezu Lazaru*, Naučni skup u Kruševcu 1971, ed. I. Božić and V. J. Đurić, Belgrade, 1975, p. 229.
[4] See ibid.   [5] See below pp. 301–2.

Kosovo to be seen as the Doomsday of national grandeur and prosperity.

The actual military magnitude of the battle also seems to be uncertain. Modern research takes us back to the early chronicles and these lead into the regions of national pride, wild speculation, and guesswork.[6] And as to the course of the battle itself —so important in the legend and the epic singing—it seems that luck was at least initially on the Serbian side. For there is no doubt that the first news about its outcome to reach the West inspired a truimphant sense of a great Christian victory; before October of the same year Ph. Mezières was thrilled by Murad's death and God's decision to put a stop to the Turkish conquest of the Balkans![7] But this good news which reached France via Florence and Venice may or may not have been deliberately misleading because it was sent by King Tvrtko of Bosnia, the holder of the prerogatives of the Serbian crown, who may have found it in his interest to present the Serbian case in the Balkans as stronger than it actually was.[8]

As regards the treason of Vuk Branković—the heart of the legend and the song—modern historians tend to renounce the views of their earlier colleagues who had proved that this was pure epic fiction. After all, the *guslar* may have been almost right; for if Vuk Branković did not betray Prince Lazar in the course of the battle, he exploited the Turkish victory for his selfish ends.[9] As he was fairly successful and the Brankovići established themselves as the new feudal lords in Serbia, it is not surprising that treachery does not figure in the early chronicles.[10] Besides, one of the Brankovići, not Vuk but Đurađ, captured John Hunyadi as he was retreating after his defeat in the Battle of Kosovo in 1448.[11] Hunyadi's misfortune made such an impact on popular Serbian imagination that this was noted in European historiography.[12] So there was, after all, apart from the treacherous politics of a Branković after a

---

[6] See *Enciklopedija Jugoslavije*, v, Zagreb, 1962, p. 336.
[7] See ibid.
[8] See ibid.
[9] See I. Božić, 'Neverstvo Vuka Brankovića', op. cit., pp. 230ff.
[10] See ibid., p. 236.
[11] See V. Ćorović, *Istorija Jugoslavije*, Belgrade, 1933, pp. 234–5.
[12] See above pp. 28–30 and note 4, p. 6.

Battle of Kosovo, also a treason of a Branković connected with a Battle of Kosovo. And as regards the other most important elements of the legend which are popularly taken as epic fiction—such as the Communion of the Serbian army and Prince Lazar's Last Supper on the eve of the battle—they appear to be historical facts.[13]

However, the magnitude of a historical event depends also on the image it makes, and there is no doubt that from the earliest days of the growth of the legend, the Battle of Kosovo was seen as an event of ultimate moral and religious significance. Thus Konstantin the Philosopher—who wrote the biography of Prince Lazar's son Stefan Lazarević about forty years after the battle—claims that the disaster was settled in advance by Providential intervention. Apparently, at first 'Lazar's men resisted and were victorious', but 'this was no time of salvation' and therefore 'the son of that [Turkish] Tsar was strengthened again during the battle itself and won because God allowed it'.[14] Lazar died crowned with 'a martyr's laurel' while his knights eagerly pleaded 'to be killed before him so that they should not witness his death'.[15] The bravest among the knights—Miloš Obilić—'a very noble man' whom 'the envious slandered to their master and accused of treason'[16]—proved his loyalty and courage by killing the Turkish Sultan Murad in spite of the insults of his own countrymen.

After several later versions of the same story, at the end of the fifteenth century Konstantin Mihailović of Ostrovica introduced the motif of discord and treachery as the explanation of the defeat. Writing with the expertise of a Serbian soldier and an ex-janissary, he was anxious to instruct the Poles and other Christians in how to resist the Turkish invasion: they must attain a strong alliance if they are to survive. 'Wherever there is

---

[13] This practice is described in Byzantine military tracts: the army takes holy communion after three days' fasting in the military fashion (i.e. after sunset only dry food is taken). See S. Radojčić, 'Kosovka djevojka', *Uzori i dela starih srpskih umetnika*, p. 240. See also J. R. Vieillefond, 'Les pratiques religieuses dans l'armée byzantine d'après les traités militaires', *Revue des études anciennes*, xxxvii (1935), pp. 322–30. See also note 56, p. 24.

[14] Konstantin Filozof, 'Život despota Stefana Lazarevića', in G. Camblak, Konstantin Filozof, Pajsije Patrijarh, *Stare srpske biografije xv i xvii veka*, iii, tr. by L. Mirković, Belgrade, 1936, pp. 59–60.

[15] Ibid., p. 60.   [16] Ibid., p. 59.

no concord, no good can come about in any way', he says and proceeds to describe the course of the Battle of Kosovo: 'The noblemen who were well-disposed towards Lazar fought bravely and loyally by his side, but others—looking through their fingers—watched the battle, and because of this disloyalty and discord (and the envy of the bad and dishonest men), the battle was lost.'[17] This introduces a major dramatic element in the legend: for the punishment of discord falls on the head of the innocent Prince Lazar and he becomes a heroic martyr expiating other men's sins. In this spirit he refuses to answer Bajazid's questions while his Duke Krajmir begs him to remember that 'the head is not like the stump of a willow tree to sprout a second time'.[18] The phrase may be ultimately of biblical origin and it is repeated in a different context in a much later decasyllabic poem,[19] but there is no doubt that the writer is imbued with Serbian folk traditions and that he is addressing European Christendom.[20]

The context of threatened Christendom is also indicated in the version of the Kosovo legend which a Slovene traveller Benedikt Kuripešić mentions in his description of his journey through the Slavonic regions of the Balkans in 1530. Kuripešić notes that the heroic deeds of Miloš Obilić (or Kobilović, as he calls him) were sung in all areas from old Serbia to western Bosnia and Croatia. In this version Miloš again appears as Lazar's bravest knight who remains loyal to his master in spite of the fact that he has been slandered and insulted even by Lazar himself. Besides, Kuripešić's story also contains a description of Lazar's Last Supper on the eve of the battle which will be such an important motif in the great poem which Karadžić was to write down about three hundred years later.[21]

From these and similar elements—which can be followed in some detail in several later versions of the legend—the singer inherited the basic themes and motifs of his poems about the Battle of Kosovo (for their topography, see Map 1). They were

[17] Konstantin Mihailović iz Ostrovice, *Janičarove uspomene*, p. 105.

[18] Ibid., p. 106.

[19] See below p. 285.

[20] See Ð. Živanović, 'Predgovor', Konstantin Mihailović iz Ostrovice, *Janičarove uspomene*, pp. 11–13.

[21] See below pp. 164–6.

sifted again and again through the needs and hopes of contemporary awareness of history: it is not insignificant that Konstantin the Philosopher, a monk himself, sees Prince Lazar as the central figure in a hagiographical story, that Konstantin of Ostrovica, an ex-janissary who fought in the Serbian army on the Turkish side when Constantinople was taken by the Turks, develops the theme of concord and discord of the Christian forces, that Benedikt Kuripešić moves the centre of the legend towards Miloš Obilić and describes him as a heroic knight who daily performed great deeds on the Christian frontier, that Miloš Obilić will later come to speak with the rough voice of a Serbian rebel in the songs which Karadžić recorded from his singers. But in spite of many different imprints of diverse political and historical realities, the legends of Kosovo were also a cluster of tales which persisted in their mythic growth—and their starting point of Providential interference in a national catastrophe has remained at the heart of their epic drama till the times of Karadžić's singers. This is why 'the honourable crosses' loom so large in the foreground of fighting in their songs and why the battle itself is seen as a choice of 'the heavenly Kingdom'.[22]

In short, some of the greatest medieval religious concepts were harnessed to the need to explain what came to be seen as a historical catastrophe, and hence became the heart of Serbian epic legends. This is perhaps why V. S. Karadžić, discussing the age and origin of Serbian epic poetry, suggested that in his opinion 'the Serbs had ancient heroic songs before Kosovo' which could not reach us because 'this change struck the people's mind so vigorously that they forgot everything that happened before and began thenceforth to sing and spin their tales anew'.[23]

2. On the Cross of Honour

In the middle of the eighteenth century a learned and conscientious Dubrovnik poet wrote down in the vicinity of his city
one of the longest *bugarštice*, the first epic poem about the
battle of Kosovo.[1] In two hundred and fifty-three long lines the
poem enumerates names and motifs which will grow later into
the material of much more dramatic decasyllabic songs: the
preparation of Bušić Stjepan for the battle, Milica's pleading to
have one of her brothers left behind, the exchange of toasts on
the eve of the battle, the slander of Miloš Obilić, the treason of
Vuk Branković, Miloš's heroic exploit and death.

But Bušić Stjepan appears here with his servant Oliver who
seems to have walked out of a French romance; and he shows
his loyalty by ignoring his wife's ominous dream and joining
Prince Lazar in time. In the decasyllabic poem Musić Stevan—
and his servant Vaistina (Verity)—will be late for the battle
but not too late to die a heroic death. Besides, it seems in the
bugarštica that Prince Lazar is leading only Hungarian forces,
and even Milica's brothers are not called Jugovići but Ugovići,
in the lines which suggest a close acoustic connection of their
name with 'ugarski', Hungarian, even if the local derivation
may also have something to do with 'Ugo'.[2] The only fully-
fledged episode in the *bugarštica* is the grand feudal scene of
Prince Lazar's conversation with the Turkish Sultan Murad and
Miloš Obilić about how they are to be buried. Miloš insists
that he be laid by Lazar's feet, not at his right hand as Lazar
proposed, because he wishes to remain Lazar's servant beyond
death. And the poem ends with two formulaic lines which
describe how Milica's heart bursts when she learns the tragic
news.[3] Several of the motifs of this *bugarštica* will recur as much

---

[1] *Pantić*, pp. 118–24 (*Bogišić*, No. 1).

[2] Ugo was a well-known foreign name in Dalmatia; this is why, for
instance, a German comic character is called Ugo Tedeško in M. Držić's
Uncle Maroje (*Dundo Maroje*), the best-known Renaissance play in Serbo-
Croat.

[3] 'Kad mi bješe Milica tužne glase razumjela, / Bješe joj se od žalosti živo
srce raspuknulo' ('When Milica had understood the grievous news, / Her

more fully-developed epic themes in the decasyllabic poems which Karadžić will write down some seventy years later from his singers.

These poems are knit together by their poetic diction, which they share with so many other poems in the Serbo-Croatian epic tradition. But they are also held together by the general outlines of their well-known story, by the frequent repetition of its major episodes and even by an occasional interplay of mutually illuminating situations, concepts, and images. The treason of Vuk Branković and the heroic exploit of Miloš Obilić can be found in several poems. Prince Lazar's curse of the traitors who fail to come to fight occurs in one of the 'Pieces from Various Kosovo Poems' which Karadžić wrote down from his father:

> 'Whoever will not fight at Kosovo,
> May nothing grow that his hand sows:
> Neither the white wheat in his field,
> Nor the vine of grapes on his mountain!'[4]

But it also recurs in a more dramatic setting in 'Musić Stefan' at the moment when the hero who is late for battle remembers what his master said:

> 'Of Serbians by nation and by birth,
> And by their blood and by their ancestry,
> Whoever does not fight at Kosovo,
> May he have no dear children born to him,
> May neither boy nor girl be born to him!
> May nothing bear fruit that his hand sows,
> Neither the white wheat nor the red wine!
> His blight rot all his brood while it endures!'[5]

---

living heart burst with sorrow', *Bogišić*, No. 1, ll. 252–3 [254–5]). A 'living heart' almost 'bursts with sorrow' in *Bogišić*, No. 35, l. 78, but the 'living heart' can also 'burst', i.e. throb, with eagerness to fight (see *Bogišić*, No. 7, l. 149 [145]).

[4] 'Ko ne dođe na boj na Kosovo, / Od ruke mu ništa ne rodilo: / Ni u polju bjelica pšenica, / Ni u brdu vinova lozica!' 'Komadi od različnijeh kosovskijeh pjesama (ii)', *Karadžić*, ii, No. 50, ll. 3–6.

[5] 'Ko je Srbin i Srpskoga roda, / I od Srpske krvi i kolena, / A ne doš'o na boj na Kosovo, / Ne imao od srca poroda! / Ni muškoga ni devojačkoga; / Od ruke mu ništa ne rodilo! / Rujno vino ni šenica bela; / Rđom kap'o, dok mu je kolena!' 'Musić Stefan', *Karadžić*, ii, No. 47, ll. 21–8.

As Lazar's words echo Jug-Bogdan's prophecy of 'the last times' ('The Wedding of Prince Lazar')[6] and the Divine punishment of mankind in the poem 'The Saints Divide the Treasure',[7] they reflect not only the range of the unity of the decasyllabic diction, but also significant relations in the whole epic landscape of Serbian history.

'The Downfall of the Serbian Empire', which was recorded from a blind woman in Srem, suggests some other interesting facets of this wide epic coherence. At the beginning of this poem the Virgin Mary sends a message to Prince Lazar which offers him the choice between 'the heavenly' and 'the earthly Kingdom' on the eve of the battle.[8] The nature of this option is also illuminated by the story of Lazar's choice in one of 'The Pieces from Various Kosovo Poems'. In this poem Sultan Murad sends the message to Prince Lazar which makes him choose between living as a Turkish vassal and dying as a hero:

> 'Oee Lazar, lord of Serbia,
> This never has been and never can be:
> One territory under two masters,
> One rayah to pay two taxes,
> We cannot both of us be ruler,
> Send every key to me and every tax,
> The keys of gold that unlock the cities,
> And the taxes on heads for seven years,
> And if you will not send these things to me,
> Then come down to Kosovo meadow,
> We shall divide up this land with our swords!'[9]

Lazar knows that he will have to fight against hopeless odds; this is why he weeps as he reads 'the book'.[10] His tears also mirror the inevitability of his honourable choice; and it is only

---

[6] See above p. 126. [7] See above pp. 108–9.

[8] '(Ili voliš) carstvu nebeskome, / (Ili voliš) carstvu zemaljskome?' 'Propast carstva srpskoga', *Karadžić*, ii, 46, ll. 13–14.

[9] 'Oj Lazare, od Srbije glavo! / Nit' je bilo, niti može biti : / Jedna zemlja, a dva gospodara; / Jedna raja, dva harača daje; / Carovati oba ne možemo, / Već mi pošlji ključe i harače, / Zlatne ključe od svijeh gradova, / I harače od sedam godina; / Ako li mi to poslati ne ćeš, / A ti hajde u Polje Kosovo, / Da sabljama zemlju dijelimo.' 'Komadi od različnijeh kosovskijeh pjesama (i)', *Karadžić*, ii, No. 50, ll. 5–15.

[10] 'Knjigu gleda, grozne suze roni', ibid., l. 17.

against this tragic background that 'The Downfall of the Serbian Empire' reveals its full pathos in the scenes in which Lazar makes his men take Holy Communion and leads them to fight a lost battle to its bitter end. The Holy Communion on the eve of the battle was, as we have seen, customary in the Byzantine and presumably in the Serbian army;[11] and the choice between the 'heavenly' and the 'earthly Kingdom' is 'a repetition and periphrasis of similar points made in Serbian historical literature in the Middle Ages'.[12] But both these details attain a rich epic life because they dramatize Lazar's predicament, his moral impulse to fight for his honour against all the odds of worldly history. However, this hagiographical illumination of the Kosovo legend runs into trouble because the singer introduces some other standard epic elements which are at odds with the general pattern of her story. Thus, for instance, when the disaster is about to occur, she suddenly changes her mind and suggests that it is not so much Lazar's choice but the treason of Vuk Branković which is the main reason for catastrophe! At this moment Lazar appears on the verge of the absurd: a martyr who, having made the choice of 'the heavenly Kingdom', narrowly misses victory:

> Lazar would have overcome the Turks,—
> God be the death of Vuk Branković![13]

This *volte-face* in the explanation of the epic story illustrates a typical difficulty of the singers who had to merge the often incompatible elements of their legends and stories. This challenge must have been particularly hard for blind women singers: doubly isolated from the human realities of the battles they described, they could not, like many male singers, particularly the fighters and outlaws, identify themselves completely with their subject-matter and in their improvisation iron out the discrepancies of the diverse sources of their material.

This explains perhaps why Karadžić wrote down one of the most successful among the Kosovo poems, 'Tsar Lazar and Tsaritsa Milica',[14] from Tešan Podrugović, an outlaw and a

---

[11] See note 13, p. 156. [12] *Matić*, p. 712.

[13] 'Tad' bi Laza nadvladao Turke, / Bog ubio Vuka Brankovića!' *Karadžić*, ii, No. 46, ll. 85–6.

[14] 'Car Lazar i carica Milica', *Karadžić*, ii, No. 45.

fighter in the Serbian Uprisings, who also told him the great patriarchal dramas of 'Simeun the Foundling' and 'Dušan's Wedding'—terse projections of the patriarchal world in the historically grand setting of the most powerful of Serbian medieval emperors.[15] Podrugović tells the story of the battle as a drama of both feudal and patriarchal concepts of honour and he succeeds in illuminating it by the emblem of the Cross which is seen again and again on Serbian banners. Sometimes there are many crosses on the banner—which might suggest an association with the pagan Slav crosses which survived in many later customs in Serbian village life.[16] But even when they are 'many', they usually turn out to be twelve—and this suggests that the older pagan association has been absorbed into the Christian concept of martyrdom and faith, of the Apostles, Golgotha, Crucifixion, and Resurrection.

The cross becomes the all-embracing symbol of the poem from the moment when Boško Jugović appears with 'the flag of the cross covering him'.[17] He feels that he has to disregard the sacred patriarchal call of his sister's love and that he cannot stay behind with her even when his master, Tsar Lazar, absolves him from his feudal pledge to his brothers and friends 'to spill his blood for the honourable cross'.[18] And, finally, when we can see Boško no more in the battlefield, after all his brothers and friends have been killed, we still watch his lonely 'flag with crosses waving over Kosovo'.[19]

The cross links Boško with his brother Voin who also refuses his sister's plea and goes to the battle 'to spill his blood for the honourable cross'.[20] It connects them with Lazar's whole army, including many of the warriors in other poems, such as, for instance, Musić Stevan who, even if late for the battle, comes to Kosovo carrying

> the silk flag of the cross,
> With twelve crosses on it.[21]

[15] See above pp. 117–23.   [16] See above pp. 19–21.
[17] 'Krstaš ga je barjak poklopio', *Karadžić*, ii, No. 45, l. 41.
[18] 'Za krst časni krvcu proljevati', ibid., l. 66.
[19] 'Krstaš mu se po Kosovu vija', ibid., l. 185.
[20] 'Za krst časni krvcu proljevati', ibid., l. 92.
[21] 'Krstat svilen barjak, / Na kome je dvanaest krstova', *Karadžić*, ii, No. 47, ll. 44–5.

The hope and the despair of the Cross—emblematic even in its physical appearance on the banner—are the warp and woof of the epic tragedy in which honourable death is seen as the pledge of the values of life.

Renunciation of life in an act of devotion to its values is also at the heart of one of the best known Kosovo 'pieces' which Karadžić wrote down from his father. It is usually entitled 'The Prince's Supper' and it probably echoes a historical feast on the eve of the battle which is mentioned in the contemporary Turkish sources and described by Kuripešić in 1530 as an unjustified humiliation of the greatest Kosovo hero Miloš Obilić.[22] As Prince Lazar was the best-known Serbian saint and martyr, inextricably connected with Kosovo, the dramatic association with the biblical story must have been unmistakable for the singer and his audience. Owing to this association the drama of treason attains an absolute status; but the biblical story is freely used by the singer. Lazar—as Christ before him—knows that he will be betrayed, but in this epic tale he suspects that he will be betrayed by his most faithful knight Miloš Obilić. The tragic irony of this situation comes out fully when Lazar, in his pathetic generosity and innocence, proposes a toast to Miloš, ready to forgive him his 'sin':

> 'Health to Miloš, the faithful traitor,
> First faithful, then a traitor!
> At Kosovo tomorrow you will desert me,
> You will run to Murad, the Emperor!
> Health to you, drink this toast,
> Drink this wine, and this cup is yours!'[23]

[22] See above pp. 23–4.

[23] 'Zdrav Milošu, vjero i nevjero! / Prva vjero, potonja nevjero! / Sjutra ćeš me izdat' na Kosovu, / I odbjeći turskom car-Muratu; / Zdrav mi budi! i zdravicu popij: / Vino popij, a na čast ti pehar!' 'Komadi od različnijeh kosovskijeh pjesama (iii)', *Karadžić*, ii, No. 50, ll. 31–6. This wording is not only closely parallel to a toast in a *bugarštica* (see note 16, p. 37), but it also repeats an earlier version of this story in which Ludovik Crijević Tubero (1450–1527), the well-known Dubrovnik historian, put the following words into Prince Lazar's mouth: 'This cup of wine is your present, Miloš, although I have been told that you will betray me' ('Na poklon ti, Milošu, ovaj pehar s vinom, iako mi je javljeno da ćeš me izdati'). See R. Samardžić, 'Oko istorijskog i legendarnog u kosovskom predanju', *Usmena narodna hronika*, p. 34.

This strange framework of ironic delusion suggests that even saints and martyrs walk the earth in Kosovo poems; hence the pathos of Lazar's magnificence which mirrors, perhaps with even greater ironic depth, the drama which we saw enacted in the earlier Serbian medieval epic landscape by Duke Momčilo and Strahinić Ban. In the world in which everything is soon to be lost, Lazar attempts to sustain the value of a generous gesture. And Miloš appreciates the nature of this gesture; he responds to it with an absolute sense of honour and loyalty:

> Miloš jumps lightly on his feet,
> He bows down to the black ground:
> 'I thank you, Lazar, glorious prince!
> I thank you for the toast you drink,
> I thank you for the toast and for the cup;
> I do not thank you for such a speech.'[24]

And, without a grain of bitterness—for Prince Lazar is only an agent of his devotion to a higher purpose—Miloš ends his speech with his dramatic promise of loyalty:

> 'Tomorrow is lovely St Vitus day
> And we shall see in Kosovo field
> Who is faithful, who is the traitor.
> The great God is my witness!
> Tomorrow I shall march on Kosovo,
> And I shall stab Murad, Tsar of Turkey,
> And stand up with his throat under my foot.'[25]

But Miloš also treads the earth; and the note of tragic serenity is broken when he turns to Vuk Branković, the prospective traitor so highly revered by Prince Lazar, and says that he will

> Tie him on his battle lance
> As a woman ties wool on a distaff.[26]

---

[24] 'Skoči Miloš na noge lagane, / Pak se klanja do zemljice crne: / "Vala tebe, slavni knez-Lazare! / Vala tebe na tvojoj zdravici, / Na zdravici i na daru tvome; / Al' ne vala na takoj besjedi" ', *Karadžić*, ii, No. 50 (iii), ll. 37–42.

[25] 'Sjutra jeste lijep Vidov-danak, / Viđećemo u Polju Kosovu, / Ko je vjera, ko li je nevjera. / A tako mi Boga velikoga! / Ja ću otić' sjutra u Kosovo, / I zaklaću turskog car-Murata, / I staću mu nogom pod gr'oce', ibid., ll. 51–7.

[26] 'Vezaću ga uz to bojno koplje, / Kao žena kuđelj' uz preslicu', ibid., ll. 61–2.

This picture in which Miloš figures as 'a woman', Vuk Branković as 'raw wool', the battle lance as 'distaff' is perhaps
parallel to the comic anticlimax of tragedy in which King
Vukašin put both his feet into one of Duke Momčilo's boots. It
is a device of domestic humour well-known in epic poetry since
Homeric times; but it is more specifically important here in so far
as it dispels the nightmarish illusion of the omnipotence of fraud
and violence, the illusion which a pure tragedy often creates.

The same kind of comic imaginative vitality which de-
mystifies the horrors of a given historical setting is also found in
the next 'piece' from Kosovo poems which describes the Serbian
spying out the Turkish army. When Ivan Kosančić, one of the
Serbian knights, comes back frightened out of his wits by what
he has seen, he phrases his fears to his blood-brother Miloš
Obilić in a way which expresses and dispels his nightmare:

> 'If all of us were turned into rock salt,
> We could not salt the dinner of the Turks'.[27]

This culinary metaphor resists a gloomy understanding of a
tragic situation; and Miloš responds in a similar way when he
asks Ivan Kosančić to hide the truth from Prince Lazar. The
idea that one should delude at such a decisive moment the
master for whom one is prepared to die shows as much the
courage of spirit as the richness of the inner resources of comedy.
And the despair of this historical predicament is indeed dissolved
in Miloš's comic wording of how the master should be deluded:

> 'The Turks have got enough of an army,
> But we have a way to strike at them,
> And to be their conquerors;
> This is not an army of fighters,
> It is all old hodjas and old hadjis,
> It is apprentices and young merchants,
> Who never saw a battle in their lives,
> Who came to the war to have bread to eat.'[28]

[27] 'Svi mi da se u so prometnemo, / Ne bi Turkom ručka osolili'. 'Komadi
od različnijeh kosovskijeh pjesama (iv)', *Karadžić*, ii, No. 50, ll. 10–11.

[28] 'Ima dosta vojske u Turaka, / Al' s' možemo s njima udariti, / I lasno
ih pridobit' možemo; / Jera nije vojska od mejdana, / Već sve stare hodže
i hadžije, / Zanatlije i mlade ćardžije, / Koji boja ni viđeli nisu, / Istom
pošli, da se ljebom rane', ibid., ll. 51–8.

Miloš refuses to read reality as a nightmare which would be worthy of his own tragic status—and this may be largely the result of an inveterate sense of humour of his soil, of the rough and wise sense of humour which is so characteristic of the epic diction which largely came into being in the outlaws' historical predicament and their response to it.

This humorous dissipation of historical nightmares, this down-to-earth illumination of tragedy should not mislead us into underplaying the moving tragic notes in these poems. They also reflect a response to several centuries of despair, of being faced and crushed by the tremendous odds of history which nothing could resist. And nature herself is seen as helpless in the struggle with such a worldly power:

> 'And if rain poured down out of heaven,
> It would not drop anywhere on to earth,
> It would drop on to good horses and heroes.'[29]

And finally in the strange processes of further epic metaphorization of history and nature the song comes to speak from the heart of the Kosovo legend with the voice which seems both to accept and resist the inevitable fate:

> 'If you had the long wings of a hawk,
> And if you fell out of clear heaven,
> Feathers would not carry the flesh away.'[30]

The effort of will cannot change the obdurate facts of reality even when Miloš kills Murad. 'The feathers' will not 'carry the flesh away'; but the image embodies the triumph of a heroic spirit which becomes the pledge of some distant, obscure historical victory. As always in great tragedies a free choice of death is the last and ultimate resort of the moral values of life, evidence that the spirit cannot be crushed. In order to live one must be prepared to die; and this is the ultimate message of the Kosovo poems.

[29] 'Da iz neba plaha kiša padne, / Niđe ne bi na zemljicu pala, / Već na dobre konje i junake', ibid., ll. 26–8.

[30] 'Da ti imaš krila sokolova, / Pak da padneš iz neba vedroga, / Perje mesa ne bi iznijelo', ibid., ll. 41–3.

3. In the Shadow of Death

Miloš Obilić, Prince Lazar, and the Jugovići choose their 'heavenly Kingdom' and fight for their 'honourable cross'. This is how the heroes of Kosovo come to be the masters of their moral fate; whatever odds they may be facing in history, death remains a possible pledge of their spiritual freedom. But the heroines—the helpless mothers, sisters, wives, and girls who have to suffer their grief for their men—are left behind. When the battle is over they can only face the wasteland of their survival and utter despair of the soul seems to be their fate. They are imprisoned in their grief in several major poems like 'Tsar Lazar and Tsaritsa Milica', 'Tsaritsa Milica and Duke Vladeta', 'The Kosovo Girl' and 'The Death of the Mother of the Jugovići'. Instead of telling a story these poems enact a tragic drama of the mind; and this gives rise to their epic idiom in which tokens and symbols work out their ominous forebodings.

Almost all the singers of these poems are either blind women or anonymous.[1] Many of their lines echo earlier dirges and songs; they do not seem to improvise so much as to repeat the lines which must have been told a thousand times before.[2] And even the heroines of these poems are, in scholarly parlance, 'unhistorical'; which is to say that the names of the grief-stricken mothers, sisters, wives, and fiancées are fictitious. The only major exception is Tsaritsa Milica; but even she is historical only by proxy, in so far as she is remembered as Tsar Lazar's wife in the largely fictitious stories about her.

[1] 'The Death of the Mother of the Jugovići' ('Smrt majke Jugovića', *Karadžić*, ii, No. 48) was sent to Karadžić by an unknown collector from Croatia (see *Matić*, p. 714). 'Tsaritsa Milica and Duke Vladeta' (Carica Milica i Vladeta vojvoda', *Karadžić*, ii, No. 49) was recorded by Karadžić from a blind woman called Stepanija (see *Matić*, p. 715). 'The Kosovo Girl' ('Kosovka djevojka', *Karadžić*, ii, No. 51) was written down for Karadžić by Lukijan Mušicki from a blind woman from the village of Grgurevci in Srem, not far away from the Monastery of Šišatovac where Mušicki was the abbot.

[2] See below pp. 319–20.

The way in which this world of echo and mute, 'unhistorical' grief emerges in the epic landscape of Kosovo can be glimpsed perhaps in Podrugović's story of how Tsaritsa Milica grasps the omens and responds to the reality of the disaster in 'Tsar Lazar and Tsaritsa Milica'. The first part of the poem seems to be in the masculine epic idiom of action and the choice of the 'honourable cross'. But the brothers' determination to fight and their refusal to stay with Milica is presented partly as the drama of her mind. This explains why Tsar Lazar—who has cursed all who do not come to die in the battle—gives his blessing to Boško Jugović, his ensign, to stay behind with his sister. The blessing fathoms the depths of her love and the despair of the approaching grief—for what else can explain Tsar Lazar's decision to grant the plea, the prayer, of his wife? And the brothers ignore her while marching by; perhaps they cannot bear to look at her because they know that they must refuse what she has to ask. Or are they evasive because they are keen to get away from a fate more terrifying than their own? When the last brother rides his horse through the city gates, Milica falls down 'on to the cold stone'[3] and Tsar Lazar's tears fathom again the nature of her misery. He orders his servant Goluban to stay behind; but even the servant has to betray her to remain true to himself.

In this tragic progress of loneliness tokens replace gestures which themselves have been ominous. The next morning does not bring back the husband and the brothers; 'two black ravens' 'drop down' on Lazar's 'white tower'[4] and their news shapes the world which Milica comes to inhabit:

> 'Out of the Turks there are men alive,
> Out of the Serbs anyone alive
> Is a wounded man dropping blood'.[5]

At this imaginative watershed—dividing the heroes' march to death from Milica's exposure to its awareness—the narrative language dissolves and the story goes on in images which are,

---

[3] '(Ona pade) na kamen studeni', 'Car Lazar i carica Milica', *Karadžić*, ii, No. 45, l. 96.

[4] 'I padoše na bijelu kulu', ibid., l. 122.

[5] 'Od Turaka nešto i ostalo, / A od Srba i što je ostalo, / Sve ranjeno i iskrvavljeno!' Ibid., ll. 143–5.

like the two black ravens, on the borderline between waking and sleeping. Such is the appearance of the servant Milutin—'carrying his right hand in his left',[6] his horse bespattered with blood. Such is the vision of the battlefield as 'broken lances':

> 'And where the glorious Prince Lazar died
> There are many broken lances,
> Broken Turkish and Serbian lances,
> More Serbian than Turkish lances'.[7]

Such is also the description of the death of the eight Jugovići who died 'where brother would not betray brother';[8] and the ninth brother is seen as hunting Turks down 'in flocks', 'a hawk over birds, over doves',[9] 'his cross waving over Kosovo'.[10] And all that remains of the heroic exploit of Miloš Obilić is 'a memory to all Serbs', a story

> To be told and told over again
> While there are people, while there is Kosovo.[11]

But whereas the heroes carry their 'honourable cross' to death, Milica is denied such a heroic gesture in reality.

A similar assumption about the tragedy of a human being who is not the subject but an object of fate is also to be found in the poem 'Tsaritsa Milica and Duke Vladeta', which Karadžić took down from blind Stepanija in Srem. The tale—in so far as there is any—circles round a cluster of tokens, signs, and images. Duke Vladeta—historically Duke Vlatko Vuković, the commander of the Bosnian army in the Battle of Kosovo—appears on a horse 'dressed in the white foam'[12] and conveys his tragic message by telling Milica about Lazar's riderless

---

[6] 'Nosi desnu u lijevoj ruku', *Karadžić*, ii, No. 45, l. 148.

[7] 'Đe pogibe slavni knez Lazare, / Tu su mloga koplja izlomljena, / Izlomljena i Turska i Srpska, / Ali više Srpska, nego Turska', ibid., ll. 173–6.

[8] 'Đe brat brata izdati ne šćede', ibid., l. 182.

[9] '(Još razgoni Turke) na buljuke, / Kao soko tice golubove', ibid., ll. 186–187.

[10] 'Krstaš mu se po Kosovu vija', ibid., l. 185.

[11] '(On ostavi) spomen rodu Srpskom, / Da se priča i pripovijeda / Dok je ljudi i dok je Kosova.' Ibid., ll. 196–8.

[12] '(Vladeta je konja oznojio) / I u b'jelu pjenu obukao', *Karadžić*, ii, No. 49, ll. 7–8. For historical information about Duke Vladeta see T. Maretić, *Naša narodna epika*, p. 231.

dapple. In his story the Jugovići are seen as facing their doom with their arms 'bloody to the shoulders' and their 'green swords to the pommel on the hilt',[13] Miloš Obilić is leaning on his broken lance, and Vuk Branković, the traitor, has not been seen at all:

'I could not see him, may the sun not see him'.[14]

The imagery mirrors again the loneliness and destitution of Milica's predicament: as there is no story, there is no expectation, there is only a retrospect of the tragic emblems of misery and misfortune.

The same loneliness of retrospect dominates the story in the two best of these poems, 'The Kosovo Girl' and 'The Death of the Mother of the Jugovići'. 'The Kosovo Girl' was written down from a blind woman in Srem and it opens with the description of a bright Sunday morning after the battle is over. A girl looks for her betrothed among the wounded and the dead, carrying white bread in her hands and two gold jugs—one filled with cold water, the other with red wine. As 'she handles the heroes in their blood',[15] it is clear from the very beginning that her youth, the brightness of the morning, and the gold of her jugs have the function of great promise which is soon to be betrayed. In the same spirit she recalls the gifts which she received before the battle from her betrothed and his two blood-brothers: 'a tunic embroidered in circles',[16] 'a gilded ring',[17] and a scarf embroidered with gold. Not only do these gifts reflect customs, but the monograms on the tunic and the gold-embroidered scarf are accurate as historical details. Even the circular patterns on the tunic are historically correct; and the most beautiful Serbian rings at the end of the fourteenth century were made not of gold but of silver gilt. This astounding accuracy of historical detail may be the result of memorization of particular formulas or of whole runs of lines in particular poems—memorization characteristic of women singers; even if

---

[13] 'Krvave im ruke do ramena / I zeleni mači do balčaka', *Karadžić*, ii, No. 49, ll. 34-5.

[14] 'Ne viđeh ga, ne vid'lo ga sunce!' Ibid., l. 51.

[15] 'Te prevrće po krvi junake', 'Kosovka djevojka', *Karadžić*, ii, No. 51, l. 13.

[16] 'Kolasta azdija', ibid., ll. 57, 60.

[17] 'Burma pozlaćena', ibid., ll. 81, 83.

a tunic embroidered with circles may have come from a fresco painting.[18] But be this as it may, this truth to distant realities gives added 'weight' to the poem in which a national catastrophe lives as a personal drama in a completely fictitious story. The story ends when a wounded hero tells the girl that her betrothed and her blood-brothers were killed. Her outcry of grief speaks again with a hundred voices of the past, with a personal sense of misery and with the full national pathos of the Kosovo legend:

> 'Unhappy, if I were to grasp a green pine,
> Even the green pine would wither.'[19]

Is it in the nature of an evergreen to wither under the touch of an innocent hand?

This inverted moral order is also mirrored in the setting of the story, in its bright Sunday morning, in the gold jugs, splendid tunics, gold embroidered scarves, and gilded rings: the darkness of their glitter is in accord with the tragic innocence of the heroine. And in this respect the poem contrasts with 'The Death of the Mother of the Jugovići', in which a mother wages her hopeless battle against her grief for her husband and her nine sons. Her love is her ultimate enemy in the tale which unfolds in pure retrospect of tokens of death working out their ominous forebodings. The poem opens with the mother's prayer for a pair of hawk's eyes and a pair of 'swan's white wings';[20] and considering her love and her anxiety for the fate of her husband and her sons, is it surprising that the prayer is immediately granted? But when the wings and the eyes take her to Kosovo, this mercy reveals a scene of death. Her husband and her sons are killed and the way she sees the disaster is reminiscent of Duke Vladeta's tale of the broken lances and riderless horses:

> The nine widows are lamenting,
> The nine children are weeping,
> The nine good horses are whinnying,

---

[18] See S. Radojčić, 'Kosovka djevojka', *Uzori i dela starih srpskih umetnika*, pp. 239–42.

[19] 'Da se, jadna, za zelen bor vatim, / I on bi se zelen osušio.' Ibid., ll. 135–6.

[20] 'I bijela krila labudova', 'Smrt majke Jugovića', *Karadžić*, ii, No. 48, ll. 7, 13.

The nine wild lions are roaring,
The nine hawks are screaming.[21]

Only the mother is speechless, 'strong-hearted'—she lets 'fall no tear from her heart'.[22] In this world of utter desolation even the appearance of a raven seems to be a relief. The raven brings the youngest son's hand, and when the mother addresses the hand, the horror of death seems to retreat into the background before the more terrifying tenderness of her words:

The mother takes Damjan's hand,
She turns it around and over,
She is whispering to the hand:
'My hand, O green apple,
Where did you grow from, where were you ripped off?
You grew on my lap,
You were ripped off on flat Kosovo!'[23]

The disruption of the normal course of things seems to mesmerize the mother's mind into the petrified calm of tenderness, more formidable than any tears could be. And when her heart breaks with pain, death comes as a relief. 'God took mercy on her', as a popular saying puts it. It would be difficult to imagine a context in which this utterance would achieve more pathos. The mother's sense of loss leads her to the fate which has been the privilege only of heroes in action. Yet, this is what comes nearer than any other kind of human love to expressing the tragic sense of Kosovo.

---

[21] 'Zakukalo devet udovica, / Zaplakalo devet sirotica, / Zavrištalo devet dobri konja, / Zalajalo devet ljuti lava, / Zakliktalo devet sokolova', ibid., ll. 33–7.

[22] '(I tu majka) tvrda srca bila, / Da od srca suze ne pustila', ibid., ll. 37–8.

[23] 'Uze majka ruku Damjanovu, / Okretala, prevrtala s njome, / Pak je ruci tijo besjedila: / "Moja ruko, zelena jabuko! / Gdje si rasla, gdje l' si ustrgnuta! / A rasla si na kriocu mome, / Ustrgnuta na Kosovu ravnom!" ' Ibid., ll. 75–81.

PART FOUR

Survival in Vassalage

1. Scapegoat or Hero?

Marko Kraljević is the most popular and the most controversial Serbian epic hero. As a hero in a poem he is mentioned for the first time in an official report of the city of Split to the Venetian Senate in 1547: apparently, a blind soldier was singing about Marko Kraljević in the streets of Split and all his audience joined in the song.[1] And a few years later we find Marko in a *bugarštica* in Serbo-Croat as a fratricide: he flares up in a quarrel and kills his magnificent brother Andrijaš because they cannot agree how to divide their loot. He will still have his hot temper in the later epic tradition, but will usually be seen in a much more favourable light. Thus in an eighteenth-century Dalmatian decasyllabic song he will revenge the death of his brother Andrijaš by killing the Turks who had murdered him.[2] In the eighteenth-century decasyllabic songs in Slavonia and Dalmatia he grows in heroic stature and moral complexity: his strength is super-human but he is also often seen as a successful trickster, he defies the Turks but he is also their vassal.[3] In the nineteenth-century poems in Karadžić's collections, which were often sung by Serbian outlaws and rebels, he is ready to die for truth and honour, but also to kill for fun or for a whim. He has a magic sword and an extraordinary horse; his hand can squeeze water out of wood which had been drying for nine years in a garret. But he sometimes has to run for his life or to win by fraud because some of his enemies are stronger than he is. He is ferocious and tender-hearted; and many of his conflicting features spring probably from diverse tales which were pinned to his name. This diversity is often puzzling and contradictory in the eighteenth-century songs about him, but the voice of Karadžić's singers merges the discrepant elements into an epic picture which meets the conflicting needs of early nineteenth-century Serbian political history. For at the beginning of the First Serbian Uprising, the rebels, like Marko,

[1] See V. M. Jovanović, 'O srpskom narodnom pesništvu', *Srpske narodne pesme—antologija*, p. xvi.

[2] See above p. 76. [3] See above pp. 76–7, 86–7.

recognized the authority of the Grand Porte and were fighting only against local military oppressors who were largely seen as insurgents by the central Ottoman authorities. So why could not a Turkish vassal be seen as a national hero? And as nobody really liked compromising with the Turks, why could he not be at the same time a scapegoat of Serbian vassalage and servitude?

The historical awareness of Marko's position—and the way it lived in the epic tradition—provided a rich starting-point for this imaginative adventure. For unlike the Kosovo martyrs who enact with grand tragic simplicity their heroic commitment to 'the honourable cross' and 'the heavenly Kingdom', Marko Kraljević is seen against the actual historical background of Serbian feudal factions and vassalage. Of course, this is not scholarly history, but many of its fictions reflect a broad historical context and illustrate how it lived in popular national awareness. And the fate of Marko Kraljević is linked as much in epic poetry as it was in actual history with that of his father King Vukašin, who refused to recognize the sovereign power of Stefan Dušan's son Uroš after his father's death. This led to factions which were a major cause of the Serbian disaster in the Battle on the Marica in 1371, which was, historically speaking, a considerably bigger affair than the more legendary Battle of Kosovo. Historians claim that it was, moreover, 'a body blow against Byzantium',[4] and therefore the most important single Ottoman victory in the conquest of the Balkans before the fall of Constantinople. King Vukašin himself was killed in this battle and it was after his death that Marko Kraljević became a Turkish vassal. In the epic picture Vukašin is seen in one or two poems as a helpless wounded hero in the river Marica after the battle, but he and his brother Despot Uglješa—who also refused to recognize Uroš's authority—live in epic memory above all as the greatest villains of Serbian factions of pre-Turkish times. Such a villainous parentage could not be lost on the patriarchal epic imagination shaping Marko's character and destiny: King Vukašin's curse consigns Marko to his prospective Turkish vassalage in 'Uroš and the Mrljavčevići'.[5] A father's curse is a father's curse—even when the father is such a scoundrel as King Vukašin.

[4] See G. Ostrogorski, *History of the Byzantine State*, Oxford, 1968, p. 541.
[5] See above pp. 140–1.

Marko Kraljević's actual position in Turkish vassalage is
marked with uncertainties and ambiguities. He was a sufficiently powerful and independent ruler to mint his own silver
coins with a Christian inscription: 'In Christ our God blessed in
faith King Marko'.[6] But does the extent of his independence
explain the fact that he did not take part in the Battle of
Kosovo on the Turkish side? Did he refuse to fight, which is
unlikely, or was he absent because Murad could not trust his
loyalty to the extent of using his forces in the battle?[7] For as he
ruled in the neighbouring area—bordering on the river Vardar,
the mountain of Šar, the lake of Ohrid and the town of Castoria
(Kostur), it is indeed strange that his name is never mentioned
either in historical sources or in epic memory in connection
with the Battle of Kosovo. But his actual historical position is
perhaps best mirrored in the songs in which he appears as a
pillar of order in the sultan's lands threatened by brigands and
by the neighbouring feudal lords (for basic epic topography,
see Map 1). And, finally, there is no doubt that Marko Kraljević was killed in Romania fighting on the Turkish side against
Duke Mirčeta in the Battle of Rovine in 1395.[8]

The first legend about him is to be found in Konstantin the
Philosopher's biography of Despot Stefan Lazarević, written
not long after the despot's death in 1427. Konstantin tells the
story which illustrates the crux of Marko's mythic status: a
heroic independence of spirit in physical Turkish servitude.
Konstantin 'quotes' what King Marko said to his closest friend
Konstantin Dejanović, who ruled, also as an unwilling Turkish
vassal, the eastern provinces bordering on Marko's state, before
both of them were killed in the Battle of Rovine: 'I say this and
pray God to give his help to the Christians, even if I am the
first to be killed in this war.'[9] In the later epic tradition Marko
and Konstantin Dejanović (Bey Kostadin) will appear as two

---

[6] 'V Hrista Boga blagoverni kralj Marko', see T. Maretić, *Naša narodna
epika*, p. 176.

[7] See ibid.

[8] See I. Božić *et al.*, *Istorija Jugoslavije*, p. 94. For a fuller discussion of the
historical and the fictitious elements connected with the epic figure of Marko
Kraljević see Lj. Zuković, 'Istorijski kralj Marko i epski Kraljević Marko',
Izraz, xviii (1974), pp. 197–232.

[9] Konstantin Filozof, 'Život despota Stefana Lazarevića' in G. Camblak,
Konstantin Filozof, Pajsije Patrijarh, *Stare srpske biografije xv i xvii veka*, iii, p. 68.

blood-brothers and their Turkish vassalage probably explains why each of them has some shortcomings in his personal character, unlike most of the other great national epic heroes. Bey Kostadin does not show the respect due to his parents and drives away poor people from the feast of his family patron saint; and Marko reprimands him duly for these faults which are very grievous sins indeed in the patriarchal moral frame-work.[10] Marko also has some faults: he is so hot-tempered that he sometimes maims or kills people for minor offences and he is so prone to drinking that a tip for wine can sometimes cool off his heroic rage.[11] But these are not such serious deficiencies; they are in fact the vices of his virtues. If he were not so hot-tempered, he could hardly be such a fighter for better social and human justice; he could hardly be so easily moved to action by other people's suffering. And wine strengthens his heroic spirit; it even heals his wounds;[12] and after all in a great hero everything has to be on a heroic scale.

In short, Marko's vices are partly reflections of his ambiguous historical status and partly comic devices which reveal his nature and his world and which shape a picture of his heroic greatness. However, in Yugoslav scholarship Marko's faults are usually underplayed as minor foibles of 'the first and best loved hero of our popular poems'.[13] On the other hand, major foreign scholars like the Chadwicks miss the whole epic context and spirit of the songs about Marko so that in their judgement he appears to be 'more of an ogre than a hero', or at least a boor

[10] See 'Marko Kraljević and Bey Kostadin' ('Marko Kraljević i beg Kostadin', *Karadžić*, ii, No. 59). See also Appendix IV.

[11] Thus, for instance, when Novak the blacksmith tells Marko that he had made a better sword than Marko's for a better hero, Marko cuts off his arm and gives him enough money to buy food for himself as long as he lives ('Marko Kraljević and Musa Kesedžija'—'Marko Kraljević i Musa Kesedžija', *Karadžić*, ii, No. 67, see in particular ll. 131–64). In another song Marko kills an Arab princess who helped him to escape from her father's dungeon: simply because he cannot stand the contrast between her white teeth and her black skin. The singer seems to realize in the end what this is about and makes Marko build 'many monasteries' to expiate his sin. ('Marko Kraljević and the Daughter of the Arab King'—'Marko Kraljević i kći kralja arapskoga', *Karadžić*, ii, No. 64). As regards Marko's readiness to be appeased if given a tip for wine, see below pp. 188–90.

[12] See below pp. 194, 197.

[13] T. Maretić, *Naša narodna epika*, pp. 182–3.

in whom 'physical strength and heavy drinking are among his chief personal characteristics'.[14] They see him as so 'low' that he comes to be summed up as a man who 'owes much to his horse Šarac, which he feeds on wine'.[15] Marko would, in fact, hardly take this as an insult; he would probably see it not only as a compliment to himself, but also to Šarac and wine. But the reason why the Chadwicks see him as 'not a very attractive hero according to modern ideas'[16] is simply that they fail to understand comedy as a device of complex imaginative discoveries. They assume, in short, the insufficient Aristotelian definition of comedy as a 'low' genre, with an appropriately 'low' social background, moral sense, and language which cannot be tolerated in heroic poetry.

But what is it that makes the epic figure of Marko Kraljević so baffling and controversial? It is partly the ambiguous historical setting of faction and vassalage in which he appears. It is partly the historical context of the best-known songs about him, the context of conflicting loyalties and divided sympathies of the Serbian outlaws and rebels who sang about him. And last but not least even the eighteenth-century decasyllabic poems in which he figures as a trickster suggest that he was particularly attractive for singers who may not have always had a refined sense of humour but were certainly keen on fun. It may also be significant that the greatest teller of songs about Marko Kraljević was Tešan Podrugović, probably the greatest master in all the Serbo-Croat epic tradition. His zest for fighting, his sense of humour, his 'scowl', his cleverness and his relative honesty, which Karadžić mentions explicitly,[17] are reflected in the great heroic spirit and the comic zeal of his poems about Marko Kraljević. Much of this spirit was already in the tradition; and there is little doubt that Podrugović shared it with many of his predecessors and contemporaries— for Marko Kraljević is indeed a great and typical national figure. But like all heroes he can be best understood in his own epic context.

[14] H. M. and Nora K. Chadwick, *The Growth of Literature*, ii, Cambridge, 1968, p. 311.
[15] Ibid.   [16] Ibid.   [17] See below pp. 311–12.

2. In Nature

It is not without its irony that Marko Kraljević appears as an ideal figure only in the poems which set their stories outside the actualities of human history. As if only outside human reality, when he has to deal with hawks or eagles, the untainted image of his noble and generous human heart could be completely achieved and fully sustained. For it is only in three or four such poems—patriarchal in their themes and imagery and akin to the epic poems about family life—that we see Marko Kraljević in anything like an ideal light.

It is significant, for instance, that in 'Marko Kraljević and the Hawk' our hero does not appear as a fighter but as a sick, wounded man lying by the road. His battle lance is planted above his head and only his great horse Šarac, tied to the lance, keeps him company. And when a hawk turns up, he is not associated—as usual in Serbo-Croat epic singing—with hunting and fighting, but with nursing the helpless:

> A hawk fell on him, grey feathered bird,
> Carrying water to him in his beak,
> And he gave water to Marko for his drink;
> He spread his wings out over Marko's head,
> He created a shadow for Marko.[1]

As so often in the poems about Marko there is both a patriarchal and a chivalric touch about this image; and what follows is a fairy tale which explains its emblematic meaning. The hawk recalls the days when the Turks cut his wings and Marko Kraljević put him high up 'in a green fir-tree'[2] so that the Turkish horses should not kill him. This network of imagery—the helpless bird, the fir-tree, the Turkish horses, the wounded hero given water by the bird and lying under the protection of its wings—suggests the same patterns of the breaking and

---

[1] 'Tu dopade soko tica siva, / U kljunu mu vode donosio, / Pa je Marka vode napojio; / Nad Markom je krila raskrilio, / Pa je Marku ladak načinio.' 'Marko Kraljević i soko', *Karadžić*, ii, No. 54, ll. 9–13.

[2] 'Na jelu zelenu', ibid., l. 26.

re-establishing of harmony between the human and the natural, between the historical and the ideal, which we find in the patriarchal poems about family relations. It is analogous to the vision of the fir between the two pines, of 'the immortelle and basil', of 'the thorns and the nettles', which tell their own story of tragic sisterly and brotherly love in 'God Leaves No Debt Unpaid'.[3]

A similar patriarchal idyll is found in the poem which Karadžić prints as another variant of 'Marko Kraljević and the Hawk', also recorded from an unknown singer. The starting point is the same: Marko again lies sick by the road, with his lance planted by his head, with Šarac tied to the lance. Instead of a hawk an eagle spreads his wings to make shade for him and brings him water in his beak. The opening lines are more vividly realized: Marko is covered by his green dolman and has a silver-embroidered scarf over his face. He does not ask the eagle why he helps him; the question is voiced by a *vila* (a mountain nymph) and the eagle's answer is richer in physical detail. The eagle reminds the *vila* of the days when his feathers were clotted with blood so that he could not fly; it was then that Marko took him 'to the green wood':

> 'And he put me high up on a fir-tree bough;
> The fine rain struck downwards from the skies,
> My wings were washed until they were clean,
> And I could spread my wings and fly with them.'[4]

And the narrative is also more elaborate; the eagle goes on to recall Marko's second good deed: when Adžaga's tower was burning, Marko saved the young eagles from their nest, kept them warm in his breast, fed them for a whole month and let them fly 'into the green wood'. The young ones come together with the old eagle; and a fundamental norm of life is re-established in the narrative which develops the initial harmony of the image of the eagle's protection of wounded Marko. But

[3] See above pp. 113–15.

[4] '(Odnese me) u goru zelenu, / Pa me metnu na jelovu granu, / Iz nebesa sitan dažd udari, / Te se moja krila poopraše, / I ja mogo s krilma poletiti', 'Marko Kraljević i orao', *Karadžić*, ii, No. 55, ll. 43–7. This is the common title of this poem, even if Karadžić calls it 'Opet to, malo drukčije' ('The same again, a little different')—as he calls all the variants of the poems which he prints in his collections. For *vila*, see Appendix III.

the story in this poem—as well as in its variant in which a hawk takes the part of the eagle—illustrates the existing harmony of man and nature; it shows that the initial ideal image has only been threatened and never destroyed in reality. And it does not come as a surprise that the ultimate origin of these stories is not to be found in Serbian history but in the Byzantine miniatures, in pictures and sculptures illustrating the legends about saints who were protected from the sun by eagles spreading their wings over them.

Such a motif is found, as S. Radojčić has pointed out, in the stories about the lives of St Servacius, St Medard and St Bertulf; in the Byzantine tradition it is connected with Emperor Markian who was also honoured as a saint. It became particularly popular owing to the chronicles of Constantine Manasses which were often illustrated by the miniatures showing Emperor Markian—very much like Marko later in the song—with an eagle over his head. Whether Markian's pillar in Constantinople with a large capital with eagles was also at the back of the legend we cannot tell; but that the poems about Marko Kraljević and the eagle or the hawk were in the tradition of such illustrations is beyond doubt[5]—even if at the same time they were also part of the living folk tradition of the songs and stories about the love between human beings and animals.[6]

[5] See S. Radojčić, 'O nekim zajedničkim motivima naše narodne pesme i našeg starog slikarstva', *Zbornik radova SAN*, xxxvi (1953)—Vizantološki institut SAN, ii, pp. 172–4. Radojčić is also right in pointing out that such epic poems are in the wider tradition of legends which grew as interpretations of pictorial and sculptural works—such as 'the tales about the saints who kill dragons, the tales about the deer with the cross, the tales about saints to whom beasts show their love' (ibid., p. 173). But it is curious to note that in his detailed analysis he makes the claim that the difference between the illustration of Manasses' text and the Serbian epic poem is that 'the imperial eagle has been replaced by the chivalric bird—the hawk' (ibid., p. 174). Has Radojčić simply overlooked Karadžić's second variant of this poem where an eagle and not a hawk actually figures? It is also worth noting that a hero in trouble addresses an eagle in the first recorded fragment of an epic song in Serbo-Croat (see above pp. 27–9).

[6] Folk tales with such motifs are innumerable; a comparatively early example of a Serbo-Croat epic song treating this theme is found in *Gesemann*, No. 86. In this song an eagle and a raven remember that a Turkish aga had given them the 'heroes' flesh to eat' ('naranio mesa junač'koga', l. 14) and their 'blood to drink' ('k'rv'ce napojio', l. 15); in return for this favour the birds fly to the wounded aga's tower and tell his mother about his predicament.

Finally, the only other poem in which Marko Kraljević appears as a saintly figure—'Marko Kraljević and Bey Kostadin'[7]—was recorded from a man who is far better known as a teller of folk tales than as a singer.[8] It is, in fact, a patriarchal moral fable with hardly any epic content in it: Marko Kraljević finds two poor women whom Kostadin drove away from his family patronal festival (*slava*). Marko gives them 'white bread to eat' and 'red wine to drink',[9] he upbraids his blood-brother for inhospitableness and proceeds to tell him about his other failings, such as his disregard of the patriarchal duty of respect for parents and elders.

But even if two of these idyllic tales about Marko Kraljević come from pictorial illustrations of Byzantine legends and the third is told by a story-teller rather than by a singer, they mirror some essential features of Marko's character as seen in the epic tradition. It would be difficult to imagine that they were pinned on to Marko's name in a completely arbitrary fashion; they could certainly never have been connected with Vuk Branković. This 'compatibility'—and compatibility is always both partial and significant—brings out Marko's noble mettle, his innate goodness, his compassion for the helpless and the weak, his attachment to basic patriarchal values. However he will be enmeshed in gory nets of history as soon as he appears in poems which represent him in epic action. In short, when he faces a wounded bird or its helpless young, he is a morally perfect and straightforward hero; but when he feels in duty and truth bound to frustrate his own father's lust for power and has to run for his life to avoid killing his own parent, the idyllic moral approach becomes a little more difficult. And matters do not become easier when he is seen as the greatest Serbian hero who, from his historical and epic position of Turkish servant and vassal, has to defend the national sense of honour.

[7] 'Marko Kraljević i beg Kostadin', *Karadžić*, ii, No. 60.

[8] See *Matić*, p. 730.

[9] 'Narani i leba bijeloga / I napoji vina crvenoga', *Karadžić*, ii, No. 60, ll. 34–5.

3. On the Sultan's Praying Rug

The recognition of limited heroic possibilities in ambiguous historical situations often leads to comedy in the poems about Marko Kraljević. Thus in 'Uroš and the Mrljavčevići', as we have seen, Marko comes to settle the dispute about Stefan Dušan's succession and he appears at first as a grand patriarchal tribune of 'the justice of the God of truth'. But at the same time he is the champion of heavenly justice on this earth; and even his truth-loving mother suspects that in this world the scales of justice are prone to tilt in the father's or the uncles' favour. Marko himself is aware of this precarious predicament of idealism in political action; he is an idealist, he refuses to tell lies in his father's or his uncles' interest and he does not 'sin against his soul'. But neither does he display excessive zeal 'to lose his life'[1]—he is not attracted by the grand tragic opportunity to die, as Miloš Obilić and Prince Lazar are.

As soon as 'the justice of the God of truth' is brought from its grand rhetorical heaven down to the political earth, as soon as Marko acts on his mother's advice and announces that Uroš is the legitimate heir of his father's empire, he has to face his own father who wants to kill him. He does not oppose his father's fury by a heroic gesture; he neither fights nor lets himself be killed. He runs for his life. And as he is a fast runner we do not see his escape as an act of cowardice so much as a realistic assessment of his predicament. There is, of course, also the moral explanation: Marko knows that it would be highly inappropriate for a dutiful son 'to fight against his own parent'.[2] But with all due respect for Marko's filial obedience, the hero has to divest himself of some of the burden of his dignity in order to take to his heels. And the chase is seen as a ring-dance round the church of the Autocrat (Samodreža), in a way which transplants a grand historical and patriarchal drama into an area of Sunday merry-making.

[1] See above pp. 138–41.
[2] '(Jer se njemu, brate, ne pristoji) / Sa svojim se biti roditeljem', 'Uroš i Mrljavčevići', *Karadžić*, ii, No. 34, ll. 217–18.

Of course, if Marko were a great pagan hero he would kill his father; if he were a genuine tragic figure in an epic poem he would probably have to speak the truth and let himself be killed and this would illuminate the depth of his attachment to the moral norm in which he had been instructed by his mother and Father Nedeljko in such a grand vocabulary. But he does not feel that 'the justice of the God of truth' is tragically and heroically binding to the end; and how could he feel bound to enact a tragedy when he is faced with such a scoundrel as his father is? Why should he not—having spoken his mind in a most heroic and disinterested spirit—run for his life? If he did not, he would hardly get a second chance of being even partially heroic.

Marko has, in short, to depend not only on his heroic heart and noble soul; he has, like Ulysses, also to use his wits to decide when it is more honourable to run away than to fight. And in many other poems we are made to feel that his success depends on survival rather than on a grand folly. All he can do in his epic landscape, and this probably reflects a historical reality, is to save, piecemeal as a rule, the little honour and justice that is left in the world as it is. There is, for instance, a fundamentally un-heroic denouement in the well-known poem 'Marko Kraljević Knows His Father's Sword', which Karadžić recorded from his best poet Tešan Podrugović. The poem opens with the vision of a compassionate Turkish girl who sees a wounded hero in the river Marica. She does not ask who he is, she accepts him as a brother-in-God and throws him a length of 'linen rag'—the same 'rag' which sisters often used, in vain, to help their brothers in need.[3] The hero turns out to be none other than King Vukašin—Marko's father who was in fact killed in the Battle on the Marica in 1371, so that there is a grain of history in this fictitious tale. However, the brother of the young Turkish girl comes to the river and kills the wounded hero because he likes his sword—and the sister curses her brother:

> 'Why have you killed my brother-in-God?
> Unhappy man, you tricked yourself,

[3] See above, pp. 74–5, 88–9, 130.

What was it for? A steel sword!
May God repay. May it cut off your head!'[4]

The dramatic impact of this curse can be grasped if we remember that it is uttered within the patriarchal assumptions about the most ideal form of human love. It is epically unprecedented: if hatred can flare up in the conflicts of interest and psychology between father and son, between two brothers, if a brother can be bewitched by the hatred of his wife to kill his sister, if even a mother can abandon her illegitimate child, yet there are no examples of a sister's hatred of her brother. And, more terrifyingly, the sister's curse comes true. When the sword is offered for sale, Marko will recognize it and kill the Turk in a scene in which we see how 'God repays'. What follows, however, brings out Marko's character in an equally significant way. Asked to report to the Sultan to answer for what he has done, Marko at first 'does not speak', he only 'sits drinking dark wine'[5]—after all, he has only killed a Turk who slew his father. Finally, annoyed by the disturbance, he picks up his heavy mace, puts on his 'sheepskin inside out'[6] and appears before the Sultan in his tent. Marko is obviously in a bad mood—even if it is difficult to say whether he minds more being interrupted in wine-drinking or being summoned to answer for inflicting a deserved punishment on a Turk:

> And Marko was so very angry,
> He sat down on the praying rug in boots.[7]

The boots and the rug define his historical position as much as the position of Serbian rebels in the First Uprising when they tried to crush the Dahijas' terror and remain loyal to the Sultan; but the image also sums up the most important facet of Marko's character and his world. The Sultan—unlike some scholars—gets Marko's point: when he sees the mace, he moves

---

[4] 'Za što zgubi moga pobratima? / Na što si se, bolan, prevario? / A na jednu sablju okovanu! / Eda Bog da, odsjekla ti glavu!!' 'Marko Kraljević poznaje očinu sablju', *Karadžić*, ii, No. 57, ll. 70–3.

[5] '(Marka zove, Marko) ne govori, / Već on sjedi, pije mrko vino', ibid., ll. 118–19.

[6] '(On) prigrnu ćurak naopako', ibid., l. 121.

[7] 'Koliko se ražljutio Marko, / U čizmama sjede na serdžadu', ibid., ll. 124–5.

away until Marko 'drives him all the way to the wall'.[8] And nothing on earth can tame Marko's rage—except perhaps a handful of ducats. So the Sultan's hand fumbles in his pockets, he takes out no less than a hundred ducats—Marko obviously has his price—and gives them to our hero to go away and get himself some wine. Marko is appeased; and he leaves telling the Sultan that he could not possibly have guaranteed the safety of his imperial person had he found his father's sword in the Sultan's hands.

The same zest of limited defiance lives in the poem 'Marko Drinks Wine in Ramadan',[9] which Karadžić wrote down from an anonymous singer. At the back of the tale there is, of course, the general prohibitionist Moslem attitude to wine, and the custom of the Ramadan fast—but its observance would not have been binding on Marko. This is why it is probable that this fictitious story originated in the actual general prohibition of wine drinking in towns during the crisis of the Turkish military and administrative system at the end of the seventeenth century when specific prohibition orders were often issued.[10] The story also partly leans on the Turkish legislation which denied the Christian population the right to wear clothes of lively colours, the 'green dolmans' of the poem.[11] The prohibition of dancing suggests further what life was 'really' like during the Turkish reign; it is not 'unhistorical' in so far as Marko expresses his defiance by dancing with Turkish girls, which social custom would have made unimaginable anyway. However, for formulaic epic reasons, as well as to add a touch of grandeur to Marko's defiance, Marko does not disregard the orders just of any sultan—but of the greatest Turkish sultan,

---

[8] 'Dok doćera cara do duvara', ibid., l. 131. The comic spirit of this and similar scenes is completely missed by scholars who see in it a great national shame; V. Đurić's patriotic assessment of such scenes is in this sense typical: 'Yes, the sultan trembled before Marko's rage, but—unfortunately—he always saved himself from that rage by putting his hand in his pocket and throwing several hundred ducats to Marko . . . In this submission to the sultan—however limited, uncertain and slight it might be—lies the deepest shame' (V. Đurić, 'Srpskohrvatska narodna epika', *Antologija narodnih junačkih pesama*, p. 60).

[9] 'Marko pije uz ramazan vino', *Karadžić*, ii, No. 71.

[10] See *Matić*, p. 745.

[11] 'Zelene dolame', *Karadžić*, ii, No. 71, ll. 3, 8 etc.

the conqueror of Hungary, Suleiman II the Magnificent (1520–66). After all Marko must find an opponent worthy of himself, and if he cannot be found in his time, or in the time of the actual prohibition of alcohol, a man from another century will do. And when Marko defies the Sultan's orders, messengers appear and ask him to report to the Sultan himself. Marko obeys the call and tries to explain to the Sultan, his 'foster father' as he calls him,[12] in the tone of a naughty foster son, why he has to wear 'a green dolman', dance with Turkish girls, and drink wine. He even comes to explain why he has to make the Turkish hodjas and hadjis keep him company in drinking:

> 'If I drink the wine in Ramadan,
> If I drink it, it accords with my faith;
> If I make hodjas and hadjis drink,
> My sense of honour cannot suffer
> That I drink and they only watch.'[13]

But who knows if the Sultan will have sufficient sense of humour to accept this as a wholly satisfactory explanation? So Marko makes sure that his sword is in his lap and his mace to hand. The message gets across; the uneasy Sultan is again driven to the wall; and a historical relationship of Marko's actual feudal vassalage is worked out in terms of a homely epic scene in which the greatest Turkish sultan is once more made to offer a Serbian king a little money for wine. The oppressed Serbian plebs, the so-called 'rayah', and their *guslar* are obviously getting their own back on the Turkish oppressors and it should not be surprising that their triumph is presented in a comic light.

But this is, of course, only a part of the epic story, and it can be appreciated only in its full context. And in this context it is clear that one could not imagine Miloš Obilić or any of the tragic Kosovo heroes as browbeating a Turkish sultan into giving them a tip for wine. Neither could any of them be imagined as defying and challenging his destiny by drinking wine, wearing a 'green dolman' or dancing with Turkish girls

---

[12] 'Poočime, (care Sulemane)!' *Karadžić*, ii, No. 71, l. 68.
[13] 'Ako pijem uz ramazan vino, / Ako pijem, vera mi donosi; / Ako nagonim odže i adžije, / Ne može mi ta obraz podneti, / Da ja pijem, oni da gledaju', ibid., ll. 69–73.

at the time of the Ramadan fast. Miloš does not tread in his boots on the sultan's praying rug while coming to make his obeisance; he pretends to bow but he kills Murad to prove his loyalty and honour and to die himself. This difference springs partly from the assumed historical and epic circumstance: the Kosovo heroes face the approaching disaster and pledge their lives to the cause of honour and moral freedom, whereas Marko lives after the disaster has taken place and is doomed to the comedy of survival. Death is the only alternative for Miloš because slavery and vassalage are unthinkable in his code of honour; but Marko is born into vassalage and the singer assumes that it is the only possible imaginative challenge for his character. It is not given to Marko even to try to make a grand tragic gesture; all he can hope to do is to laugh the bitterness of reality away and patch up the national sense of honour as best he can. But even if Marko and Miloš embody two different myths about two radically distinct historical situations, even if they express two diametrically opposite responses to life, they are—like Don Quixote and Sancho Panza—complementary and necessary to each other, because their contrasting brings out in full relief many significant details in the epic landscape of Serbian history.

So for instance when Miloš is slandered by a traitor, he swears that Kosovo will show 'who is faithful, who is the traitor'.[14] And this is magnificently shown when he kills Murad and dies in glory. 'The faith' is all of a piece, and so is, for that matter, the 'treason'. Miloš has nothing to do with it; it is the province of the character of Vuk Branković. Everything is heroically simple and dignified; how could there be any ambiguities about the tragedy of the greatest national ordeal? But Marko treads a world in which the ordeal is over; the question is not how one could most honourably die, but how one could survive with as little dishonour and shame as possible in the circumstances. This is why for Marko the 'firm faith'[15] is

[14] 'Ko je vjera, ko li je nevjera', 'Komadi od različnijeh kosovskijeh pjesama (iii)', *Karadžić*, ii, No. 50, l. 53.

[15] The concept of 'firm faith' was used in medieval documents (see above p. 21); it is found already in *bugarštice* (see notes 86, 87, p. 48). Marko Kraljević is probably the only epic hero in the tradition who can play tricks with this sacrosanct concept.

above all inspiring when it can serve a useful comic purpose. Thus in 'Marko Kraljević and the Daughter of the Arab King', again recorded from Tešan Podrugović, Marko is moved to great eloquence in a scene in which he uses his 'faith' for the purpose of perjury. As he has no other way of getting out of the Arab prison, he swears to the King's daughter that he will never leave her if she helps him to escape.[16] In his perjury he invokes cosmic powers to witness his trick: he puts his cap on his knee and swears loyalty in fact to the cap when he promises to be more 'faithful' to his word than the changing sun which does not give as much heat in winter as it does in the summer![17] And the epic tale lives as long as it sustains its comedy; its epic texture cracks when it becomes 'serious', when Marko kills the girl who has helped him because he cannot stand the sight of her white teeth against her black skin and proceeds to expiate his sin by building many monasteries. Similarly, in another epic tale which also tells the story of Marko's imprisonment—based, we are told, on the historical fact that another man with the same name was imprisoned by the Turks[18]—the most lively lines identify 'faith' with 'uncertain credit' because Marko cannot find anyone to guarantee that he will pay his ransom as he promises.[19]

In short, at his liveliest Marko Kraljević moves in a tricky world in which he has to shape his moral stature in a highly ambivalent fashion. His character feeds on the discrepancies of life and history which suggest that the man and the world have not been cut to quite the same measure. This is why in the motley of the ideals and the historical experience which went into his making, he can never achieve the simple grandeur and dignity which would suggest that man has been put on this earth for some grand tragic purpose. In short, history and

[16] 'By firm faith I will not leave you!' ('Tvrda vjera, ostavit te neću', 'Marko Kraljević i kći kralja arapskoga', *Karadžić*, ii, No. 64, l. 54).

[17] See ibid., ll. 51–8.

[18] See below p. 196.

[19] See 'Marko Kraljević in the Azak Gaol' ('Marko Kraljević u azačkoj tamnici', *Karadžić*, ii, No. 65, ll. 31–2). In these lines Marko pleads with the daughter of the Arab king to ask her father to let him out of gaol even if he has no one to guarantee that he will pay his ransom, to let him out on his word of honour, 'on faith and on uncertain credit' ('a na vjeru i na veresiju', l. 32).

cosmos, together with the greatest moral notions, have to be reduced to a human scale; and, perhaps not surprisingly, everything becomes easier and brighter. For the result is that the assessment of the human situation and possibility becomes far less radical and a little more merciful. A rich compromise embraces the radical element, but history is no longer just a grand stage on which only a tragic gesture can be worthy of the décor. It is also seen, partly at least, as a circus; so why should not a great hero—having told the truth to his father's and his uncle's faces—run for his life and hop in a dance around a church? And are not the boots on the sultan's praying rug foolhardy enough? This image of grandeur and courage is hardly less genuine for being a little ironical.

4. In Single Combat

The horse, the arms, the equipment, and the appearance of a hero, his manner of fighting reveal his mettle and the nature of the imaginative world in which he moves. The appearance of Marlo Kraljević—to keep mainly to the poems which Kara-džić recorded from Tešan Podrugović, the man with an outlaw's sense of humour—is always connected with his fat, piebald horse Šarac which is not

> like other horses are
> But spotted like a cow.[1]

A skin of wine is an important part of the equipment; appar-ently, nothing else could quite balance the heavy mace so that 'neither side should overweigh'.[2] Wine is, moreover, an important feature of Marko's strategy as well as of his tactics. When he gets seventy heavy wounds in his fight with the Arab army,

> Marko does not go off to a doctor,
> He goes from one inn to the other,
> To find out where is the best wine.[3]

And, of course, as soon as he had drunk enough wine,

> His terrible wounds began to heal over.[4]

Wine becomes particularly important in epic action in the poem 'Marko Kraljević and Đemo of the Mountain' in which Podrugović, an outlaw himself, sees Marko as fighting against brigandage and keeping order in the sultan's lands. Does Podrugović identify himself partly with the brigand when he

---

[1] 'Kakvino su konji, / Veće šaren, kako i goveče', 'Marko Kraljević and General Vuča'—'Marko Kraljević i Vuča dženeral', *Karadžić*, ii, No. 42, ll. 129–30.

[2] 'Da ne kriva ni tamo ni amo', ibid., l. 87.

[3] 'Ali Marko ne traži ećima, / Već on ide iz krčme u krčmu, / Te on traži, đe je bolje vino.' 'Marko Kraljević i Mina od Kostura', *Karadžić*, ii, No. 62, ll. 190–2.

[4] 'I grdne mu rane zarastoše.' Ibid., ll. 194.

makes Marko Kraljević run away? Not quite perhaps—for
Marko is unarmed and, anyway, he has to win in the end. But
he wins by fraud, using wine literally as the most important
weapon against his enemy. When Đemo takes Marko, with his
hands in iron fetters, to a tavern, Marko himself is worried
about what will happen because he has left so many of his wine
bills unpaid. But there is a maid called Janja in the tavern; and
Janja is a standing name for such heroines who were, of course,
also important historical figures, particularly for outlaws and
caravans. For apart from wine and feminine charms they could
also provide information—to one or to the other side, or to
both. In this poem Janja is so important that even the mountain
where she lives is called Janjina; and in spite of Marko's
worries about his unpaid bills, he is obviously Janja's favourite,
among other reasons perhaps because he owes her so much
money for wine. So there is sufficient motivation for Janja to
put 'all kinds of herbs' into Đemo's wine;[5] and Đemo will fall
asleep—in the wording again characteristic of the comic spirit
of the poem—'with his head without a pillow'.[6] Janja will undo
Marko's iron fetters and set him free, so that we shall witness a
comic triumph of our hero in which wine is the decisive factor
in his victory over a stronger enemy.

A similar comic triumph by cunning is also to be found in
one of the best known poems in which Marko fights Mina of
Kostur (Castoria). As the city of Kostur lay near the south-
western border of King Marko's state, the historical Mina—
Duke Mihailo of Sibinj, usually called Mihna in chronicles—
came to be seen as Marko's victim in epic poems even if he was
in fact killed by Dmitar Jakšić, another Serbian feudal lord, in
1510, more than a hundred years after Marko's time.[7] Several
versions of this story—a *bugarštica*, some eighteenth-century
decasyllabic poems and the poem which Karadžić recorded
from an anonymous singer—describe Marko as a comic hero
who kills his enemy by disguising himself as a monk.[8] This
suggests the singers' kinship in comic spirit, even if none of the

---

[5] 'Bilje svakojako', 'Marko Kraljević i Đemo Brđanin', *Karadžić*, ii, No.
68, l. 164.
[6] '(Pade Đemo) glavom bez uzglavlja', ibid., l. 165.
[7] See *Matić*, p. 733. See also T. Maretić, *Naša narodna epika*, pp. 191–2.
[8] *Bogišić*, Nos. 7, 86, 87; *Karadžić*, ii, No. 62. See above p. 77.

earlier versions is so fully developed in comic details as the one which Karadžić wrote down. In this version Marko puts on his head 'a monk's tall hat',[9] he grows a black beard down to his waist, dresses in a monk's apparel and comes in this disguise to marry Mina—

Who to? To his own love.[10]

He hops a little monkish dance in this wedding; under his light feet the house-beams begin to tremble in the ground and he draws his rusted sword, cuts off Mina's head and goes back home 'singing and singing his song'.[11]

In 'Marko Kraljević and Musa Kesedžija', one of the best and most popular Serbo-Croat epic poems, which Karadžić recorded from Tešan Podrugović about Easter time in 1815 in Sremski Karlovci, we are again faced with so much cunning and so many tricks that the poem can be appreciated only as a very ambiguous monument to the greatest Serbian hero. The actual historical background of the poem is most uncertain: Musa may be nominally connected with Bajazid's son Musa who fought for the Turkish throne and was killed in the battle in which a Serbian feudal lord took part.[12] But as he is called Musa Arbanasa, his name is obviously connected with Albania; and as he is represented as plundering the Sultan's caravans, the scale of his rebellion would suggest Balkan history in the eighteenth and nineteenth centuries. Musa has three hearts, like Virgil's Erul in *The Aeneid* (Canto VIII); and at the beginning of the poem Marko is found in the Sultan's prison, which suggests a sixteenth-century Knight Marko, a Serb from Dalmatia, who was taken prisoner by the Turks at the time when he was in the service of a Romanian feudal lord.[13] As this knight was a popular figure in Serbian and Romanian epic songs, it is not difficult to imagine how these songs were partly absorbed in the epic traditions about Marko Kraljević. Finally, the description of Marko's 'rotting bones' in the

[9] '(A na glavu) kapu kamilavku', 'Marko Kraljević i Mina od Kostura', *Karadžić*, ii, No. 62, l. 260.
[10] 'Da sa kime, već sa svojom ljubom!' Ibid., l. 293.
[11] 'Pjevajući i pop'jevajući', ibid., l. 336.
[12] See *Matić*, pp. 739–40. Cf. T. Maretić, *Naša narodna epika*, pp. 195–6.
[13] See *Matić*, pp. 736–7. Cf. T. Maretić, op. cit., pp. 195–6.

prison comes from the story about 'Akir the Wise' which was well known in Serbian medieval literature.[14] The food which Marko eats—he grew up on 'honey and sugar'—comes from the tables of the Bosnian Moslem beys' families of Podrugović's times.[15]

All these diverse elements, however, are merged into a lively epic tale in which Podrugović displays his mastery of comic tone in a rich interplay of colourful details. To begin with, the Sultan is driven by desperate need to let Marko out of prison—for there is no other hero in the world who could kill Musa. When he sets Marko free, three barbers are needed to make our hero look like a man again: the first to wash him, the second to shave his beard, and the third to cut his nails. It is clear that Podrugović is telling his story—tongue in cheek— with great warmth and zest; and when Marko is made presentable, he begins to make himself fit for fighting by drinking wine and slivovits. Eventually, drink restores his heroic spirit, but even so in the central scene in the story Musa turns out to be a much better man. He knocks Marko down and sits on 'his heroic breast'.[16] At this moment Marko begins to squeal and curse the *vila*, his blood-sister ('posestrima'), accusing her of perjury because she had sworn to help him in need and nothing is being done about his precious life in such mortal danger. The *vila* appears in the clouds; she tries at least to save his honour by explaining to him that it would never do for the two of them to fight against a lone enemy. In the same breath she hints at how Marko could outwit and cheat Musa:

> 'It is a shame for two to fight one,
> Where are the vipers you have hidden?'[17]

Musa looks up to see who Marko is talking to and at this moment Marko draws out his daggers, his 'hidden vipers', and slashes him 'from his belly-band to his white throat'.[18] The

---

[14] See *Matić*, p. 740.

[15] See ibid., p. 741.

[16] '(Pak mu sjede) na prsi junačke', 'Marko Kraljević i Musa Kesedžija', *Karadžić*, ii, No. 67, l. 233.

[17] 'Sramota je dvome na jednoga; / Đe su tebe guje iz potaje?' Ibid., ll. 244–5. The appearance of the *vila* from the clouds and her moral ambiguity are in accord with widespread popular beliefs. See Appendix III.

[18] 'Od učkura do bijela grla', *Karadžić*, ii, No. 67, l. 249.

trick succeeds; the *vila*'s logical *non-sequitur* and Marko's subsequent action also succeed in illuminating the comic discrepancies between their words and their actions, so characteristic of Marko's world in which one could hardly engage in saving honour alone. It would hardly be worth it; there was so little of it left anyway.

In the same spirit Marko wriggles from underneath Musa's dead body and the grotesqueness of this triumph continues while 'dead Musa goes hopping on the bare land',[19] until Marko cuts off his head to take it as a trophy to the Sultan. For, after all, Marko defends law and order and Musa is an outlaw here; and there is no end to this comedy of heroic vassalage even when Marko throws Musa's head in front of the Sultan's feet:

> And the Sultan leapt to his feet in fear.[20]

Marko asks him wryly how he could have met a living Musa when he goes 'dancing away from the dead head'.[21] And there is, finally, the usual happy ending of the Sultan's rich tip— this time it is three loads of treasure! In short, the nature of violence and force is unmasked in the manner of their presentation in the triumphs of Marko Kraljević.

Force and violence also appear in a comic light in the poems in which Marko suffers severe blows, but fails to respond by an appropriate amount of pain and anguish. Thus, for instance, while Vilip the Hungarian—possibly a historical figure, an Italian knight in the Hungarian service[22]—keeps striking Marko with his heavy mace, Marko tells him:

> 'Do not wake up the fleas in my sheepskin'.[23]

Similarly, in the poem 'Marko Kraljević Abolishes the Wedding Tax'—recorded from a blind woman in the village of Grgurevci in Srem and referring not to Marko's times but to the much later social history when the Turks were fully

[19] 'Mrtav Musa po ledini skače', *Karadžić*, ii, No. 67, l. 259.
[20] 'Car je od stra' na noge skočio', ibid., l. 273.
[21] '(Kad) od mrtve glave poigravaš', ibid., l. 277.
[22] See T. Maretić, *Naša narodna epika*, pp. 164–6.
[23] 'Ne budi mi po kožuhu buha', 'Marko Kraljević i Filip Madžarin', *Karadžić*, ii, No. 59, l. 166.

established in the Balkans[24]—Marko asks a black Arab who keeps beating him:

> 'Are you joking or beating me in earnest?'[25]

After all, there may be some consolation in the thought that the endurance of blows may be greater than the enemy's ability to inflict them; 'Heaven save us from what we could stand'[26]—as an old proverb puts it, somewhat ambiguously perhaps. But what can force and violence achieve if the victim refuses to succumb to the mystique of their power and logic? For this is basically what happens while Marko endures the blows and even when he comes to respond to the Arab's beating with an almost innocent glee before he kills him:

> 'I also have some sort of mace,
> To give you three or four knocks'.[27]

Similar elements of the heroic fraud and comedy—as a medium of unmasking the nature of violence—are also mirrored in the strange mixture of the historical, the legendary, the factual and the anachronistic in the poem 'Marko Kraljević and Alil-aga'. Karadžić recorded this poem from the blind woman called Živana who—as he tells us—was born in Serbia but wandered in many different regions including Bulgaria[28] where Marko Kraljević was also a popular epic hero.[29] This may go some way towards explaining the diversity of the sources behind this poem and the comic impact which is achieved by their unusual imaginative combination. For the poem is indeed a great crossroads of different times and social customs: it seems to be set both in a vague tradition of chivalric tournaments and the much later times of Turkish terror. Marko knows, for instance, the protocol of chivalric fighting

---

[24] See *Matić*, p. 743.

[25] 'Il' se šališ, il' od zbilje biješ?' 'Marko Kraljević ukida svadbarinu', *Karadžić*, ii, No. 69, l. 202.

[26] 'Ne daj Bože što se durat može.'

[27] 'I ja imam nešto buzdovana, / Da te kucnem tri četiri puta', *Karadžić*, ii, No. 69, ll. 208–9.

[28] See V. S. Karadžić, 'Predgovor', *Karadžić*, iv, p. 370.

[29] So for instance the Miladinov brothers, as W. J. Entwistle points out, 'collected twenty-four Bulgarian ballads of Marko Kraljević' (*European Balladry*, Oxford, 1939, p. 329).

and insists that Alil-aga must shoot his arrow first because he
has challenged him to the contest. But even this point of
chivalric protocol is undercut by the derisory suggestion that
Alil-aga, being a Turk and belonging to the ruling race, would
have to have priority anyway. As Marko tells him:

> 'You are my senior,
> Because yours is the lordship and the empire,
> And your contest is senior to mine
> Because you challenged me to the contest.'[30]

It has been suggested that Alil-aga was the actual Turkish
vizier at the time of the Battle of Kosovo,[31] but this is a very
common name, sometimes associated in Serbo-Croat with
great strength. Similarly, Marko's wife is called Jelica in this
poem—and this is not only historically correct but also one of
the commonest epic names for wives and sisters. His blood-
brother, Bey Kostadin, is his historical eastern feudal neighbour and Marko wins the contest because Kostadin brings him
the required 'Tatars' arrow', which seems also to be some kind
of historical reference because Tatars are often mentioned as
Turkish soldiers in the Serbian chronicles between the thirteenth and the eighteenth century.[32]

All these diverse elements—and many others—are interwoven into a mock-heroic tale which sustains its ambivalent
tone from beginning to end. Riding towards Constantinople
with Bey Kostadin Marko decides to feign illness—'not because
he is ill, but because he is so wise'.[33] Alil-aga rises to the bait
and sees this as an opportunity for contest which should not be
missed. He pledges his wife and all his riches and asks only for
the right to hang Marko and take his horse if he wins. Thus we
are faced from the beginning not so much with a legendary
chivalric contest as with a parody of its knightly customs. And
the next step in this parody takes us to the regions of the
proverbially corrupt Turkish administration and judicial
system. Alil-aga trusts, of course, Marko's illness for his success;

---

[30] 'Ali ti si od mene stariji, / Jer je vaše gospodstvo i carstvo, / Tvoj je
mejdan stariji od moga, / Jer si mene na mejdan zazvao', 'Marko Kraljević
i Alil-aga', *Karadžić*, ii, No. 61, ll. 101–4.

[31] See *Matić*, p. 731.   [32] See ibid., p. 732.

[33] 'Bez bolesti, od mudrosti teške', *Karadžić*, ii, No. 61, l. 13.

but he also bribes the judge who verifies the terms of their agreement so that he would issue Marko with a false contract about what the winner gets. However, Marko has rich administrative experience and he sees immediately through the Turkish fraud. While speaking to the judge he appears to be innocently engaged in playing with his heavy mace in his lap; his voice vibrates with the realities of the treacherous world he lives in:

'Do you hear me, efendi-judge!
Give me a true and not a false contract,
Can you see this six-feathered gilded mace?
If I start to beat you with it,
You will need no balms,
You will forget about your court,
And you will never see the ducats!'[34]

As a Turkish lawyer the judge has a highly developed sense of the weight of a genuine argument: this is why a fever shakes him and his hand trembles as he spells out a true contract. This is, of course, as much Serbian history as it is folk daydreaming about the cunning and intrigue which would be up to the legal procedures of Turkish courts where, in one of the Serbian proverbs, you often find that the man who brings the accusation passes the sentence.[35] The comedy culminates when Marko outshoots Alil-aga: Alil-aga offers him a tie of brotherhood-in-God, his wife and 'white palaces' and Marko responds by a set of jokes about the possibilities of Turco-Serbian brotherhood and Islamic polygamy:

'I have no need of your wife,
We are not like the people of the Turks—
The women of our house are like sisters,
And I have another faithful love at home.'[36]

[34] 'Čuješ li me, efendi-kadija! / Daj ti mene pravog sindžilata, / Jer vidiš li šestoper pozlaćen, / Ako t' odem udarati njime, / Neće tebe melem trebovati, / Mešćemu ćeš i zaboraviti / A dukate ni videti nećeš!' Ibid., ll. 78–84.
[35] 'Kadija te tuži, kadija ti sudi.'
[36] 'Mene tvoja žena ne trebuje, / U nas nije, kano u Turaka, / Snašica je, kano i sestrica; / Ja na domu imam ljubu vernu', *Karadžić*, ii, No. 61, ll. 136–9.

The same comic heroic spirit in which Marko fights this fraudulent and treacherous chivalric contest, in which he beats Musa, abolishes the wedding taxes and outwits Đemo of the Mountain, is characteristic of almost everything he ever does when we see him in his characteristic quasi-historical setting. He has to depend on all the resources of his muscles and wits to preserve the vestiges of humanity and normality against the Turkish force and judiciary; and, ultimately, the only way to succeed is to dispel the nightmare of violence and its historical reality, to reduce them to the small tricks of everyday life. For Marko is a great comic epic character not only when he obeys the Sultan's summons and comes to express his defiance by treading in his boots on the Sultan's praying rug, not only when he has to beat a stronger man than himself, but also when he appears as a cavalier and lover, even when he comes to face death.

5. In Love

The character of a great hero—universally known in an epic tradition—colours everything that comes into his orbit. This explains the difference between the Kosovo girl in the shadow of Miloš's tragic death and the same heroine when she comes to meet Marko Kraljević. Both poems—'The Kosovo Girl' and 'Marko Kraljević Abolishes the Wedding Tax'—were recorded by Lukijan Mušicki, a friend of Vuk Karadžić and the abbot of the monastery of Šišatovac in Srem, from a blind woman who lived in Grgurevci, a small nearby village.[1] In the first of the two poems the heroine treads a legendary land; as we have seen, she walks in the battlefield after everything has been lost and recalls Miloš Obilić and his two blood-brothers, one of whom is her betrothed. She remembers their splendid presents and when she learns about the fate of her betrothed, she cries out that even a green pine would wither if touched by her hand. However, in 'Marko Kraljević Abolishes the Wedding Tax' the same heroine is no longer a very young girl; in fact, she seems to be almost on the spinsterish side. As Marko puts it, not without a certain warmth of feeling, but perhaps a little awkwardly for a gallant cavalier who will play such a chivalric role in saving the honour of his protégée:

> 'You were fair, sister, when you were younger!
> Your waist and your stature are lovely,
> Your rosy cheeks, your noblewoman's look!
> But your hair, sister, has spoilt you;
> For what man have you gone so grey, sister?
> Who has taken away your young luck?'[2]

This is not a reference to the grief caused by the death of the beloved; the misery springs from the prohibitively high wedding

---

[1] See 'Predgovor', *Karadžić*, iv, p. 373.

[2] 'Lepa ti si, seko, mlađa bila! / Krasna ti si stasa i uzrasta! / Rumenila, gospodska pogleda! / Al' te, seko, kosa pokvarila; / Jer si tako, seko, osedila? / S kog' si mlada sreću izgubila?' 'Marko Kraljević ukida svadbarinu', *Karadžić*, ii, No. 69, ll. 11–16.

taxes imposed by an Arab in the area of Kosovo. Not only that the girl cannot marry her betrothed; now she cannot marry anyone at all. And there is little consolation in the Arab's insistence on his right of the first night with all brides and virgins; the girl complains to Marko and tells him in despair that her turn has come. This is obviously a very different Kosovo from the one inhabited by Miloš Obilić; and if there is, as there is, genuine pain and misery here, we see it in a setting which is not without prosaic touches. Such touches accumulate in the course of the story in which Marko performs his chivalric role in his usual comic spirit: he offers a ridiculously small deposit for his wedding taxes and requests credit, he laughs at the Arab who beats him with his mace and asks if he really means it seriously.

However, the colour this comic spirit gives to the epic landscape in which young girls appear in Marko Kraljević's company can be best seen in 'The Wedding of Marko Kraljević'. Karadžić recorded this poem from Tešan Podrugović;[3] and the outlaw's recital marked the ultimate achievement in the decasyllabic epics in which great heroes appear as comic lovers. It seems again that the fictitious story has some sort of uncertain factual background behind it: there are references in the contemporary historical sources to Marko's unruly marriage and an unsuccessful wooing.[4] In an early seventeenth-century history—in which facts and fantasies live happily together—one learns that Marko drove out his unfaithful wife,[5] even if he may not have been the only epic hero to whose name such mishaps could be ascribed with some historical justification. But there are also some other semi-historical elements in the poem: the Bulgarian King Šišman was Marko's contemporary although not his father-in-law; the tricks and treacheries of Marko's best man, the Doge of Venice, reflect some Serbian prejudices which are rooted in actual history. And last but not least, most of the marriage customs in the poem belong to Karadžić's and Podrugović's times, even if some of them go back much further. The gifts which Marko's father-in-law gives Marko and his entourage—shirts, towels, scarfs, stockings—are standard in Serbian patriarchal village custom, but there is also a sprinkling of some epic gold and jewels.[6]

[3] See 'Predgovor', *Karadžić*, iv, p. 363.
[4] See *Matić*, pp. 698–9.
[5] See ibid.
[6] See ibid., pp. 724–6.

The poem is interesting, however, because it comes to see Marko Kraljević as a completely comic character in a mock-heroic parody which makes fun of some of the most sacred customs and norms of Serbian patriarchal civilization. Of course, this comic spirit is part of that civilization itself; even if a rich sense of humour has always been much more prominent in the actual observance of these customs than in the ethnological writings about them. The poem opens with a light touch of patriarchal comedy: Marko's old mother has to remind her heroic son that he should marry, as if the idea had never occurred to him. A richer vein of the patriarchal sense of humour emerges when Marko explains that none of the girls that he felt like marrying would have provided a suitable daughter-in-law for his patriarchal mother. On the other hand, however, he failed to be in the least excited by any of the girls that might have been eligible as a decent wife:

> 'Wherever I found a girl who suited me,
> I have not found a family for you;
> And wherever I found a family for you,
> I have not found a girl who suited me.'[7]

Eventually, after some perseverance and visits to nine kingdoms and an empire, an exciting bride is found in a decent family; but our hero falls in love with her so wholeheartedly that he again appears funny:

> 'When she came in my sight, old mother,
> The green grass turned around and around me!'[8]

On the whole, perhaps, this is most appropriate; but the bride inspires the same kind of feeling in Marko's best man, the Doge of Venice:

> And the Doge of Venice has seen her face,
> And the Doge's head is aching in his pain,
> He can hardly wait for the night to fall.[9]

[7] 'Đe ja nađoh za mene đevojku, / Onđe nema za te prijatelja; / Đe ja nađoh za te prijatelja, / Onđe nema za mene đevojke', 'Ženidba Marka Kraljevića', *Karadžić*, ii, No. 56, ll. 14–17.

[8] 'Kad je viđeh, moja stara majko! / Oko mene trava okrenu se!' Ibid., ll. 22–3.

[9] 'Viđe lice dužde od Mletaka, / Od muke ga glava zaboljela, / Jedva čeka, kad će noćca doći', ibid., ll. 146–8.

This seems to ridicule not only a fairly common foible, but also the patriarchal sacred norms among which the obligations of the best man (*kum*) stood so high that the end of the world, 'the last times', has been sometimes seen as an adequate punishment for their disregard.[10] Even allowing for the fact that the man who disregards these obligations is a Venetian, one of the 'old tricksters',[11] it is still worth noting that the relationship which is the holy of holies in the patriarchal world is invoked here in order to show how real life plays its tricks upon it.

Moreover, when Marko's best man offers his bride his amorous services, she defends herself in a grand speech which displays her heroic sense of honour. She tells the Doge that a bride must not be caressed, that 'the earth would tremble to bits under their feet', and 'heaven would crack open over their heads'.[12] This heroic stylization of the bride's sense of honour reflects the belief that an immoral human act disturbs the cosmic natural order—the belief common in all agricultural civilizations and found in many decasyllabic folk epic poems, particularly those which mirror the norms of patriarchal family life ('The Saints Divide the Treasure', 'God Leaves No Debt Unpaid' and others). But the tragic dignity of language is questionable because it appears so suddenly in a story so rich in comic overtones; and yet, together with the heroic scale of the punishment which will befall the bride and her best man if they break the sacred norms of their relationship, it creates a medium of high moral tone and heroic language which reveal their purpose only in the lines which follow. And the use of the heroic language in these lines is analogous to that of *The Battle of Mice and Frogs* or *The Rape of the Lock*; it is in such mock-heroic spirit that the Doge opposes to the bride's grand moral visions his personal remarks on his own experience and reality:

[10] See above pp. 103, 108, 125–6. See also note 30, p. 115.

[11] Venetians are usually referred to as 'old tricksters' ('stare varalice'). Even if Tešan Podrugović does not make this specific reference to the Venetians in 'The Wedding of Marko Kraljević', the whole story suggests that he shares this epic assumption. Besides, the standard line—'The Latins are old tricksters' ('Latini su stare varalice')—can be found in his poem about 'Dušan's Wedding' (*Karadžić*, ii, No. 29, l. 112).

[12] 'Pod nam' će se zemlja provaliti, / A više nas nebo prolomiti', *Karadžić*, ii, No. 56, ll. 189–90.

'My kinswoman, my dear, do not be silly!
There are nine I have undone down to this time,
My kinswoman, all kin by baptism,
And twenty-four kinswomen, by marriage!
Not one time did the earth tremble to bits,
Or heaven crack open above my head.'[13]

All our imaginative sympathies are on the bride's side and she has, like Marko Kraljević on many other occasions, to face an enemy who is much stronger than she is. So she is obliged to defend her honour, like Marko, by fraud and cunning, by fooling and outwitting her enemy. And is there a sweeter victory than the one in which the hero will expose his enemy not only as a scoundrel but also as a fool? It is in this spirit that the girl will make the Doge shave his beard by telling him, with double irony, that she had sworn to her mother that she would never kiss old men—

'But only a young hero with no beard,
Like Marko, like the Prince'.[14]

Apart from the implied difference between Marko's youth and the Doge's old age, there is also the comedy of the Doge's impatience which leads him to misunderstand the insult and 'summon his quick barbers'.[15] He is obviously in a hurry; but the bride will snatch his shaven beard and rush with such a *corpus delicti* to Marko:

The shaving of a beard is not a joke![16]

But this is not the end of the joke, of the tricks and misunderstandings in the poem. Suddenly woken up—and he is a sound sleeper—Marko is unaware of what is going on, and imagines that his bride has come on a different business in the middle of the night:

[13] 'Oj ne luduj, moja mila kumo! / Ja sam dosad devet obljubio, / Kumo moja! kuma krštenijeh, / A vjenčane dvadest i četiri; / Ni jednom se zemlja ne provali, / Nit' se nebo više nas prolomi', ibid., ll. 193–8.
[14] 'Već junaka mlada golobrada, / Kao što je Kraljeviću Marko', ibid., ll. 204–5.
[15] '(On) berbere hitre dobavio', ibid., l. 207.
[16] 'Nije šala obrijana brada!' Ibid., l. 279.

'Were you not able to wait for me,
Until we come to my white halls
And carry out a Christian marriage?'[17]

Even when the drowsy hero comes to see what it is all about, he
will not think that an attempt at the seduction of his bride is
sufficient reason for interrupting his sleep. He goes on sleeping,
and only on the following morning does the imbroglio of
Marko's wedding begin to be disentangled in the Doge's inept
defense before angry Marko:

'The natures of people are various,
One can no longer have a joke in peace.'[18]

And who should know this better than the Doge, the crafty
best man who was so fooled by an innocent bride and so richly
paid back in his own coin of fraud and cunning? Once this
point has been established—the natures of people are indeed
various—the deserved punishment follows; but even in the way
in which Marko kills the Doge there seems to be an overtone of
comedy:

And of one body, he made two bodies.[19]

Is it possible that Marko and his world are so funny that they
make fun even of death itself?

[17] 'Zar ne može mene pričekati / Dok dođemo do bijela dvora / I rišćanski
zakon savršimo?' *Karadžić*, ii, No. 56, ll. 242–5.
[18] 'Sad su ljudi svakojake ćudi, / Sad se nije ni našalit' s mirom', ibid., ll.
275–6.
[19] 'Od jednoga dvojicu ogradi', ibid., l. 287.

6. Facing Death

Humour has always been one of the most desperate means of self-defence. All that is unacceptable, all that one cannot come to grips with in any other way, all the discrepancies of life and history which make one utterly helpless, can be, at least, mocked and laughed away. Laughter thus becomes a kind of power for the helpless; and this ancient function of comedy in life and art is nowhere so richly mirrored in Serbo-Croatian epic singing as in the poems about Marko Kraljević and, particularly, in the poem which describes his death. For not even Marko Kraljević can escape death, but his departure from history is presented so that the tragedy of the inevitable end seems to dissolve in the epic hotch-potch through which the hero wades all the way to the grave and a little beyond it.

When Marko dies we are still faced with the world in which other people have developed the habit of being frightened, of avoiding all that can be avoided, of getting out of everybody's way. This is why these people—obliged by law to get out of the way of every Turk on a horse and pay their homage to him— are afraid even of their own champion of justice. Such an extreme love of justice, such excessive courage, inevitably connected with a hot temper, are, after all, unpredictable— heaven knows what they might turn into! This is why Marko is left to lie dead by a water-spring for a whole week before anyone dares to approach him:

> Whoever passed along the wide track,
> Observing Marko the Prince,
> He thought he saw Marko sleeping,
> He went a long way round to pass by,
> For fear he might wake him.[1]

This is not only how Filip Višnjić, the most popular of all Karadžić's singers, envisages Marko's death, but also a picture of a world of the inveterate habit of fear which makes these

[1] 'Kogod prođe drumom širokijem, / Te opazi Kraljevića Marka, / Svatko misli, da tu spava Marko, / Oko njega daleko oblazi, / Jer se boji, da ga ne probudi.' 'Smrt Marka Kraljevića,' *Karadžić*, ii, No. 74, ll. 124–8.

people go such a long way round not to come too near to their greatest and best-loved hero. Even a holy father from Mount Athos, who does not have much to lose and who is initiated into 'the justice of the God of truth' as much as Marko is, warns his novice to be careful:

> 'Son, go quietly, not to wake him,
> Marko rouses from sleep bloody-minded,
> He might murder us both.'[2]

This is perhaps the ultimate irony of an attitude of a whole people to its own image of the greatest hero; and this is perhaps the ultimate grain of the historical truth in this poem, the truth of fear of courage and justice. In all the other semi-factual details history is much more deeply immersed in legends: it is true that Marko's bequest of his treasure for prayers and alms follows the usual forms of the last will of the Serbian medieval rulers, but even the basic circumstances of his death are seen in a completely fictitious light. The mountain Urvina replaces the Romanian village Rovine where Marko was killed fighting on the Turkish side in 1395; and it is conveniently placed by the sea so that the hero can dispose of his mace in the proper fashion. Besides, Marko receives the intimations of his approaching death by looking into a water-spring and he weeps because he has lived for only three hundred years and enjoyed the company of his Šarac for just one hundred and sixty years. In short, most of the 'facts' in the poem reflect—in a slightly comic light—much older legends and some of the customs of pagan times.[3]

But what is Marko's ultimate farewell to life? Before he leaves the tricky world which he has enjoyed so much, he will leave his last message which has largely been ignored in the patriotic assessments of the epic poetry about him and which can be fully appreciated only in his full comic contrast to the tragic character of Miloš Obilić. It is the message of the epic hero who appeared in the first complete epic song in the language and has lived—apparently—to the present day, longer than any other epic hero, in fact more than three

---

[2] 'Lakše, sinko, da ga ne probudiš, / Jer je Marko iza sna zlovoljan, / Pa nas može oba pogubiti.' *Karadžić*, ii, No. 74, ll. 137–9.

[3] See *Matić*, pp. 747–50.

hundred years. Perhaps because he preferred survival to heroic death; and this is certainly a reflection of a sense of history at least as authentic and as rich as Miloš's desire to die and show 'who is faithful, who is the traitor'.[4] And it is owing to his impulse to live by mere survival that Marko remained so free in his slavery, so defiant in his vassalage, ready not merely to die a heroic death but also to pay the price of survival in the world which he has neither created nor chosen by his own act of free will—so that, in strict moral logic, he should have no reason to feel personally responsible for everything that keeps happening in it. But within this framework, within the given human and historical possibilities, Marko remained, in a way, in the only way which he was granted, true to himself. Prepared to risk everything and take all precautions; ready—above all—to look at life with the courage of fully open eyes.

This is why his farewell to the world is as puzzling as his appearance in history and his epic character, as his ideal goodness of heart which dominates so splendidly the poems which move in the epic landscape outside the realities of human history, the poems in which he has to deal only with hawks and eagles. He is, in short, a hero who has tasted the bitterness of life to the full without being embittered, let alone poisoned by it. This is why his wisdom still speaks with the nobility and honesty of a spiritual insight which has no need to overestimate itself—in a metaphor which is much richer than it was at the time when it first appeared in Serbian spiritual history. For Marko shows the ultimate generosity of impulse which has no need to beautify the world which he sees or to ask the question whether the world—such as it is—deserves all the love which he has to give it. In his love of the world, the love which needs no illusions, Marko shows his true heroic spirit, the spirit of the man whose love of life is neither less exciting nor less authentic for being fully mature.

'Deceiving world, my sweet flower'[5]

is his last word on himself and human life as he has come to know it.

---

[4] 'Ko je vjera, ko li je nevjera,' 'Komadi od različnijeh kosovskijeh pjesama (iii)', *Karadžić*, ii, No. 50, l. 53.

[5] 'Laživ sv'jete, moj lijepi cv'jete!' *Karadžić*, ii, No. 74, l. 68.

PART FIVE

The Outlaws and the Border Raiders

1. In History

Highway robbery, at least ever since the Middle Ages, has been an important corrective in social distribution of wealth in the Balkans. During the intervals of peace the demobbed soldiery often had no other way of making a living on its skills. There were also times when the destitute peasantry were driven to the woods by economic despair; and fear of legal prosecution—for a petty offence, for a major crime—added moral colour to and furthered the prosperity of the trade. This is why an outlaw as a social victim is so difficult to distinguish from a highway robber; they behaved in the same way and, indeed, were often one and the same person. This social tradition goes back to pre-Turkish times in Balkan history; but during the Turkish rule—particularly from the seventeenth century when monstrous forms of taxation began to be levied on a large scale by a corrupt administration—outlawry became a widespread form of social protest, gaining in scope and in moral interest. The existing historical evidence shows that from this time outlawry 'often attained the scale of mass movements, growing at certain moments into true rebellions of some parts of the country against the Turks'.[1] The culminating point of this process was the First Serbian Uprising against the Turks at the beginning of the nineteenth century: outlaw companies, led by their experienced captains ('harambaše'), joined the fighting for national independence and were recognized in the epic songs as outstandingly qualified for the task.[2] Indeed, some of these companies came from Bosnia and Herzegovina in order to fight in Serbia; and the story of a brigand growing into a national hero, or moving into no-man's land between the two, is not uncommon.[3]

This general historical and moral pattern is reflected in the lives of some of the greatest of Karadžić's singers. The epic

---

[1] S. Nazečić, *Iz naše narodne epike*, Sarajevo, 1959, p. 223.

[2] See below pp. 287–9.

[3] This was the case with Karadžić's most gifted epic poet Tešan Podrugović. See below pp. 311–14.

pilgrimage of Filip Višnjić, the most popular of all these singers, began when the uncle with whom the boy lived was hanged for having killed in blood-vengeance some Turks who raped one of the women in the family.[4] Old Milija—the singer of 'Banović Strahinja', the most fully developed and the best single epic poem in Karadžić's collection—was also uprooted from his native Herzegovina by conflicts with the Turks; Karadžić records that all his head was scarred with vivid memories of these encounters.[5] And Karadžić's best poet Tešan Podrugović was at first a merchant in Bosnia and Herzegovina until he 'killed a Turk who had tried to kill him and so dispersed his home and became an outlaw'.[6]

This type of outlawry, widespread in depopulated Serbia and in Bosnia and Herzegovina, particularly along the major caravan routes in the range of the mountain Romanija, is described with considerable historical and moral perception by Karadžić himself:

Our people think and sing in their songs that men became outlaws ('hajduci') in Serbia as the result of Turkish terror and misrule. It should be said that some went off to be outlaws without being forced to it, in order to wear what clothes and carry what weapons they liked or to take revenge on someone; but the full truth is that the milder the Turkish government, the fewer outlaws there were in the land, and the worse and more arbitrary it was, the more outlaws there were.[7]

As the Ottoman legislation entitled only the Moslems to carry weapons and wear clothes of lively colours, the Christians were clearly dressed as targets in many of the everyday conflicting situations during the Turkish times. In a brawl in a tavern, in a quarrel which so easily flared up during the tax-collecting, when a Christian parent tried to keep his child which was being forcefully taken away to be trained as a Turkish janissary or when he opposed the rape of his daughter or wife—in all such situations the unarmed non-Moslem plebs, the 'rayah', had to deal with armed rulers. Perhaps the only deterrent in

[4] See below p. 306.
[5] See below p. 311.
[6] 'Predgovor', Karadžić, i, p. 537.
[7] V. S. Karadžić, Srpski rječnik, p. 826. The passages from this article are quoted—with some minor changes and corrections—in D. Wilson's translation. See The Life and Times of Vuk Stefanović Karadžić, 1787–1864, pp. 32–4.

such cases was the moral duty and social custom of blood-vengeance; but to oppose the oppressor or exercise this moral duty usually meant to be forced to become an outlaw.

But when one became an outlaw—whether as an innocent victim of a monstrous social order or as a criminal or for mixed reasons—one shared the same actual and moral predicament in what must have always been mixed company:

The truth is that many become outlaws without thought of doing evil, but when men, and particularly simple folk, are once cut off from human society and take leave of all authority, they begin—especially when banded together—to do wrong. So the outlaws do wrong to their own people who still love and pity them when faced with the Turks; but even now it is the greatest shame and reproach for an outlaw to be called a thief and 'scourge of women' ('pržibaba').[8]

In short, the outlaws often had to behave and live as robbers even if it was social despair that drove them to the woods, even if they had to cultivate high ideals of personal courage and loyalty, even if their 'cause' often had, particularly during the rebellions, the colouring of fighting for national independence and better social justice. This moral ambivalence will grow into the central imaginative challenge of some of the best poems about them and Karadžić's account also brings out some of these conflicting moral features in their actual and epic stature:

In the old times, as is sung in the songs, the outlaws liked best to lie in wait for the Turks when they were carrying tax-money. That has rarely happened in our time; they lie in wait for merchants and other travellers and sometimes attack the houses of people who are thought to have money or fine clothes and weapons. When they attack a house and do not find money, but think that there is some, they find a son or brother of the owner, take him off and keep him with them until the ransom is paid.[9]

It is, in short, clear, that the outlaws could hardly afford to indulge in fine moral and social discriminations between the rich local people, Turks, merchants, and travellers as different sources of their income. And the epic singer is not only aware of this—he takes it for granted. His greatest hero Old Vujadin, for instance, remembers the days when he watched from high in the mountain his approaching prey: 'the Turks and the

[8] V. S. Karadžić, *Srpski rječnik*, p. 826.   [9] Ibid.

traders'.[10] Of course, it is not only for alliterative reasons that these two different, if sometimes overlapping, categories of people are seen in the way which suggests that for our hero's purposes one was as good as another. However, the moral interest of this historical situation springs from the fact that so many people, with a highly developed sense of partiarchal honour and justice, found themselves in such a predicament. For their fanatical loyalty and courage were not only the morality of bandits—they gave a tragic moral colouring to the historical forms of outlawry:

> Outlaws keep to their faith, fast and pray like other people, and when they are taken to be impaled and the Turks offer to spare their lives if they convert, they curse Mohammed, saying 'As if I wasn't going to die some time anyhow!' Outlaws all regard themselves as great heroes, and it is rare that any dares to join them who is not self-reliant.
>
> When they are caught and taken to be impaled, they usually sing at the top of their voice, to show that they care not at all for their lives. Even a surrendered outlaw is always bold-mannered and bluffer than other people; he will allow no liberties to be taken with him, and all are rather afraid of him.[11]

So apart from the basic reality of robbery, there was also the historical background of social victimization of vast numbers of brave, pious, and honourable men, the dignity of personal freedom in national and social slavery, the pathos of lonely fighters defying common destiny in the historical and epic landscape of outlawry. This gave rise to the characteristic heroic epic figure usually represented with a tragic moral flaw; and this figure is not only largely true to the broad facts of Balkan social history but its epic setting mirrors many of the historical details which are found in Karadžić's description of the life of the outlaws in Serbia in his time:

> In the summer, they live in the woods and come to their peasant 'protectors' ('jataci') who feed them—for example they will come in the evening, and the 'protector' will give them food to take away in baskets, enough to feed them till the next evening. Sometimes the 'protector' will install them somewhere in the woods, and bring them dinner and supper himself. When winter comes, they part company,

---

[10] 'Turci i trgovci', 'Stari Vujadin', *Karadžić*, iii, No. 50, l. 66.
[11] V. S. Karadžić, *Srpski rječnik*, p. 827.

and go off each to his own friends for winter quarters, after having agreed how and where to meet in the spring. In winter quarters, some of them lie up for the day in cellars or other buildings, and at night they feast and sing to the *gusle*; others dress in ordinary clothes and herd cattle or sheep for people as servants. If anyone fails to come at the appointed time to the place agreed, the company go to look for him. If it happens that a 'protector' has betrayed or killed an outlaw in winter quarters, all the others will look to their revenge as long as fifty years afterwards.

The outlaws of our time in Serbia usually wore bright blue cloth trousers, with stockings and soft shoes on their feet, a cloth waistcoat and sleeved jacket on top, and sometimes a blue or green jacket, with an ordinary cloak over all. . . . They particularly liked to wear silver discs on their breast, and those who could not yet afford these, would sew on heavy silver coins. For weapons they would carry a long rifle, two small ones and a large knife.

While the Turks ruled in Serbia, there was in practically every subdistrict one commander with a number of guards, among whom there were Serbs as well as Turks. They hunted the outlaws, and sometimes, when many outlaws had appeared and there was much killing and robbing, the Turks would gather the whole population for a 'drive' . . . When the guards killed anyone, they would cut off his head, take it into the town and put it on a pole on the ramparts. Anyone who fell into the hands of the Turks alive would be impaled. When not even a drive had any effect on the outlaws, the Turks would go out on a *teftish*—that is to say some high Turkish officer would go among the people with a good number of young men, and by imprisonment, terror and fines would drive the headmen and everyone in the outlaws' native village to find out the 'protectors' and to capture the outlaws (but except for the *teftishes* against the outlaws' village, no one harmed their wives and children, if they had any, and these lived at peace in their homes). . . .

When a man had had his fill of being an outlaw, or had been talked over into giving it up, he would surrender himself and ask the headman to produce a guarantee for him from the Pasha; he could then go around again among the people and after that no one would dare to remind him of what he had done in his time as an outlaw. Surrendered outlaws usually become official guards, because they have become unused to doing normal work; but a former outlaw cannot become a chief.[12]

However, this kind of outlaw—a social desperado with his own code of honour, living freely in the woods in the summer

[12] Ibid., pp. 826–7.

and hiding in winter, existing on plunder and robbery if often fighting the hated foreign oppressor—was characteristic primarily of Serbia, Bosnia, and Herzegovina. But the same term was often applied to the Montenegrin and Dalmatian fighters, border raiders and pirates; and indeed the different features of their actual historical setting have been absorbed in the epic tradition and merged with the image of Serbian and Bosnian outlawry.

The Turkish control of Montenegro was never as complete as that of Serbia and Bosnia: the Montenegrins fought successfully against their own Islamized countrymen as well as against the Turkish military units which attempted to re-establish their uncertain rights of taxation. This often led to Montengrin campaigns of blood-vengeance not only in Montenegro but also in the neighbouring Herzegovina controlled by the Turks; and the plunder of sheep and cattle along the borders was a heavy two-way traffic and an important feature of the general historical picture. Sometimes the border robberies and skirmishes led to Turkish military expeditions into Montenegro and the Montenegrin armed farmers and cattle breeders were forced to keep outside Turkish reach and lived temporarily in inaccessible areas. But even if they found themselves for protracted periods in the predicament approaching that of the homeless Serbian and Bosnian outlaws, even if there were actual outlaws among them on such occasions, when fighting was over, the Montenegrin border fighters and raiders had homes and families to return to and most of the time they lived on their land. Thus the epic poems about them present a general picture of the Montenegrin wars of independence even if they include many of the features of the poems about outlaws and border raiders.[13]

However, on the Montenegrin coast in the Bay of Kotor, which was also a soil very rich in epic tradition and singing, the Venetian presence gave a different historical imprint to the border fighting against the Turks. This was the area where Stefan Nemanja, the founder of the Serbian medieval state,

---

[13] This is why Karadžić included them in his fourth volume—among 'the heroic songs of more recent times about the wars for independence' ('pjesme junačke novijih vremena o vojevanju za slobodu'). These Montenegrin songs are dealt with in Part VI of this book.

built his court, where his son St Sava built a church and whose inhabitants held high offices in medieval Serbian courts. This explains perhaps the flourishing of feudal oral epic *bugarštice* in the seventeenth and eighteenth centuries; but the local singing did not feed only on Serbian medieval feudal themes and forms, but also on its own immediate history. At the heart of this history was the fighting for Herceg-Novi, the fortress which commands the entrance to the Bay and which was for two centuries, until 1687, the stronghold of the Turkish naval and commercial presence in the Adriatic. Severe border fighting was going on here, particularly during the major Turco-Venetian wars in the seventeenth century, and the border fighters were, as in all Dalmatia, local Slavs in regular Venetian military service—living on their salaries in times of war and depending on private enterprise in times of peace:

Along the Dalmatian border with Turkey Venice established, in the course of its wars with Turkey during the seventeenth century, a complete defensive system, which was upheld for the most part by the local population. In the garrisons along the border, there were regular Venetian soldiers and officers, but the local population liked best to serve under its native leaders, as Petar Ćivran, the Governor of Dalmatia, pointed out in his report to the Venetian senate. They were organized into companies of cavalry or infantry, fifty or sixty each. . . . The local people who were able to carry arms received from the Venetian authorities their arms, ammunition, bread and rusks while they fought or were on a definite military errand. The more renowned people were given the title of captain ('harambaša') and the most distinguished ones, like the Smiljanići and the Jankovići, received the title of sirdar ('serdar'). For special merits the captains could get permanent monthly salaries, or could be put on the list of a company for their salaries and living, but without the obligation to serve in the company itself. Under such dispensation the main source of income had to be plunder and military booty.[14]

In the official documents in Dubrovnik all these Slav soldiers in Venetian temporary military service were called 'outlaws' ('hajduci'), whereas the Venetian documents make a distinction between 'outlaws' (the fighters in the Bay of Kotor and the littoral of Makarska) and the 'Morlachians' (the fighters in the vicinity of Šibenik and Zadar).[15] In the oral epic tradition these

---

[14] S. Nazečić, *Iz naše narodne epike*, p. 224.   [15] See ibid., pp. 224–6.

border fighters and raiders are also merged in the general picture of outlaw fighting inasmuch as their heroes are also richly dressed, their leaders have to gather their companies for particular exploits, these exploits are usually raids on 'the Turks and traders', the cult of loyalty, courage and honour is expressed in the same formulaic language.

However, the historical picture behind this epic landscape is further complicated by the actions of the sixteenth and seventeenth century fighters from Senj—to whom, and to whom only, the name of border raiders ('uskoci') was historically applied.[16] They operated as outlaws and pirates from their harbour in the northern Adriatic, which was controlled by Austria. Initially, they were a group of retreating warriors who came from Herzegovina and defended the fortress of Klis, near Split. After this fortress was taken by the Turks in 1537, they went far north to Senj and were established as semi-regular Austrian military units operating from small fast ships, manned by thirty to fifty people who were both oarsmen and fighters armed with rifles, axes and daggers. They fought both against the Turkish and against the Venetian fleet: in 1597, for instance, about five hundred of them on seventeen ships captured, in a single night attack, all the Turkish and Venetian ships in the harbour of Rovinj. The dread of the Adriatic, they also ravaged Turkish inland territories; among the most successful raids was their landing near Dubrovnik in 1605 when they went as far inland as Trebinje in Herzegovina. Although their numbers never exceeded five to six hundred men, major Venetian naval operations against them were of no avail; and they made life very colourful along the Adriatic coast until Venice reached an agreement with Austria in 1618 and they were exiled from Senj.[17]

In the epic tradition, however, many features of these different types of 'outlaws' are merged, for historical and poetic reasons, into a fairly coherent general picture of lonely fighting of small companies against the Turkish invaders. Their raids on towns, caravans and villages could hardly

[16] See S. Nazečić, loc. cit.

[17] G. Stanojević, *Senjski uskoci*, Belgrade, 1973, gives a detailed account of the actions and the general historical background of the border raiders of Senj.

appear—and in fact they hardly were—very different from one another. Who, for instance, in Herzegovina—usually considered a cradle and certainly an important crossroad of epic singing—would see much point in differentiating between the groups of armed men who might suddenly attack a Turkish caravan or garrison and quickly retreat with their booty? Whether they were local outlaws, pirates coming from Senj, armed cattle raisers from neighbouring Montenegro or a band of Venetian ex-soldiers, there was little difference in what they were doing and in the moral qualities necessary for such exploits. And there was even less reason to doubt that they were all fighting against the hated Turkish oppressors. It was this general historical appearance and feeling, the common epic diction and the fact that many of the outlaws and border fighters were singers themselves, that created the imaginative landscape of outlawry in which the heroes challenge their national fate and history. But what is of ultimate interest, of course, is the range of the moral and imaginative sense of history which these poems embody.

2. In the Bondage of History

The captain of an outlaw company could be a criminal or a petty delinquent, the head of an honourable Serbian patriarchal family or a professional highway robber, an armed Montenegrin farmer with a tribal sense of honour or a destitute social desperado, an ex-soldier or a great Venetian military commander, a pirate protected by the Austrian military establishment in Senj (for basic epic topography of these poems, see Map 1). He could be also several of these characters in succession and, indeed, at the same time. And this protean historical figure offered a great imaginative challenge which was sometimes duly met; but in many of the poems about outlaws and their captains the memory of the traditional epic formulas seems to be bewildered by the range of their historical and moral reference.

This is what happens, for instance, in 'The Wedding of Ivan of Risan' which tells the story of the competition of suitors and the kidnapping of the bride on her wedding journey, a common subject in Serbo-Croatian epic singing. The story is set in the social realities and fictions of the Montenegrin border fighting against the Turks in the Bay of Kotor at the time when this fighting was supported by the Venetian Republic because Herceg-Novi was the most important outpost of the Turkish naval and military presence in the Adriatic (1481–1687). Ivan, the hero of the story, is an outlaw captain living in the small town of Risan in the Bay of Kotor—in all probability as one of the distinguished, paid Venetian officers who commanded the companies of their Slav countrymen who defended themselves and the Venetian Republic and often had to live by raiding the neighbouring Turkish territory.

However, as the poem is told by Tešan Podrugović, who fought in far more primitive and 'heroic' conditions of Bosnian and Serbian outlawry, the social misunderstandings between the poet and his material are of considerable interest. To begin with, Ivan, the captain of an outlaw company, is competing as a suitor with no less a figure than the Turkish military

commander of Herceg-Novi for the hand of a fictitious king's
daughter living in a neighbouring legendary city. The trouble
begins as soon as the Turkish commander writes to the royal
father of his prospective bride calling her 'honey Jefimija'.[1]
This is absurd for more than one reason,[2] but it is not as absurd
as the reply of the king who tries to refuse the proposal and calm
down the Turkish military suitor by telling him that the girl
had already been promised to his enemy, an outlaw captain in
Risan, a man who cannot be refused because he is such a
heroic nuisance that he would make life difficult for both of
them:

> The men of Risan are famous heroes,
> They will make much trouble for both of us.[3]

This suggests some epic self-esteem in the fighters from the area
of Risan where the poem must have originated: but the
commercial code of values of the small maritime town which
provided some admirals for the Venetian fleet is certainly as
important. For what most worries the royal father of the bride
is that he has to choose between a Turk and an outlaw; he has
no chance of marrying his daughter to one of the really great
'naval generals' of Risan.[4] And the full tonal breakdown of the
story is achieved when the father exclaims:

> 'My daughter, honey Jefimija!
> Why are you so beautiful,
> I wish that God had made you blind!'[5]

The poetic stammer goes on and a little later the king comes to
describe the approaching wedding and the arrival of the
commander of Herceg-Novi with considerable enthusiasm:

---

[1] 'Dilber Jefimija', 'Ženidba Ivana Rišnjanina', *Karadžić*, iii, No. 34, l. 6.

[2] The epithet 'dilber' ('darling') is a homely word of Turkish origin; it
sounds absurd when attached to a name like Jefimija—rich in historical
associations, particularly in connection with the wife of Despot Uglješa, well-
known in old Serbian literature for her praise of Prince Lazar.

[3] 'Rišnjani su na glasu junaci, / Dosadiće i mene i tebe', *Karadžić*, iii, No.
34, ll. 18–19.

[4] 'Morski dženerali', ibid., l. 38.

[5] 'Šćeri moja, dilber Jefimija! / Što si mene odviše lijepa, / Da je bog d'o
da si mi slijepa!' Ibid., ll. 34–5.

'There he comes with a thousand wedding guests,
My daughter, on the following Sunday.'[6]

In the second part of the poem the story grows much taller: the outlaw captain of Risan is seen on his 'slender tower'[7] with his servant Oblačić Rade, a legendary hero of several other poems and, in the opinion of some scholars, no less a figure than Đurđe Radič, one of the chieftains ('čelnik') of Stefan Lazarević, Prince Lazar's son who ruled Serbia as a Turkish vassal in the early fifteenth century.[8] Leaving aside the question whether this kind of scholarly speculation is even taller than the story itself, suffice it to say that the outlaw captain and his lordly servant do not waste time waiting for the other outlaws to come and help them; the two of them attack a thousand Turkish wedding guests and take away the bride in triumph. However, tall as this ending is, it is only here that Ivan of Risan emerges as an outlaw hero and that some of the lines describing him in action achieve some of the usual expressive force of Tešan Podrugović. Such is, for instance, the description of the flight of the Turks who are seen in a comic ellipsis as running so fast that they literally disappear into 'trees and stones'.[9] But in spite of such sporadic achievement when the poet's voice rises to the occasion which he feels and understands, the poem as a whole reads like a parody of its heroic intentions, because the diverse, historical, legendary and local elements, alien to Podrugović and the mainstream of the tradition, fail to achieve the imaginative welding of great epic poetry.

This kind of epic failure is due to the migration of the story through different historical settings and social codes and customs as much as to the discrepancies between the local and the heroic, the actual and the mythic. It is not surprising, of course, that we see it as the failure of the epic diction to fully adapt to the historical change and the transformation of social code and custom; and in this sense it is analogous to the failure of many *bugarštice* which were also recorded in the area of the Bay of Kotor.[10] But what is even more specifically

---

[6] 'Eto nam ga sa hiljadu svata, / Šćeri moja! u neđelju prvu', *Karadžić*, iii, No. 34, ll. 43–4.   [7] '(Ivan sjedi na) tananoj kuli', ibid., l. 73.

[8] See T. Maretić, *Naša narodna epika*, pp. 202–3.

[9] '(Sve uteklo) drvlju i kamenju', *Karadžić*, iii, No. 34, l. 261.

[10] See above pp. 63–73.

characteristic of the failure of many of the mediocre or poor decasyllabic songs about outlaws is their cult of righteous cruelty and violence. The singer's imagination—and the singers were often outlaws themselves—is obsessed by such hatred of the enemy that the song ends up by glorifying the hero who can match up the enemy in cunning, cruelty, and devising ingenious forms of torture.

It is exactly this that happens, for instance, in such poems as 'Captain Kostreš'. History knows nothing about Kostreš, but he is also mentioned in some of the Moslem poems as an outlaw who made himself a nuisance not only to the living but also to the dead. The mountain Tijana, his abode in the poem, is also fictitious; but as the task of killing Kostreš is given to the commander of Udbina, we should perhaps remember that Udbina, lying in the field of Krbava, was the most important Turkish outpost for further invasion towards Senj in the sixteenth and seventeenth centuries. So perhaps the general historical background of the poem may be connected with the border raiders of Senj, even if we are told that the Turkish commander will have very far to go to get to the mountain of Tijana, thirty nights to get to the sea and thirty-four along the coast. The basic plot of the poem is heroically simple and historically typical: the Turks organize a 'drive' to kill Kostreš, but he makes an ambush and kills them all. But what is it that 'our' Kostreš has to oppose to the Turkish terror and violence? In the first part of the poem the Turkish ensign tells his commander of his previous encounter with the outlaw captain: Kostreš intercepted them as they were escorting 'a mighty giaour'[11] and killed their best three men. This may be understood as deserved punishment of the Turkish oppressors; but the way in which justice triumphs is perhaps more telling:

> 'He did not want to kill the thirty of us,
> He only left his mark on everyone,
> On me by cutting off both of my ears.'[12]

The poem ends on a similar triumphant note: the commander of the Turkish fortress is caught, bound, and brought to Kostreš,

---

[11] 'Silna kaurina', 'Kostreš harambaša', *Karadžić*, iii, No. 46, l. 64.
[12] 'Nas trideset ne šće pogubiti, / No udari svakom po biljegu; / Mene j' onda uši osjekao', ibid., ll. 73–5.

while the outlaws hang the Turks whom they have taken prisoner. There is no trace of the awareness that the hanging of prisoners and the cutting off of ears as keepsakes might give rise to any other human feeling but mirth. This is what the poem opposes—in imaginative and human terms—to the Turkish oppression and violence.

And it is not significantly different from what we find in 'Mato of Horvat', which is also historically confused but should be basically connected with the traditions about the seventeenth-century border fighting in the area of the Bay of Kotor. Admittedly, the name of the hero might suggest a different connection: Horvati was an old estate in Srem, near Vinkovci, and a feudal family, important in the history of Hungarian and Croatian relations, was named after it. But whether the name of the hero merely echoes the name of a grand family or simply suggests that he is a Croat ('Hrvat'), or both, or neither, it is impossible to tell. As regards the names of the Turkish heroes who figure in the poem, Vizier Muhamed Ćuprilić and his son Ahmed Ćuprilić, a Grand Vizier, were two successive com-manders of the Turkish forces during the Candian War (1645–1669) in which the Turks captured Crete (Candia).[13] At this time severe fighting went on along the Montenegrin and Dalmatian parts of the Turkish and Venetian borderland, and particularly in the area of the Bay of Kotor where the Vene-tians helped the local Slav outlaws and border raiders in their actions against the Turks. As the story takes place on the Adriatic coast and mentions Vizier Ćuprilić by name, its general historical and geographical setting seems to be clear enough. The reference to the 'Serbian lords'[14]—to whom the Vizier is taken at the end of the poem—may be anachronistic; but whether it reflects the medieval times when Kotor was an important administrative centre of the Serbian empire or the later period when Serbian feudal lords retreated to Dubrovnik and the Bay of Kotor, it connects the poem with this same area.

The poem opens with a hunting scene: Vizier Ćuprilić fails

---

[13] See N. Banašević, 'Beleške i objašnjenja' in V. S. Karadžić, *Srpske narodne pjesme*, iii, Belgrade, 1958, pp. 588–9, 607, 644–6. Banašević's 'Beleške i objašnjenja' ('Notes and Explanations') in this edition will henceforth be referred to as *Banašević*.

[14] 'Gospoda Srpska', 'Od Horvata Mato', *Karadžić*, iii, No. 48, l. 179.

to catch either 'a stag or a giaour', 'either a doe or a giaour woman',[15] but he captures at least Mato of Horvat and throws him into his dungeon. Mato promises a rich ransom, far beyond the means of any outlaw, and the Vizier lets him go when a Turkish aga volunteers to be kept as a hostage until Mato returns. As Mato does not come back after three days, the Vizier gives orders to have the hostage burnt on a pyre:

> They built up a good pillar of fire . . .
> And burnt the unhappy on the fire.[16]

But what is it that Mato and the poem as an image of what he does have to oppose to the bestiality of the Vizier? When Mato returns with his ransom, in a boat with a jewel which shines like daylight, and sees what the Vizier has done, he catches the Vizier:

> A good pillar of fire they made,
> And they burnt him on the fire.[17]

The example is interesting in so far as it identifies in the same wording the logic of the victim with that of the murderer.

However, the examples of the broader moral identifications of the Turks and the outlaws in action—presented as essentially and ultimately the same without a grain of awareness of what this implies—are much more numerous. Thus, for instance, in 'The Two Kurtići and Alil Boičić' the great hero Stojan Janković, more a Venetian feudal dignitary than an outlaw captain in seventeenth-century Dalmatia, kills the greatest hero of the Moslem epic poems Tale the Fool (Budalina Tale) in such a way that he appears even more cruel than Tale himself; the poem ends with a magnificent cracking of Tale's bones:

> Tale's bones began to crack,
> Like a seven-year old wooden fence.[18]

In another poem, written down from Filip Višnjić, the most

---

[15] 'Ni jelena niti kaurina, / Ni košute niti kaurkinje', ibid., ll. 7–8.

[16] 'Dobar tumbas vatre načiniše, / . . . Na vatri ga jadna sagoreše', ibid., ll. 110, 113.

[17] 'Dobar tumbas vatre načiniše, / I na vatri njega sagoreše.' Ibid., ll. 185–186.

[18] 'Stade praska u Talu koščina, / Kano plota od sedam godina', 'Dva Kurtića i Boičić Alil', *Karadžić*, iii, No. 35, ll. 230–1.

popular of all singers, St Sava, an image of enlightened Serbian Christianity, digs out Hasan Pasha's eyes at a moment of a maliciously gleeful triumph of the epic spirit:

The Pasha screams like a swallow.[19]

And even when the saint—having manifested the terror of his powers—returns the eyes and brings back life to Pasha's paralysed hands and legs, the singer makes the malicious point that

The whole of him was a little giddy
And he will never be just as he was.[20]

Justice also often triumphs when the enemy's 'white livers' show in broad daylight. Such is, for instance, the moral aura of the happy ending of 'Vuk Jerinić and Zukan the Ensign'[21]— the poem recorded from Stojan the Outlaw who was later imprisoned for having killed a woman, presumably a witch, who had eaten his child.[22] Such and similar poems—and they are many—need no other comment except perhaps the observation that history triumphs over poetry in them. Least of all do they need the comment of scholars who have often been tempted to explain their cruelty of feeling by the ancient times and bad customs of a more primitive civilization. For such explanations suggest some very naïve illusions about the ways in which a highly developed civilization tends to affect human life in history. And if one were to accept them, the triumphs of great poetry in many other poems about outlaws would be inexplicable; and so, for that matter, would much of central European twentieth-century history.

[19] 'Cvili paša, kako lastavica', 'Sveti Savo i Hasan-paša' ('Saint Sava and Hasan Pasha'), *Karadžić*, iii, No. 14, l. 118.
[20] 'Ali i to sve je vrtoglavo, / Nit' će igda biti k'o je bilo'. Ibid., ll. 151–2.
[21] '(Vide mu se) b'jele džigerice', 'Vuk Jerinić i Zukan barjaktar', *Karadžić*, iii, No. 54, l. 213.
[22] See 'Predgovor', *Karadžić*, iv, p. 368.

3. In the Cracked Mirror

Despite the flaws of a confused social setting and glorified cruelty, some of the poems about outlaws contain magnificent achievements which illustrate how history becomes fully articulate in language, the ancient 'home and haven of sense and beauty'.[1] Such are, above all, the two great poems 'The Betrayal of Grujo's Love' and 'What Vengeance Does' recorded from anonymous singers and 'Captain Gavran and Limo' recorded from Old Milija, one of the greatest masters in the tradition. Each of these poems seems to hover between a document of bloodshed and a vision of gore: each shows how cruel historical material reveals sporadic visionary glimpses of human reality. There are large blind spots in these poems, but they are ultimately interesting because cruelty and violence, historically 'accurate', suddenly deviate into illumination.

The most drastic examples of such flawed greatness are to be found in 'The Betrayal of Grujo's Love'. Grujo is a young 'unhistorical' outlaw, but scholars tell us that he has two different historical fathers merged in the single figure of Old Novak who usually appears, together with his son, in the Bosnian mountain Romanija, the traditional and most popular resort of Bosnian outlaws.[2] In this poem Grujo is referred to several times as a 'knight' and the appearance of his wife, with gold embroidery, in front of his tent, suggests a mixture of a grand feudal and a humble outlaw setting. The poem tells the story of how the treacherous wife betrayed her heroic husband to the Turks, how he set himself free and punished her for her crime. The punishment takes a fairly standard epic form: Grujo spreads wax, tar, and sulphur over his wife's body and lets her slowly burn while he sits down to drink his 'cool wine'.[3]

---

[1] B. Pasternak, *Doktor Zhivago*, Milan, 1961, Chapter xiv, Section 8, p. 448.

[2] See *Banašević*, pp. 576–7. 'Novak's Cave' is still a climbing attraction on Mount Romanija.

[3] '(A on sede piti) vino ladno', 'Nevjera ljube Gruičine', *Karadžić*, iii, No. 7, l. 286.

However, this cruelty is not the ultimate reason for the imaginative flaw in this scene; physical horrors—like Gloucester's blinding or Desdemona's stifling—may yet have a function in a work of art. The flaw cannot be assessed even in terms of the question whether this punishment is proportionate to the crime, perhaps because the crime itself is so monstrous that any kind of moral 'proportion' is hardly conceivable in this instance. The trouble is that this horror is presented as meaningful, and proportionate—almost as providential; the terrifying lines which describe the tortures are meant to ring as a kind of hymn to justice. What kind of justice is being enacted is mirrored in the cynicism of the question which Grujo asks his wife before deciding how to kill her:

> 'Maksimija, faithless creature!
> Would you like to give me candlelight?
> Or would you like to kiss my sword?'[4]

Maksimija does not understand what this question means; monstrous as she has proved herself in the poem, she is still innocent enough to miss Grujo's point and let slip this opportunity of choosing the manner of her execution. This is why she answers that the sword is 'foul with all sorts of misdeeds'[5] and that she would rather hold his candle for him even if she is not going to get any sleep. The helplessness and the innocence of her answer suggest a moving misunderstanding; the language refuses to accept the cynical meaning which is imposed upon it—instead of expressing the idea of a deserved punishment, it seems to suggest that Maksimija, after the betrayal of her husband and her cruelty to her son, is still less inhuman than Grujo.

However, this displacement of moral focus is found side by side with great imaginative insights. Such is, for instance, the evocation of Maksimija's character in its unearthly combination of beauty and cruelty:

> Such beauty is not to be found in the land,
> Her face is worth all Constantinople.[6]

---

[4] 'Maksimija, koleno neverno! / Ili voliš svećom svijetliti? / Il' mi voliš sablju celivati?' *Karadžić*, iii, No. 7, ll. 265–7.

[5] 'Sablja (ti) je od svašta skrnavna', ibid., l. 271.

[6] 'Lepote joj na krajini nema, / Lice joj je vredno Carigrada.' Ibid., ll. 136–7.

But this beauty which can be measured only by the distant glamour of an Oriental city is matched in the story by the perversity and the cruelty of the mother who stops her son from warning his father of the approaching Turkish danger:

> The child went to wake his father,
> But his mother Maksimija ran after him,
> She caught him at the entrance of the tent,
> She hit her own child on the cheek
> So lightly, lightly she struck him,
> The child turned over three times on the ground
> And three of the sound teeth jumped out of him.[7]

The mother's cruelty will be later mirrored in the child's helpless effort to keep pace with the Turkish horses:

> 'But I cannot keep up with the horses,
> The Turks do not let me stay in the woods,
> They whip me across the eyes.'[8]

And this magic of Maksimija's beauty and cruelty lives in the story with powerful inevitability of its dramatic function. It provides the narrative background for the response to the great lines in which her son, unable to watch the scene of his mother's punishment, tells his father:

> 'My mother's breasts are burning,
> Which nursed me, father,
> Which put me on my feet.'[9]

The daring of this pleading stops short of becoming a request; this is how the inarticulate poignancy of the son's pity provides a partial dramatic justification of the cruel scene of the mother's burning. However, the ultimate tragic fulfilment of the scene is never achieved, largely owing to the narrative and moral confusion of Grujo's malice and Maksimija's innocence.

[7] 'Nego pođe da probudi babu, / Za njim trči Maksimija majka, / Dostiže ga šatoru na vrati, / Udari ga rukom uz obraze, / Kako ga je lako udarila, / Tri puta se dete premetnulo, / Tri mu zdrava iskočila zuba', ibid., ll. 23–9.

[8] 'Već ne mogu s konjma putovati, / Turc' u gori ostati ne dadu, / Kamdžijama biju po očiju.' Ibid., ll. 102–4.

[9] 'Izgoreše mojoj majci dojke, / Koje su me odranile, babo, / Koje su me na noge podigle.' Ibid., ll. 314–16.

This is why Stevan's voice remains only a pledge of a tragic possibility in this scene, the pledge of the grand helplessness which was more fully embodied in the preceding scene in which Stevan had stolen the heavy knives from the sleeping mother and the Turks in order to set his father free. He is described as dragging the knives with both his hands:

> The knives are heavy and the child is weak.[10]

He does not even cut the ropes with which his father is tied— he 'leans the knives against the ropes'[11] so that he cuts not only the ropes but also his father's hand. There is no need to explain why 'the black blood'[12] runs from the outlaw's hand: there are physical, historical, and metaphorical reasons for it. The father's impulse to spare his son's feelings is also expressed in a few splendid lines:

> 'Do not fear, Stevan, my child!
> Blood is not coming from your father's hand,
> The blood is coming out of the rope.'[13]

In short, the fatherly tenderness is expressed in a lie which suggests that a rope is bleeding. This image sums up a sense of tragic national fate and it defines both the predicament and the spiritual effort of a great outlaw, the situation in which nothing makes sense and everything is possible, in which ultimate loyalties are expressed in cruel gestures, in which a primal moral impulse is in total revolt against reality. For as a rope cannot bleed—and yet it does; so a lie about a bleeding hand grows into the final truth of human affection. The cruel predicament of an outlaw becomes paradoxically an area which comes to test the nobility of the human mind.

Of course, this does not reflect a merely technical, stylistic feature characteristic of some poems about outlaws. Their imaginative range is a reflection of the nature of the outlaws' historical commitment; and it is also worth noting how it is mirrored in the most realistic descriptive details. So, for

[10] 'Noži teški, a dete nejako', *Karadžić*, iii, No. 7, l. 204.
[11] '(Te) nasloni nože na konopce', ibid., l. 207.
[12] 'Crna krvca', ibid., l. 211.
[13] 'A ne boj se, Stevo, čedo moje! / Krv ne ide iz babine ruke, / Nego ide krvca iz konopca.' Ibid., ll. 215–17.

instance, in the poem 'Novak and Radivoje Sell Gruica', recorded from Tešan Podrugović, perhaps the greatest outlaw and the greatest master in the tradition, Grujo appears as a black devil riding a white devil:

> If anyone were present to see this!—
> A devil riding on a devil's back,
> A mountain outlaw on a furious white horse.[14]

Not only that the attribute 'mountain' defining the outlaw does not suggest a pure idyll, not only that the fury of the horse is also a description of his master, but Grujo's appearance also shows the moral 'outlawry' of the image which identifies the hero and his horse with the devil.

Similarly, the comparisons and the epithets grow imperceptibly into symbols and metaphors which sum up the nature of outlawry in the description of Grujo's father Old Novak in 'The Wedding of Gruica Novaković' which was recorded from Old Raško, one of the best singers of Karadžić's times. The ultimate historical ancestor of Old Novak might have been a Novak Debelić who was sung in the mid-sixteenth-century Bulgarian poems as a hero who, together with Marko Kraljević, defended his country from the Turks. He may have also been a late sixteenth-century Papa Novak (Baba Novak), described in the chronicles as fighting against the Turks and the Hungarians.[15] But the epic singer sees him as a homeless outlaw of the Bosnian mountain Romanija:

> He had on him a coat of a bear's skin,
> And on his head a cap of a wolf's skin,
> And in his cap the white wing of a swan,
> And his eyes were two deep glasses of wine.[16]

The 'coat of a bear's skin' and the 'cap of a wolf's skin' do not merely describe his clothes: a coat of lambskin or a cap of

[14] 'Da je kome pogledati bilo, / Kad usjede đavo na đavola; / Gorski hajduk na b'jesna đogata', 'Novak i Radivoje prodaju Gruicu', *Karadžić*, iii, No. 2, ll. 142–5.

[15] See *Banašević*, p. 575. See also T. Maretić, *Naša narodna epika*, pp. 213–214.

[16] 'Na njemu je kožuh od međeda, / Na glavi mu kapa vučetina, / I za kapom krilo od labuda, / Oči su mu dvije kupe vina', 'Ženidba Gruice Novakovića', *Karadžić*, iii, No. 6, ll. 258–61.

hareskin would have been a much more obviously realistic choice of garments. Their imaginative interplay with the 'white wing of a swan' suggests the outlaws' imaginative effort to break through the nature of their own historical realities; and the eyes, seen as 'two deep glasses of wine', with their associations of feudal banquets and gory realities, also embody a total awareness of the historical, moral, and imaginative nature of the material.

Thus the mode in which the outlaws' predicament is expressed reflects the paradox of the implacable historical bondage and the total imaginative freedom in which the singer sees his material. This is why realistic descriptions of outlaws are visions which sum up the nature of outlawry in a far more complex and vivid way than a historical assessment of this subject could ever hope to attain, reaching at the same time what the sword could only strive to touch. The achievement—and it is ultimately the achievement of total imaginative freedom from the historical weight of its material—is also often realized in the visions of the helpless victims whom the outlaw heroes tried to defend. Thus in the anonymous poem 'What Vengeance Does'—set in the borderland of Montenegro and Herzegovina with the names of some of the late seventeenth-century outlaws in the Venetian military service in the Bay of Kotor[17]—the misery of a Montenegrin woman who had run away to live in the woods, after a Turkish raid and the betrayal of her own kin who should have offered protection, is described as an inverted idyll of the traditional patriarchal vision of nature:

> 'I ran away to the green wood,
> I walked, so young, in the green wood,
> I grazed the grass for fifteen days,
> I grazed the grass as a doe does
> And I did not see a mouthful of bread.'[18]

[17] The main characters in this poem are unhistorical, but Bajo Pivljanin and Captain Limo are the historical names of two well-known outlaw captains who were in the Venetian service in the seventeenth century. See *Banašević*, pp. 690–1, 694.

[18] 'Ja utekoh u goru zelenu, / Hodih mlada po gori zelenoj, / Pasoh travu za petnaest dana, / Pasoh travu, kakono i srna, / I ne viđeh ljeba zalogaja.' 'Šta osveta čini', *Karadžić*, iii, No. 69, ll. 16–20. In l. 17 'Hodit' has been corrected to 'Hodih' as in V. S. Karadžić, *Srpske narodne pjesme*, iii, Vienna, 1846, No. 69.

In oral epic singing, particularly in the poems about family life, the green woods, the grass, and the doe have usually suggested the ultimate possibilities of the harmony of man and nature. But here nature is seen as the last resort; it offers a kind of physical hardship which at least can be humanly faced.

It is within this setting that the heroine asks her brother-in-law Tašo Nikolić, a captain of the Montenegrin border fighters, to come and kill his own sister and her husband who had betrayed her to the hated Turks. In case he should refuse, she promises to send him 'a spindle and a distaff',[19] and faced with the message containing such misery and such a promise of ridicule, Tašo calls his outlaws and other captains, among them the famous Bajo Pivljanin, who actually lived in Perast in the Bay of Kotor. The message is again set in a highly paradoxical wording:

> 'My brother in God, Bajo Pivljanin,
> Unfurl your silken banner,
> Smear with blood the apple on the flagpole.'[20]

The planting of the banner in the earth so that the outlaws should gather around it reflects a historical outlaw custom of feudal origin. But even if we cannot tell if the 'smearing of the apple on the flagpole' reflects a historical custom (and it would be difficult to imagine that it does not), even if the 'apple' denotes here the ball at the top of a flagpole, the expressive force of the image springs from its veiled association with one of the most traditional patriarchal tokens of love. For as apples were given as gifts and tokens of love, the word itself came to denote a 'gift', more specifically the gift which the bride gives to her prospective bridegroom and, hence, 'betrothal'.[21] In epic poetry it is sometimes used to express the mother's love for her son or the husband's love for his wife, usually in the tragic

---

[19] 'Drûgu i preslicu', ibid., l. 26.

[20] 'Bogom brate, Pivljanine Bajo! / Razvijder mi svilena barjaka, / Okrvavi na koplju jabuku', ibid., ll. 33–5.

[21] An example of this meaning of the word 'apple' ('jabuka') is quoted in M. Stevanović *et al.*, eds., *Rečnik srpskohrvatskoga književnog jezika*, ii, p. 550: 'Spremite sve što treba za jabuku i svadbu' ('Prepare everything that is necessary for the betrothal and the wedding').

context of death ('The Death of the Mother of the Jugovići', 'The Building of Skadar')[22]

In 'What Vengeance Does' the 'apple', smeared with blood, suggests the way in which Tašo will come to express his love for his sister-in-law. And a fundamentally analogous paradox of patriarchal love and bloodshed is further developed in the lines which describe the call for the muster of the outlaws in which the spiritual pendulum swings from the imagery of home-life, of the affection of father, mother and wife, to the wasteland of outlaws' predicament, their homelessness, their swords, rifles, and guns:

> Go then and gather heroes to the flag,
> The homeless heroes with blood-stained hands,
> Who have no father and have no mother,
> Who have never known a faithful love,
> Whose home is nothing but a mountain-cloak,
> Sword and rifle father and mother,
> And two guns for two brothers by blood,
> Who feed by sword in the border countrey,
> As hawk on wing hanging among clouds.[23]

The 'mountain-cloak' is, of course, literally, physically, an outlaw's home and a token which suggests, with ironic pathos, that he has no home; his sword and gun are his only protection, his father and mother, because he has no father and no mother and because, in the wider context of this poem, they will enable him to express his sense of justice and human affection. And the whole of this semantic adventure comes together in the picture

[22] 'My hand, O green apple, / Where did you grow from, where were you ripped off?' ('Moja ruko, zelena jabuko! / Gdje si rasla, gdje l' si ustrgnuta!' 'Smrt majke Jugovića', *Karadžić*, ii, No. 48, ll. 78–9). Similarly, when Gojko sees that his young wife will be walled up in 'The Building of Skadar' he exclaims that he had had 'a gold apple', but it fell into the river Bojana ('Imao sam od zlata jabuku, / Pa mi danas pade u Bojanu', 'Zidanje Skadra', *Karadžić*, ii, No. 26, ll. 165–6).

[23] 'Pak ti kupi pod barjak junake, / Sve krvnike i beskućanike, / Koji nema ni oca ni majke, / A za vjernu ljubu i ne znade; / Kom je kuća divan-kabanica, / Mač i puška i otac i majka, / Dva pištolja dva brata rođena; / Koj' se rani mačem po krajini / Kao soko kril'ma po oblaku.' *Karadžić*, iii, No. 69, ll. 36–44. In l. 40 'divna kabanica' has been corrected to 'divan-kabanica' as in V. S. Karadžić, *Srpske narodne pjesme*, iii, Vienna, 1846, No. 69.

of a lonely hawk, the free bird feeding among clouds. But in all these details we also witness the merging of two different historical backgrounds: the predicament of the Montenegrin border fighters, who had their homes and lived with their fathers, mothers, and faithful loves, is seen in terms of homeless outlawry, more characteristic perhaps of inland regions in Bosnia and Serbia.

This imaginative merging and the highly metaphorical nature of the language used for what appears also to be a realistic description mirrors the paradoxes of the singer's imaginative awareness of the outlaws' predicament. The outlaws are obviously seen as the apostles of justice and freedom in a world of violence and treachery, but they have to express their affections and loyalties in the form of bloodshed, vengeance, and hatred. They have to pay the price for their freedom and dignity not only by their lives but also by their way of life. And it is not perhaps insignificant that under this historical and imaginative burden this pattern falls to pieces at the end of the poem, in the scene in which Tašo comes to fulfil his duty and kill his sister. The outburst of cynical cruelty is analogous, in fact, to the ending of 'The Betrayal of Grujo's Love'. The parallel lies not only in the zest of vengeance but also in the cynicism of moral feeling, even in the nature of the language:

> 'Stand by, my sister, till we exchange our gifts!'
> And he drew his dagger from his thigh,
> And struck his sister on her silken waist,
> She tumbled into two halves on the ground,[24]

—and, to make the triumph of justice complete:

> Her baby boy fell out from her belly,
> And rolled away dead on the green grass.[25]

This 'gift' of love sums up the significance of the smeared 'apple' on the flagpole. The scene is analogous to the cynicism of the situation in which Grujo's wife is offered the choice between a sword and a candle; and the unborn baby, rolling 'on the

[24] ' "Stani, sestro, dok se darujemo!" / Pak poteže mača od bedrice, / Ud'ri sestru po svilenu pasu, / Dvije pole na zemlju padoše', ibid., ll. 79–82.
[25] 'Iz nje pade ono muško čedo, / Pa se valja po zelenoj travi.' Ibid., ll. 83–4.

green grass', mirrors the same confusion of moral sympathies which we found in Stevan's pity for his burning mother. For how can one—faced with this pity or with the rolling unborn baby—accept the scene in the way in which it is obviously meant, as a form of deserved punishment?

In the poems about the outlaws we are sometimes faced with a much more pedestrian breakdown of epic communication. Thus in 'Captain Gavran and Limo' Old Milija, one of the greatest of Karadžić's singers, seems to be nodding most of the time, to wake up only at the end of the poem. Geographically, his story seems to be connected with western Bosnia, the area of Bihać, in which one of the outlaw captains nicknamed Gavran, historically probably connected with the distant littoral area of Zadar, organizes a raid on the Turkish tax-collectors. He asks for help from another outlaw captain called Limo, whose name is historically connected with the area of the Bay of Kotor, also controlled by the Venetians but certainly too far from Zadar for a joint outlaw effort.[26] Thus distant and different historical backgrounds are again merged in a story which has partly a legendary character in so far as it embodies a typical moral justification of the outlaws' heroism, that of raiding the Turkish tax-collectors. The singer seems to be partly and vaguely aware of the nature of his material—he makes Limo's party complain of their very long journey while they are on the way to western Bosnia. And the sequence of the story is mostly logical and 'clean'; it only lacks colour and movement. Occasionally there is a lively descriptive detail; thus the two companies of outlaws agree to meet

> In a place by a dry-headed fir-tree,
> Beside a white stone under the fir-tree,
> At a cold spring of water by the stone.[27]

But even if the lonely white stone, the dry-headed fir-tree and a spring of cold water are in a sense suggestive of a quality of the outlaws' way of life, they are far less dramatically suggestive

[26] On Captain Gavran see *Banašević*, p. 655. On Limo see Karadžić's note, *Karadžić*, iii, p. 215. See also Karadžić's *Srpski rječnik*, p. 334 (Limo).

[27] 'Đeno ima suhovrha jela, / I pod jelom jedan bijel kamen, / Kod kamena jedna voda ladna', 'Gavran harambaša i Limo', *Karadžić*, iii, No. 42, ll. 20–2.

than Grujo's bleeding ropes, his devilish appearance on his horse, Old Novak's 'cap of a wolf's skin', Tašo's 'apple smeared with blood'. And, similarly, the description of the outlaws' starvation in the wood, of the long hours of waiting in what appears to be a vain ambush, is also up to a good standard of story-telling, but it never touches the great imaginative strings of the Serbo-Croatian oral epic singing at its best:

> And the heroes were weary with this pain,
> But the heroes are harder than stone is,
> They suffer hunger and heroic thirst,
> And not one says a word.[28]

And thus the story meanders on—occasionally enlivened with vivid observation—until it comes to describe the actual fighting with the Turkish tax-collectors led by the terrifying native hero Petar Mrkonjić who is in their service. At this moment the poem falls into the standard pitfall of a malicious triumph in blood-shed, particularly in the lines describing how beautifully one of the outlaw captains shot Petar Mrkonjić, a native in the enemy's service:

> He tore off his head at the shoulder,
> A sword could not have trimmed a finer edge.[29]

However, even if the feeling of *Schadenfreude* hardly makes this an enlightened or an enlightening line, it is at least set in a battle-scene, not in the situation of a warrior punishing a helpless wife or sister. Besides, this is a detail; this triumph of justice does not dominate this poem to the same extent to which 'The Betrayal of Grujo's Love' and 'What Vengeance Does' are dominated by their barbaric endings. Finally, the drowsy story-telling has at least one saving grace, in so far as it makes us skim over such lines half-asleep; and, besides, this moment does not contain, fortunately, a 'point' which would bring together some important threads in the story. However, the point—a very great point indeed—comes, as if by the way, at the end of the poem. As if poor Old Milija, the notoriously

---

[28] 'Junacima muka dosadila, / Al' junaci tvrđi od kamenja, / Trpe glađu i junačku žeđu, / Niti kakav riječi besjedi', ibid., ll. 80–3.

[29] 'Do ramena otkide mu glavu, / Ne bi sablja ljevše porubila', ibid., ll. 259–60.

drunken singer, had suddenly sobered up when Rosnić Stevan
came to divide the plunder:

> He divided the treasure beautifully,
> Not by counting or by calculation,
> But Captain Limo's helmet for measure;
> How justly he divided the treasure,
> Evenly among living and dead.
> The living took their treasure on their backs,
> The treasure of the dead remained in heaps.[30]

The way in which the treasure is divided seems to reflect the
outlaws' thirst for a heavenly kind of justice. After the gathering,
the ambush and the clash, after the lurid image of 'blood-
smeared' cobbles and spruces,[31] the singer presents an emblematic moral gesture of an outlaw, the gesture which pushes
beyond the reasons and realities of history. For the justice which
leaves the dead outlaws their share of the booty—in the
strangely ambivalent form of the burial mounds by their heads
—reflects the ultimate triumph of moral imagination over
experience, even if it must have been inspired by the historical
custom which demanded that the booty be shared with the
families of those who were killed in action.[32] The custom itself
was rooted, of course, in the local history of the areas where
outlawry was a major branch of the national economy and
often the only means of survival. But the imaginative achievement which flourished on this custom brings us to the threshold
of the ultimate possibilities of the Serbo-Croatian epic vision of
the outlaws' actual predicament.

[30] 'On lijepo blago dijeljaše, / Ne dijeli brojem ni hesapom, / No kalpakom
harambaše Lima; / Kako pravo blago podijeli, / Sve na mrtva kao i na
živa. / Živi svoje blago uprtiše, / A mrtvijem osta na kupove', *Karadžić*, iii,
No. 42, ll. 386–92.

[31] 'Krvavo je (po drumu) kamenje, / Krvave su (vite) omorike', ibid., ll.
360–1.

[32] See D. J. Popović, *O hajducima*, ii, Belgrade, 1931, p. 34.

4. In Imaginative Reality

In some of the greatest poems about outlaws the hero is not seen in triumphant action but as a victim of his tragic fate. Thus in 'Old Vujadin' he is caught and tortured; in 'The Death of Ivo of Senj' he is hunted like a beast; in 'Predrag and Nenad' he kills, unawares, his own loving brother. In such poems a great outlaw who has renounced society comes to show his mettle by a desperate gesture which proves his ultimate loyalty to himself and his kin. This is sometimes done in the full awareness of the moral and human curse of the historical commitment to outlawry, and in this respect 'Old Vujadin' is the most fascinating of all the poems about outlaws.

This poem was recorded from an anonymous singer who spoke with the tongues of many earlier songs. One of them—a very rudimentary version—was recorded more than a hundred years earlier along the northern Turkish frontier with Austria: it also describes the torturing of captured outlaws and their heroic loyalty to their friends, some of its heroes' names are similar to those of the later version (Milivoje and Vukoje as compared to Milić and Vulić) and it is also set in the town of Livno in southern Bosnia, along the Turco-Venetian frontier.[1] Livno was until the middle of the seventeenth century a major Turkish administrative centre from which the beys of the Sandjak of Klis ruled western Bosnia, Lika and parts of Dalmatia, but after the Turkish defeats in Dalmatia during the Morean War Livno was reduced to a frontier outpost with a Turkish garrison which was exposed to Venetian attacks and the raids of local outlaws. As Livno lay on a major commercial route from the Adriatic coast to central Bosnia, the decasyllabic accounts of the attacks of the mountain outlaws on caravans could be easily adorned with some of the grand elements of the Venetian military establishment, particularly as many Slav outlaws served as soldiers and officers in Venetian military units.

'Old Vujadin' opens with a traditional formulaic curse—a young girl curses her own eyes for not having seen three outlaws

[1] See *Gesemann*, No. 168. See also above pp. 84–5.

in splendid clothing, captured by the Turks and led to Livno to be tortured. Old Vujadin is described as wearing a gold-embroidered gown, the usual garment of the Turkish pashas and viziers;[2] one of his sons has feathers of gold on his helmet. This is not pure epic fiction and it does not reflect only the general taste of the outlaws for gaudy apparel. The outlaws' captains and sirdars in the Venetian military service were sometimes dressed in a combination of Oriental costume and the clothes of a European feudal lord, as an existing portrait of Stojan Janković shows.[3] (See Pl. 4.) And silver feathers, worn on the helmet, were actually given to the outlaws and their captains in recognition of their service in the Venetian regular military units.[4] However, the basic epic situation which is assumed in the poem does not reflect so much the predicament of Venetian soldiers and officers as the situation of much more romantic and 'heroic' outlaws living freely in the woods. This is clear from what the old father tells his two sons as they approach Livno:

'O my sons, O my young hawks!
Can your eyes make out Livno of the curse
And the white tower that is in Livno?
There they will whip us and will torture us,
And they will break our feet and hands
And they will dig away our dark eyes.
O my sons, O my young hawks!
Do not show the heart of a widow,
But show the heart of a hero,
Do not betray a single friend,
Do not betray those that have sheltered us
Where we have spent winters, left treasure;
And do not betray any young girls
Who poured us out the red wine in taverns,
The red wine that we drank in our hiding.'[5]

[2] See *Banašević*, p. 668.

[3] A copy of this portrait is on display in The Historical Museum of Croatia, Department of Serles in Croatia, Zagreb.

[4] See *Banašević*, p. 617.

[5] 'O sinovi, moji sokolovi! / Vidite li prokleto Lijevno, / Đe u njemu bijeli se kula? / Onđe će nas biti i mučiti: / Prebijati i noge i ruke, / I vaditi naše oči čarne; / O sinovi, moji sokolovi! / Ne budite srca udovička, / No

In short, the grand gold-embroidered gown and silver feathers
on the helmet are only splendid details in the homely epic
setting of inland outlaws with their hiding places and secret
protectors, their girls and taverns, the setting which corresponds
to Karadžić's description of the life of outlaws in Serbia.[6] And
it is within this setting that Old Vujadin—a captured, feeble
old man—grows into a heroic martyr of his fate. When the
Turks break 'both his feet and hands', when they begin 'to dig
away his dark eyes'[7] and offer him the choice between treason
and death, his answer displays a cool heroic attitude defying
not only his enemy but his own historical commitment:

'Do not talk foolishly, Turks of Livno!
I did not speak for those swift feet,
Which could outrun horses;
I did not speak for the heroic hands,
Which could snap lances in two
And strike against a naked sword,—
I will not speak for the deceiving eyes
Which led me to evil
Watching from the highest mountain,
Watching the highroads below
Where Turks and traders pass.'[8]

The contrast between the present and the past, the old age and
youth, the broken feet and the times when they 'could outrun
horses', the broken hands and the days when they 'could strike
against a naked sword' is as fascinating as the hero's moral order
in which the 'feet' and the 'hands' are valued far above the
'eyes'. The daring of the way in which the old captured outlaw
comes to see himself and his life is equal to his physical courage:

budite srca junačkoga, / Ne odajte druga nijednoga, / Ne odajte vi jatake
naše / Kod kojih smo zime zimovali, / Zimovali, blago ostavljali; / Ne
odajte krčmarice mlade, / Kod kojih smo rujno vino pili, / Rujno vino pili u
potaji.' 'Stari Vujadin', *Karadžić*, iii, No. 50, ll. 21–36.

[6] See above pp. 216–20.

[7] '(Prebiše mu) i noge i ruke; / (Kad stadoše) oči vadit' čarne', ibid., ll.
44–5.

[8] 'Ne ludujte, Turci Lijevnjani! / Kad ne kazah za te hitre noge, /
Kojeno su konjma utjecale; / I ne kazah za junačke ruke, / Kojeno su koplja
prelamale / I na gole sablje udarale; / Ja ne kazah za lažljive oči, / Koje su
me na zlo navodile / Gledajući s najviše planine, / Gledajući dolje na
drumove, / Kud prolaze Turci i trgovci.' Ibid., ll. 56–66.

his vision has not been blurred by his historical commitment. This is what enables him to refer to his 'deceiving eyes' which 'led him to evil' and yet to remain true to himself, in the full awareness of the moral nature of his historical commitment. Of course, this is not only an accidental reference to the evil of outlawry; in 'Old Novak and Chief Bogosav', written down from the great outlaw poet Tešan Podrugović, Old Novak is also asked what 'trouble' made him

> 'Break his neck, walk the mountain,
> In outlawry, the bad craft,
> And in old age which is no time for it?'[9]

His answer suggests that the economic terror of a Serbian feudal ruler and Turkish violence turned him into an outlaw, and it ends on a heroic note defining himself as a man who is brave

> And fit to overtake and run away
> And to endure in terrible places
> And to fear no one but God Himself.[10]

But interesting as this poem is for the understanding of the epic insight into the social origins and heroic ideals of outlawry, it does not embody, like 'Old Vujadin', the moral drama of the tortured hero who remains true to his historical commitment in spite of his clear awareness of its moral nature. This courage of spirit which pushes beyond the immediate needs of history makes 'Old Vujadin' one of the most fascinating songs in the tradition.

In such a vision of history the epic language seems to take upon itself the whole of the spiritual burden of a historical reality, giving it a mythic imaginative significance. Of course, it could never do so had its subject not been deeply rooted in such common historical realities as the torturing of outlaws. Similarly, one of the most fantastic epic poems in the Serbo-Croat tradition, 'The Death of Ivo of Senj', spins its story out of dreams and nightmares which spring from clearly recognizable

[9] 'Vrat lomiti, po gori hoditi, / Po hajduci, po lošu zanatu, / A pod starost, kad ti nije vrime?' 'Starina Novak i knez Bogosav', *Karadžić*, iii, No. 1, ll. 10–12.

[10] 'A kadar sam stići i uteći / I na strašnu mjestu postajati, / Ne bojim se nikoga do Boga!' Ibid., ll. 90–2.

historical realities. Written down from an anonymous singer, this poem is obviously connected with the actions of the sixteenth- and the early seventeenth-century border raiders (*uskoci*) who attacked Venetian and Turkish ships and territories from the harbour of Senj, which was controlled by Austria. The poem describes the hero's nightmarish sense of being pursued after a raid on the territory controlled by the Venetian Republic, 'the country of Italy'[11] as he calls it. Besides, a dream comes to be interpreted in the poem as a prophecy that Senj will be 'laid waste',[12] which is clearly a reference to the later banishment of all the border raiders from Senj after the agreement reached by Austria and Venice in 1618. Finally, the hero of the poem, Ivo of Senj—as the editors tell us with charming innocence—'was a historical personality, but it is difficult to establish which, because Ivan was the name of several well-known, and undoubtedly also of some unknown, heroes from Senj, the town of border raiders'.[13] But whereas Maretić quotes a military list from 1551 and finds that Ivo of Senj must have been an ordinary soldier,[14] some other scholars take a more exalted social view of him and claim that he must have been the duke of border raiders Ivan Novaković-Vlatković, unless he was 'Captain Ivan Lenković, a military commander of Senj'.[15] However, the poem reads like anything but a factual account of what 'really' happened even if its subject—the pursuit of a border raider—must have been a common occurrence. It opens with a portentous dream of a mother which forebodes, among other things, the death of her son. Of course, the dream lends itself, like most dreams, to a 'realistic' interpretation; and this is how Father Nedeljko— almost as formulaic as dreams in Serbo-Croat epic singing— interprets it to the mother. But what follows is not so much an account of reality as of the nightmare of Ivo's sense of being pursued—by enemy soldiers who become fateful apparitions from which he can never hope to run away.

In short, the dream in which the mother sees 'the clear sky'

[11] 'Zemlja Talija', 'Smrt Senjanina Iva', *Karadžić*, iii, No. 31, ll. 46, 48.
[12] '(Ono će ti) pusto ostanuti', ibid., l. 20.
[13] See *Banašević*, pp. 629–30.
[14] See T. Maretić, *Naša narodna epika*, pp. 210–11.
[15] *Banašević*, pp. 629–30.

which 'has broken', 'the shining moon fallen to the earth', 'the stars' which have 'escaped to the border of the sky' and 'the morning star' which has 'risen blood-stained'[16] are not so much the clues to what will 'happen' as an imaginative dramatization of the essential historical predicament of a border raider, of his perpetual race for life which has to be repeated until he falls dead. In this sense the mother's dream is further developed in the way in which her son sees his pursuers, in the mythopoeic quality of his vision of what was quite clearly 'actual' history. In the first round of his attempt to escape Ivo sees his pursuers as 'black horses' and 'black riders';[17] and in the second round they appear to him as 'white horses' and 'more furious heroes'.[18] However, having escaped two pursuing parties, he will be soon followed up by the third:

> 'There the third pursuit caught up with us,
> With black plaids, with long rifles,
> Their legs burnt away to their knees'.[19]

The black plaids and the long rifles intensify the sense of approaching danger, and the legs burnt 'to the knees' express Ivo's mad hope and his maddening desire to escape. The illogical dislocation of the image—for Ivo seems to be running away before the pursuers whose legs have been burnt—embodies the effect which this situation has on Ivo's mind. And the same fantastic logic—in which history, experience and myth-making come together—is carried on in the tragic irony at the end of the poem. For Ivo will return to his mother, he will bring her his own hand instead of a gift and die after he has succeeded in running away:

> 'Here's my right hand in my left!'
> Thus he speaks, he struggles with his soul,
> This he said, he let his light soul go.[20]

---

[16] '(Đe se) vedro nebo prolomilo, / Sjajan mjesec pao na zemljicu, / . . . (Đe) zvijezde kraju pribjegnule, / (A) Danica krvava izljegla', *Karadžić*, iii, No. 31, ll. 3–4, 6–7.

[17] 'Crni konji, a crni junaci', ibid., l. 54.

[18] 'B'jeli konji, a bješnji junaci', ibid., l. 61.

[19] 'Tu nas stiže i treća poćera, / Crna struka, a dugačka puška, / Pregorele noge do koljena', ibid., ll. 67–9.

[20] ' "Evo desne u lijevoj ruke!" / To govori, a s dušom se bori, / To izusti, laku dušu pusti', ibid., ll. 76–8.

The same sense of the tragically dislocated personal life under the unlucky star of history, of the human predicament of the outlaws and border raiders, is also reflected in the poems which tell the stories of their loves. 'Predrag and Nenad' is the most 'unhistorical' among them, perhaps because it was recorded far from the regions of the fighting of outlaws and border raiders. It was sent to Karadžić by the Serbian writer Jovan Berić from Budim; except for one reference to the mountain Garevica—which might just conceivably be connected with the name of a Serbian village in Croatia[21] even if it is more probably just an epic reference to an imaginary 'soot-black' (*garav*) mountain—there is nothing in it to indicate a geographical or a historical connection. This is why it reads more like a kind of fairy-tale in which the theme of brotherly love and fratricide, so central to the Serbian patriarchal culture, has been harnessed to the need of expressing the poignancy of the outlaws' personal fate. Even the names of the two brothers suggest a fairy-tale rather than an epic background: Predrag denotes the dearest of the dear and Nenad, his parents' unhoped-for joy. It is in this imaginary setting that we see Predrag fleeing to the woods to live freely as an outlaw as soon as he is 'tall enough to mount a horse'.[22] Nenad, the unhoped-for joy, had no chance of even remembering his elder brother. But when Nenad also becomes a captain of an outlaw company, he comes to realize—while dividing booty—that he is the only outlaw, as he thinks, who has no sister and no brother to swear by. And it is this interplay of a patriarchal fairy-tale of brotherly affection and the cruel realities of the outlaws' life that gives this poem its unique ring. Eventually, Predrag will inflict a deadly wound on Nenad when Nenad, driven by his thirst for brotherly love, comes to look for him in the mountain, and Nenad will die grateful for the first and last chance of seeing his brother:

[21] See *Matić*, pp. 650–1.

[22] '(Predrag majci) do konja doraste', 'Predrag i Nenad', *Karadžić*, ii, No. 16, l. 6. This poem follows the general pattern of legends about fratricide; this is why Karadžić classified it among the poems of 'the oldest times' in the second volume of his definitive edition. However, the poem sets its story in a specified outlaw setting in which it can be profitably considered.

'O this is you, my own brother!
Thank God that I have seen you with my eyes
And my living desire has passed from me!'[23]

Predrag's dirge for his dead brother rings a similar note of tragic pathos: he sees his dead younger brother as his 'hot sun'[24] which has risen early and had to set so early, as 'sweet basil from the green garden'.[25] The traditional patriarchal imagery of the harmony of nature and human life has an inverted tragic function, and in the same spirit of the inversion of the natural order of things the outlaw comes to affirm his love for his brother by suicide. As in 'Old Vujadin' the outlaw's free choice of death is seen as the ultimate affirmation of his sense of honour, of the only possible form of human love in his historical setting.

Among the tragic poems about the outlaws 'The Wedding of Milić the Ensign' is possibly the ultimate achievement, even if it is far less connected with a typical 'outlaw' situation, or the situation which is meant to bring out the tragic essence of the outlaws' historical commitment. It was also recorded from an unknown singer, its hero is unknown to history and it is not placed in a specific historical and geographical setting. Some of the references suggest the borderland of Herzegovina and Montenegro, others connect the story with the famous seventeenth-century outlaw captains in Venetian service, operating from the Bay of Kotor to Šibenik and Zadar (Stojan Janković, Bajo Pivljanin, Vuk Mandušić).[26] The wedding customs and the funeral customs show some distinct Montenegrin features; in all probability the epic singer assumed that Milić the Ensign was a border fighter from Herzegovina or Montenegro and that his journey to his prospective bride had taken him far away to the north, to the inland mountain region near the Dalmatian coast

---

[23] 'Ta ti li si, moj brate rođeni! / Vala bogu kad sam te video, / Te me živa moja želja minu,' *Karadžić*, ii, No. 16, ll. 177–9.

[24] 'Jarko sunce', ibid., l. 184.

[25] '(Moj) bosiljče iz zelene bašče!' Ibid., l. 187. In Serbian mythology basil has a protective magic function: it is used to protect a newborn baby and after the christening the hair cut by the godfather is kept in basil. The girl promised in marriage sends her fiancé a bunch of basil. But basil is also used in funeral rites: it is put round the hand of the dead and is planted on graves. See Š. Kulišić *et al.*, *Srpski mitološki rečnik*, pp. 41–2.

[26] See *Banašević*, pp. 616, 690, 614–15, 707.

(Zagorje). But the imaginative framework of the poem—that of human grandeur and affection born under an unlucky star—is analogous to what we find in most of the greatest imaginative insights into the outlaws' and the border raiders' predicament. This drama opens at the very beginning of the poem when Milić the Ensign, dazzled by the beauty of his bride, asks her mother whether she had 'cast her of gold', 'hammered her of silver' or 'snatched her away from the sun'.[27] Even if the mother answers that God had given her such a beautiful daughter, there is a strong suggestion that such beauty is always doomed. For the mother also says that all her beautiful daughters had died on their way to the wedding, and this might be historically connected with the outlaws' raids on wedding parties:

> 'I had nine like this one,
> For eight of them their mother found husbands,
> But not one of them has she visited,
> They were born under bad stars, poor creatures,
> And arrows kill them on their way.'[28]

The point is not, however, so much that the wedding parties provided worthwhile targets for outlaws and border raiders, but that the greatest occasion of joy and beauty in human life is seen as being under the unlucky star of the outlaws' fate. This is why—in the ensuing scene—the mother 'gives through tears her gift to her son-in-law',[29] for even if her tears could be understood for the moment as an expression of her sorrow at parting with her daughter, they will grow as an ominous foreboding in the narrative development of the poem.

And when the bride and the groom die on their way to their happiness, their burial and the expressions of grief will follow an inverted pattern of the wedding expectations. The bride will be buried 'whence the clear sun rises'[30] and the groom 'whither

---

[27] '(Ili si je) od zlata salila? / (Ili si je) od srebra skovala? / (Ili si je) od sunca otela?' 'Ženidba Milića barjaktara', *Karadžić*, iii, No. 78, ll. 95–8.

[28] 'Devet sam ih takijeh imala, / Osam ih je udomila majka, / Ni jedne ih nije pohodila, / Jer su jadne roda urokljiva, / Na putu ih ustrijeli str'jela', ibid., ll. 107–11.

[29] 'Kroz plač zeta punica dariva', ibid., l. 112.

[30] 'Otkuda se jasno sunce rađa', ibid., l. 193.

the hot sun sets';[31] this sunrise and sunset sum up a wedding day and appear as a symbolic vision of the outlaws' predicament and fate. For at the heart of this image cluster is the vision of the sun as a symbol of death; and this iconic suggestion is rooted in the mother's grief. The lonely helpless mother comes to the foreground of her son's earthly lot:

> The lone mother remained;
> She howled like a cuckoo bird;
> She rolled like a swallow in air;
> She went to her vineyard,
> She cut her hair, she tied the vines,
> She wept and watered the vinestock with her tears,
> She spoke softly to the vineyard:
> 'O vineyard, planted by a dear hand!
> He who planted you
> Will never pluck your grapes again!'[32]

This tragic inversion of the harmony of man and nature is further developed in the poignancy of the mother's insane waiting for the impossible to happen. For after her son's death— even if she knows all there is to know and suffers all there is to suffer—the mother looks, with implacable logic, at the setting sun:

> She speaks, she follows with her eyes the sun:
> 'Thank God for such a blessing!
> Blessed am I, there comes my son!'[33]

The mad gaze of the mother's love, fixed at the sun which had set, wandering after her departed son, is not the end of the nightmare. The mother goes on gazing and catches a glimpse of the rising sun:

> When the sun is in the east,
> Milić's mother comes out,

---

[31] 'Kuda jarko smiruje se sunce', *Karadžić*, iii, No. 78, l. 255.

[32] 'Osta jadna samorana majka, / Ona kuka kako kukavica, / A prevrće kako lastavica; / Ona ide svome vinogradu, / Kosu reže, pa vinograd veže, / Suze lije, čokoće zal'jeva, / Vinogradu tiho progovara: / "Vinograde, mili rukosade! / Ko je tebe mene zasadio, / Nikada te veće brati neće!"' Ibid., ll. 256–65.

[33] 'Pa govori, a za suncem gleda: / "Blago mene i do Boga moga! / Blago mene, eto sina moga!"' Ibid., ll. 268–71.

She looks at the sun and says:
'Blessed am I, there comes my daughter-in-law!
She comes from the spring, she brings cold water,
She is taking my place in my old age!'[34]

The tragically illuminated figures of the son and the daughter-in-law in the nightmare of the mother's grief mirror the nature of the outlaws' dreams and destinies in the epic landscape of the Serbo-Croatian heroic songs. For they suggest a reaching after the impossible, the irrational spiritual courage of an imaginative effort which defies realities. This form of defiance of the actual is lit by a tragic irony from within; the irony springs from the mother's madness which is the only possible form which her love can take.

Finally, it is also significant that at the end of the poem the wedding customs are also inverted for the purposes of a burial ceremony. Instead of the songs of joy and the display of weapons

They reversed their spears,
They led their ring dance in reverse.[35]

As Karadžić tells us in his book about Montenegro, this reflects an actual custom, the Montenegrin custom of approaching a dead friend with the rifle reversed on one's shoulder.[36] There is also some evidence of the reversal of the ring dance, from right to left, as a funeral custom[37] and the inversion implied in these customs is also mirrored in the description of Milić's coffin which is 'sword-hewn'.[38] In short, the inversion of the wedding customs and of the use of weapons is analogous to the inversion of the patriarchal image of harmony between man and nature— the image which lives in the mother's walk in the vineyard and in her eyes which are fixed at the sun. This inversion, this rapture of hopeless expectation, expresses the tragic irony which lies at the heart of the best poems about outlaws and border

[34] 'Kada bude na istoku sunce, / Izilazi Milićeva majka, / Sunce gleda pake progovara: / "Blago mene, eto mi snašice! / Ide s vode, nosi vode ladne, / Hoće mene staru zam'jeniti!" ' Ibid., ll. 274–9.
[35] 'Naopako koplja okrenuše, / Naopako kolo povedoše', ibid., ll. 249–50.
[36] See V. S. Karadžić, *O Crnoj Gori—Razni spisi*, ed. G. Dobrašinović, *Sabrana dela*, xviii, Belgrade, 1972, p. 680.
[37] See *Banašević*, p. 709.
[38] 'Sabljama (mu sanduk) satesaše', loc. cit., l. 252.

raiders. For this is the meaning of history which is voiced in the vision of Old Vujadin's crucifixion on the cross of honour—the crucifixion in which a captured outlaw, old and helpless, with his hands and feet broken, reveals his own self and the commitment, such as it is, for which he has lived and for which he dies. Is not the same kind of inversion—for historically the strength of youth and the terror of a successful raid were certainly much more 'typical' ideals—characteristic of Ivo of Senj who brings 'his right hand in his left' and presents it to his mother as a gift at the moment when he dies, having run away and seen his life as a nightmare of pursuit from which no one can escape? The ultimate purpose of such visionary scenes—in which a whole landscape of actual historical ideals is inverted—can also be glimpsed in Rosnić's division of the plunder in equal shares among the living and the dead, in Grujo's fatherly tenderness, in his effort to console his son by telling him a lie and making him believe that it is only the ropes which are bleeding.

PART SIX

The Struggle for Independence

1. Serbian Rebels and Montenegrin Tribal Warriors

The crisis of the Turkish administrative and military system in the eighteenth century made the taxation in Serbia heavier and more arbitrary. This often led to violence and increased outlawry, and the reforms of Selim III at the end of the century were aimed at curbing the power of the janissaries and making the population along the Turkish borders less hostile to the Ottoman administration. However, in the mounting international crisis which was to lead to the Napoleonic wars, Mustapha Pasha, who ruled Serbia, was forced to welcome janissaries back, among others Osman Pazvan Oglu, who had ruled as an independent military despot in the neighbouring borderland in Romania. The initial intention of the Porte was probably to get an unreliable military leader away from his immediate military support, but the result was that Mustapha Pasha was murdered in 1801 and the four janissary commanders, the four great Dahijas (deys), had a free hand in Serbia. Their economic and military terror antagonized the Turkish spahis as much as the Serbian peasants; and in 1802 many of the spahis were executed after an unsuccessful attempt at a rebellion. During the next two years the Dahijas recruited their own private armies and reduced the new Vizier Hasan Pasha to a puppet in their hands, but the number of outlaws grew. When the Sultan sent a ferman to the Dahijas hinting that he might arm Serbs against them, they decided, in February 1804, to murder all the Serbian district chiefs ('knezovi'). The decision was carried out fairly successfully and the Dahijas survived it for a few months: by August they had all been killed in the revolt of the Serbian population led by Karađorđe.

Initially, the First Serbian Uprising was not a revolt 'against the Sultan, nor necessarily against the highest nominal Turkish authorities in Serbia (the Pashas), nor against the local Turkish landlords, but against an irresponsible soldiery, who reacted violently against attempts from Constantinople to curb their power'.[1] But at the same time the spirit of the rebellion was also shaped from the beginning by the rebels' revolt at the murder of the district chiefs and in this sense it was felt as a desperate national move. Karadžić reports that Karađorđe encouraged the spirit of rebellion by the argument that Turks have decided 'to cut us all down and kill us': 'If we are otherwise going to be bound and die like women at the hands of their horsemen, it is better to die like heroes and men, to make them pay for our lives and to avenge our brothers.'[2]

In the years which followed—owing to Russian help and pressure on Turkey, to the failure of many rounds of negotiation with the Grand Porte and, above all, to the great Serbian victories over several major Ottoman armies—the spirit of desperate rebellion grew into the defiant mood of fighting for total national freedom. The first major victory for the rebels came in 1805 when Hafiz Pasha, the newly nominated Vizier of Belgrade, led his army of about twenty thousand men to Serbia. In Paraćin he refused the rebels' demand to use the old route, the Sultan's highway, leading from Jagodina to Grocka through dangerous gorges and forests. He started with several cartloads of small caps, instead of fezzes, and plenty of hangman's halters for any who might welcome him in a different spirit. He decided to do away with the Serbian rebels' trenches defended by about two thousand and five hundred men at Ivankovac, near the monastery of Ravanica. He did not think of this undertaking as a major battle, but on the first day of fighting his losses were heavy and on the second day Karađorđe came to help with five thousand men and three cannon. The Turkish army dispersed in panic and the Pasha himself retreated as far as Niš where he died suddenly. A little later Smederevo on the Danube, the strongest Turkish fortress in Serbia, was also taken by the rebels. And the next year brought the greatest military triumph for Karađorđe and his fighters: the Serbian forces, estimated at about five to seven thousand soldiers, about one thousand and five hundred to two thousand horsemen and four cannon, defeated the Turkish army which

---

[1] D. Wilson, *The Life and Times of Vuk Stefanović Karadžić 1787–1864*, p. 28. Chapter Three of this book gives a good account of the social and historical background of the First Serbian Uprising.

[2] See ibid., p. 38.

came from Bosnia and consisted of about forty thousand men and strong artillery, in the Battle of Mišar, near Šabac in Mačva.[3] Is it surprising that such great victories should become immediately subjects for heroic songs? For at this time—as Karadžić tells us—there was a *gusle* in every peasant house in the mountainous areas of southern Serbia where every adult peasant knew at least some fragments of several heroic songs.[4] And, of course, many of the old songs came to a new epic life in the changed historical circumstances of the First Serbian Uprising.

However, the heroic singing about the struggle for independence was not shaped only by a sense of triumph but also by an awareness of great ordeals and disasters. In 1809, for instance, major Turkish military operations against the Serbian rebels were for the first time successful. The Turkish forces defeated the Serbian rebels who were defending their trenches on Mount Čegar near the village of Kamenica, commanding access to Niš which was not only an important stronghold of the rebels but also on their major route of communication with the Russian forces. But when the Turks invaded the trenches after bitter resistance, Serbian commander Sinđelić fired his revolver at his own ammunition reserves and caused an explosion in which he was killed with all his troops, together with many of the advancing Turkish soldiers. The Pasha of Niš commemorated his victory by having about a thousand Serbian skulls built into a square tower. Thus he immortalized both himself and his enemies in a war memorial which still stands on the right side of the road leading from Niš to Pirot.

But this did not really help. In 1810 the Serbian rebels held again all the lost territories in Serbia and it was not until 1813, when Serbia was attacked by Turkish armies from all sides, that the Ottoman rule was re-established, at least for the next two years. At this time, however, tens of thousands of Serbs emigrated temporarily across the river Sava to the territories controlled by the Austrians—among them Vuk Stefanović Karadžić and some of his best poets, like Tešan Podrugović and Filip Višnjić. Many of the best poems in Karadžić's collections were recorded in this area—some in the interval before the

---

[3] See *Enciklopedija Jugoslavije*, vi, Zagreb, 1965, p. 136.
[4] See 'Predgovor', *Karadžić*, i, p. 529.

struggle for independence flamed up again in 1815 and, led by Miloš Obrenović, resulted in a combination of fighting and diplomacy, a succession of agreements and mutual deceptions, which brought, step by step, Serbian autonomy and complete independence in the decades to come.

The Montenegrin struggle for independence was in a sense analogous in so far as it was carried out by most members of the adult male population in political circumstances in which the Turkish authority could never be fully exercised. But the struggle went on for centuries, and was marked by Montenegrin tribal organization and the poverty of the land in the valleys among the karst mountains where communications were difficult and some of the areas practically inaccessible. Very soon after the conquest of Montenegro in 1499 the Ottoman administration was made to realize that it could not introduce its feudal system of spahis who would provide military service, keeping the taxes for themselves. Instead, in the early sixteenth century the system of hearth-tax was introduced: it meant that no poll-tax could be levied, that the inhabitants lived on the sultan's land, were spared the evils of arbitrary local Turkish rule and had to help the Turkish army only on their territory. Whether this privilege is to be explained by local poverty, by the heroic Montenegrin resistance, by its geography or by the vicinity of Venetian Dalmatia, it meant considerable local autonomy for the Montenegrins and sharpened their appetite for more.

During the Turco-Venetian wars in the sixteenth and the seventeenth centuries Montenegrins sided with Venice and often had to fight off the raids of the Turkish military expeditions which kept coming back to re-establish their rule. The Montenegrin participation in the Russo-Turkish war in 1711 ended in a Turkish military expedition which devastated Montenegro two years later, but very soon Montenegro had to be reconquered. In 1756 the Montenegrin tribal warriors defeated the Turkish armies which attacked their country from three main directions, but in 1785 Mahmud Bušatlija led a Turkish army which took Cetinje. However, the fighting went on and in the later battles at the end of the century Bušatlija was killed and his forces defeated and driven out of the country. In short, right from the sixteenth to the beginning of the nineteenth century there was hardly any lack of heroic subjects in which the clashes with the Turks could be seen on a large scale.

The deep historical analogy between the Serbian and the Montenegrin struggle for independence is not surprising: in medieval times Serbia and Montenegro were one state; there was also the bond of a common religion and many customs and later links between the Montenegrin monastic life and the retreating Serbian culture, as well as the common expectations from and historical sympathies for Russia. Even if the Montenegrin organized struggle went on for a much longer time, at the beginning of the nineteenth century the battle was waged in both countries by desperately courageous fighters united into major armies not by training or recruitment, not by the morality of a band of outlaws living in the woods, but by their determination to survive in spite of the political, military, and economic odds of history. The fact that Petar Petrović Njegoš, the greatest figure in Montenegrin political, ecclesiastic and spiritual history, dedicated his masterpiece *The Mountain Wreath* (1847) to Karađorđe, the leader of the Serbian rebels, is perhaps only a political gesture and a literary symbol of this historical sharing and communion. But its human reality can be best grasped in the heroic songs about the Serbian and Montenegrin struggle for independence, in the unity of their moral idiom and poetic language, with all that this implies.

2. To the Last Man

In the early nineteenth century heroic songs the contemporary historical subjects were largely seen through the eyes of the epic tradition and its imaginative and moral idiom which had the continuity of several centuries behind it. Thus in 'The Battle of Loznica', recorded in the monastery of Šišatovac in Srem in 1815, the most popular blind *guslar* Filip Višnjić tells the story of the siege of a Serbian town in which, only five years earlier, he himself kept up the rebels' spirit of resistance by his song.[1] But when he describes the meeting of the captains of the Serbian army which will come to rescue the besieged town, he phrases the commander's call for battle in the formula of the curse on the prospective traitor:

> 'Who betrays us, may summer betray him!
> May he have no harvest of white grain!
> May his old mother never look on him!
> May his dear sister never swear by him!'[2]

Not only that the 'old mother' takes us back to many of the earlier *bugarštice* and decasyllabic poems;[3] but so does the formal pattern of the curse on the prospective traitor. Moreover, the wording of the curse—which must be rooted deeply in much earlier unrecorded folklore past—is so universal that we find it in the poems recorded from many other singers: blind Stepanija's 'Saints Divide the Treasure', Old Raško's 'Wedding

[1] See V. Nedić, 'Filip Višnjić' in V. Nedić, ed., *Narodna književnost*, pp. 325–7 (this article was first published as a separate booklet: *Filip Višnjić*, Belgrade, 1961).

[2] 'Ko izdao, izdalo ga ljeto! / Bijelo mu žito ne rodilo! / Stara njega majka ne viđela! / Njim se mila sestra ne zaklela!' 'Boj na Loznici', *Karadžić*, iv, No. 33, ll. 421–4.

[3] See, for instance, *Bogišić*, No. 7, ll. 16, 31, 70, 80; No. 21, ll. 25, 81, 87; No. 45, ll. 1, 14, 88 (as Bogišić breaks l. 26 into two lines, this is l. 87 in PS, No. 12). For the occurrence of 'old mother' ('stara majka') in the decasyllabic poems see *Bogišić*, No. 68, l. 13 (in fact l. 14 as l. 13 is missing; cf. Mazarović–Pantić, No. 485); *Gesemann*, No. 58, l. 59; No. 82, l. 7; No. 129, ll. 2, 128.

of Prince Lazar' and, in the most closely parallel form, in 'The Various Pieces from Kosovo Poems' which Karadžić recorded from his father.[4]

And when in the same poem—'The Battle of Loznica'—the rescue army comes to rest on its way to the battle, their rest is described in the lines which follow the syntactic and phrasal patterns of the songs which had been recorded much earlier:

> Whoever is hot is chilled with water,
> Whoever is thirsty drinks cold water.[5]

Is this not an echo of the voice which was also recorded in an eighteenth-century Dalmatian decasyllabic song in the description of the rose on a girl's grave:

> Round the rose water was channelled . . .
> Who is fine, let him pluck the rose,
> Who is thirsty, let him drink the water.[6]

And does not the phrase 'who is thirsty, let him drink the water' also occur in two poems recorded in Slavonia about 1720 in *The Erlangen Manuscript*—again connected with funeral customs which take us back to the distant past?[7] But the repetition of this phrasing is perhaps as characteristic as the radical change of its meaning and context in Višnjić's poem. The whole formulaic pattern has been deprived of its ancient funereal connotations and harnessed to describe the Serbian rebels on their march to victory.

Similarly in 'The Battle of Čačak'—written down from an unknown Serbian peasant in the district of Rudnik—the gathering of the Turkish army is represented in the formulaic patterns which were often used to describe the gatherings of outlaws and can be traced back to the earliest recorded decasyllabic songs. But at the same time the description

---

[4] See above pp. 108–9, 126 and particularly p. 160 (the wording of Prince Lazar's curse of prospective traitors here is very close to Višnjic's wording in 'The Battle of Loznica').

[5] 'Ko s' ugrij'o, vodom s' razlađuje, / Ko je žedan, ladnu vodu pije', *Karadžić*, iv, No. 33, ll. 448–9.

[6] 'Oko ruže vodu navratili . . . / Ko je gizdav neka ružu bere, / Ko je žedan neka vodu pije.' *Bogišić*, No. 95, ll. 115, 117–18. See above pp. 78–9.

[7] See note 53, p. 79.

sparkles with a mischievous parody which was never associated
with these formulas before:

> Under the banner he gathered heroes,
> And each of them was drunker than the next,
> And each a better hero than the next,
> And fit to overtake and run away
> And to endure in terrible places,
> The hero who cares not if he is killed,
> Whose sword is his father and mother,
> His mountain-cloak—his home when he needs it,
> Who does not know any faithful love,
> But thinks to marry soon
> A girl from Morava or Šumadija.[8]

Of course, the mustering of the fighters under the banner is both
a historical custom[9] and an epic formula; the ability 'to overtake and run away', 'to endure in terrible places', the readiness
to die, the patriarchal sense of loneliness of 'the mountain-
cloak' as a 'home' in which swords replace parents and in which
there are no 'faithful loves'—all these are elements of the
standard run of formulas embodying the outlaws' historical
situation, their mood and their sense of their own destiny.[10] On
the other hand, however, they had never been described as
'drunkards' or eager to marry foreign wives: the halo of
ancient epic dignity is used here for mock-heroic purposes
because traditional formulas serve the additional function of
ridiculing the enemy's army. Even if the device of parodic
usage is not fully controlled and far from being mastered in tone,
the freedom of its usage mirrors the spirit in which the rebels
challenge their fate, their past, and their future.

It is not, however, only this calmly defiant mood which is
the most characteristic feature of the poems about the struggle

---

[8] 'Pod barjake pokupi junake, / Sve bekriju goreg od gorega, / A junaka
boljeg od boljega, / Koji može stići i uteći / I na strašnom mjestu postajati, /
A ne žali junak poginuti; / Kom je sablja i otac i majka, / Kabanica kuća đe
mu drago, / A za vjernu ljubav i ne znade, / No se misli skoro oženiti / Ja
Moravkom, ja li Šumadinkom', 'Boj na Čačku', *Karadžić*, iv, No. 46, ll. 56–66.

[9] See V. Latković, 'Beleške i objašnjenja' in V. S. Karadžić, *Srpske narodne
pjesme*, iv, Belgrade, 1958, p. 584. Latković's 'Beleške i objašnjenja' will
henceforth be referred to as *Latković*.

[10] See above pp. 69–70, 237–9, 246.

for independence. They are also rooted in the awareness that their subject is not a single combat or a local raid, but the fighting which has nation-wide scope and significance. Every particular detail is seen in them as part of the decisive battle which has flamed up on all sides. Thus a new mythic situation is born out of contemporary history: the fighting does not begin or end in a green wood, the fighters do not come together on St George's Day in spring to disperse again on St Demetrius' Day in the middle of autumn.[11] They do not attack only from ambush or kill only for plunder; they assault the whole of their historical future and their voice thunders from the threshold of freedom even if it vibrates with all the memories of the national martyrdom which live in the epic diction inherited from the past.

This new awareness and its corresponding epic mood pervades, for instance, the great Montenegrin poem 'The Piperi and Tahir Pasha' in which a Montenegrin tribe refuses the Turkish Pasha's request for tax in blood. Finally, a seventeen year old boy leads his tribe from 'their caves, the walled up houses',[12] the ancient resort of the outlaws but now the abode of the whole tribe, and drives the Turkish army away from his part of the country. The same historical voice thunders in 'The Beginning of the Revolt Against the Dahijas', the greatest Serbian epic poem about the struggle for freedom. The scope and the mood of the prospective fighting are clearly outlined in Karađorđe's address to the Turks:

> 'Even if all seven kings should arise
> To quiet us, they could not reconcile us,
> We shall fight to the last man, my friends!'[13]

[11] Hence the popular decasyllabic utterance which Karadžić quotes as a proverb: 'St George's Day—outlaws' meeting, / St Demetrius' Day—outlaw's parting' ('Đurđev danak hajdučki sastanak, / Mitrov danak hajdučki rastanak.' *Srpske narodne poslovice*, p. 105). St George's Day falls on April 23, St Demetrius' Day on October 26 according to the Orthodox Calendar—this is what made the two well-known Christian festivals the meeting and the parting days for outlaws.

[12] '(I) pećine kuće zazidane', 'Piperi i Tahir-paša', *Karadžić*, iv, No. 6, l. 118.

[13] 'Da ustane svi sedam kraljeva, / Da nas mire, pomirit' nas ne će: / Bićemo se, more, do jednoga!' 'Početak bune protiv dahija', *Karadžić*, iv, No. 24, ll. 585-7.

This readiness of the whole nation to fight 'to the last man' introduces a new protagonist into the epic landscape—'the poor rayah',[14] the non-Moslem plebs, who have been roused by despair to wage their battle for life or death, who have come to disregard not only the odds of history but also the voice of their own village headmen and district chiefs who still believe in negotiating with Turkish rulers. And the toiling pariahs of the Turkish social dispensation 'grow like grass out of the earth'[15]—with blind, primal force which nothing can stop. The quality of this force has something of a natural phenomenon about it; this is why in 'The Battle of Loznica' Bogićević Anto keeps up the spirit of the defenders by shouting like 'a hawk' from the ramparts of the fortress.[16] And this is why in 'The Battle of Montenegrins Against Mahmut Pasha' the fighters appear as 'the dark wolves of the mountains',[17] their captains as 'winged eagles',[18] their ensigns as 'grey hawks',[19] even if it is clear from the context that these tokens of woods and beasts do not refer to a band of outlaws but to the army of a prince bishop.

The imagery in which a collective struggle is seen as a natural phenomenon is particularly characteristic of many of the songs which Karadžić wrote down from his most popular singer Filip Višnjić. Thus in his 'Battle of Salaš'—in which the Serbian rayah is clearly the main protagonist—the bleating sheep and bellowing cattle grieve for their native land while they are being driven away by the Turks so that their voices would 'break the heart of a wild beast'.[20] And in the vision of this blind singer the battle itself is seen through the 'fog' spreading 'from the earth to the sky', hiding the 'clouds' and the 'sun'.[21] Similarly, in 'Stanić Stanojlo' the shot of a rifle cracks 'like the thunder of

---

[14] 'Sirotinja raja' (or, more rarely, 'raja sirotinja'), *Karadžić*, iv, No. 24, ll. 145, 182.

[15] 'Usta (raja) k'o iz zemlje trava', ibid., l. 569.

[16] '(Viče Anto, k'o da) soko (klikće)' *Karadžić*, iv, No. 33, l. 158.

[17] '(To su) mrki od planine vuci', 'Boj Crnogoraca s Mahmut-pašom', *Karadžić*, iv, No. 10, l. 216.

[18] 'Krilati orlovi', ibid., l. 218.

[19] 'Sivi sokolovi', ibid., l. 220.

[20] 'U zvjerki bi srce prepuknulo', 'Boj na Salašu', *Karadžić*, iv, No. 28, l. 278. See below pp. 340–1.

[21] '(Pade) magla od neba do zemlje, / (Nit' se vidi) neba ni oblaka, / (Viš' njih jarko pomrčalo) sunce', ibid., ll. 309–11.

heaven'[22] and in 'The Battle of Loznica' the earth 'groans', the
skies 'rattle'[23] and 'the red flame' is 'tied into the sky'.[24] The
same sweep of the 'natural' imagery of the collective bloodbath
of history is to be found in 'Bjelić Ignjatije' in the description
of a grand outlaw captain who has grown into a leader of the
rebels' army, of the Serbian soldiery as destitute as the fighters
in the woods:

> When Zeko shouted at them,
> He tied a red flame into the sky,
> And the leaves flew off the trees.[25]

Such image clusters, deeply rooted in the natural world, sum up
the collective spirit and the historical mood of the myth about
the Serbian and Montenegrin struggle for freedom.

However, the road from a historical myth to great epic
poetry is always uncertain and particularly tricky when it has
to be built with the themes of immediate, contemporary history.
This is why—with the exception of several major poems and
many details which show that the singer's imagination has come
to full grips with his material—the vision of historical cruelties
and conflicts is not always meaningful and is often enslaved in
the nature of its material. Such failures are not perhaps as many
as the material seems to promise, but it is significant that in the
Montenegrin poems Krsto Kresojević, for instance, triumphs
over his enemy by 'slaughtering him like a living sheep',[26]
that Mujo Marunović spills his enemy's 'guts over the vale',[27]
that Pero Mrkonjić 'opens a window' in his enemy's back.[28]
As regards the Serbian poems such instances of faithful re-
production of history can be seen in the occasional malicious
presentation of the sorrow of the Turkish wives and mothers,[29]

[22] '(Puče puška,) k'o grom od nebesa', 'Stanić Stanojlo', *Karadžić*, iv, No. 43, l. 73.

[23] 'Zemlja ječi, vedro nebo zveči', *Karadžić*, iv, No. 33, l. 597.

[24] 'Crven plamen do neba svezali', ibid., l. 546.

[25] 'Kade Zeko na njih podviknuo, / Crven plamen za nebo svezao, / Sve sa gore odlijeće lišće', 'Bjelić Ignjatije', *Karadžić*, iv, No. 35, ll. 351–3.

[26] '(Pa) ga zakla kako živa brava', 'Po smrti Uskok-Karimana' ('After the Death of Kariman the Border Raider'), *Karadžić*, iv, No. 15, l. 105.

[27] 'I prosu mu trbuh po dolini', ibid., l. 114.

[28] 'I na leđi pendžer otvorio', *Karadžić*, iv, No. 16, l. 136.

[29] A major instance can be found in the famous 'Battle of Mišar' ('Boj na Mišaru', *Karadžić*, iv, No. 30). See below pp. 281–2.

in the request that the river Sava should 'eat up our enemies',[30] in the way in which Luko Lazarević 'slaughters' his enemy 'like a white lamb',[31] in the scene in which an enemy 'puts a belt of guts around his waist',[32] and in the standard couplet in which the Serbian 'swords' keep 'flashing' and 'the dead Turkish heads yawning'.[33] There are, finally, a few colourful curses, but surprisingly enough—considering the richness of the historical material—this exhausts the list.

However, this cruel and lively kitsch is not the weakest spot of these poems. A far more widespread and, perhaps, more serious flaw is their imaginative monotony that stems from the singer's urge not to leave anything unsaid. The issues of contemporary history must have been so fascinating for the singers and their audience that even the most gifted among them felt no need to leave anything out, to 'improve' on the material which gave so much satisfaction in its raw form. For after all the basic aim of these songs was not, like that of many others, to invoke the ghosts of history in forms which would make them speak to the present, but to keep the audience informed about what was going on and sharpen its appetite for more and greater triumphs. How could a singer or his audience ever tire of hearing enumerated all the Turkish captains who were killed in the battle of Mišar? Could anything be more exciting than the tale of the Turkish vizier who, after the initial Serbian success in the first two years of the uprising, called up his army from twelve different regions of the country in 1806 in order to attack the Serbian fortifications on the main Constantinople highway, between Belgrade and Niš, at Deligrad, the fortifications which commanded the access to Karađorđe's Serbia? Does not each of the twelve regions deserve at least three or four lines? And is it not equally exciting to listen to the singer tell, at the same length and in the same sequence, how

[30] 'Žderi, Savo, naše dušmanine', *Karadžić*, iv, No. 30, l. 143.

[31] 'Zakla (Pejzu) kao jagnje b'jelo', 'Luko Lazarević i Pejzo' ('Luko Lazarević and Pejzo'), *Karadžić*, iv, No. 34, l. 284.

[32] 'Opasa se crijevima (Suljo)', 'Pop Dragović i Marko Taušan' ('Father Dragović and Marko Taušan'), *Karadžić*, iv, No. 42, l. 248.

[33] 'Kako Srpske sablje sijevaju, / Mrtve Turske glave zijevaju', 'Miloš Stoićević i Meho Orugdžijć' ('Miloš Stoićević and Meho Orugdžijć'), *Karadžić*, iv, No. 32, ll. 319–20. See also *Karadžić*, iv, No. 33, ll. 614–15; No. 39, ll. 396–7.

the commanders of all the regions receive the call, even if their response is bound to be the same—as it is in 'The Battle of Deligrad'?[34] And is not the traditional language of heroic poetry the most resonant medium for all the news which has to be told? And perhaps even the description of maces and spears in the historical battles which were largely fought with rifles and cannon are not as anachronistic as they seem to the modern reader. For after all many of the rebels were armed initially with clubs and pitchforks which could be seen with more truth and dignity as traditional weapons than could more recent military equipment.

And, last but not least, the traditional language of heroic poetry was easy to understand and in this sense ideally suited for the purposes of political propaganda. This is why the informative and persuasive functions of language in these poems often threaten its potential imaginative life; what is, however, more surprising is that great poetry so often survives. A sporadic word or image suddenly makes a lively imaginative response to an actual historical detail or perception; the immediacy and the poignancy of an occasional motif carries the singer away; the historical situations and personalities, the customs deeply rooted in the local soil, take on a moving significance and the representation of history comes to live also as part of a wider mythic landscape. In this landscape the songs about the Serbian rebels and the Montenegrin tribal warriors have many basic features in common, but they also abound in the distinctive characteristics of their local social and historical circumstances, which can be grasped more easily within their immediate context and invite a separate examination.

[34] 'Boj na Deligradu', *Karadžić*, iv, No. 31.

3. In Montenegro

Harsh and monotonous as the karst on which they flourished, the Montenegrin poems in Karadžić's collection remember well, sometimes too well, the history which went into their making (for their basic epic topography see Map 1). Many of them tell of the Turkish military expeditions and punitive drives into Montenegro; some describe the desperate resistance to the brutal forms of tax-collecting, or the race for life of the Montenegrins who escape from Turkish prisons.

Most of these poems, however, seldom offer more than documentary historical interest—moving and significant as this often is. Thus in 'Lazar Pecirep'—which Karadžić recorded from a Montenegrin farm-labourer who came to Serbia from the Montenegrin area of Morača—the great outlaw remembers his younger days when he lived happily as a cattle raiser in the neighbouring mountains in Herzegovina until a party of forty Moslem townsmen killed forty of his lambs for dinner. The greatest scene in the poem—as lifelike as it is moving—is the moment when Lazar cannot stand the sad look in the eyes of his ewes which miss their young ones: he comes to clash with the Turks and his triumph results in a Turkish punitive military expedition which destroys his home and turns him into an outlaw. But the enumeration of his later victories over the Turkish heroes is far less compelling than the editor's note from which we learn that Lazar actually developed a zest for burning and impaling his Turkish enemies until he was caught by them and ended up on a Turkish pale, smoking defiantly for three days before he died.[1]

Similarly, perhaps, there is considerable intrinsic documentary interest in the decasyllabic tales about Kariman, the border raider, who was killed by a young Serb while trying to rape his mother and whose death the Moslems of Herzegovina tried in vain to avenge. But typical and significant as rape and vengeance were historically, there is again perhaps more intrinsic human drama and interest in Karadžić's note which

[1] 'Lazar Pecirep', *Karadžić*, iv, No. 7. See *Latković*, p. 495.

tells us how Kariman came to accept Islam. He lived, we are told, as a poor and lonely Montenegrin farmer until he gave up his Christian faith, embittered because one of his high-handed Montenegrin neighbours robbed his mother and sister when they were carrying home wine to celebrate their family patronal festival. It was this, apparently, that made him move to neighbouring Herzegovina and become the scourge of the Montenegrin borderlands.[2]

An interest more historical and human than imaginative is also found in the versified tales in which the vengeance motif operates from a more remote background. Thus 'The Death of Alaj-bey Čengijć'—sent to Karadžić from Cetinje and recorded from a singer in the vicinity of Trebinje in Herzegovina[3]—is interesting because it connects the epic landscape of the well-to-do border raiders in semi-regular Venetian service in the Bay of Kotor with the fighting of the inland Montenegrin tribal warriors. Besides, the murder of the hated Turkish oppressor in this poem is instigated as much by the Montenegrin zest for plunder as by the urge to avenge the condition of 'the poor rayah', their Christian brethren in Herzegovina, who have to toil for the Bey who whips them until 'he drives the flesh into the shirt'.[4] This, of course, suggests a significant historical step in the struggle for independence, the moment when the tribal loyalties begin to be shaped into some form of national awareness which also has its social colouring; and the ensuing pursuit and the successful escape are also a reliable part of the general historical picture.

The realistic texture is equally dense in the poems which describe the fighting of the Montenegrin tribes among themselves, sometimes divided by the Montenegrin and Turkish frontiers but often connected by mutual treacheries ('The Montenegrin Priest and Vuk Koprivica').[5] The stories about tribal bloodshed because of family quarrels ('Janko Laketić and Petar Bošković')[6] or because of sheep-stealing ('The Piperi

---

[2] See the introductory note to 'Uskok Kariman' ('Kariman the Border Raider'), *Karadžić*, iv, No. 14, p. 77.
[3] 'Smrt Alaj-bega Čengijća', *Karadžić*, iv, No. 8. See *Latković*, p. 498.
[4] 'Ućeriva u košulju meso', *Karadžić*, iv, No. 8, l. 156.
[5] 'Pop Crnogorac i Vuk Koprivica', *Karadžić*, iv, No. 3.
[6] 'Janko Laketić i Petar Bošković', *Karadžić*, iv, No. 17.

and the Crnčani')[7] also add to the versatility and colour of the general historical picture, even if they raise the question whether a prosaic and less 'heroic' literary form would have been more suitable to their content.

But apart from the interest of a rich chronicle of the times which were exceptionally colourful even by the standards of Balkan history, some of the Montenegrin epics show a deeper imaginative response to their fascinating material. Sometimes an epic chronicle moves towards the regions of great poetry, and so we find, for instance, several powerful dramatic scenes in the fairly ineptly told story about Vuk Mićunović, an early eighteenth-century commander of the Montenegrin border fighters who won the highest Venetian decorations, including a gold medal for courage and the title of a 'sirdar'. Such is the evocation of the moment after Vuk Mićunović has called his followers, his 'hawks',[8] to the decisive assault of the city gates of Trebinje:

> He seized the iron ring with his hand,
> He struck against the gate with his foot,
> And then Vuk looked round,
> But there was no one else with him,
> The whole army was in the flat meadow
> And Vuk was alone at the white gate.[9]

In the intense authenticity of such a detail of heroic loneliness the 'bush' of history 'burns' with considerable imaginative fire, perhaps only matched again at the end of this mediocre poem. In the last scene Vuk Mićunović is dying together with his wounded fellow-fighter Ivan Popović who had also shown mad daring in action:

> All the night Vuk Mićunović asked
> About Ivan Popović of the Njeguši,
> Whether his soul would leave his body,
> Ivan kept asking if Vuk was dying,

[7] 'Piperi i Crnčani', *Karadžić*, iv, No. 21.

[8] 'Moji sokolovi', 'Pogibija Vuka Mićunovića' ('The Death of Vuk Mićunović'), *Karadžić*, iv, No. 2, l. 68.

[9] 'Za brnjicu rukom dovatio, / I u vrata nogom udario, / Pa pogleda oko sebe Vuko, / Al' sa Vukom niđe niko nema, / No sva vojska nasred polja ramna, / A sam Vuko na bijela vrata.' Ibid., ll. 72–7.

3. Tsar Uroš in the Church of the Holy Trinity in Pljevlja.

4. Stojan Janković, Historical Museum of Croatia, Department of Serbs in Croatia, Zagreb.

> Until both their souls left their bodies,
> Each one asking about the other.[10]

But this compelling simplicity is not achieved only in such highly exceptional scenes, as lonely in the epic tradition as the assault of the deserted captain on a hard city gate or the warriors who ask after each other's health as both lie dying, but also in some of the motifs which have much wider historical and epic currency. Such is, for instance, the poignant gradation of loss in 'The Three Prisoners', when the captured Montenegrin heroes come to bewail their fate. The first grieves for his young wife whom he has left at home uncaressed, the second for his great treasure, a helpless mother and 'a sister without a brother to swear by'.[11] But their misery becomes only the framework of what the third has to say:

> 'I also have my house and my estate,
> And in the house my old mother,
> The true love who was brought me recently,
> And a dear sister unmarried;
> But I grieve for none of these,
> I grieve that I will die,
> Die today without having avenged myself.'[12]

The scope of destitution is mirrored in the afterthought which overshoots even the concept of blood vengeance, the ultimate hope in the Montenegrin historical despair. And the same kind of epic take-off from the runway of mediocre epic singing is achieved again at the end of this poem when Duke Vuksan outwits his executioner, runs like a hunted beast, and answers the men who warn him not to cross the bridge on the Bojana because he will be in mortal danger:

> 'If there is no way forward,
> There is no way back either.'[13]

[10] 'Pita svu noć Mićunović-Vuče / Za Njeguša Popović-Ivana, / Hoće li mu ispanuti duša, / Ivan pita, umrije li Vuko, / Dok objema ispanula duša, / Pitajući jedan za drugoga.' Ibid., ll. 155–60.

[11] 'I sestrica bez bratske zakletve', 'Tri sužnja', *Karadžić*, iv, No. 4, l. 32.

[12] 'I ja imam dvore i timare, / I u dvoru ostarilu majku, / Vjernu ljubu skoro dovedenu / I sestricu milu neudatu; / Al' ja toga sad ništa ne žalim, / Već ja žalim, đe ću poginuti, / Poginuti danas bez zamjene.' Ibid., ll. 37–43.

[13] 'Ako tamo kud naprijed nemam, / Ni natrag se nemam kud vratiti.' Ibid., ll. 118–19.

The serene spirit of this awareness that one has to face history even when there is no way out, round or through touches one of the most characteristic heroic chords of the Montenegrin singing—the chord of calm, unpretentious dignity in despair. And the same heroic clarity of mind—which has no need to close its eyes in the face of the inevitable realities—is also found in another poem when a mother comes to instruct her son to accept the challenge of the Turkish aga to fight him:

'I had better be left without you, my only son,
Than have you live in such shame.'[14]

Finally, some such moments of transitory epic illumination show a deep formulaic kinship with the Serbian poems about the predicament of the Bosnian and Serbian outlaws. Thus the claim of the great Bosnian outlaw Old Novak that he 'can catch up and run away' and 'endure in terrible places' is varied in the request of the Montenegrin outlaw Lazar Pecirep, when he tells his blood-brother that each of the fighters left with him must be a man

'Who is fit to overtake and run away,
And stand his ground in a tight place,
And give his hand to a wounded friend,
And strike his sword against the sharp sword,
Who does not care if he should die.'[15]

The substitution of the 'tight' place for the 'terrible' place and the addition of the moral duty to help a wounded friend are perhaps as significant as the repetition of the standard run of formulas which mirror such an intense sense of the Montenegrin history.

And yet such an illumination of history in Montenegrin heroic songs is fully achieved and sustained on a large narrative and dramatic scale in only one of the Montenegrin poems in Karadžić's collection. It is perhaps significant that this poem— 'The Piperi and Tahir Pasha'—has a major feature in common

[14] 'Radija sam bez tebe jednoga, / No da tako pod sramotu živiš.' 'Aga od Meduna i Jovan Babović' ('The Aga of Medun and Jovan Babović'), *Karadžić*, iv, No. 19, ll. 19–20.

[15] 'Koji može stići i uteći, / Na tijesnu mjestu pričekati, / Za ranjena privatiti druga, / I na oštru udariti ćordu, / Kome nije žao poginuti', 'Lazar Pecirep', *Karadžić*, iv, No. 7, ll. 317–21. See also above p. 246.

with 'The Beginning of the Revolt Against the Dahijas', the greatest heroic song about the Serbian Uprising: the distant epic perspective in which history is dispersed and transformed into a great number of vivid if unreliable details which hold together as a myth illuminating a historical moment in terms of an intense human and moral drama. Both poems were written down from blind singers—the Serbian one from the great master Filip Višnjić and the Montenegrin from Đuro Milutinović-Montenegrin who brought a message from the Montenegrin Prince Bishop to Karađorđe in 1809, at the critical time of the Turkish successes and the great crisis of the First Serbian Uprising.[16] The distant perspective, the imaginative moulding of the material and its mythic unity are achieved in Višnjić's poem by the singer's command of many of the different voices of the traditional decasyllabic diction so that all the past is brought to a head in a vision of a moment of contemporary history, whereas Milutinović picks up a distant subject from early eighteenth-century Montenegrin history, which enables him to work freely into it his own dramatic sense and wide experience of the Montenegrin struggle for survival. The distance of the historical theme enables him to get many of the actual details 'wrong', to reshape them or displace them so that they should fit his general imaginative pattern.

His poem tells the story of Montenegrin opposition to the brutal forms of Turkish tax-collecting—a story particularly typical and 'true' in its setting and time for the area of the tribe of the Piperi in the early eighteenth century. The Piperi had lived for centuries in the north of Podgorica (Titograd), on the right bank of the river Morača, mostly as farmers and cattle raisers. Apart from the good farmland by the river and excellent climate in the valley opening to the Mediterranean south and the lake of Skadar, there were also good pastures on the slopes of the rising mountains and, higher up, plenty of rock, stone and karst to take refuge in. In the vicinity, a little further up the river, there was also the great monastery of Morača, founded by a grandson of Stefan Nemanja, an important religious, cultural, and political centre and, further beyond it, wild mountains closing the area from the north. As this area was not

[16] See V. S. Karadžić, 'Predgovor', *Karadžić*, iv, p. 369.

a part of Montenegro at the beginning of the eighteenth century, its population had to pay poll-tax (*harač*) and was often exposed to the military terror of the neighbouring Turkish garrisons in Podgorica and Nikšić. So when Milutinović sings about Tahir Pasha—who was actually the Turkish vizier in Skadar from 1708 to 1712—and his order that the Piperi should pay their poll-tax or have their villages burnt, the general picture is true to history, even if the lively details of the Turkish request for twelve hostages and eight girls may have only a very distant historical root. As regards the historical stature of the hero of the poem—the seventeen-year old boy Pejo Mrčarić—scholars tell us that there was in fact a Pejo Mrčarica living in the tribe of Piperi at the beginning of the eighteenth century.[17] And who can prove that the singer did not have him in mind? Of course, it is quite obvious why a patriotic Montenegrin singer found it easier to remember correctly the name of the Turkish vizier than that of his own hero who had also lived a century earlier; and it may be worth noting that the singer invented some epically sonorous names for the local villages and got some of the other names, including those of the neighbouring tribes, wrong —probably, we are told, because he had been living for quite some time in Serbia when his poem was written down.[18] How important his contact with Serbian epic singing must have been in his dramatic and powerful shaping of his story is another question; that he knew it well is clearly mirrored in Karadžić's statement that Milutinović succeeded in getting more people to subscribe to his collections than anyone else.[19] But there is little doubt that this contact and the imaginative freedom offered by his distant historical subject account for the superiority of his achievement over the Montenegrin and many Serbian songs which were made up of detailed knowledge of actual contemporary history.

The imaginative liveliness of many diverse details clustering into a great epic theme is clearly foreshadowed at the very beginning of this poem. In the opening lines the Turkish Pasha threatens that he will 'burn all the Piperi to the last house',[20]

---

[17] See *Latković*, p. 494.   [18] See ibid.

[19] See 'Predgovor', *Karadžić*, iv, p. 369.

[20] 'Sve Pipere listom popaliti', 'Piperi i Tahir-paša', *Karadžić*, iv, No. 6, l. 27.

unless the tribe and their priest agree to pay the poll-tax for
seven years, give eight of their girls to his soldiers and send
twelve of their best men as hostages, including the young
seventeen-year-old boy Pejo Mrčarić—

> 'Without Pejo I will not accept one'.[21]

This opening reveals a reliable command of an exciting epic and
historical voice, and the moment when the Piperi hold council
and decide how to face Pasha's threat is also given with the
dramatic sense characteristic of Karadžić's singers at their best.
The Piperi are 'bitterly frightened'[22] as soon as they come to
understand Pasha's 'book'; they seem to be frightened out of
their wits and agree to meet Pasha's demand. But this pattern
is broken by the voice of Pejo Mrčarić, the young boy who will
grow into the hero of the poem. Once he has reminded them of
their sense of honour which is threatened, he argues with sad
wisdom that the tax should be paid, that the hostages should
be given, but,

> 'How can you send eight girls,
> This would be a great sin before God,
> And a scandal and a shame before men;
> It would be better for us all to die
> Than to give girls into the hands of Turks.'[23]

This touches the tribe to the quick: the choice of honourable
death echoes in their defiant reply and leads to their defence.
The stone of Montenegro and its history become one in the
resolution of the tribe to retreat into the karst mountains and
their caves which had been their fathers' traditional resort
before the Turkish expeditions:

> 'The caves, the walled-up houses,
> Which were walled-up by their ancestors,
> Because of the great fear and evil deeds,
> The evil deeds done by the Ottomans.'[24]

[21] 'Bez Peja ti neću nijednoga', ibid., l. 22.

[22] '(Piperi se) prepadoše ljuto', ibid., l. 37.

[23] 'Al' što šljete osam đevojaka, / Od Boga je velika grijota, / A od ljudi
pokor i sramota: / Bolje nam je svima izginuti, / No u Turke davati đevojke.'
Ibid., ll. 51–5.

[24] 'I pećine kuće zazidane, / Što su njini stari zazidali / Od velika straha
i zuluma, / Od zuluma od Otmanovića', ibid., ll. 63–6.

This is as much a description of a landscape and a history which
has grown into it as a description of the mettle of men who live
there, who have decided to give nothing to the Pasha, 'nothing
but stone'—

> 'That it may strike both your shoulders!'[25]

What this line exactly means, no one seems to know, but it is
usually suggested that an image of a tax-collector, with his bag
full of stones instead of money on his back, is behind it.[26]

The ensuing burning of the villages, the Piperi's defence and
their assault from one of their 'towers' also breathes Montenegrin stone and history, particularly at the moment when the
young boy comes to call his tribesmen to leave their 'caves',
their 'walled-up houses' and attack the Turks. At the moment of
triumph, however, his voice will be for ever silenced by a
Turkish gun, and the singer leaves us wondering about the
promise of a great heroic life which has never been fully
achieved:

> Had Mrčarić Pejo grown up,
> Had he grown up, as he did not grow up,
> (He was no more than seventeen),
> He would have made a better hero,
> A better hero than Marko, the Prince,
> Or than Relja, the Hawk of Bosnia.[27]

So the assault of the Montenegrins from their 'walled-up houses'
into history finds at least one rich and dramatic illumination in
a great poem about the struggle for honourable survival. It is
this poem—together with many a powerful note in the epic
voice of the others—that erodes Karadžić's judgement that the
Montenegrin poems contain 'more history than poetry'.[28] Of
course, one can read this judgement today in more than one
way; but even taken in its context as a deprecatory remark
attached to a single poem, it does not necessarily imply that

[25] '(Ne damo ti) ništa do kamena, / Da s' nijim biješ u oba ramena.'
Karadžić, iv, No. 6, ll. 69–70.

[26] See *Latković*, p. 494.

[27] 'Da doraste Mrčariću Pejo, / Da doraste, kako ne doraste, / (Nemaše
mu no sedamn'est ljeta), / Bolji ćaše biti na junaštvu / Od junaka Kraljevića
Marka / I sokola Relja Bošnjanina.' Ibid., ll. 147–52.

[28] See Karadžić's note to 'Ivan Nikolin', *Karadžić*, iv, No. 22, p. 98.

there is *no* poetry in these poems. However it was so often dug out by later scholars that it came to be regarded as a general judgement on the limitations of the Montenegrin epic genius.[29] In a recent collection Radovan Zogović has demonstrated how untenable it is as a sweeping statement,[30] and his study has opened new vistas which reveal how deeply the Montenegrin epic singing is rooted in the customs and realities of a hard soil and harsh history. But once this point is grasped, it should also be added that the ultimate achievement of the Montenegrin epic genius is to be found in the work of Petar Petrović Njegoš, the great collector and even greater poet in whose *Mountain Wreath* the Montenegrin oral heroic poetry became only a rich historical, cultural, and literary heritage.

[29] So for instance P. Popović quotes Karadžić's judgement and claims that in the Montenegrin poems there is 'no imagination and no sense of humour'; there is 'only a certain sober realism in the description'. P. Popović, *Pregled srpske književnosti*, Belgrade, 1931, p. 84.

[30] See R. Zogović, 'Predgovor', *Crnogorske epske pjesme raznih vremena*, p. 67.

4. In Serbia

The name of Filip Višnjić—more than that of any other single singer—has come to stand for the Serbian epic bard ('guslar'), the blind seer, partly because Karadžić wrote down from him almost all the best known and most popular poems about the First Serbian Uprising (for their topography, see Map 1). These poems describe the slaughter of the Serbian district chiefs and the beginning of the revolt against the Turkish janissaries,[1] the Battle of Čokešina in 1804 in which several hundred Serbian fighters were killed almost to the last man, inflicting such heavy casualties on much stronger Turkish forces that they had to retreat,[2] and many of the great Serbian victories, such as the Battle of Salaš, or the Battle of Mišar in 1806 in which a Turkish army almost eight times the strength of the Serbian forces was completely defeated.[3] Višnjić's heroes include many of the greatest and most famous historical leaders of the Serbian rebels—the quick and hot-tempered Karađorđe whose cunning matched his daring, the sturdy peasants of Mačva who became Karađorđe's dukes, their orderlies like Simeun Katić and Ignjatije Bjelić who rose to the rank of captains during the Uprising, the outlaw captains who joined the rebels, like Jovan Gligorijević (Zeko Buljubaša) who 'tied the red flame into the sky'.[4] Besides, there are also some less obvious figures: the Turks whose desire to treat the Serbs humanely was tragically at odds with their own politics, the innumerable peasantry and such characters as Ivan Knežević, the district chief in the border region of Bosnia who bought off his own people when the Turks captured them and sold them as slaves in reprisal for the military successes of the rebels in Serbia in 1806.

[1] 'Početak bune protiv dahija' ('The Beginning of the Revolt Against the Dahijas'), *Karadžić*, iv, No. 24.

[2] 'Boj na Čokešini' ('The Battle of Čokešina'), *Karadžić*, iv, No. 26.

[3] 'Boj na Salašu' ('The Battle of Salaš'), 'Boj na Mišaru' ('The Battle of Mišar'), *Karadžić*, iv, Nos. 28, 30.

[4] 'Crven plamen za nebo svezao', 'Bjelić Ignjatije', *Karadžić*, iv, No. 35, l. 352.

This was much more living than legendary history—both for Višnjić and for his audience; and when Karadžić tells us that Višnjić was 'making up new songs all by himself',[5] he means probably that Višnjić was putting the contemporary news into a highly traditional epic language. Of course, a singer has to know many songs before he can do this—in Karadžić's opinion at least about fifty.[6] And in this respect Višnjić was also outstanding: he could not have been a wartime professional singer exploiting his craft on the spur of the moment, had he not also known the peacetime drudgery of earning his living by his songs, of making up happy endings even for Moslem beys in Bosnia whom he had also entertained. In short, neither the initial range, not the immediate impulse were lacking, when Višnjić found himself in the historical turmoil of the First Serbian Uprising as the singer of an illiterate army fighting for survival.

And yet, Višnjić's epic achievement is both impressive and disappointing. As he lived at the heart of the Serbian Uprising, within a rich epic tradition, one might be tempted to think that he could hardly have chosen a better place and time for the purpose of oral epic singing. But he was also too close to history —which had all to be sung and therefore was more frequently versified than sung. Hence the discursive touch and the endless enumerations—the passion not to leave out a single detail almost equal to Old Raško's maniacal monotony in 'The Battle of Deligrad'.[7] This is why most of Višnjić's poems are much more rigidly formulaic than those of the great masters, like Old Milija and Tešan Podrugović, usually are. As a ready-made language was at hand and the historical turmoil offered an overwhelming richness of subject-matter, who could bother about making up a relationship or a phrasal combination of ultimate originality and precision—particularly as everything, or almost everything, could be expressed in phrases and patterns which were so easily available? For after all, there seemed to be so much to say.

It might almost be worth quoting the whole of the famous

[5] 'Predgovor', *Karadžić*, iv, p. 365.

[6] 'It is easy for a man who knows fifty different songs (if he is any good at this work) to make up a new song.' 'Predgovor', *Karadžić*, i, p. 530.

[7] See above p. 268–9.

'Battle of Mišar' to show how extensively Višnjić's decasyllabics are clichetic, how little variation one finds in his formulas, how lacking is the originality of their usage which is so characteristic of the greatest singers at their best. The two standard black ravens at the beginning of this poem have—like their brethren in a poem in *The Erlangen Manuscript* (No. 179)—their beaks bloodied up to their eyes, but—and this is what makes them different from their 'Erlangen' ancestors—instead of having their wings bloodied to their shoulders, they have their feet bloodied to their knees! This is, undoubtedly, a variation, but is the introduction of the ravens' knees really an improvement on the wings or merely a clumsy image? At the end of this poem the death of the wife of the defeated Turkish commander will be described in vocabulary suggesting the dying of an animal and not of a human being ('crći'), which is hardly an improvement on the more standard 'parting' with 'the soul'.[8] But it is in keeping with the use of the standard ravens—maliciously foreboding an enemy's death—at the beginning of the poem, so that more than one formulaic element which used to be the vehicle of tragedy is reduced here to the function of sneering *Schadenfreude*. Of course, as the poetic language—deeply steeped in traditional moral and spiritual generosity—cannot bear this burden, a malicious intent becomes inevitably self-defeating if not self-parodying. Similarly, among many of the traditional epithets which Višnjić uses in this poem—the 'rich' Mačva, the 'wavy' Drina, the 'wide' field of Mišar, the 'white' city of Šabac—we also find the standard 'honourable' Bosnia.[9] But as the Turkish armies come from Bosnia to attack the Serbian rebels in this poem, it is clear that Bosnia is 'honourable' for no apparent or intrinsic reason in so far as this poem is concerned. But what is it then—in spite of such extensive use and occasionally unfortunate variation of clichés—which makes Višnjić nevertheless a singer of outstanding stature?

To begin with, many of Višnjić's poems have sufficient merit to atone for all the singer's 'sins'. Thus in his song about the heroic Serbian resistance and defeat at Čokešina he creates one

---

[8] See note 71, p. 46.

[9] 'Bogata Mačva', 'Boj na Mišaru', *Karadžić*, iv, No. 30, l. 6; 'valovita Drina', ibid., l. 7; 'Sa Mišara, polja širokoga', ibid., l. 2; 'A od Šapca, grada bijeloga', ibid., l. 3; 'čestita Bosna', ibid., l. 8.

of the most moving epic scenes in the whole tradition: the rebels run out of ammunition and continue to fight until each of their 'rifles is broken into seven pieces'[10] in their desperate resistance. Equally sparse and poignant are his epic devices in the description of the Turkish devastation of the 'rich' Mačva, in his picture of the bleating of the homesick sheep and cattle.[11] Apart from such achievements—which in their originality and sturdy homeliness testify to the powers of a great epic imagination—Višnjić introduced a major new protagonist into the Serbo-Croatian epic in the making: the 'poor rayah', the non-Moslem plebs, compared to trodden grass,[12] becomes in his poems the moving spirit of history. The dispossessed make several dramatic appearances in his poems and they are, undoubtedly, the chosen people of his epic landscape. And, last but not least, Višnjić weaves his sense of contemporary burning history into the moral and spiritual patterns of the traditional epic fabric which he knows and 'feels' so richly. Thus he creates an epic landscape in which—more than in any other—the traditional and the living meet and merge, the landscape illuminated from within by a cluster of images which—dispersed and repeated in many poems—live together in a kinship which spells out the closing chapter in the Serbian national epic in the making.

This imagery—the fog of gunpowder, the eclipsed sun, the dawn which has not yet reddened the horizons, the red flames which have been 'tied into the sky'[13]—reflects the general mood and the historical outlines of the Uprising. But the full rapport between what happens and the human response to it is also mirrored in far more numerous and intimate ways in the texture of this epic fabric. Thus the scarlet cloth rips on the knee of Luko Lazarević when he jumps to put on his belt and arm himself for the battle.[14] He has in his hands 'the rifle of the Turkish outlaws',[15] a rifle with 'twelve letters', each 'tempered

[10] 'Izlomiše puške na sedmoro', 'Boj na Čokešini,' *Karadžić*, iv, No. 26, l. 283.
[11] See below pp. 340–1.
[12] See above pp. 216–17, 266, and below pp. 286–7, 293–4.
[13] See above pp. 266–7.
[14] 'Luko Lazarević i Pejzo' ('Luko Lazarević and Pejzo'), *Karadžić*, iv, No. 34, ll. 120–1.
[15] 'Puška krdžalijnka', ibid., l. 266.

in blood', so that 'it beats every amulet'.[16] Equally characteristic of this 'feel' of history is the fact that a rifle is sometimes
not just taken up into the hands but 'embraced'—both in 'The
Battle of Loznica' and in 'Stanić Stanojlo'.[17] The same rich and
immediate relationship of the epic poet to his subject-matter
lights up the description of Miloš Stoićević when he prepares
to fight Meho Orugdžijć:

> When Miloš tightens his white horse's girth,
> The horse senses the battle,
> And paws the ground with his front hooves,
> Paws the ground, pricks up his ears,
> The living heart in Miloš laughs.[18]

And finally Višnjić is also capable of suggesting some of the
'lower', prosaic and comic facets of the moment which he sees
primarily as a great historical apocalypse. He also shares, in
short, the rich tradition of the Serbo-Croatian epic comedy—
the tradition reflected, for instance, in Kosančić's spying on the
Turks in Kosovo and in Marko Kraljević's tricks which almost
match the treacheries of the world and history he has to face.[19]
It is in this way that Višnjić describes the outlaw Captain
Ćurčija, who spies on the Turkish army in 'The Battle of
Čokešina'. While spying on the Turks during a Serbian fast he
is prepared to eat forbidden food with the enemy; moreover,
he tries to keep his Orthodox faith while praying in a mosque:

> 'I bow like a Turk, I pray like a Serb.'[20]

His character could hardly have found a better place and
occasion to express itself—a whole philosophy of life, or a
comedy of a philosophy of life, peeps from behind his wording.

---

[16] '(Na kojoj je do) dvanaest slova, / Svako slovo u krv' okaljeno, / . . .
Ona bije svaku amajliju', *Karadžić*, iv, No. 34, ll. 272–3, 275.

[17] '(A pješaci puške) zagrliše', *Karadžić*, iv, No. 33, l. 563; (Sedefliju
pušku) zagrlio', *Karadžić*, iv, No. 43, l. 38.

[18] 'Kada Miloš đogu kolan steže, / Tu se đogat boju osjetio, / Pa prvijem
zakopa nogama, / Nogam' kopa, a ušima striže, / Milošu se živo srce smije',
'Miloš Stoićević i Meho Orugdžijć' ('Miloš Stoićević and Meho Orugdžijć'),
Karadžić, iv, No. 32, ll. 98–102.

[19] See above pp. 166–7, 194–202.

[20] 'Turski klanjam, Srpski Boga molim.' 'Boj na Čokešini', *Karadžić*, iv,
No. 26, l. 113.

But had he not already shown how much he would like to have
it both ways when he requested the Serbian commander Jakov
Valjevac to bring more troops to the battle so that he could
risk joining in and being a hero on the winning side:

> 'Would you bring more troops, my friend?
> If you will not bring more troops,
> I will be the first who will not fight the Turks,
> For I am not a willow tree,
> To sprout new branches when I am cut down
> And be a willow as it was before,
> But I am Ćurčija, mountain captain,
> And when they cut me down, I sprout no more.'[21]

Of course, this contrast between a man and a tree is ultimately
of biblical origin: 'For there is hope of a tree, if it be cut down,
that it will sprout again, and that the tender branch thereof will
not cease', 'but man dieth, and wasteth away: yea, man giveth
up the ghost, and where *is* he?'[22] It may also be worth noting
that in a fifteenth-century version of the Serbian legends about
Prince Lazar's death, Duke Krajmir warns the Prince not to
defy the enemy who has captured him because 'the head is not
like the stump of a willow tree to sprout a second time'.[23] But
of course Višnjić uses this traditional formulaic contrast in a
completely new spirit: he gives it a comic dramatic status
which makes the Serbian commander retort by telling Ćurčija
that he is no soldier but 'a scourge of old women'[24] and that his
ancestors were no warriors but kept cows in Srem (Sirmium),
on the other bank of the river Sava, in the territories which
were not ruled by the Turks since the end of the seventeenth
century.

It is also significant perhaps that on this occasion—as well as
in the description of Kosančić's spying on the Turks before the
Battle of Kosovo and in many of the situations which Marko
Kraljević has to face—the comic element is introduced to dispel

---

[21] 'Oćeš, bolan, više dovest' vojske? / Ako l' ne ćeš više dovest vojske, / Ja
se prvi s Turci biti ne ću: / Jer ja nisam drvo vrbovina, / Kad pos'jeku, da s'
omladit mogu, / Pa da budem vrba, k'o i bila, / Već Ćurčija, gorski aram-
baša, / Kad pos'jeku, omladit' se ne ću.' Ibid., ll. 97–104.

[22] Job 14: 7.   [23] See above p. 157.

[24] '(Ti, Ćurčija, jedan) pržibabo!' *Karadžić*, iv, No. 26, l. 124.

the gloom of the hopeless odds of actual history. For in the Battle of Čokešina the Serbian rebels were also facing an over-whelming enemy: Jakov Nenadović had only three or four hundred men with him when he tried to intercept the advancing Turkish reinforcement of two to three thousand men who were on their way to Šabac in order to help the besieged Turkish garrison in that town. Small wonder that Nenadović had difficulties in agreeing about the position of his forces with the local leader Đorđe Ćurčija and his outlaws. When the Battle was finally fought and lost—in April 1804 near the monastery of Čokešina, about thirty kilometres to the south-west of Šabac —the outlaws and their commander were among the very few Serbs who survived the disaster. A sense of humour was obviously needed to face this situation as an imaginative epic challenge, even if the Turkish losses were so heavy that their army had to retreat.

Similarly, in Višnjić's poem about 'The Battle of Salaš'— which took place in 1806 in the north-west of Mačva, near the borderland with Bosnia—the Serbian heroes fight against such tremendous odds that they have to be disguised as Turks and strengthened by slivovits to face them.[25] However, another 'low' element—but a 'low' element which achieves a 'high' imaginative status—is far more significant in this song. Unlike the socially exalted heroes of the 'older' songs—the Serbian medieval kings and feudal lords, Marko Kraljević and the outlaw captains in the rich feudal costumes of the Venetian and Austrian military leaders—the main protagonist is 'the poor rayah', the human grass of history. This humble and nameless soldiery bears the brunt of the suffering and is seen both as the thunderer and the thunderbolt in this epic landscape. While the three grand military leaders—seen as the traditional epic 'dukes'—drink wine and wonder in drink who will come to rule Mačva in the end, a young sentry, bareheaded and bare-footed, runs in:

> Without shoes, without his long rifle,
> Torn with forest thorns,[26]

---

[25] See 'Boj na Salašu', *Karadžić*, iv, No. 28, ll. 237–47.
[26] 'Bez obuće i bez duge puške; / Od šumskoga trnja oderano', ibid., ll. 36–7.

to tell them that the rayah 'wails in misery' while they feast.[27] He also reminds them who it was that 'supplied them with their horses', 'cut their clothes' and 'forged their arms'.[28] The destiny of the 'rayah' is also the moral gauge of the Uprising: the dukes who started the battle with the Turks must *win* it to save their honour—even if they were to die a heroic death and lose the battle their souls would never 'see God's face' because their deeds would have led to the woe and misery of the rayah. This is, of course, a complete reversal of the myth of Kosovo— defeat is no more the ultimate source of moral significance and dignity, victory has become the *sine qua non* of atonement.

In Višnjić's poem 'Luko Lazarević and Pejzo'—describing one of the many defeats of the Turkish armies which invaded western Serbia from Bosnia in 1806—the rayah appears under the leadership of the outlaw captain Zeko Buljubaša. This man —his historical name was Jovan Gligorijević—was one of the great heroes of the Serbian Uprising. He commanded a company of homeless fighters in the borderland along the river Drina, until in 1813 the company ran out of ammunition and was killed to the last man in a desperate attack on the Turks with knives. The social status and the spirit of these fighters are richly suggested in Višnjić's description of their appearance:

> 'What heroes are these ragged children!
> They would kill a crane under a cloud,
> Let alone a hero walking the earth!'[29]

The 'ragged children' of Zeko Buljubaša also figure in Višnjić's poem 'Bjelić Ignjatije' which is again set in the borderland along the river Drina. But this time a Serbian raid into Bosnia is described and it is both historically and socially significant that its hero Ignjatije Bjelić is not one of the Serbian great military commanders but a minor officer. For the action takes place during one of the actual historical periods when the leaders of the Serbian Uprising made some sort of provisional

[27] '(Sirotinja) u nevolji cvili', ibid., l. 45.
[28] 'Tko je vama konje nabavio? / Tko je vama čohu porezao? / Tko li vam je pokov'o oružje?' Ibid., ll. 64–6.
[29] 'Da kakvi su golaći junaci! / Ubili bi pod oblakom ždrala, / A kamo li na zemlji junaka!' 'Luko Lazarević i Pejzo', *Karažić*, iv, No. 34, ll. 155–7.

agreement with the Grand Porte and it is within this context that Ignjatije Bjelić—historically a servant and later a captain of the great military leader Stojan Čupić—comes to complain to his master that the Turks keep breaking faith, crossing the river Drina, killing Serbian soldiers and stealing horses. He threatens that he will become an outlaw if he is curbed in his revenge. But Stojan Čupić gives his secret blessing to Bjelić's avenging expedition to Bosnia, advises him 'to go wisely, not to get killed like a fool'[30] and, if possible, to get help from the 'ragged children' of Zeko Buljubaša. In fact, Zeko and his 'ragged children'—who know the paths on the other bank of the river Drina[31]—are vividly seen as loyal and equal to each other in their ultimate destitution. As soon as they are called, when their captain fires a shot in the mountain—

> All the ragged children recognize the rifle,[32]

and respond immediately to the call. As their captain has to choose only ninety men, the others complain that they are no worse fighters than their chosen comrades and Zeko has to tell them that someone must stay behind to guard the border:

> 'You are not worse, you are all equal to me,
> Who will guard the Parašnica?'[33]

It is also interesting that Zeko himself is called 'a ragged child' and that he—and not his military superior in rank Ignjatije Bjelić—is made the commander of the raid. This is not merely a matter of obvious military convenience (an outlaw captain being more competent in leading a raid), but also a situation which is exploited with sharp and subtle social sense and wit. Thus when the captain of the 'ragged children' comes to make the arrangements for the attack on the approaching Turks, he gives orders to his military superior Simeun Katić—calling him 'master' and asking him to block the road on which the Turks are expected to come:

[30] 'Hodi mudro, ne pogini ludo', 'Bjelić Ignjatije', *Karadžić*, iv, No. 35, l. 43.

[31] 'Koji znadu staze preko Drine' ('Who know the paths on the other side of the Drina'), ibid., l. 50.

[32] 'Svi golaći pušku poznadoše', ibid., l. 113.

[33] 'Niste gori, već meni jednaci, / Ko će more čuvat' Parašnicu?' Ibid., ll. 127–8.

'For the masters own the highways and roads,
And the outlaws—the narrow mountain passes.'[34]

But in spite of this sharp sense of the social realities of the
outlaws and the 'poor rayah', this new collective epic protagonist
of the poems about the Uprising partakes some of the legendary
epic glory through the language and customs which connect it
with the medieval kings and their feudal lords. Apart from the
most obvious historical connection—that of the outlaw captains
who had a feudal social status as military leaders in the Venetian
and Austrian armies—there is also the fundamental link of the
same epic tradition. In 'The Battle of Čokešina', for instance,
all the army takes communion before the fighting begins—
which is both in keeping with the medieval Byzantine and
Serbian military code and with the later epic poems about the
Battle of Kosovo.[35] Moreover, when the defeat has to be faced
at Čokešina we do not find only the obviously contemporary
detail of the desperate resistance with empty rifles, but also the
curse of the traitors which takes us much further back in the
history of epic singing and folk customs. In 'The Battle of
Salaš' the curse of the traitors uses a similar formulaic wording
which can be found in Prince Lazar's curse in a poem which
Karadžić wrote down from his father;[36] and in 'The Battle of
Loznica' the Turkish army is described almost exactly in the
same wording which Kosančić Ivan used to describe his spying
on the enemy in a poem also recorded from Karadžić's father:

> Horse by horse, hero by hero,
> Battle lances like a black forest,—
> Banners waving in the field,
> Like black clouds in the sky.[37]

[34] 'Gospodski su puti i drumovi, / A hajdučki tijesni bogazi!' Ibid., ll.
232–3.

[35] See above pp. 24, 156, 162.   [36] See above p. 160.

[37] 'Konj do konja, junak do junaka, / Bojna koplja kano čarna gora, /
Sve s' vijaju po polju barjaci / Kano mrki po nebu oblaci', 'Boj na Loznici',
Karadžić, iv, No. 33, ll. 122–5. Cf. 'Konj do konja, junak do junaka, / Bojna
koplja kao čarna gora, / Sve barjaci kao i oblaci' ('Horse by horse, hero by
hero, / Battle lances like a black forest, / Banners everywhere like clouds',
'Komadi od različnijeh kosovskijeh pjesama (iv)', *Karadžić*, ii, No. 50, ll.
22–4. Another variant of this run of formulas can be found in 'Rastanak
Kara-Đorđija sa Srbijom' ('Karađorđe's Parting with Serbia'), *Karadžić*,
iv, No. 40, ll. 30–3.

Such formulaic links point both to a kinship of the contemporary mood and to the sharing of an inherited epic language and its conventions. But in no other poem has this unity of a mythic sense of history and of a whole tradition of epic singing grown into such a splendid vision uniting the past and the present as in Višnjić's greatest song 'The Beginning of the Revolt Against the Dahijas'.

Karadžić wrote down this poem—together with fourteen others—from Visnjić in the monastery of Šišatovac where he was staying in 1815 with his learned friend the literary abbot Lukijan Mušicki. The recording went on for days, sometimes graced by the presence of the learned archimandrite. But he usually left Karadžić and Višnjić alone after the first few lines were sung: 'the learned versifier could not listen to the poet'.[38] The date of the recording—soon after Easter in 1815—is also significant; for it was at a gathering on Palm Sunday that year that the decision to start a second round of fighting against the Turks was made in the village of Takovo in Serbia, and it was this struggle—combined with politics and diplomacy—that eventually brought national freedom to Serbia. So Višnjić was in fact singing from the historical threshold of Serbian national freedom about the events which led to the First Serbian Uprising in 1804 and to the ensuing glorious years. Višnjić himself had witnessed this turmoil as the greatest singer of the Serbian rebels' army until it was defeated in 1813 when Višnjić—together with Karadžić and tens of thousands of other Serbs—had to leave Serbia and come to Srem which was controlled by Austrians.

'The Beginning of the Revolt Against the Dahijas' is, in short, one of the greatest swan songs in the whole Serbo-Croatian oral epic tradition sung at the historical watershed dividing the heroic age from the ensuing era of national freedom, social conflicts, and party politics. It is this historical change which will soon make it impossible for any singer to produce a major song about contemporary history in the old heroic idiom. However, Višnjić's greatest song is still set in the historical circumstances in which it was possible to interweave dozens of contemporary historical facts and details into the grand landscape of traditional epic singing. Višnjić's description of

[38] V. Nedić, 'Filip Višnjić', *Narodna književnost*, p. 326.

the terror of the janissary commanders in Serbia, for instance, is true to historical facts. And so are his pictures of the Dahijas' decision to execute all the Serbian district chiefs and village headmen, of Karađorđe's escape from the Turks who had come to kill him, of the outbreak of the Uprising and the rebels' conquest of the Serbian towns in which the Turkish military garrisons had been situated. The names of the Turkish commanders are accurate and the basic substance of the epic report on the meeting at which they reached their decision to kill the Serbian district chiefs and village headmen is in accord with known historical facts, even if the conflicting opinions are seen in the poem, for dramatic reasons, as the clash of a wise old father (Old Fočo) and his foolhardy young son (Memed-aga). The names of the slaughtered Serbian leaders are also accurately given, although in one or two instances they were not the victims of the first round of the Turkish slaughter but were killed in battle a little later. Some of the circumstances of their execution are accurately reported, some are left out. Thus the execution of Aleksa Nenadović and Ilija Birčanin in Valjevo on the bridge over the river Kolubara is true to historical fact. Hadži-Ruvim, Marko Čarapić and many other Serbian chiefs and headmen were actually executed by the Turks as described in the poem; Vasa Čarapić was not executed but was killed in battle a little later; whereas the description of the death of Hadži-Ruvim, the Archimandrite of the monastery of Bogovađa near Valjevo, is true to historical fact in so far as it takes place 'in the midst of Belgrade', even if the singer does not mention—probably because he does not know—that Hadži-Ruvim actually refused to betray the work of the Serbian chiefs while his flesh was torn off his body with a pair of pliers.[39] And, perhaps more significantly, the poem rests on a fairly reliable general sense of history, particularly in its evocation of the distant background of the Battle of Kosovo, Sultan Murad's death, the early days of the comparatively humane Turkish rule and the later economic, political, and military terror. Moreover, Višnjić knows what are believed to be historical facts about Sultan Murad's death in the Battle of Kosovo—his Sultan also survives his death wound until the battle is over. Finally, the description of the blood boiling up out of the earth

[39] See *Latković*, pp. 525–8.

as a call for vengeance reflects a widespread popular belief; and it has been pointed out that even the supernatural framework of the poem—the partial eclipse of the moon, the appearance of a comet—corresponds to the actual meteorological phenomena recorded at this time in the chronicles.[40] However, such a framing of an oral poem is also part of the traditional epic technique and a good example can be found in the imagery of breaking skies, falling stars and flying snakes at the beginning of an early Dalmatian decasyllabic poem about the liberation of Herceg-Novi.[41]

In fact, the most fascinating feature of 'The Beginning of the Revolt Against the Dahijas' is the imaginative interplay of the traditional epic techniques and the 'contemporary' historical facts. In no other 'contemporary' oral epic in Serbo-Croat has the present been so extensively, and so intensely, seen with the eyes of all the epic heritage in the language. What is in many respects a historical chronicle is at the same time illuminated by a rich imaginative awareness of its mythic significance. In its basic structure the poem is conceived as an inversion of the Kosovo myth—the ancient omens forebode again, as in Raško's 'Wedding of Prince Lazar', the approach of 'the last times', but 'the last times' of the Turkish janissaries are seen here as a dawn for the Serbian rebels. However, this inversion does not develop in the direction of *Schadenfreude*—which it could, and did, so easily take in some other poems. Instead, it builds a dramatic historical landscape irradiated by a great epic wisdom and excitement: Sultan Murad, the commander of the enemy army, is seen as a prudent and generous man who forgives the great Serbian hero the death wound which he had inflicted upon him:

'The fortune of the soldier brought me that'.[42]

Moreover, his last word to his viziers is a warning not to 'deal bitterly with the rayah'.[43] Of course, this mirrors an awareness of the comparatively humane beginning of the Turkish rule of the Balkans, of its later terror and the helplessness of the Grand

---

[40] See *Latković*, pp. 522–3.   [41] See above pp. 73–4.

[42] 'To je sreća vojnička don'jela', 'Početak bune protiv dahija', *Karadžić*, iv, No. 24, l. 122.

[43] '(Vi nemojte) raji gorki biti', ibid., l. 112.

Porte to control it in Serbia, particularly in the years preceding
the Uprising, but above all it creates an epic tension in which
the traditional black-and-white schematism of moral vision is
eroded so that the poetic imagination feeds on the ways in which
universal human history tends to go astray.

This broad and dramatic tension is also captured in the
opening imagery of the blood boiling up out of the earth, of the
struggle of the moon against its eclipse, of the bloodied banners
marching across the sky, of the winter thundering and the sun
struggling to dawn. The failure of the later Turkish rulers to
follow Murad's wise and just advice is thus seen as part of a
cosmic drama—but it is a cosmic drama which is often cut down
in the poem to 'realistic', prosaic and comic forms which
enable the epic imagination to come to full human grips with
it. Thus in one of the ensuing scenes the Serbian district chief
Ilija Birčanin defies the grand Dahija Memed-aga almost in the
same comic spirit in which Marko Kraljević used to challenge
the Sultan whenever he obeyed his call and appeared in his
boots on the Sultan's praying rug. As Marko used—in his
ambivalent display of courage—to make the Sultan retreat to
the wall, so Ilija Birčanin 'shoots with his eyes'[44] when he gives,
haughtily, but still gives the tax-money which he has brought
to Memed-aga:

> 'Memed-aga, are you counting this tax?
> I have already counted what I pay.'[45]

And as 'the honourable tsar' usually had second thoughts about
his original intentions when faced with Marko, so Memed-aga,
at the end of his tether, can hardly 'wait for that curse to go
away'.[46] In short, this poem is capable of assimilating not only
the tradition of 'the last times' and the approaching Kosovo,
but also the epic massif of Kosovo legends, of the later terror and
outlawry, of the many-voiced songs about heroism in vassalage
which is so characteristic of the poems about Marko Kraljević.
It is in this rich unison of different epic voices that contemporary
history is seen as the time 'when the pick rises, when the long

[44] 'Očima strijelja', ibid., l. 277.
[45] 'Memed-aga! zar ćeš je brojati? / Ta ja sam je jednom izbrojio.' Ibid.,
ll. 278–9.
[46] 'Jedva čekam, da se skine b'jeda', ibid., l. 282.

hoe rises',[47] when 'the rayah grows like grass out of the earth'.[48]

Within a magnificent supernatural frame—analogous to the openings of such outstanding epics as 'The Death of the Mother of the Jugovići' and 'God Leaves No Debt Unpaid'—history moves with the inevitability of natural phenomena. And historical issues are no more a limiting imaginative factor here than they are in 'The Death of Duke Prijezda' or 'Old Vujadin'; the actual conflicts seem to radiate their own all-embracing drama. In short, the epic imagination works with almost 'tangible', but 'burning' historical material; in fact, the Turkish burning of the Serbian villages is seen by a wise old Turk as an attempt to extinguish 'a living fire' by waving a handful of straw over it.[49] And this 'straw' and 'fire' re-emerge at the end of the poem in the literal burning of the Turkish towns and fortifications; and 'the poor rayah' which 'grows like grass out of the earth' now thunders its revenge on the Turks:

'And the grass will grow up from your hearth-stones'.[50]

In this web of interwoven historical details and poetic imagery we also see the eclipse of the sun when the district chiefs Aleksa Nenadović and Ilija Birčanin are slaughtered. Is it 'historical' or biblical, is it an extension of the introductory struggle of the moon against its eclipse—or is it only 'traditional', the reflection of the standard epic technique in which the physical so often breathes the spiritual?

In this sense 'The Beginning of the Revolt Against the Dahijas' is the summing up of the traditional oral epic singing in Serbo-Croat. For the song seems to have fathomed its ultimate imaginative depths a little after the First Serbian Uprising—all the poems about the second uprising show, by universal agreement, a sharp imaginative decline. Clearly, the heroic song ceased to be a major way of understanding history and responding to its challenge as soon as the political conditions were changed so radically that party tactics and politics

---

[47] 'Kad ustane kuka i motika', *Karadžić*, iv, No. 24, l. 146.

[48] 'Usta raja k'o iz zemlje trava', ibid., l. 569.

[49] 'Uzmi slame u bijelu ruku, / Mani slamom preko vatre žive' ('Take up some straw in your white hand, / Wave it about over a living fire'), ibid., ll. 339–40.

[50] 'Iz ognjišta pronić' će vam trava', ibid., l. 154.

came to the historical foreground of national existence. The collective epic language could no more establish a creative relationship with the burning issues of the present—even if it could survive in many epic oases as a nostalgic memory of a great imaginative past. The singing went on, but it was no more the central form of awareness of history and it soon stopped being its most powerful mythic and mythopoeic shaping force. It could be remembered, its heritage could be used and manipulated by major poets in the language— particularly for ironic or comic purposes. However, whenever used to describe contemporary history it sounded hollow, dead and mechanical—if not, indeed, unintentionally funny.[51] The discrepancy between the conventions of the epic language, its social and historical assumptions, and actual modern history made a gap which no traditional epic voice could ever bridge again.

[51] See, for instance, notes 166, 167, p. 65.

PART SEVEN

The Epic Setting

1. The Singer and the Song

The general picture of chronology, geography and achievement of Serbo-Croat oral epics seems to be fairly clear in its main outlines. The first Slav singers in the Balkans used their cithers as disguise in espionage near Constantinople in the seventh century and they gave their name to the professional practitioners of this art in the Hungarian language. But their pagan world survived only sporadically in some of the village customs in much later times. Medieval Christian Serbia, however, gave a much stronger imprint to the whole tradition of the epic art: its history provided some of the major later themes and motifs, its monastic literature left the heritage of several major legal and moral concepts as well as a few skeletons of much older Eastern legends, its frescoes kept in vivid memory the outward appearance of the medieval feudal lords, their gowns, rings, and pitchers. During the Turkish conquests and the dissolution of this medieval world in the fifteenth century, the feudal professional singers cultivated their distinctive 'Serbian manner' in their retreat in Hungary at least until the middle of the sixteenth century. The same 'manner' was absorbed into the much more popular and plebeian forms of epic singing in the Christian urban setting of some prosperous cities along the Adriatic coast. It was in this environment that the old feudal *bugarštice* were written down as they were dying from the end of the fifteenth to the end of the eighteenth century. Their debris left a rich bequest of themes and motifs, stock phrases, formulas and formulaic expressions, stylistic and narrative devices to the flourishing tradition of decasyllabic village singing.

On the other hand, the irrefutable early sixteenth-century evidence makes it clear that the epic songs about the Battle of Kosovo (1389) were widely cultivated among the Christian population in the central Balkan area spreading from old medieval Serbia to Herzegovina and Bosnia, all the way to the western Turkish frontier with Croatia. For obvious political and cultural reasons these popular village songs could not be recorded, but this area, particularly the region of Herzegovina and Montenegro, is generally assumed to be the cradle of decasyllabic village singing. The earliest collection of these songs—which an unknown German wrote down, probably in or near the military camps along the northern Balkan Christian frontier in Slavonia—dates from about 1720 and its linguistic features as well as some of its subjects reflect the long travels of the epic voice through many regions, from old medieval Serbia and the Adriatic coast, to Herzegovina, Bosnia, and Croatia. This evidence also shows that many Croatian and Moslem singers must have contributed a great deal to the oral epic diction in Serbo-Croat, but as their respective cultures were dominated by urban centres which provided different modes for cultural expression, it was only among the Serbs that oral epic singing absorbed for a long time most of the available artistic national talent. The central function which epic singing had in Serbian village life and the enormous pressure of historical circumstance, particularly on some of the greatest singers, explain perhaps how the debris of the 'high' monastic medieval culture could come so fully alive in the 'low' social setting of the later epic songs. The shape and the ornamentation of some humble products of nineteenth-century village craftsmen mirror clearly what actually happened. Their chairs and flasks, for instance, often embody in an impressively simplified design their grand medieval ancestors. Thus the finely-wrought and yet sturdy village chair of Berane (Ethnographical Museum, Belgrade) reflects the medieval design of such lofty objects as the throne in the fifteenth-century Church of the Ascension in Leskovec near Ohrid. (See Pl. 5.) And the crude specimen of a popular nineteenth-century flask (Ethnographical Museum, Belgrade) was obviously inspired in its form by medieval pitchers—such as the fifteenth-century one in the Museum of Applied Art in Belgrade, or the earlier one which Moses holds on a fourteenth-century fresco painting in the monastery of Dečani.[1] (See Pl. 6.)

The most extensive and valuable body of decasyllabic oral epics, which were collected by V. S. Karadžić, represents a similar kind of achievement. But these epics also bear the social

[1] See V. Han, 'Putevima narodne tradicije od srednjovekovnih fresaka do folklornih originala', *Zbornik Svetozara Radojčića*, Filozofski fakultet, Belgrade, 1969, pp. 391–8.

and historical imprint of the First and the Second Serbian Uprisings, 'the first of the great nationalist movements of the nineteenth century'.[2] And it is, of course, significant that the geography of the oral epic song in its golden age shows that the greatest poems come from the areas in which epic singing was most intensely and widely cultivated. 'At the present time', claims Karadžić writing in 1823,

heroic songs are most widespread and most lively in Bosnia and Herzegovina, in Montenegro and in the hilly southern regions of Serbia. In these regions even today there is a *gusle* in every house, and particularly in the shepherds' summer huts in the mountains. And it is difficult to find a man who does not know how to play the *gusle*, and many women and girls know it too. In the lower regions of Serbia (along the Sava and the Danube), the *gusle* are more rare in people's houses, but I still think that in every village (particularly on the left bank of the Morava) one could be found.[3]

On the northern banks of the Sava and the Danube, in Srem, Bačka, and Banat, which were more prosperous and had been for a long time under the Austrian and Hungarian rule, only blind men had the *gusle* and sang oral epic songs. Apparently, 'other people were ashamed to hang blind men's *gusle* in their houses'.[4] And it is this distribution which explains, in Karadžić's opinion, the difference in the poetic achievement in various areas:

the epic poems in Srem, Bačka, and Banat are worse sung than in Serbia, in Serbia along the Sava and the Danube they are worse sung than further inland, especially in Bosnia and Herzegovina. In the same way, as we move westwards from Srem through Slavonia to Croatia and Dalmatia, heroic songs are more and more cultivated by the people.[5]

This geographical picture shows that heroic songs were most widespread and best sung in the heart of the central mountain ranges in Herzegovina, Bosnia, Montenegro, and Serbia, as well as along the military frontiers of Slavonia, Croatia, and Venetian Dalmatia.

This agrees with the general directions of the major Balkan

---

[2] D. Wilson, *The Life and Times of Vuk Stefanović Karadžić 1787–1864*, p. 28.
[3] 'Predgovor', *Karadžić*, i, p. 529.
[4] Ibid., pp. 529–30.   [5] Ibid.

migrations from the fourteenth to the nineteenth century—the migrations which were so extensive that in this period 'almost all the population in the area from the Canyon of Veles on the river Vardar (Macedonia) to the Mountain of Zagreb (Zagre-bačka gora, Croatia) changed its abode'.[6] (See Map 4.) Hundreds of thousands of people were moved by force from Serbia all over the Turkish Empire during the fifteenth century: during the single decade after the fall of Constantinople (1453) over three hundred thousand Serbs were displaced in this way.[7] During this heavy depopulation of Serbia in the fifteenth century the bulk of the refugees moved along the central Dinaric mountains to the regions which, a little later, supplied most of the Serbian migrants moving to the areas of the Slavonian, Croatian, and Dalmatian frontiers. The second wave of Serbian migrations during the great Turco-Austrian wars in the seventeenth century left dozens of villages completely uninhabited and many towns with only a handful of people in them. Austrian reports on the demographic situation in Serbia from the beginning of the eighteenth century show that the number of deserted settlements exceeded that of inhabited ones: at this time there were probably only about one hundred thousand people in the whole of Serbia (four to five per square kilometre).[8]

These migrations supplied a vast army for the Hungarian, Austrian, and Venetian military frontiers. The nineteenth century, however, marked the beginning of vast movements in the opposite direction: the extent of the repopulation of liberated Serbia is reflected in the fact that in the area of the river Morava and the river Drina about eighty per cent of the total population at the beginning of the twentieth century had come from somewhere else.[9] The linguistic and thematic impact of these migrations on the art of oral epic singing can hardly be overestimated: it explains why this art had to be not only 'anachronistic' but also 'anatopistic' from the moment when the first two complete songs were written down in the middle of the sixteenth century.[10]

For the singer and the song followed these main historical streams, and not only their social status but also the range of

[6] *Enciklopedija Jugoslavije*, vii, p. 506.   [7] See ibid.
[8] See ibid.   [9] See ibid., pp. 506–7.   [10] See above pp. 49–58.

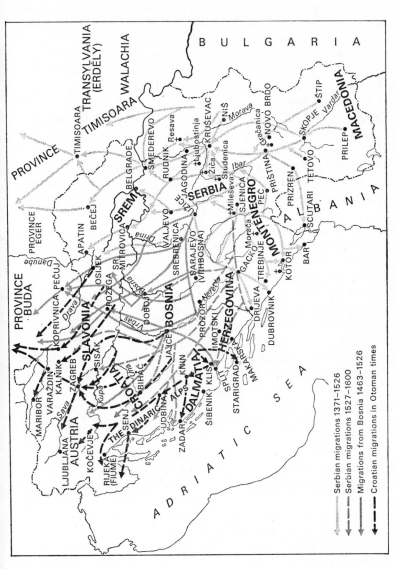

4. Serbian and Croatian Migrations

their voice was affected. The pre-Christian Slav singers in the Balkans seem to have been ordinary people sharing in a popular entertainment, but in the early Christian times they were already known as professionals in Hungary and among some other nations. In the monastic literature of feudal times there are references to 'the devilish songs' of common people,[11] to the lascivious 'harmful songs of youthful desires', to the collective epic singing about themes of public importance, to the various forms of royal and feudal entertainment by professional singers.[12] The evidence of strong epic traditions, absorbing hagiographical legends and apocryphal material, in the patrician setting of Bar is also significant.[13] However, the whole world of medieval feudal song—performed by foreign and native *jongleurs*, by various types of medieval entertainers, singers, actors and drummers, by wandering scholars ('dijaci') and composers of popular religious songs ('začinjavci')—was mainly absorbed either into the literary or into the oral culture in the sixteenth century.[14] The new type of popular epic singer was a different man in a different social setting.

To begin with, he might have been just any peasant, farmer or fisherman, in any rural area under the Turkish rule, or in any village or city on the Christian side of Turco-Christian frontiers. More specifically, he was often an outlaw, a border raider, a soldier, a gifted articulate man often from a distinguished village family in a patriarchal community, a slightly bohemian or artistic 'misfit', a village 'character', a self-made merchant, a clever shepherd, a blind man or woman making a living by his art. However, the popular image of the *guslar* as a blind visionary is exaggerated, even if it is a true description of Filip Višnjić, the most popular and perhaps the only true professional among Karadžić's best singers. But how did the personality, the biography, and the social setting of the greatest singers affect their art? There is sufficient evidence about some of the greatest of the nineteenth-century singers to suggest in outline some answers to this question.

[11] See V. Latković, 'O pevačima srpskohrvatskih narodnih epskih pesama do kraja xviii veka', *Prilozi za književnost, jezik, istoriju i folklor*, xx (1954), p. 188.

[12] See above pp. 12–15.   [13] See above pp. 16–19.

[14] See V. Latković, op. cit., pp. 191–2.

5(a). Throne from the Church of the Ascension in Leskovec, fifteenth century.

5(b). Chair from the village of Berane, nineteenth century, Ethnographical Museum, Belgrade.

6(a). Lead pitcher with representation of a chalice, fifteenth century, Museum of Applied Art, Belgrade.

6(b). Pitcher held by Moses, fourteenth century, Monastery of Dečani.

6(c). Flask from Pirot with the head of Prince Mihajlo Obrenović, nineteenth century, Ethnographical Museum, Belgrade.

Karadžić's family history is in itself significant. The family of the great collector came originally from Herzegovina, the heart and cradle of Serbo-Croat decasyllabic heroic songs. They lived at Tršić, near Loznica, in the hills of north-western Serbia, where the neighbouring monastery provided not only the initial education for the greatest Serbian man of letters, but also ammunition for the Serbian rebels and fighters against the Turks. And it is not surprising that Karadžić himself, one of the few literate laymen in his country, served as a clerk in the rebels' army during the First Serbian Uprising. When this Uprising was crushed in 1813, Karadžić crossed the river Sava and emigrated, with tens of thousands of his compatriots, to Austrian teritory. It was here—near the monastery of Šišatovac —that he recorded many of his songs. And it was from his father that he wrote down the few fragments of Kosovo poems, perhaps among the finest in the language, and certainly central in the general epic landscape of the whole tradition.[15] His father was a pious and serious farmer—perhaps not too serious to indulge in epic song-making, but certainly serious enough not to admit to the indulgence. Karadžić—who made it clear on many occasions that poems were improvised rather than memorized[16]—seems to have believed his father when he told him that he was not responsible for the songs, because they were, in fact, old grandfather's responsibility.[17] There was also an uncle in the family who was capable of making up heroic songs as soon as the occasion arose—for instance, four or five days after Smail-bey Begzadić was killed.[18] This song is not a particularly significant achievement, but it is a clear and adequate description of a contemporary event of public importance. There are no jarring notes in it and this suggests a correspondence between the whole of the traditional epic diction (its formulas, its stylistic and narrative devices, its basic moral concepts) and the popular response to history as well as the way in which it was immediately understood and interpreted.

[15] See above pp. 160–1, 164–7.   [16] See below p. 322.

[17] Karadžić refers to his father as 'a pious and earnest man who cared little for songs except in so far as he memorized them, almost accidentally, from his father Joksim and his brother Toma, who not only knew many songs and were glad to sing and tell them, but also made up songs themselves' ('Predgovor', *Karadžić*, iv, p. 374).

[18] See ibid., pp. 374–5.

This situation will soon change, but it can be most clearly demonstrated in the life and work of Filip Višnjić, Karadžić's most popular singer. He was a man who carefully collected first-hand information from the Serbian rebels about the battles in which they fought and which became the subjects of his songs.[19] At the same time, however, he was a man 'who could move his audience to tears'.[20] This can be explained, in so far as such things can be explained, by his command of the epic language and by his imaginative gifts, but it might also have something to do with his own personal experience of history. He was born in Bosnia, 'on the other side of the river Drina',[21] and it was in his native part of the country, in the vicinity of Bijeljina, that he came to witness some of the common forms of Turkish terror. When he was twenty, blind after smallpox from the age of eight, a group of Turks raped one of the women in his uncle's household, where he lived after the death of his father. In revenge the family killed a Turk and 'hanged another one on a plum tree by his horse's halter'.[22] As a result all the members of the family were tortured and most of them killed. What survived this punishment was the story of his heroic uncle Marko, the head of this large farming household, who 'sang through the town of Zvornik as he was going to the gallows'.[23] Homeless Filip, a very gifted young man, travelled for years and lived on his voice. He sang to the Christian rayah in many Bosnian villages and to the crowds on popular feast days at the monasteries. But he also cultivated a special repertoire for 'the great Turks' whom he entertained when his travels took him to towns.[24] During the First Serbian Uprising his native region was sometimes a major battlefield: in 1809,

---

[19] 'Višnjić told Lukijan Mušicki how he began his songs about the Uprising. He asked the fighters, he said, as they were coming back from the battlefield: "who was their commander", where they fought, "who was killed, who they fought against". This is to say—he collected his material. The singer did not tell Mušicki how he turned the dry details into poetry. He himself was not aware of the secret.' V. Nedić, 'Filip Višnjić', *Narodna književnost*, p. 331.

[20] L. Ranke, *A History of Servia and the Servian Revolution*, London, 1847, p. 76. See also below pp. 322–3.

[21] V. S. Karadžić, 'Predgovor', *Karadžić*, iv, p. 365.

[22] V. Nedić, 'Filip Višnjić', *Narodna književnost*, p. 324.

[23] Ibid.   [24] Ibid.

for instance, the Serbian rebels crossed the river Drina and, under the command of Stojan Čupić and Luko Lazarević, who were to become great heroes in Filip's songs,[25] besieged Bijeljina and fought some severe battles in this region. When they were forced to retreat, Filip joined them. Stojan Čupić, who had risen from the position of a servant to that of a great captain of the rebels' army, gave Filip a white horse for his song 'The Battle of Salaš'. The song described one of the major battles in 1806 and Stojan Čupić is presented in it as a man of immense courage and equal sensitivity for the social position and suffering of his peasants.[26] During 1810—after Višnjić's retreat to Serbia—his song kept up the spirit of the twelve hundred rebels, besieged in Loznica and exposed to Turkish fire and poisoned water supply. They waited for twelve days for the relief which was led by Karađorđe himself, the chief commander of the Serbian armies. After the Serbian victory Višnjić's song moved Karađorđe who, 'a man of few words', came to talk to him.[27] After the Uprising was crushed in 1813, Višnjić crossed the river Sava and came to live in Srem. He had a hut in a farmer's courtyard and some stools for the villagers who would come to listen to him during the winter. In summer he travelled round the villages in the whole area and wherever he came he was well-received and richly rewarded for his songs. The peasants in his own village Grk remembered him for a long time; when he died in 1834, they carved a *gusle* on his oak cross.

The nature of Višnjić's achievement becomes clearer in the light of his personal and historical fate. It is the fate of a blind seer who experienced some of the most atrocious forms of Turkish terror in his young days and found himself at the heart of one of the greatest historical national upheavals. But it is also the fate of a persevering and widely travelled craftsman who learned his art in the large central areas of oral epic singing where he mastered its full range. For Višnjić sings about Stefan Nemanja, St Sava, Marko Kraljević, the outlaws and the

[25] Both these heroes figure in the famous 'Battle of Loznica' (*Karadžić*, iv, No. 33) and 'Luko Lazarević and Pejzo' (*Karadžić*, iv, No. 34). Stojan Čupić also figures in 'Čupić's Boast' ('Hvala Čupićeva', *Karadžić*, iv, No. 36) and in 'The Battle of Salaš' (*Karadžić*, iv, No. 28).

[26] See above pp. 286–7 and below pp. 340–1.

[27] V. Nedić, 'Filip Višnjić', *Narodna književnost*, p. 325.

border raiders and, above all, about the greatest captains and the common soldiery of the First Serbian Uprising. Moreover, he also sings about Sultan Murad, the Great Dahijas, many Turkish and Moslem heroes, their mothers and wives—often at considerable length and sometimes with a vocabulary which reflects his appreciation of their human involvement in tragic history. This is why his dramatic sense of history, his intense feeling for concrete detail, his visionary image of the whole landscape and his imaginative response to the human impact of gory realities are so impressive.

His blindness explains why in his songs St Sava claims that his father Stefan Nemanja spent his treasure not only building churches and monasteries but also, among other things, 'giving alms to the crippled and to the blind'[28]—a detail not to be found in blind Stepanija's version of this poem who did not respond so quickly to the occasion of interweaving a moving personal element into a traditional epic tale.[29] And this ability is not mirrored only in Višnjić's long list of monasteries which Nemanja built, including many Bosnian ones which Nemanja did not build but which Višnjić, a widely travelled singer, knew. It is even more clearly demonstrated in Marko Kraljević's bequest of his treasure—part of which is again to be given 'to the crippled and to the blind':

> 'Let the blind walk the roads of the world
> And let them sing of Marko in their songs'.[30]

Besides, as blind professional singers were much more dependent on their public performances, often at the monasteries on great festivals, and as they were generally much more influenced by hagiographical literature, it may be also Višnjić's blindness which accounts partly for his outstanding sense of the miraculous—sometimes according to the epic standard, but often quite exceptional in its frequency and in the importance of its epic function. Thus, for instance, the ominous dream at the beginning of 'St Sava and Hasan Pasha'

---

[28] 'Dijeleći kljastu i slijepu', 'Sveti Savo', *Karadžić*, ii, No. 24, l. 42.

[29] See above pp. 142–3.

[30] '(Treći ćemer) kljastu i slijepu, / Nek slijepi po svijetu hode, / Nek pjevaju i spominju Marka'. 'Smrt Marka Kraljevića', *Karadžić*, ii, No. 74, ll. 110–12.

is a standard epic narrative device, but the melting of the
Pasha's sword when he tries to slash the relics of St Sava, the
fire which burns his tents, the Pasha's blinding and the crippling
of his arms and legs, his wailing for mercy, the abbot's prayer
and the miraculous healing of the Pasha are much more in
keeping with the song's distinctly hagiographical tenor which is
usually characteristic of blind singers.[31] Some of the miraculous
elements in the story about the death of Marko Kraljević—
particularly the appearance of the *vila* and her prophecy of
Marko's death—are also according to the epic standard. But
the ominous stumbling and weeping of Marko's horse, the
evocation of ancient beliefs in the miraculous properties of
water, Marko's reflection in a well which forebodes his death
—these give the whole tale a visionary colouring which is not
common in the songs about Marko.[32] And the heavenly omens
in 'The Beginning of the Revolt Against the Dahijas' as well as
the stars, 'trapped' in a dish of water which mirrors the headless
bodies of the Turkish rulers, are certainly quite unique in a
story about a contemporary historical subject.[33]

But in Višnjić's poems the visionary and the miraculous—
and in this he is different from many other blind singers—often
illuminate the historical and the immediate which are given
with exceptional factual accuracy. For Višnjić is above all the
singer of contemporary history and his descriptions of the
beginning of the Serbian revolt and many of the historical
battles—at Čokešina (1804), near Salaš (1806), in the field of
Mišar (1806), at Loznica (1810)—are not only broadly true to
historical facts but also distinguished by a lively sense of many
particular details. The shortage of ammunition in 'The Battle of
Čokešina' and the subsequent use of guns as clubs, the bleating
sheep and the lowing cattle which are driven away from their
homeland in 'The Battle of Salaš' and many other of Višnjić's
great scenes are unique both in their physical precision and

[31] See 'St Sava and Hasan Pasha' ('Sveti Savo i Hasan-paša'), *Karadžić*,
iii, No. 14. For the miraculous element in the songs of blind singers see
above pp. 107–9 and, particularly, pp. 161–2.
[32] See 'The Death of Marko Kraljević', *Karadžić*, ii, No. 74, ll. 12–14,
49–66.
[33] See 'The Beginning of the Revolt Against the Dahijas', *Karadžić*, iv,
No. 24, ll. 1–68.

their imaginative sense of the Serbian soil and history.[34] More-over, Višnjić's sense of realistic detail ranges from the heroic and the tragic to the genuinely comic and humorous. Such are the moments when Ilija Bírčanín frightens the powerful Dahija out of his wits as he throws at him the bag with the tax-money which he had collected, when the cowardly Captain Ćurčija explains that he cannot afford to fight a stronger enemy because he is not like a willow-tree, once cut, to sprout again, when Bey Ljubović challenges Bajo Pivljanin to a duel and threatens, if the challenge is refused, that he will send his enemy raw wool and a distaff to make a shirt and a pair of pants for himself.[35] Similarly, we well may ask why it is that the hands of the great Serbian captain Anto Bogićević tremble so that he cannot write a message requesting help for besieged Loznica. Is he so frightened of the Turks, or is he illiterate and frightened of paper—or perhaps just an old man with trembling hands?[36]

The interplay of such vivid realistic elements with the invocations of Kosovo itself, with the visionary and miraculous illuminations of history suggest an almost medieval imaginative genius flourishing in the setting of much later times. Višnjić's ability to merge such diverse and often anachronistic elements into a unified vision of his tales make him an exemplary epic singer. In short, his 'darkened sun' is as much a heavenly omen as it is the result of the fog of gunpowder in Mačva and this is perhaps why he succeeded—to paraphrase his favourite image —in 'tying the red flame into the skies'.[37] And last but not least, it was perhaps his singing to 'the great Turks' in Bosnia that enabled him to master their moral and psychological idiom and push the frontiers of the epic drama so far as to include the great and humane Turkish characters, like Sultan Murad and Old Fočo, within the scope of his vision.[38] In short, the maturity of his epic voice—that of a young blind boy, a victim of Turkish terror, a professional singer and craftsman, an entertainer of the Serbian rebels and an elderly exiled man—was not unearned.

[34] See above pp. 280–95 and below pp. 340–2.
[35] See 'Bajo Pivljanin and Bey Ljubović' ('Bajo Pivljanin i beg Ljubović'), *Karadžić*, iii, No. 70, ll. 14–19.
[36] See 'The Battle of Loznica', *Karadžić*, iv, No. 33, ll. 291–2.
[37] See above p. 267. [38] See above pp. 292–4.

A different but equally significant historical and biographical pattern is reflected in the life of Tešan Podrugović, the greatest of Karadžić's poets—for he did not sing but used to 'speak' his poems. He was born in the village of Kazanci in Herzegovina and he also travelled quite extensively, at first making his living as a trader. He was a huge man—as big as a man and a half (*po drugog čoveka*); hence Podrugović instead of Gavrilović which was in fact his original family name.[39] His courage equalled his stature: as a young man he was unperturbed when a group of Turks tried to rape one of the girls in his household and everyone ran away. He killed one of the Turks and drove away the others, so that at the age of about twenty-five he had to leave his home and take to the woods. As an outlaw he made a name for himself; when the Serbian Uprising broke out he crossed the river Drina and joined the rebels. He distinguished himself in the battles near the river Drina, but when his captain did him an injustice, he left the Serbian army so that he should not have to kill his superior. Before the defeat of Serbian rebels in 1813 he crossed the river Sava and came to live in Srem in utter poverty.[40] Karadžić found him making his living by cutting reeds and selling them in towns—a reticent and serious man, with a strange sense of humour, 'scowling' as he told his often funny stories.[41]

'He was clever and, for an outlaw, an honest man';[42] and it was at this time, when Podrugović was about forty, that Karadžić recorded twenty-two poems from him. 'I have never found anyone who knew the poems as well as he did. Each of his poems was a good one, because he—particularly as he did not sing but spoke his poems—understood and felt them, and he thought about what he said.'[43] He had a large repertoire and knew, in Karadžić's opinion, at least another hundred poems apart from the recorded ones; moreover, Karadžić claims that if Podrugović were 'to hear the worst poem, after a few days he would speak it beautifully and in proper order which was characteristic of his other songs, or he would not remember it at all, and he would say that it was silly, not worth remembering

[39] See V. S. Karadžić, 'Predgovor', *Karadžić*, iv, p. 364.
[40] See V. Nedić, 'Tešan Podrugović', *Narodna književnost*, pp. 344–6.
[41] See 'Predgovor', *Karadžić*, iv, p. 364.
[42] Ibid.   [43] Ibid., pp. 364–5.

or telling.'[44] However, Karadžić's recording of Podrugović's songs in the monastery of Šišatovac in Srem was suddenly interrupted. About Easter time in 1815 the news came that the second round of fighting against the Turks in Serbia had just started; it was, Karadžić tells us, 'as if a hundred thorns had got under his skin'.[45] And it was with great effort that Karadžić kept him for a few more days to write down some more of his poems before Podrugović left for Serbia to' fight the Turks again'.[46] Obviously, he had more important business on hand than the most enlightened man in Serbia of his time could understand.

However, in the summer of the same year, he left the Serbian army again, went to Bosnia, killed a bey and became an outlaw. A little later he tried to get back to Serbia, but on his way he quarrelled with some Turks in an inn. He killed a few of them and, himself wounded, tried to escape. However, the Turks caught up with him and as he had no ammunition, he defended himself by throwing stones as he retreated up the mountain. With two more wounds he managed to escape, but they went bad and he had to return to a village in which he died a few days later.[47]

Podrugović's courage and suffering, his physical stature and his irascible temper, his grand sense of personal, family, and national honour, his love of funny stories defying his experience of history suggest the characteristic figure of a great outlaw who becomes a fighter for national independence at the beginning of the nineteenth century. Besides, his personal fate and character also explain his imaginative attachment to certain themes. His sense of patriarchal loyalties—which turned him into an outlaw at the age of twenty-five—is clearly mirrored, for instance, in the poems in which the ideals of family village life dominate the heroic feudal scene. Thus in 'Dušan's Wedding' Miloš Voinović, the historical military commander who represented the emperor in his dealings with Dubrovnik, is turned into a shepherd who rides a horse covered by a bear-skin and defends his imperial uncle in spite of the latter's credulity and slanderous insults. His outstanding stature, cunning and courage, and above all his skill in outwitting his

---

[44] 'Predgovor', *Karadžić*, iv, p. 378.   [45] Ibid., p. 364.   [46] Ibid.
[47] See V. Nedić, 'Tešan Podrugović', *Narodna književnost*, p. 346.

enemies and making fools of them are clearly the reflections of Podrugović's own personality. A sense of patriarchal values also dominates his great song about the Battle of Kosovo in which Tsaritsa Milica obtains Tsar Lazar's blessing to have one of her brothers stay with her, but each of them feels in duty bound to die in the battle. Similarly, when a Turkish girl helps the wounded King Vukašin and accepts him as her brother-in-God but is betrayed by her own brother, Marko Kraljević will kill the treacherous brother when he offers King Vukašin's sword for sale ('Marko Kraljević Knows His Father's Sword').

However, Podrugović's greatest heroes—like Miloš Voinović who can jump over three horses with three fiery swords on them, or Marko Kraljević who plays by throwing his mace into the clouds and catching it again—are not only men of uncommon physical strength. They also illustrate Podrugović's unique sense of realistic comedy which often takes place within the framework of exalted heroic ideals. Thus Karadžić's claim that Podrugović liked to tell funny stories with a scowl defines the comic tenor of 'Marko Kraljević and Ljutica Bogdan' in which two hot-headed Serbian heroes come to blows and frighten each other so much that their final reconciliation reflects above all their desire never to meet again.[48] An equally rich and often much more complex sense of comedy pervades, as we have seen, Podrugović's greatest songs about Marko Kraljević: 'The Wedding of Marko Kraljević', 'Marko Kraljević Knows His Father's Sword', 'Marko Kraljević and the Daughter of the Arab King', 'Marko Kraljević and Musa Kesedžija', 'Marko Kraljević and Đemo of the Mountain'. For it was in the traditional songs about Marko Kraljević and his exploits that Podrugović found the richest scope for the expression of his own genius—the genius of great comic dignity, of a hot-headed, irascible and clumsy, but also exalted sense of personal and communal honour. And, finally, it is also significant that this great outlaw has left us several of the classic lines about 'the bad craft' of outlawry,[49] about the 'bitterness' of the outlaws' fate, about the skill and courage of the man

---

[48] See 'Marko Kraljević i Ljutica Bogdan', *Karadžić*, ii, No. 39, ll. 12–37, 113–16.

[49] See above p. 246.

Fit to overtake and run away
And stand his ground in terrible places . . .
Who fears no one but God Himself.[50]

To sum up, Karadžić's greatest epic poet, who knew that fighting was more important than singing, created the heroes who have to face—and use—the tricks and treacheries of history and Realpolitik to defend the dignity of human life on this earth.

The links between the singer's personal fate, his interest in particular themes of the epic heritage and his ability to make them live as poetry can also be discerned in the four outstanding songs—running to almost three thousand lines—which Karadžić recorded from Old Milija (Starac Milija). The honorary title of 'starac' was not the privilege of 'just any elderly man', but of 'the wise man and the sage who knew the tradition', who was held in high esteem, next to the village chief.[51] This suggests that Karadžić's recording of Old Milija's songs took place when a wise and, as we shall see, tough man was breaking under the burden of old age, personal misfortunes and drink. For Old Milija was also, like Podrugović, born in old Herzegovina, in the vicinity of Kolašin (now in Montenegro) and, like Podrugović, he was also involved in a fight against 'some Turks', which forced him to leave his native area.[52] Unlike Podrugović, however, he was not twenty at the time, but at least in his fifties. This is not the age when a farmer would easily leave his land; and there is no doubt that some great trouble must have driven Old Milija to escape to Serbia.[53] When Karadžić met him in 1822 in Kragujevac, the souvenirs of this trouble were still vivid: 'all his head was scarred with cuts', Karadžić tells us.[54] Besides, Karadžić had

[50] See note 10, p. 246.

[51] M. Lutovac, 'Ibarski Kolašin', *Srpski etnografski zbornik*, lxvii (1954), p. 114.

[52] 'Predgovor', *Karadžić*, iv, p. 366.

[53] Lj. Zuković suggests that Old Milija was, if not a 'real outlaw', at least 'an outlaw of the Montenegrin type, i.e. from time to time he joined an outlaw company and when the danger was over, he returned home' ('Vukov pjevač starac Milija', *Putevi*, xi [1965], p. 604). Zuković's argument rests partly on the interpretation of Karadžić's note that Old Milija 'escaped to' ('dobežao'), not just 'came' or 'moved' to Serbia.

[54] 'Predgovor', *Karadžić*, iv, p. 367.

great difficulty getting in touch with the gifted, decrepit singer: the efforts of the head of the Serbian administration in the district of Požega were not sufficient to secure his presence. So in the autumn of 1822, when Karadžić came to Serbia on the invitation of its ruler Prince Miloš Obrenović, the illiterate Prince himself gave strict orders to his head clerk 'to have Milija brought alive or dead'[55] and make special arrangements for normal work on Milija's farm in his absence. When Old Milija turned up, he was so weak with old age and his wounds that he was unable, and unwilling, to sing without 'slivovits'. As soon as the drink was brought, he would pour it all into his own flask and disregarding the custom of offering it to other people present, he would start sipping and singing. People in the audience often teased him about this and asked him what the 'slivovits' was like. 'He used to answer, shuddering and frowning: "Awful, my son, so bad, it couldn't be worse; Heaven forbid that you should drink it!" '[56] The recording itself did not go smoothly: Milija was unable to sing his songs with the required pauses. So he drawled out his phrases as best he could and Karadžić wrote as fast as he could, and this had to be repeated several times for each song. Four songs took more than fifteen days to write down. Finally, one of the loitering local louts—'such as can be found in many courts, worrying only about how to turn everything into a joke'[57]— persuaded Milija that all his harvest would go to the dogs if he went on wasting his time with such an irresponsible and mad fellow as Karadžić who cared, obviously, only for songs.[58] Milija soon disappeared—having collected his fee from the Prince's office—in the utmost secrecy. When Karadžić enquired about him again a year later, he was already dead.[59]

Milija's personal misfortune which struck him in old age and drove him away from home is mirrored in all his poems in the imagery of ravaged homes when the heroes are far away or terrible miseries which befall them on their long journeys. In 'Banović Strahinja'—running into eight hundred and ten lines, probably the greatest single epic poem in the language—the hero's home is devastated, his mother and his love are captured, while he feasts far away with his in-laws. This provides not only

---

[55] See ibid.   [56] Ibid.   [57] Ibid.
[58] See ibid.   [59] See ibid., pp. 367–8.

the moving force of the narrative, but also the most important inner link of Ban's sympathy with a noble-minded old Turkish dervish, a solo drinker like Milija himself.[60] For the two enemies understand each other much better than any of their friends: the old dervish had been humanely treated as Ban's prisoner a long time ago and he touches Ban to the quick when he tells him his story of his return to his ravaged home in which elder had come to grow in the doorposts. In 'The Wedding of Maksim Crnojević'—one of the outstanding poems in the epic tradition, running to 1,226 lines[61]—the hero is disfigured with smallpox while his father is far away in Venice, looking for a bride for him. The universal catastrophe—the quarrel and the slaughter of the wedding party with far-reaching historical consequences—also occurs on their journey, far away from home. The long journey which takes Marko Kraljević, Miloš Obilić, and Winged Relja of Pazar to Captain Leka's castle results in the tragic maiming and blinding of the prospective bride who insults her great Serbian suitors ('Captain Leka's Sister').[62] And in 'Captain Gavran and Limo'—with its magnificent image of the loot equally divided among the living and the dead outlaws—there is also a very long journey which takes the Montenegrin fighters to north-western Bosnia and the frontier area near the town of Bihać.[63] Long journeys are not, of course, uncommon in the epic tradition, but no other singer makes them a source of personal tragedies in all his poems. It is in this sense that Milija's songs embody a vivid awareness of his own personal tragedy as well as a wider concept of partiarchal village culture, the assumption that being far away from home is one of the main sources of misfortune and misery in human life.

Karadžić's description makes it clear that Old Milija tried to extinguish his sense of misfortune and misery in drinking, just as the old Turkish dervish does in 'Banović Strahinja'. Besides, Milija's representation of Marko Kraljević, a notorious drinker in the songs of many other singers, is outstanding, not perhaps because Milija's Marko drinks a whole 'tub' of wine

[60] See above p. 136.
[61] 'Ženidba Maksima Crnojevića', *Karadžić*, ii, No. 89.
[62] 'Sestra Leke kapetana', *Karadžić*, ii, No. 40.
[63] See above p. 240–2.

and gives one to his horse, but because this enormous amount of wine makes the horse red up to his ears and Marko only to his eyes![64] And when the wedding party in 'The Wedding of Maksim Crnojević' comes to the sea, everyone does what he likes best:

<blockquote>Every drunkard tips up his flask.[65]</blockquote>

The number of drunkards suggested shows that a common element in the tradition must have been exceptionally near to the singer's heart.

Finally, the poetic genius of the unfortunate old drunkard saw everything on a magnificent scale. His Strahinić Ban is not only richly dressed like so many other epic heroes: the rosy colour of his clothes surpasses that of the sun, their redness is redder than water—presumably at sunset.[66] In 'Captain Leka's Sister' Marko Kraljević appears all in gold and his horse is covered in lynx fur;[67] Miloš Obilić has 'three storeys' of rich clothes on him;[68] the Winged Relja of Pazar makes both of them look shabby by his appearance.[69] The gold shirt which the mother-in-law gives to the prospective bridegroom in 'The Wedding of Maksim Crnojević' has a serpent's head under the throat with a precious stone so brilliant that the groom will need no candle when he takes his bride to their bedroom.[70] Moreover, the cruelties of Milija's heroes and heroines are on the same scale: no other epic heroine ever dared insult the three great Serbian dukes as Captain Leko's sister did, no other epic hero was as generous as Strahinić Ban who spared the life of his unfaithful love. This is why it has sometimes been claimed —not perhaps with any reliability and certainly with little sense of what Old Milija's art is about—that the behaviour of his heroes and heroines suggests a certain decline of patriarchal moral norms in actual life, characteristic of Milija's times and perhaps of his own personal experience.[71] Be that as it may, in

---

[64] See 'Sestra Leke kapetana', *Karadžić*, ii, No. 40, ll. 56–63.

[65] 'Ko l' bekrija, naginje čuturom', *Karadžić*, ii, No. 89, l. 594.

[66] 'The cloth was redder than the water, / The cloth was pinker than the sun' ('Što od vode čoha crvenija, / A od sunca čoha rumenija'), 'Banović Strahinja', *Karadžić*, ii, No. 44, ll. 24–5.

[67] See 'Sestra Leke kapetana', *Karadžić*, ii, No. 40, l. 54.

[68] 'Tri kata haljina', ibid., l. 144.   [69] See ibid., ll. 187–92.

[70] See 'Ženidba Maksima Crnojevića', *Karadžić*, ii, No. 89, ll. 791–8.

[71] See P. Bakotić, 'Starac Milija', *Školski vjesnik*, xii (1962), No. 8, p. 26.

Milija's songs we are faced with a tragic range and intensity which endorse the broken moral patterns and reveal an outstandingly generous and perceptive poetic mind.

Far less is known about Karadžić's other singers. But it is worth noting that Old Raško—the singer of several of the best poems with motifs from Serbian medieval history, such as the splendid, if highly controversial 'Building of Skadar' and the universally acknowledged 'Uroš and the Mrljavčevići'—was also born in Kolašin, in old Herzegovina, and came to Serbia at the beginning of the First Serbian Uprising.[72] Stojan the Outlaw —the singer of 'The Wedding of King Vukašin', one of the greatest poems with medieval heroes—was also born in Herzegovina. But when he came to Serbia and gave up out-lawry, he ran into trouble for having killed an old woman who, he believed, was a witch who had 'eaten' his child.[73] His idea of women and witches may go some way towards explaining his interest in such characters as the faithless Vidosava, the villain in the story of 'The Wedding of King Vukašin' and one of the greatest 'bitches' in the Serbo-Croat epic tradition.[74] It is also noteworthy that the greatest of Karadžić's Montenegrin singers Đuro Milutinović, the singer of the two best poems from this area, 'Perović Batrić' and 'The Piperi and Tahir Pasha', was a blind man who brought a letter from the Montenegrin Prince Bishop to Karađorđe in 1809 and stayed in Serbia.[75]

To sum up, the existing evidence about Karadžić's greatest singers—and it is evidence recorded by an outstandingly shrewd and objective observer, whose sober judgement is illustrated by everything he wrote, including his historical writings, his great dictionary and grammar—seems to point not only to the basic routes of the Serbian migrations but also to a very lively interplay of the oral epic traditions with the personal

---

[72] See 'Predgovor', *Karadžić*, iv, p. 368. For the discussion of 'Uroš and the Mrljavčevići' and 'The Building of Skadar' see above pp. 138-41, 147-151.

[73] See above p. 127 and particularly note 10 on that page.

[74] See above pp. 128-31. There is also an example of a treacherous wife in Stojan the Outlaw's song 'Vuk Jerinić and Zukan the Ensign': Hajka, Zukan's 'faithful love', takes hold of a broken sword and helps Zukan's enemy to slaughter her husband (see 'Vuk Jerinić i Zukan barjaktar', *Karadžić*, iii, No. 54, ll. 209-17).

[75] See 'Predgovor', *Karadžić*, iv, p. 369.

involvement of the singers in the burning issues of contemporary
history. But if this is a major part of the picture there is also
another vast and important area which tells a completely
different story and which is not usually fully recognized. It is
the area of the great epic songs of blind, pious old women who
did not move about and were sometimes linked with particular
monasteries. Their greatest achievements are to be found in the
songs about medieval feudal times and their sense of the distant
past seems to be stronger and sometimes more accurate than
that of other singers. So, for instance, 'Momir the Foundling'—
a great song originating perhaps from a *bugarštica* which derived
its story from Byzantine sources and, ultimately, from *1001
Nights*—was recorded from 'blind Živana who sat in Zemun'.[76]
Two more songs about Marko Kraljević—one of them being
'Marko Kraljević and Alil-aga', one of the finest in Karadžić's
collection—were written down from the same singer.[77] Blind
Jeca who, apparently, also 'sat' in Zemun was the singer of
'The Death of Duke Prijezda', deservedly one of the best-known
poems in the language, the greatest example of a tragic feudal
drama in the Serbo-Croat oral epic tradition.[78] One of the very
few songs about the Battle of Kosovo in Karadžić's collection,
'Tsaritsa Milica and Duke Vladeta', was written down from
blind Stepanija of whom we know only that she was born in
Jadar in Serbia.[79] Karadžić also notes that he received a
variant of this song—'almost the same as this one'—from
another source.[80] What 'almost the same' exactly means is
difficult to say—but does it suggest a higher degree of memorizing than we usually find in the tradition? And last but not
least Lukijan Mušicki, a learned versifier and the abbot of the
monastery of Šišatovac in Srem, recorded—or had someone
record for him—from a blind woman in the neighbouring
village of Grgurevci some of the finest poems about feudal
times in Karadžić's collection: 'The Downfall of the Serbian
Empire', 'The Kosovo Girl' and 'Marko Kraljević Abolishes

---

[76] Ibid., p. 370. See also above pp. 115–17.

[77] See above pp. 199–201. The other song which Karadžić recorded from
blind Živana is 'Marko Kraljević and the Twelve Arabs' ('Marko Kraljević
i 12 Arapa', *Karadžić*, ii, No. 63).

[78] See above pp. 89–91 and below pp. 337–8.

[79] See 'Predgovor', *Karadžić*, iv, p. 372. See also above pp. 170–1.

[80] 'Predgovor', *Karadžić*, iv, p. 372.

the Wedding Tax'.[81] 'The Kosovo Girl' is one of the finest songs in the tradition and it is astoundingly accurate in historical detail—the communion of the Serbian army on the eve of the battle, and the representation of the silver gilt rings, feudal gowns with monograms and circular ornaments, the scarves woven with gold threads and given in token of betrothal. S. Radojčić—one of the most distinguished Serbian art historians —has checked these details against the evidence of contemporary Byzantine military tracts, Serbian monastic literature and medieval fresco painting. This has led him to claim that their survival can only be explained by the assumption that the poem was memorized by generations of singers and repeated 'like Paternoster—with or without understanding—but accurately, line by line'.[82]

Of course, this need not have been the case. But even if generations of singers memorized only stock phrases, formulas, and clusters of formulas hardly ever running beyond a few lines, even if they learned only how to handle some specific narrative and stylistic structures, this does not imply merely the command of a poetic language. This language itself was a way of memorizing history, many of its physical details, actual events and social concepts. At the same time this language was not being mastered in the abstract, but within narrative structures which were a way of responding to history and interpreting its significance. These narrative structures were open to change and adaptation, they could absorb new concepts and new material; and it was in a dramatic interplay of the past and the present, the imaginative interplay of anachronistic and anatopistic features, that the singers created their greatest achievements. For the oral epic singing at its best was both a way of coming to terms with history and a means of getting out of it. This is why its ultimate significance cannot be grasped in the analysis either of the technique of its composition or of the diverse historical sources of its social concepts, motifs, and themes. For a song about fighting is not the same thing as fighting or even as the recording of an actual response to it. Similarly, songs about great defeats, vassalage, outlawry, or

[81] See above pp. 161–2, 171–2, 203–4.
[82] S. Radojčić, 'Kosovka djevojka', *Uzori i dela starih srpskih umetnika*, p. 239.

rebellions attempt to grasp in language not only their historical but also their moral significance. They interpret the actual in terms of what it means as a challenge to the human spirit and to the whole tradition of oral poetic language in which it expresses itself. This is why the way in which diverse stylistic and narrative devices, the whole anachronistic heritage of the historical material embedded in the nature of the oral epic convention itself, has to be the object of inquiry: what sense— if any—does the Serbo-Croat oral epic language at its best make of what it remembers of several centuries of the Balkan history?

2. Technique and Achievement

Describing the growth of heroic poems Karadžić claims—and he was at the heart of a flourishing tradition—that they come into being slowly and never reach an enduring form:

The poems have not immediately, in their beginning, become as they are, but one man begins and composes as he can, and then going from mouth to mouth the poem grows and becomes more beautiful, and sometimes shrivels and is spoilt; for as one man can talk more clearly and beautifully than another, so he can sing and speak poems.[1]

This is why 'even if there are many people who know many poems, it is still difficult to find a man who knows poems beautifully and clearly'.[2] However, when a great oral poet, like Tešan Podrugović, is found, 'each of his poems is good (particularly as he did not sing but only spoke his poems) . . . because he understands and feels the poems and thinks about what he says'.[3]

Leopold Ranke—one of the greatest German historians of the nineteenth century who depended heavily on Karadžić for his information about the Serbian Uprising and Serbian heroic poetry—also stresses the importance of improvisation and personal talent in traditional epic singing:

The very song which is disliked when given by an inferior singer excites enthusiasm when sung by a more successful performer—by one possessing more of the national talent and spirit. . . We must not suppose the singer to be a mere declaimer: he is obliged by his own poetical talent to reproduce the poem which was handed down to him.[4]

It is this possession of 'the national sentiment and spirit' that enables singers of genius, 'the men of real poetic talent, like

[1] 'Predgovor', *Karadžić*, i, p. 536.   [2] Ibid., p. 537.

[3] 'Predgovor', *Karadžić*, iv, pp. 364–5. It is also of some interest to note that 'speaking' was, apparently, a more 'homely' manner of performance: old men usually 'spoke' their poems to children and many people could be more easily persuaded to 'speak' than to sing poems (see ibid., p. 365, note).

[4] L. Ranke, *A History of Servia and the Servian Revolution*, p. 74.

Philip Wishnitsch from Bosnia' to 'move their audience to tears'.[5]

This pitch of communication was achieved at a flashpoint of history and it depended as much on the genius of a particular singer as on the collective epic language. This language stored up in its formulas not only a rich range of the elements for easy story-telling, but also an exciting awareness of the past, framed within several major moral concepts of biblical, feudal, and patriarchal origin. The formulas included the grand opening scenes in 'white palaces', where heroes 'held council', 'drank wine' or 'wrote' their 'thin' or 'small-lettered books'. Such openings were usually followed by long journeys on which 'cold water' or, preferably, 'cool' or 'red wine' had to be drunk. The journeys resulted in battles or single combats, with their 'good horses', 'battles lances', 'razor-sharp swords' and 'heavy maces'. The battles led to 'heavy' or 'fierce wounds', the 'parting with sinful souls', 'terrible tears' streamed down 'white faces'; and 'black' was not only the colour of mourning clothes and gunpowder, but also of blood, earth, and birds, particularly ravens. This historical world was further framed in the natural imagery of 'the supple fir-trees' and 'the hot sun' in 'the clear sky'.[6] Numerous other stylistic devices added to the exciting interplay of the historical and natural world: in the poems opening with paradoxical Slavonic antitheses the human world was often deceptively seen in terms of natural imagery mirroring a divine order. This illusion was always immediately dispelled and the implied moral order destroyed in the reality of the story to emerge again as a tragic ideal moral norm at the end.[7]

Finally, many of the best songs were illuminated from within by formulas rich in association with legendary heroic concepts of biblical or feudal origin. The world on the eve of the Turkish conquest was seen as 'the last times' of Serbian history, and this concept of Doomsday re-emerged when history came full circle: in the great poem describing 'The Beginning of the Revolt Against the Dahijas', where old books were brought again to foretell to the Turkish rulers what would happen 'in the end'.[8]

---

[5] Ibid., p. 76.   [6] See above pp. 43–9.   [7] See above pp. 38, 113–15.

[8] '(Šta će nama biti) do pošljetka', 'Početak bune protiv dahija', *Karadžić*, iv, No. 24, l. 87.

Similarly, the decision to die for a lost cause and fight the
Battle of Kosovo was seen as the renunciation of 'the earthly'
and the choice of 'the heavenly Kingdom', which reiterates a
formula from medieval historical literature.[9] 'God's faith' was
often the test of 'who is faithful, who is the traitor', of 'firm
faith'—itself a medieval legal concept.[10] It gave added historical
dignity to many of the later instances of partiarchal loyalty—as
important in the poems about family life as in those about
Kosovo or the actions of outlaws. And finally, the demand to
surrender 'the good horse' and—or—the weapons as the ultimatum at the beginning of several poems reflected a major
medieval legal and moral concept, even if it was sometimes
blurred in the context of outlawry.[11] Free creative use of such
phrases and concepts, stylistic and narrative devices, explains
why 'any particular song is different in the mouth of each of its
singers' and even 'different at different stages of his career'.[12]
In short, the creative effort of the epic singer is largely directed
towards an inventive combination of his ready-made formulas;
he has to create as he sings—and the art is fundamentally not
one of memorizing but of improvisation. 'The poetic grammar
of oral epic singing is and must be based on formula. It is a
grammar of parataxis and of frequently used and useful
phrases.'[13]

Moreover, the decasyllabic formulas and their parataxis owe
very much to all the other forms of folk oral culture. Many of
the singers were also story-tellers and they must have known,
probably much better than most other people, many proverbs,
riddles, curses, incantations, dirges, and toasts—all of which
were formulaically suitable for diverse great and small occasions
of patriarchal life. Is it surprising that the singers often used the
motifs, formulas, and structural models of such utterances for
their epic purposes? It is clear, for instance, that many of the
comparatively few miraculous elements in Serbo-Croat heroic
poetry originated from widely known folk tales. Of course, such
elements had to be used sparsely in the predominantly historical
and 'realistic' epic medium to be effective at all. This explains
why such poems as 'Jovan and the Giant Master', and 'The
Serpent Bridegroom' which abound in miracles and depend on

[9] See above p. 162.   [10] See above p. 21.   [11] See above pp. 22, 53, 89–90.
[12] A. B. Lord, *The Singer of Tales*, p. 100.   [13] Ibid., p. 65.

them for their narrative movement, fail to attain the epic tenor of heroic poetry. Is it surprising that the former contains many elements of the earlier prose legends[14] and that the latter has been recorded in a much more coherent form as a folk tale.[15] This is also why some of the old feudal *bugarštice* which abound in miracles make slightly absurd reading: the predominantly historical tenor of the epic idiom cannot come to terms, for instance, with the repetitive miracles in the song about the crowning of King Matijaš. Repetition is, of course, a standard epic device; but when the crown, thrown into the air, miraculously falls for the third time on Matijaš's head, the effect is disastrously cumulative.[16] An occasional miraculous detail in *bugarštice*—such as the appearance of the girls with 'crowns of gold and pearls'[17] and 'helmets of pure gold'[18] on 'the green mountain'[19] before Marko Kraljević or Duke Janko's shooting of the miraculous 'fierce winged snake'[20] which brings about Ban Sekula's death—is usually much more successful. But how effectively it can be used at a decisive moment in a heroic poem is best seen in the appearance of the mountain nymph (*vila*) in many of the poems about Marko Kraljević. The richest interweaving of the realistic and the miraculous is probably to be found in the highly ambiguous appearance of the *vila* in Marko Kraljević's crisis during his combat with Musa Kesedžija: the *vila* tells Marko Kraljević that it would be a shame if the two of them were to fight against a single enemy and at the same time hints how he can defeat him by using his secret daggers.[21]

However, an occasional interweaving of a miraculous folk-tale element into the 'historical' illusion of a heroic poem is not perhaps the greatest debt of the epic world to the folk-tale.

[14] 'Jovan and the Giant Master' ('Jovan i divski starješina', *Karadžić*, ii, No. 8) echoes some legends about Hercules and Samson (see *Matić*, pp. 634–5).

[15] 'The Serpent Bridegroom' ('Zmija mladoženja', *Karadžić*, ii, Nos. 12, 13) can be found, also in two versions, in the form of a folk tale in V. S. Karadžić, *Srpske narodne pripovijetke*, Belgrade, 1969, pp. 46–52.

[16] See *Bogišić*, No. 30.

[17] 'Zlatne krune od bisera', *Bogišić*, No. 3, ll. 7, 9 (owing to different arrangement of lines these are ll. 6, 8 in PS, No. 75).

[18] 'Žarkula od suha zlata', ibid., l. 8 [7].

[19] 'Planinom zelenom', ibid., l. 2.

[20] 'Ljuta zmija krilatica', *Bogišić*, No. 19, ll. 13, 31, 40.

[21] See above pp. 197–8 and Appendix III.

This debt is also mirrored in the technique of epic story-telling, in the crystal-clear narrative interweaving of numerous and many-coloured threads in the best heroic poems. For the two forms lived side by side; and it was the clarity of a rich narration that struck Jacob Grimm as the most significant feature of Serbo-Croat heroic poetry when he claimed that it excelled in having no gaps in the story-telling and in being 'intelligible and clear from beginning to end'.[22] One should remember *Beowulf* or the *Nibelungenlied* to appreciate this point.

Of course, the easy spinning of complex tales is itself an expression of the inner composure of the patriarchal civilization which was so clear-headed in its moral and imaginative assessment of the historical turmoil and the human suffering in it. This mature and lucid response to the complexity of actual experience also found rich expression in many proverbs. This is why they were often taken over ready-made, if with a slight metrical adjustment, as formulas into epic poetry; and if none was readily available for a particular occasion, their syntactic and semantic structure could at least provide a generative model for an *ad hoc* maxim which the singer felt particularly pertinent to his story. So for instance in the *bugarštica* which describes the historical confusion of local betrayals, of Spanish, Venetian, and Turkish conflicts in the Bay of Kotor after the Turks recaptured Herceg-Novi, the singer sums up the scene in an *ad hoc* proverb which is a shrewd expression of his own deliberately bewildered point of view:

Where armies swell, reasons vanish![23]

The terse irony of this maxim and its syntactic balance clearly reflect the tone and structure of some Serbo-Croat proverbs, but it is, like many of the greatest lines in Serbo-Croat heroic songs, fundamentally non-formulaic—a single example of a great utterance. It is 'only' this achievement which makes it different from some other unique, *ad hoc* proverbs in *bugarštice*—the 'proverbs' which do not come off because they make a banal didactic point after it has been already worked to death in a long-winded story.[24]

[22] 'Narodne Srpske Piesme', *Kleinere Schriften*, iv, p. 199.

[23] 'Đe su sile velike, razlozi se izgubiše!' *Bogišić*, No. 73, l. 6.

[24] Such an example can be found, for instance, at the end of the same poem: the vengeance of treachery is explained in the following terms: 'For

However, proverbs and *ad hoc* proverbs—unique maxims moulded on their syntactic models—had a much richer life in the decasyllabic poems. The shorter line was obviously more suited to their economy of expression but they were also used, or made up, in a more ingenious creative spirit. So, for instance, a standard proverb lives in a specific dramatic context in one of the great scenes of Old Milija's 'Banović Strahinja'. A Turkish dervish, a poor drunken devil like Milija himself, explains to his opponent why he failed, his riches gone, to pay him the promised ransom after he was set free on trust:

'When riches go, friends go.'[25]

It is only because the old dervish expects more understanding from his Serbian enemy than he got from his Turkish friends that this proverb comes alive and outlines, among other things, his loneliness, his assumptions about generosity and his frustrated faithfulness.

Similarly Tešan Podrugović—in the last line of his famous 'Dušan's Wedding'—sums up in a standard proverb his story about Miloš Voinović's loyalty to his foolish uncle, his suzerain who had snubbed him:

Woe wherever is no next of kin![26]

The patriarchal wisdom of this proverb lives on the centuries of political and economic migration, on the suffering and the

---

the good is remembered and the evil is not forgotten' ('Er se dobro pametuje, a zlo se ne zaboravlja', *Bogišić*, No. 73, l. 99). Another example of platitudinous statement masquerading as proverbial wisdom can be found in the long-winded utterance near the end of the *bugarštica* which tells the story of the Paštrovići who, misled by the slander of one of their girls who claimed to have been dishonoured by a young man from Perast, kill this man and get killed themselves: 'May everyone meet such an end, who does evil without thinking, / What may befall him. / Because before you do evil, think what it might turn into.' ('Tako svaki dovršio, koji zlo čini bez razmisli, / Što mu može biti. / Jer prije neg' si zlo činio, misli na što može izaći.' *Bogišić*, No. 61, ll. 85–7—'učinio' in l. 87 corrected to 'činio' as in Balović–Pantić, No. 154). Leaving aside all the absurd implications of such a wording, suffice it to note that it is not unique in *bugarštice*.

[25] 'Nesta blaga, nesta prijatelja', 'Banović Strahinja', *Karadžić*, ii, No. 44, l. 421. See also V. S. Karadžić, *Srpske narodne poslovice*, p. 204.

[26] 'Teško svuda svome bez svojega', 'Ženidba Dušanova', *Karadžić*, ii, No. 29, l. 690. See also V. S. Karadžić, *Srpske narodne poslovice*, p. 285.

helplessness involved, but it comes to a richer imaginative life in the story based on the moral irony of ultimate loyalty to the kinsman and the suzerain who does not deserve it by personal merit and behaviour.

However, the best example of a standard proverb richly inlaid into an epic story is to be found in the well-known poem 'The Wedding of King Vukašin.' Duke Momčilo, on the threshold of disaster, tells his treacherous wife, with compelling innocence, his ominous dreams which forebode the oncoming doom. But she consoles him—having already betrayed him to the enemy—in a standard proverb which is normally used to dispel the fear of bad dreams in someone we love:

'The dream deceives, God is truth.'[27]

It is the husband's innocence and gullibility which make this utterance possible and dramatically convincing and this is how a standard proverb, in its 'normal' meaning, least suited to the occasion, illuminates the central moral conflict of the characters in this poem.

Each of these decasyllabic gnomic utterances can be found in identical phrasings in Karadžić's collection of *Serbian Popular Proverbs*.[28] Even if practically all the proverbs which Karadžić quotes in his collection are in prose, one has a strong sense that these decasyllabic utterances must have been proverbs before they were used in epic poetry—partly because of their wide circulation and appeal, partly because they embody a down-to-earth view of things, the realistic widsom, the conformist spirit which has no epic high-mindedness about it, the spirit characteristic of the practical wisdom of proverbs. The question whether in such instances an existing proverb might have been slightly adapted to fit the decasyllabic line and its caesura after the fourth syllable, whether such an adaptation

---

[27] 'San je laža, a Bog je istina!' 'Ženidba kralja Vukašina', *Karadžić*, ii, No. 25, l. 152. See also V. S. Karadžić, *Srpske narodne poslovice*, p. 253. This proverb is quoted in slightly different wording in an earlier version of this poem recorded in Dalmatia in the eighteenth century: 'San je klapnja, sam Bog je istina' ('Dreams delude, God Himself is truth'), *Bogišić*, No. 97, l. 47. This suggests perhaps that this proverb has not been quite stabilized at this time, for as a rule proverbs are usually more stable in their wording than the lines in epic poetry. See also above pp. 75, 129–30.

[28] See the preceding notes, 25–7.

might have made such proverbs more easily memorable and helped their circulation, must remain in the area of speculation. There is, of course, no doubt that such an adaptation sometimes occurred: in his collection Karadžić quotes, for instance, the well-known patriarchal judgement of feminine wisdom: 'Long braids—short brains' and adds as an illustration two lines from 'The Wedding of Maksim Crnojević' in which this proverb occurs in a semantic and metrical form adapted to decasyllabic singing. [29]

However, when a proverb runs to more than one perfect decasyllabic line—even if decasyllabics are almost as natural to Serbo-Croat speech as blank verse to English—one begins to wonder whether it came into being initially in the medium of epic poetry and, sometimes, if it is a proverb at all, regardless of the fact that it is quoted as such by Karadžić. An example of the former kind—of what might be a proverb but must have come into being in epic poetry—can be found in Podrugović's deservedly famous 'Dušan's Wedding.' When Miloš Voinović, the honest and devoted, but rough-mannered nephew of Tsar Stefan Dušan the Mighty, is faced with the task of leaping over three steeds with three fiery swords on their backs, the Emperor curses the tailor who had 'cut' such a long mountain-cloak for Miloš. Miloš answers with unperturbed calm in the lines which sum up not only his response to the Emperor's silly concern with technicalities on such a grand occasion, but also a deep patriarchal sense of loyalty and belonging, of fully accepting the world which one has been born into:

> 'When a sheep is fretting over its own fleece,
> There will be no sheep, there will be no fleece'. [30]

---

[29] 'U žene je duga kosa, a kratka pamet.' V. S. Karadžić, *Srpske narodne poslovice*, p. 294. This quotation is followed by Karadžić's comment: 'Here one might also mention what the love of Ivan Crnojević said: "Who would listen to his love's advice, / With her long braids, but her short brains?" ' ('Kog' su ljube dosle sjetovale, / S dugom kosom, a pameću kratkom?' 'Ženidba Maksima Crnojevića', *Karadžić*, ii, No. 89, ll. 226, 228.)—In modern usage this proverb appears in shorter form: 'Duga kosa, kratka pamet' ('Long braids, short brains').

[30] 'Kojoj ovci svoje runo smeta, / Onđe nije ni ovce ni runa!' 'Ženidba Dušanova', *Karadžić*, ii, No. 29, ll. 483–4. See also V. S. Karadžić, *Srpske narodne poslovice*, p. 154.

There is, of course, no reason why such a concept may not have a universal proverbial appeal in the patriarchal society; it is only the two perfect decasyllabics, involving in the original an unusual poetic shift of syntactic and semantic relations, that make one suspect that this utterance must have been of decasyllabic origin if it ever had a wide enough circulation to be called a proverb.

An analogous example of an epic *ad hoc* proverb—made to the specific measure of an epic story if hardly qualifying as an item in a handbook of practical wisdom—can be found in Old Raško's 'Uroš and the Mrljavčevići'. Marko Kraljević's mother advises her son who has to decide the question of lawful succession to the Serbian throne and she asks him to speak 'not for his father's sake or his uncle's',

> 'Because it is better to lose your life
> Than sin against your soul!'[31]

The syntactic pattern—it is better to do this than that—is common to many proverbs[32] and 'losing one's life' and 'sinning against one's soul' are not only part of the highly formulaic epic diction but also very common idioms in the language. However, when Karadžić lists these two lines as proverbs,[33] one remembers that they are unique in epic poetry, that Old Raško has been pushed into originality by a specific epic situation in which a mother has to act in the spirit of heroic high-mindedness. In short, it is difficult to imagine very many actual occasions in which such a statement would be offered as ancient wisdom in the form of practical advice.

Finally, there are also several major instances in Serbo-Croat epic singing in which the singer was pushed into a gnomic utterance even if he did not have a ready-made formula of a proverb at hand, so that in fact he had to make up a proverb himself which would suit his purpose. Thus in one of

[31] 'Ni po babu, ni po stričevima, / . . . Bolje ti je izgubiti glavu, / Nego svoju ogr'ješiti dušu.' 'Uroš i Mrljavčevići', *Karadžić*, ii, No. 34, ll. 129, 132–3.

[32] e.g. 'Better to fight a good man than kiss a bad one.' ('Bolje ti se s čoekom ubiti no s rđom ljubiti', V. S. Karadžić, *Srpske narodne poslovice*, p. 66.) In Karadžić's collection there are several pages of proverbs beginning with the word '*bolje*' (better).

[33] See ibid., p. 66.

Višnjić's poems his great hero Miloš of Pocerje comes to explain his love for his common soldiery after he has risked his life to spare theirs:

> 'Every mother's glad to see her son'.[34]

It is only this dramatic context of self-sacrifice which brings out the epic high-mindedness of what would have been otherwise only a piece of practical, platitudinous proverbial wisdom, based perhaps partly on a proverbial syntactic model.[35]

Such *ad hoc* proverbs can also be completely independent of either epic or proverbial formulas. The greatest instance is perhaps one of the best known lines in the whole epic tradition —the tragic cry of grief at the end of 'The Kosovo Girl'. After her betrothed had been killed in battle the heroine expresses her sense of her own fate in a gnomic utterance which not only sums up in highly personal terms the significance of the story, but also shows a universal sense of history and the symbolic interplay of the historical, the personal and the natural which has often been so characteristic of the Serbo-Croatian epic expression at its best:

> 'Unhappy, if I were to touch a green pine,
> Even the green pine would wither.'[36]

This is again an example of a unique proverbial utterance— proverbial only in its gnomic spirit and 'formulaic' only in its ultimate syntactic origin, in the sense in which almost every- thing is 'formulaic' in language from the point of view of generative grammar. Like so many of the greatest lines, it occurs only at a great moment in one of the greatest songs; it is not to be found anywhere else in the thousands of lines which had been recorded before. In short, a gifted singer can rise to an exceptional and unique epic occasion, even when this means pushing beyond the limits of the standard formulaic epic language.

[34] 'Svaka majka rada viđet' sina', 'Miloš Stoićević i Meho Orugdžijć', *Karadžić*, iv, No. 32, l. 194.

[35] Many proverbs in Karadžić's collection begin with the word 'svaki' (every, each). For instance: 'Svaka tica k svome jatu (leti)' ('Birds of a feather flock together"), *Srpske narodne poslovice*, p. 255.

[36] 'Da se, jadna, za zelen bor vatim, / I on bi se zelen osušio!' 'Kosovka djevojka', *Karadžić*, ii, No. 51, ll. 135–6.

Similarly, it could be easily shown that there are very significant unique elements in the many highly formulaic lines in the sections of epic poems which were shaped on the basic patterns of riddles, such as enigmatic dreams[37] and bewildering questions or comparisons at the beginning of many Slavonic antitheses.[38] It should not come as a surprise that the greatest instance of an enigmatic, dream-like quality which reality takes in an epic poem is found in one of the greatest poems about border raiders, 'The Death of Ivo of Senj'. There is, of course, in this poem, as in many others, the mother's traditional and 'formulaic' ominous dream and its standard interpretation. But nowhere else do the border raiders see their pursuers as 'black riders' on 'black horses', a little later—in the second round of pursuit and running for their lives—as 'white riders' on 'more furious horses' and, finally, as riders 'with black plaids', with 'their legs burnt away to their knees'.[39] It is the last, completely non-formulaic phrase which expresses the despair of the border raiders' wishful thinking, their vain hope that they might escape their fate. And if most of the Slavonic antitheses ask standard questions and give standard answers, this stylistic device is used at the beginning of the greatest of all family poems—'God Leaves No Debt Unpaid'—in a unique way. The vision of the harmony of the ideal brotherly and sisterly love—outlined in the image of a supple fir-tree protected by two green pines—provides a starting point for a rich interplay of the human, the natural and the moral world, which could hardly be exploited more than once in the same terms.[40]

The incantations and the curses are also usually standard and formulaic and can be followed in several poems in closely parallel phrasings.[41] But in one of the greatest of Kosovo poems —'Musić Stefan'—Prince Lazar's curse on any traitor who might fail to come to the Battle of Kosovo ends with:

'His blight rot all his brood while it endures!'[42]

The line is repeated once more in the same poem, but it is not to be found anywhere else, not even in another of Lazar's

---

[37] See above pp. 73–4, 129–30, 246–8.   [38] See note 17 on p. 38.

[39] See above p. 248.   [40] See above pp. 113–15.

[41] See above pp. 108–9, 126, 160–1, 262–3, 289.

[42] 'Rđom kap'o, dok mu je kolena!' 'Musić Stefan', *Karadžić*, ii, No. 47, ll. 28, 83.

curses which repeats the other standard elements, the curse of sterility and the destruction of harvest and vineyards.[43] So it is not a traditional formula, even if it is on the threshold of becoming the singer's personal formula which he could use only in a very specific and limited context.

As regards the dirges in the *bugarštice* and the decasyllabic poems, they are more widely spread and often phrased in the formulaic language which mirrors the customs and the conventions of an oral folk form which had its independent life outside epic poetry.[44] But when incorporated into some of the greatest epic poems, they often reflect a rich interplay of the formulaic and the unique. Thus the mother's maddened grief for her son at the end of 'The Wedding of Milić the Ensign' is expressed in the lines which mirror custom and formulas in a unique description of sorrow:

> She cut her hair, she tied the vines,
> She wept and watered the vinestock with her tears.[45]

The tears and weeping, the cutting of hair are customary and formulaic, but nowhere else have the vines been tied with the mother's hair and vinestock watered with her tears. Similarly, the greatest of all the dirges in Serbo-Croat epic poetry—that of the Mother of the Jugovići—begins in a formulaic description and comes to a unique climax:

> The mother takes Damjan's hand,
> She turns it around and over,
> She is whispering to the hand:
> 'My hand, O green apple!
> Where did you grow from, where were you ripped off?
> You grew on my lap,
> You were ripped off on flat Kosovo!'[46]

[43] See above pp. 160–1.

[44] See Lj. Zuković, 'O tužbalicama naročito s obzirom na ostale vrste naših narodnih pjesama', *Radovi Filozofskog fakulteta u Sarajevu*, v (1968–9), pp. 293–307.

[45] 'Kosu reže, pa vinograd veže, / Suze lije, čokoće zal'jeva', 'Ženidba Milića barjaktara', *Karadžić*, iii, No. 78, ll. 260–1.

[46] 'Uze majka ruku Damjanovu, / Okretala, prevrtala s njome, / Pak je ruci tijo besjedila: / "Moja ruko, zelena jabuko! / Gdje si rasla, gdje l' si ustrgnuta! / A rasla si na kriocu mome, / Ustrgnuta na Kosovu ravnom!" ' 'Smrt majke Jugovića', *Karadžić*, ii, No. 48, ll. 75–81.

The last three lines—with the exception of the second part of the last line—are unique, but their basic semantic components ('grow', 'grew', 'ripped off') are repetitive, so that this suggests the birth of a new formulaic pattern. If the epic language were not formulopoeic as well as formulaic, it would be difficult indeed to imagine how a single formula could have come into being.

Finally, many of the toasts needed only a little metrical adjustment to be taken over from feudal or village customs into epic poetry. Such is, for instance, the greatest of all of the exchanges of toasts in Serbo-Croat epic poetry—Prince Lazar's toast to Miloš and Miloš's reply on the eve of the Battle of Kosovo, in one of the greatest poems which Karadžić wrote down from his father.[47] This exchange is set in a dramatically modified framework of the Last Supper situation: Prince Lazar proposes a toast to Miloš Obilić, his bravest knight, forgiving him in advance his prospective betrayal in the Battle of Kosovo. But as Prince Lazar has unjustly accused his most faithful knight, Miloš's answer brings out the enormity of this mistake. It culminates in his prophetic accusation of Vuk Branković for treason and his promise to 'tie' the traitor 'on his battle lance':

'As a woman ties raw wool on a distaff!'[48]

How could this be part of the epic formula for a toast—even if the promise of the present of raw wool and distaff is a fairly standard form of mockery of cowardice.[49] Such outstandingly suggestive moments often contain no formulas even if they are based on the syntactic patterns of the highly formulaic forms of oral folk culture.[50] They are as significant as they are statistically negligible, like many of the other greatest and unique lines of Karadžić's poets and singers. Thus most of the lines in the anonymous and mediocre Montenegrin version of 'The Saints Divide the Treasure' are formulaic—except the genuinely powerful ones which describe the drought in the highly original

---

[47] See above pp. 164–5.

[48] 'Kao žena kuđelj' uz preslicu', 'Komadi od različnijeh kosovskijeh pjesama (iii)', *Karadžić*, ii, No. 50, l. 62.

[49] See above pp. 165–6, 237.

[50] For an example of the development of a formulaic pattern crowned by a unique line, see, for instance, above pp. 70, 83, 238–9.

imagery of 'the heroes' brains broiling', 'the rocks cracking open in the woods', 'the woods drying up in the mountains', 'the black earth cracking' and 'the heroes and the horses breaking'.[51] The Montenegrin soil—as well as a spark of inspiration—were necessary for this. Similarly, in 'Milan-bey and Dragutin-bey' the great image of brotherly love—'their horses kissed under them'[52]—is not to be found anywhere else. And neither is the image of brotherly and sisterly love—after the innocent victims meet their tragic end in 'Momir the Foundling' and a pine and vines grow on their graves:

> The vines have entwined the pine
> As a sister's arm round her brother.[53]

Of course, it was the sister's embrace that misled the Emperor to suspect incest and execute Momir; the impact of the line depends on the discrepancy of the meaning of the sister's embrace in the human and in the natural world.

The most moving line in Stojan the Outlaw's 'Wedding o King Vukašin' is also unique: Momčilo advises his murderer not to marry his 'unfaithful love' but to 'take' his loving sister who will be always true to him:

> She will bear you a hero as I was.[54]

This is perhaps one of the most moving lines in the whole of the Serbo-Croat epic tradition; if one made the effort to imagine it as being standard and formulaic, it would be absurd. And equally non-formulaic is the great comic ending of this poem in which dwarfish Vukašin puts three fingers in Momčilo's gold ring and both his feet in one of Momčilo's boots. Many of the most lively lines in 'Banović Strahinja' also contain no formulas for the simple reason that they express ideas beyond the common pale of the Serbian patriarchal culture: the father condemning his daughter as a whore because he is a coward and cannot face the risk of rescuing her from the enemy camp, the hero's ability

[51] See above pp. 108–9.

[52] 'Pod njima se dobri konji ljube', 'Milan-beg i Dragutin-beg', *Karadžić*, ii, No. 10, l. 4.

[53] 'Savila se loza oko bora, / K'o sestrina oko brata ruka.' 'Nahod Momir', *Karadžić*, ii, No. 30, ll. 393–4.

[54] 'Rodiće ti, k'o i ja, junaka.' 'Ženidba kralja Vukašina', *Karadžić*, ii, No. 25, l. 258.

to communicate more humanely with an old Turkish dervish than with his in-laws, his pardon of his wife's life in spite of her treason. Even the great ending introduces an unexpected turn to the standard image of collective drinking; having exposed his in-laws as cruel cowards, the brave and generous hero remains lonely and destitute—and all he can tell his in-laws is:

> 'I have no one to drink the red wine with.'[55]

But is not this enough? The whole formula of drinking together had to be reversed to fathom the hero's loneliness.

This was, of course, an example of a partly formulaic and partly non-formulaic line; but some of the highlights of 'The Building of Ravanica' are completely non-formulaic. Such is, for instance, the irony in the line exposing the nature of Tsar Lazar's desire to build in gold and pearls:

> 'Let it shine, let the world know who I am!'[56]

And such are also the last lines in which the glamour of the church strikes the horse in the eye so that he rears up and throws the Tsar to the ground. And the well-known description of the Turkish army on the eve of the Battle of Kosovo is also given in lines in which there are no formulas:

> 'If all of us were turned into rock salt,
> We could not salt the dinner of the Turks!'[57]

This is obviously the kind of image which is so striking that it can be used successfully once and once only—repetition in similar contexts would make it absurd. And when Marko Kraljević comes to the wedding of his wife and fools his enemy Mina of Kostur (Castoria) by dancing a little monkish dance

[55] 'Nemam s kime ladno piti vino', 'Banović Strahinja', *Karadžić*, ii, No. 44, l. 807. It is only in another poem by the same singer, Old Milija, who could not even sing his songs without drinking slivovits, that we find another, positive variant of this expression. When Marko Kraljević learns of the beauty of the girl whom he decides to ask to be his wife, he remembers her rich and dignified father and thinks that 'he would have someone to drink wine with' ('imao bi s kime piti vino', 'Sestra Leke kapetana'—'Captain Leka's Sister'—*Karadžić*, ii, No. 40, l. 26).

[56] 'Nek se sjaje, nek se moje znaje.' 'Zidanje Ravanice', *Karadžić*, ii, No. 36, l. 65.

[57] 'Svi mi da se u so prometnemo, / Ne bi Turkom ručka osolili', 'Komadi od različnijeh kosovskijeh pjesama (iv)', *Karadžić*, ii, No. 50, ll. 10–11.

and pretending to marry Mina 'Who to? To his own love',[58] when he obeys his mother's advice to give up slaughtering people and make ploughing his profession, his triumph—after he had ploughed the Emperor's roads and plundered the soldiers who tried to stop him—has to be non-formulaic:

> 'Mother, this is what I ploughed up for you today.'[59]

Such lines—which are distinctly non-formulaic, but prominent in the imaginative landscape of great poems—can be also found in the heroic songs about later feudal lords, border raiders and outlaws. As a rule, however, we do not find them in the earlier eighteenth-century variants, but only in those which Karadžić published in his collections. Thus both versions of 'The Death of Duke Prijezda' describe the heroic defence of the besieged fortress of Stalać; in both variants the commander of the fortress, Duke Prijezda, and his wife choose death when further resistance becomes impossible. But whereas in the stuttering version which was recorded in the early eighteenth century in *The Erlangen Manuscript* Duke Prijezda says to his wife at the end of the poem:

> 'Come on, love, to the Morava water',[60]

in the corresponding moment of the great song which was published in Karadžić's collection, it is the wife who speaks to the husband:

> 'The Morava water has bred us up,
> Let the Morava water bury us!'[61]

Instead of the absurdly gallant offer of a defeated warrior to take his wife with him to death, we face the wife's self-effacing readiness to lead her husband to the only honourable end for both. There is not a single formula in the two lines, but they are traditional in a different sense. The two words repeated in both lines—the 'water' and its name Morava—supply, as it were, the solid ground for the contrast between 'bred' and

---

[58] 'Da sa kime, već sa svojom ljubom!' 'Marko Kraljević i Mina od Kostura', *Karadžić*, ii, No. 62, l. 293.

[59] 'To sam tebe danas izorao.' 'Oranje Marka Kraljevića', *Karadžić*, ii, No. 73, l. 30.

[60] 'Aidi ljubo u moravu vodu', *Gesemann*, No. 70, l. 118.

[61] 'Morava nas voda odranila, / Nek Morava voda i sarani!' 'Smrt vojvode Prijezde', *Karadžić*, ii, No. 84, ll. 104–5.

'bury', the two fundamental concepts expressed in a pair of
antonyms which are phonetically and etymologically so close
in Serbo-Croat ('odraniti', 'saraniti'). This contrast itself
embodies the traditional paradox of many songs about the
Morava, the life-giving river which often threatens death.[62]
Its phrasing is certainly shaped on the standard semantic
gnomic pattern;[63] but deeply immersed as the two lines are in
traditional language and some of its major moral paradoxes,
they are not to be found anywhere else in Serbo-Croat oral epic
poetry. 'Formulaic' as they appear to be in the structure of
their contrast, they are quite original and unique in their
dramatic impact and meaning; this is how an imaginative
triumph is achieved in a great creative moment of oral epic
poetry. In short, there are occasions in which the singer cannot
meet the great imaginative challenge of his material in any
other way.

The poems about more recent or contemporary history—
about the outlaws, the border raiders, and the later Serbian
rebels—also contain some of the greatest unique, non-formulaic
or only partly formulaic, lines which are sometimes soon
forgotten and sometimes remembered in the oral transmission
for a very long time. Thus a century divides the two variants
of 'The Betrayal of Grujo's Love'—and the song which Karadžić wrote down is superior in clarity of narration, in character-
drawing and in motivation to the *Erlangen* variant.[64] Its
greatest lines describe the decisive moment when the weak son
cuts his father's hand while trying to release him from his ropes:

> 'Do not fear, Stevan, my child!
> Blood is not coming from your father's hand,
> The blood is coming out of the rope.'[65]

[62] The best known among these songs is 'Oj, Moravo' in which the
attachment to the life-giving river is also expressed as a question about why
it has to flood vast areas.

[63] Similar examples can be found in many proverbs; e.g. 'He who flies
high, falls low' ('Ko visoko leti, nisko pada', V. S. Karadžić, *Srpske narodne
poslovice*, p. 148). 'Fly' and 'fall', 'high' and 'low' are contrasted in an
analogous way as 'breed' and 'bury', even if the syntactic structure is, of
course, different.

[64] See above pp. 86, 231–4.

[65] 'A ne boj se, Stevo, čedo moje! / Krv ne ide iz babine ruke, / Nego ide
krvca iz konopca.' 'Nevjera ljube Gruičine', *Karadžić*, iii, No. 7, ll. 215–17.

The situation is unique and there could not have been a formula readily available to express the father's tenderness in the image of bleeding ropes. But the same scene is found in the much inferior variant which was recorded about a hundred years earlier in closely parallel phrasing:

> 'Do not fear, Stevan, my son,
> You have not cut me, my son,
> Black blood is dripping from the ropes.'[66]

In this instance the unique lines—they are not, of course, to be found in other poems—survived perhaps because they deserved to survive and because they expressed so much of the general 'national sentiment'.

But the existing material does not always offer such ground for optimistic speculation about poetic survival. Some of the best lines—partly formulaic and partly non-formulaic—in the *Erlangen* version of the story about the outlaws waiting in vain for a very long time in ambush had a different fate. It is only in this version that the outlaws waited from St George's Day to St Demetrius' Day (the two traditional days when the outlaws came together and parted ways)[67] and it is only in this version that during their waiting:

> The leaf dropped and the snow covered the earth.[68]

This is not to say that this is a superior song; Old Milija's variant is a much more fully and much more clearly developed story and it is only in his poem, 'Captain Gavran and Limo', that we find the grand run of non-formulaic lines which describe the unique division of booty among the living and the dead:

> How justly he divided the treasure,
> Evenly among living and dead.
> The living took their treasure on their backs,
> The treasure of the dead remained in heaps.[69]

[66] 'Neboimi se dejete stipane / Nisi sin'ko mene porezao / Iz litara cer'na krv'ca suri', *Gesemann*, No. 117, ll. 81–3.

[67] See note 11, p. 265.

[68] 'List opade a snijeg zapade', *Gesemann*, No. 17, l. 16.

[69] 'Kako pravo blago podijeli, / Sve na mrtva, kao i na živa. / Živi svoje blago uprtiše, / A mrtvijem osta na kupove', 'Gavran harambaša i Limo', *Karadžić*, iii, No. 42, ll. 389–92.

The lines have to be unique among other reasons, because they push beyond social custom and reality.

However, the richest evidence of the interplay of the formulaic, the formulopoeic and the unique is to be found in the songs of Filip Višnjić, Karadžić's greatest singer of contemporary history. He is most traditionally formulaic in some of his mediocre songs—such as 'The Battle of Mišar'.[70] His language is highly formulopoeic in his best song 'The Beginning of Revolt Against the Dahijas': the heavenly omens are worked out in such detail that they require new phrases for their expression, but as soon as they are made up, they are repeated and varied in the description of the further omens. This is how they become formulas and provide formulaic possibilities for the progress of the narrative. This is also true—to a lesser extent—of the many other elements in this story: the council held by the great Dahijas, Murad's humane advice and the execution of the Serbian headmen.[71] This process—which provides rich illustration for A. B. Lord's theory of oral composition and shows how far it goes—can be perhaps more significantly observed in Visnjić's magnificent description of the misery of the cattle which the Turks drive away in 'The Battle of Salaš'. Of course, as the grief of sheep, goats, cows and oxen is not a common epic subject, new phrases are necessary to express it, but it should be observed how easily they become formulaic:

> And the sheep go bleating after their lambs,
> And the lambs go mewling after their ewes,
> And the goats go baaing after their kids,
> And the kids go screaming after nannies;
> And the cows bellow after their calves,
> And the calves bleat after the cows;
> And the bulls of Mačva keep roaring,
> Because they do not see their own shepherds—
> The cattle see the road they will travel
> And all the cattle sorrow for their home.[72]

[70] See above pp. 281–2.
[71] See above pp. 290–4.
[72] 'Stoji bleka ovac' za janjcima, / Stoji meka janjac' za ovcama, / Veka stoji koza za jarići, / A jarića dreka za kozama; / Stoji rika krava za teladma, / A teladi meka za kravama; / Buka stoji Mačvanskih volova, / Ne

The introductory line—in spite of its formulaic opening—has to be unique because the subject has not been tackled in epic poetry before, but it sets a formulaic pattern for the lines which follow. Yet the culmination of the whole description—in the last three lines—remains unique for obvious semantic reasons: the grief of the cattle is not a standard epic subject, even if it can express a kind of helpless homesickness more movingly than more articulate creatures could ever hope to do. This is, among other reasons, also due to the fact that the great oral poet, who has the whole epic tradition at his fingertips, is not here tackling an epic motif or theme, but introducing a new one as a historical witness. For the most important hero in this poem is Stojan Čupić, the Serbian captain who brought Višnjić to Serbia after one of his raids into Bosnia and was his patron later.

But Višnjić did not only introduce new formulas—specifically suitable for some of the great scenes in his songs. He also introduced and exploited the formulaic cluster which represents the First Serbian Uprising as a battle unprecedented in scope: this is why in 'Stanić Stanojlo' the shot of a rifle cracks 'like the thunder of heaven' and in his 'Battle of Loznica' as well as in 'Bjelić Ignjatije' 'the red flame' is 'tied into the sky'.[73] And it was also he who introduced the Serbian rayah as the main protagonist in the epic poems about the Uprising. His ease in making up new formulas is as impressive as the extent of his command of the traditional ones, and yet some of his best known and greatest lines are unique. Such are some of the omens in the opening lines of his greatest song 'The Beginning of the Revolt Against the Dahijas': 'the blood has boiled up out of the earth',[74] 'bloody banners of war passed overhead',[75] 'loud thunder claps on St Sava's Day',[76] the image of the Dahijas 'trapping the stars of heaven in a dish',[77] Murad's advice to the Turkish rulers 'not to deal bitterly with the rayah', but 'to deal

poznaju svojijeh čobana, / Vidi stoka, đe će putovati, / Pake žali svoga zavičaja', 'Boj na Salašu', *Karadžić*, iv, No. 28, ll. 258–67.

[73] See above pp. 266–7.
[74] '(Jer) je krvca iz zemlje provrela', *Karadžić*, iv, No. 24, l. 11.
[75] '(Sve) barjaci krvavi idoše', ibid., l. 25.
[76] 'Grom zagrmi na svetoga Savu', ibid., l. 30.
[77] 'U tepsiju zv'jezde povataše', ibid., l. 61.

with them very easily',[78] the image of the bewildered Old Fočo 'biting his white beard'[79] and his subsequent advice to the Dahijas to refrain from slaughter:

> 'Take up, my son, Fočić Memed-aga,
> Take up straw in your white hand,
> Wave it about over a living flame:
> Will you put out the fire waving straw,
> Or will you stir it up?'[80]

'My son', the 'white hand' and the 'living flame' are formulas, but the whole run of these lines—'take up straw', 'wave it about', 'will you put out the fire', 'or will you stir it up'—is overwhelmingly original in its phrasing: it reflects a strong response to the imaginative challenge of a particular scene. Lines such as these—including the image of 'the rayah growing like grass out of the earth'[81]—provide the heart of this great poem.

To sum up, the evidence of the heroic songs and poems which Karadžić recorded from his singers at the time of the greatest flowering of heroic poetry in Serbo-Croat modifies to a certain extent A. B. Lord's theory of the formulaic nature of oral epic composition. On the one hand, all these songs—particularly if set against the existing contemporary or earlier variants— confirm A. B. Lord's claim that oral epic composition is an art of improvisation which 'must be based on the formula'.[82] But Karadžić's singers and their audience were personally involved in oral epic composition as the most exciting form of their awareness of contemporary history and this is why many of their greatest lines are sometimes altogether unique and some- times a combination of the formulaic, the formulopoeic, and the unique. They could hardly help this—not because they cared to be *avant-garde*, but because their personal fate often mirrored major aspects of contemporary history and was sometimes

---

[78] (Vi) nemojte raji gorki biti, / Veće raji vrlo dobri bud'te', *Karadžić*, iv, No. 24, ll. 112–13.

[79] '(Starac Fočo podavio) bradu, / Pa je b'jelu (sa zubima) grize', ibid., ll. 169–70.

[80] 'Uzmi sinko, Fočić Memed-aga, / Uzmi slame u bijelu ruku, / Mani slamom preko vatre žive: / Il' ćeš vatru sa tim ugasiti, / Ili ćeš je većma raspaliti?' Ibid., ll. 338–42.

[81] 'Usta raja k'o iz zemlje trava', ibid., l. 569.

[82] A. B. Lord, *The Singer of Tales*, p. 65.

interwoven into their stories, because they sometimes happened
to bump into a subject which had never been treated before or
stumble on a great image which suddenly illuminated an
ancient theme as it had never been illuminated before. But
apart from such instances which, like so much of human
achievement, have to be explained *par hasard et par génie*, there
were also imaginative and moral reasons for the deviation into
originality in many of the greatest lines in Serbo-Croat oral
epic poetry.

Was Andrijaš illustrating a historical moral norm when he—
with his brother's sword in his heart—invented a generous lie
to beguile their mother and promised to help his murderer in
need beyond the grave? And why did Duke Momčilo feel
compelled to advise his murderer to take his loving sister
instead of his treacherous wife, promising his enemy that she
will bear him a hero as he, Momčilo, was? And why did
Strahinić Ban spare the life of his treacherous wife—instead of
tying her in the proper epic fashion to the horses' tails? And how
dared he find a better understanding with his enemy than with
his powerful and glorious in-laws? Could any social or moral
custom explain Lazar's choice of 'the heavenly Kingdom', his
resolution to fight the battle which had been lost in advance?
How can one understand this in historical terms? And why
were Lazar's brothers-in-law, the Jugovići, deaf to their sister's
call, the most sacred call of the purest form of love in the
patriarchal world, defying, moreover, their suzerain's strict
orders? And why should the great outlaw Rosnić Stevan
divide the loot so justly that heaps of gold were left beside the
heads of his friends who had been killed in action?

All this goes against the grain of history and social norms, and
one could hardly expect that ready-made phrases could have
been available for such magnificent insights into the moral
possibilities of human life, defying all the odds of history. For
such insights open imaginative vistas far beyond the actualities,
customs, and social norms of the feudal and patriarchal Slav
civilizations in the Balkans—this is why they express their spirit
far better than their realities. After all, the greatest lines in the
heroic songs in Serbo-Croat did not only echo the voices of
troubled history but also those of its visionary martyrs who, at
least in their poetry, were sung to their final rest.

Appendices

I. Karadžić's Collections

As V. Nedić points out, Karadžić started his work on Serbo-Croat oral poetry in Vienna after the First Serbian Uprising was crushed in 1813.[1] He wrote down mostly lyrical, 'women's poems' ('ženske pjesme') from his own memory; he also recorded many such poems from the recitals of his relative Savka Živković and other Serbian exiles. A year later he published his first collection: *Mala prostonarodnja slaveno-serbska pjesnarica* (*A Small Simple-Folk Slavonic-Serbian Song-Book*), Vienna, 1814. It contained a hundred 'women's' and only eight 'heroic poems' ('junačke pjesme'): Karadžić was still reluctant to publish what were pejoratively called 'blind men's poems' ('sljepačke pjesme').

From the end of 1814 to the middle of 1815 Karadžić lived in Srem, whence tens of thousands of Serbs had escaped after 1813. He wrote down over two hundred 'women's' and several dozen 'heroic' poems, many of them from his greatest oral poets, such as Tešan Podrugović, Filip Višnjić, blind Živana and others. These provided the basis for his next collection: *Narodna srbska pjesnarica* (*Serbian Folk Song-Book*), Vienna, 1815, which contained some of the best heroic poems about the Battle of Kosovo, Marko Kraljević and the First Serbian Uprising. It also showed greater respect for the singers' language: the words of Oriental origin were no longer replaced by the 'pure', native ones. There is a good modern edition of these two collections: V. Nedić, ed., *Mala prostonarodnja slaveno-serbska pjesnarica* (*1814*)—*Narodna srbska pjesnarica* (*1815*), Belgrade, 1965.

From 1816 to 1833 Karadžić often visited Srem and Serbia and wrote down many more poems, including such famous ones as Stojan the Outlaw's 'The Wedding of King Vukašin', Old Milija's 'Banović Strahinja', and Old Raško's 'The Building of Skadar'. The next, the so-called 'Leipzig' edition—*Narodne srpske pjesme* (*Serbian Folk Poems*)—was a much bigger and richer collection. The first volume (Leipzig, 1824) contained only 'women's' poems. The second volume (Leipzig, 1823) included most of Karadžić's best material: the 'oldest' heroic poems about subjects from medieval history and the heroes who lived when firearms were not in use. The third volume (Leipzig, 1823) contained mostly the poems about outlaws

---

[1] See 'Pogovor' in V. S. Karadžić, *Srpske narodne pjesme*, iv, Belgrade, 1969, pp. 385–92. This appendix is partly a summary of Nedić's text.

and the Turkish times. The fourth volume (Vienna, 1833) included the poems about the Montenegrin and Serbian wars of independence. This division set the basic pattern for all later editions.

From 1834 to 1841 Karadžić travelled in Montenegro, the Bay of Kotor, Dubrovnik, Dalmatia, and Lika—the well-known epic regions which he had not visited before. He looked not only for new poems but also for the best variants of those he had already written down. He also had many poems sent to him by other people. His definitive Viennese edition contained one thousand and forty-five separate pieces, among them several hundred new ones. It was published under the title *Srpske narodne pjesme* (*Serbian Folk Poems*) in four volumes in 1841, 1845, 1846 and 1862 respectively. The best modern edition, closely following Karadžić's text and correcting only misprints, is: V. Nedić, ed., *Srpske narodne pjesme*, i–iv, Belgrade, 1969, 1976.

Karadžić was not a folklorist but a critical genius. He sometimes looked for years for a good variant of a poem which did not quite satisfy him, and he sometimes spent years tracing a man who had the reputation of a good singer: he found Stojan the Outlaw in a prison in Brusnica and recorded from him one of the finest poems in the language ('The Wedding of King Vukašin'). His manuscripts show, as V. Nedić has pointed out, that he had a greater respect for the original text of the recording than any of his contemporaries. Finally, he also left over two thousand unpublished poems in his collections in Belgrade and Leningrad.

Karadžić had little luck with the various scholarly and state committees which attempted to produce a complete edition of his works. The first of these committees was founded in 1885, two years before the centenary of Karadžić's birth. The committee had higher criteria of taste than of accuracy: it produced an edition of a single volume, Karadžić's best, the second volume of heroic poems, but with so many errors and misprints that it had to be destroyed.

A new committee planned the so-called 'state edition' ('državno izdanje') in twenty-eight volumes. The first of the twenty-three published volumes was produced in 1891 and the last in 1913; the publication could not be completed because of World War I. It included, however, a rich collection of oral poetry: *Srpske narodne pjesme*, i–ix, Belgrade, 1891–1902 edited by Lj. Stojanović. The editor did not completely reveal his textual principles: he claimed, for instance, in his foreword to volume six that he had closely followed Karadžić's text changing nothing except punctuation and emending these misprints which he knew how to correct (see 'Predgovor', *Srpske narodne pjesme*, vi, Belgrade, 1899, p. xiii). A note to a later reprint, however, shows that this time the editor's standards of decency surpassed those of accuracy: all the 'indecent' words were replaced by 'more appropriate' ones ('O ovome izdanju', *Srpske narodne pjesme*, vi, Belgrade, 1935, p. ix). This must have been quite an achievement, but it did not produce a reliable text. This edition was reprinted between the two wars.

In 1937—on the occasion of the hundred and fiftieth anniversary of Karadžić's birth—a new committee was founded for the publication of Karadžić's works, but it could not do anything before World War II.

As the centenary of Karadžić's death approached a new committee was founded in 1963 with the task of arranging the publication of a critical edition of *The Collected Works of Vuk Karadžić* (*Sabrana dela Vuka Karadžića*, Belgrade, 1965–), but not a single volume of heroic poems has been published in this edition so far.

V. Nedić's edition of *Srpske narodne pjesme*, i–iv, Belgrade, 1969, 1976 provides the most reliable text but gives no comments or explanations. The best annotated modern edition is *Srpske narodne pjesme*, i–iv, Belgrade, 1958–64 (first edition 1953–4). The four volumes are edited by V. Đurić, S. Matić, N. Banašević and V. Latković respectively; their text, however, is given in modern orthography which makes it considerably different from what Karadžić wrote down.

Finally, the material of the nine volumes of the pre-war 'state edition' has been supplemented by *Srpske narodne pjesme iz neobjavljenih rukopisa Vuka Stef. Karadžića* (*Serbian Folk Poems from the Unpublished Manuscripts of Vul Stef. Karadžić*), Ž. Mladenović, V. Nedić, eds., general editor V. Đurić, i–v, Belgrade, 1973–4. This edition reflects new standards of decency: instead of 'improving' on the indecent poems and words, the editors have put such poems in the last volume which is not offered for sale to private persons so that only public institutions are entitled to this treat. However, a selection of 'the best' of these poems is now readily available (V. S. Karadžić, *Crven ban*, ed. B. Jastrebić, Belgrade, 1979) in Prosveta's series 'Erotikon', which includes such classics as the Marquis de Sade.

II. Some Early Assessments of Homeric Relevance

Many of the earliest references to Serbo-Croat oral poetry raise the question of its Homeric relevance. At the heart of these discussions is the problem whether the singers memorize or improvise their songs. So Fortis—after comparing the 'Morlacchian' songs to 'the ancient Provençal Romances' and 'the poems of the celebrated

Scotch bard'—points out that they reflect 'the simplicity of Homeric times' and goes on to observe that some singers add, at the end of their songs, some 'extempore verses in praise of the personage by whom they are employed; and some of them are capable of singing extempore during the whole entertainment, always accompanying the voice with the *guzlas*' (*Travels into Dalmatia*, London, 1778, pp. 83–6). K. Szyrma also refers to 'a Morlacchian Improvisatore' (*Letters on Poland*, Edinburgh, 1823, p. 52), and the great German historian Leopold Ranke had a very clear sense of what improvisation involved (see above p. 322). A British reviewer of the original German version of Ranke's work clearly sensed what was to attract later Homeric and comparative scholars to the field of Serbo-Croat oral epic singing: 'The scholar and the critic, who may wish to study the growth and the vigour of poetical feeling in a nation, may here, in the almost only remaining living school of the kind, carry his researches further than scholiasts or grammarians would guide him' ('*Die Serbische Revolution* . . . von Leopold Ranke', *The British and Foreign Review*, xii (1841), p. 554).

In another review there is a characteristic reference to 'an honourable peculiarity of the Servians' who 'possess a store of old poetry which is capable of forming itself into epic unity and continuity, like that of pre-Homeric Greeks, or the Teutonic singers of Siegfried' ('Marko Kralievitch: The Mythical Hero of Servia', *Macmillan's Magazine*, xxxv [January 1877], p. 222). Another reviewer calls the singers 'improvisatori' and in his discussion of Petranović's and Karadžić's collections suggests that 'it is certainly a curious phenomenon that in such modern times we should find a class of Homeridae chanting to such primitive music the heroic achievement of their ancestors' ('The Literature of the Servians and Croats', *The Westminster and Foreign Quarterly Review*, New Series, liii [1 April 1878], p. 311). It was not, however, until M. Parry's and A. B. Lord's work was published that the Homeric relevance of Yugoslav oral epics was fully recognized in international scholarship.

III. THE VILAS

In popular belief a *vila* is a supernatural being, usually seen as a beautiful young girl in lovely transparent robes, but her beauty is sometimes marred by ugly legs which she tries to hide (the legs are usually those of a horse, a donkey or a goat). The *vila* is born out of dew and herbs; she lives in mountains, in plants and trees, in clouds or in lakes—which suggests that originally she was a nature spirit. The *vilas* are miraculous healers; they can fly and are usually seen as friends and sometimes as mothers or blood-sisters of the great epic heroes, but they can also be envious and vindictive. They often figure in the poems about Marko Kraljević. Thus in 'Marko Kraljević and the *Vila*' ('Marko Kraljević i vila', *Karadžić*, ii, No. 38; for two other variants see Ž. Mladenović, V. Nedić, eds., *Srpske narodne pjesme iz neobjavljenih rukopisa Vuka Stef. Karadžića*, ii, Nos. 35, 36) a *vila* shoots Miloš Obilić, Marko's blood-brother, because she envies him the beauty of his voice, but Marko hits the *vila* with his mace and compels her to heal Miloš's wounds. In 'Marko Karljević and Musa Kesedžija' ('Marko Kraljević i Musa Kesedžija', *Karadžić*, ii, No. 67) the *vila* is seen as Marko's blood-sister who helps him to overcome his enemy by fraud (see above pp. 197–8). In 'Marko Kraljević and the *Vila* of the Ford' ('Marko Kraljević i vila brodarica' in V. S. Karadžić, *Srpske narodne pjesme*, vi, Belgrade, 1935, No. 23; another variant in Ž. Mladenović, V. Nedić, eds., op. cit., No. 37) Marko is so thirsty that he feels like drinking his horse's blood, but a *vila* shows him a spring of water in the mountain. However, when she demands the water-tax, Marko kills her. In 'The Death of Marko Kraljević' ('Smrt Marka Kraljevića', *Karadžić*, ii, No. 74) a *vila* has the gift of prophecy: she foretells Marko's approaching end. For further information about *vilas* see Š. Kulišić *et al.*, *Srpski mitološki rečnik*, pp. 66–8.

IV. SLAVA

In its origin the festival of *slava* celebrates the day of the saint adopted as patron by the ancestors of a family when they received Christianity. The basic rites of *slava* go back to very ancient times. The breaking of a round loaf even suggests the time when no knives were available (see P. Ž. Petrović, 'Krsno ime' in Š. Kulišić *et al.*, *Srpski mitološki rečnik*, p. 177). The dish of boiled grains of wheat ('koljivo') may go back to the days before wheat was ground (see V. Čajkanović, 'Slava' in S. Stanojević, ed., *Narodna enciklopedija srpsko-hrvatsko-slovenačka*, iv, Zagreb, 1929, p. 145). The burning of the candle is a substitute for pre-Christian sacrifices to fire (see P. Ž. Petrović, op. cit., p. 176). The question whether this festival is connected with the cult of the dead or of the living is controversial. The dish of boiled grains of wheat is used in the rites connected with the cult of the dead, but the prevailing mood before and during the feast to its end is that of merriment (see V. Čajkanović, loc. cit.; *Mit i religija u Srba*, pp. 148, 263; cf. P. Ž. Petrović, op. cit., p. 175).

The importance of this festival in village life is clearly reflected in Karadžić's claim that the head of a Serbian peasant household 'makes careful preparations during the whole year' for its celebration (see 'Krsno ime' in *Srpski rječnik*, p. 317). The basic social features of *slava* are hospitality (food and drink must be offered to whoever comes along) and toasts which used to be and in some regions still are a flourishing form of oral culture. The failure to observe the obligations of equal hospitality to rich and poor alike is the subject of the epic poem 'Marko Kraljević and Bey Kostadin' ('Marko Kraljević i beg Kostadin', *Karadžić*, ii, No. 60). With persistent guests the obligations of hospitality can lead to comic situations: the refusal of the guests to leave for days and the host's efforts to entertain them are the subject of the classic short story 'Ivko's *slava*' by S. Sremac (see D. Mikashinovich, D. Milivojević, V. D. Mihailovich, eds., *Yugoslav Literature*, New York, 1973, pp. 115–21).

V. SERBO-CROAT HEROIC SONGS IN ENGLISH TRANSLATIONS

Many of the heroic songs about medieval Serbia, which are discussed at some length in this book, can be found in English in R. P. Noyes's and L. Bacon's *Heroic Ballads of Servia*, Boston, 1913: 'The Brothers and Their Sister' ('Sister and Brother'), 'Uroš and the Mrljavčevići' ('Uroš and the Sons of Marnyava'), 'Banović Strahinja' ('Ban Strahin'), 'The Building of Ravanica', 'The Building of Skadar', 'Pieces from Various Kosovo Poems' ('Fragments of Kosovo Ballads'), 'Tsar Lazar and Tsaritsa Milica', 'The Downfall of the Serbian Empire' ('The Battle of Kosovo'), 'Tsaritsa Milica and Duke Vladeta' ('Tsaritsa Militsa and Vladeta the Voyvoda'), 'The Death of the Mother of the Jugovići', 'The Kosovo Girl' ('The Maid of Kosovo'). This list can be supplemented, in great need, by the very poetical prose versions of the following songs in W. M. Petrovitch's *Hero Tales and Legends of the Serbians*, London, 1914: 'The Saints Divide the Treasure', 'Dušan's Wedding' ('The Marriage of Tsar Doushan the Mighty'), 'The Wedding of King Vukašin' ('The Marriage of King Voukashin').

The latter is also found in a much more workable translation in D. H. Low's *The Ballads of Marko Kraljević*, Cambridge, 1922. This work also contains many of the best songs about Marko Kraljević: both variants of 'Marko Kraljević and the Hawk' ('Marko Kraljević and the Falcon'), 'Marko Kraljević and Mina of Kostur', 'Marko Kraljević and Alil-aga', 'Marko Kraljević and Musa Kesedžija' ('Marko Kraljević and Musa the Outlaw'), 'Marko Kraljević and Đemo of the Mountain' ('Marko Kraljević and Djemo the Mountaineer'), 'Marko Kraljević and Filip the Hungarian' ('Marko

Kraljević and Philip the Magyar'), 'Marko Kraljević Knows His Father's Sword' ('Marko Kraljević Recognizes His Father's Sword'), 'Marko Kraljević Drinks Wine In Ramadan', 'Marko Kraljević Abolishes the Wedding Tax' ('Marko Kraljević Abolishes the Marriage-Tax'), 'The Wedding of Marko Kraljević' ('The Marriage of Marko Kraljević'), 'The Death of Marko Kraljević' and some others. Most of these songs can also be found in G. R. Noyes's and L. Bacon's collection.

This collection also contains several poems about outlaws and border raiders, including 'The Death of Ivo of Senj' and 'Predrag and Nenad'. The former can also be found in M. Mügge's *Serbian Folk Songs, Fairy Tales and Proverbs*, London, 1916, together with several Kosovo poems and some others.

The rebels of the First Serbian Uprising seem to have done much better in English translations than their outlaw predecessors. W. A. Morison's *The Revolt of the Serbs Against the Turks*, Cambridge, 1942, contains some of the most notable poems about them, including 'The Beginning of the Revolt Against the Dahijas', 'The Battle of Mišar', 'The Battle of Deligrad', 'Luko Lazarević and Pejzo', 'Miloš Stoićević and Meho Orugdžijć', and others.

Most of these translations vary in accuracy, in literary and non-literary tastes—not always in the most desirable direction. But they are at least less exuberant than the nineteenth-century versions of John Bowring and Owen Meredith, even if they lack their exotic historical interest. A new selection of Serbo-Croat heroic songs, in the translation of Anne Pennington and Peter Levi, is forthcoming.

Bibliography

This is a selective list of the most important collections, editions, critical and historical studies of the Serbo-Croat oral epic poems which were written down by V. S. Karadžić (1787–1864) and the earlier collectors. Later field-work and studies of Serbo-Croat oral epic oases—in which old songs survived mostly in poorer variants and new subjects were tackled in unintentionally mock-heroic spirit—are, of course, of considerable theoretical and comparative interest. But they raise for the most part a different set of issues and only major works in this area have been cited in this Bibliography.

Many of the quoted books and studies contain useful bibliographies. For a good general selective bibliography see V. Nedić, 'Bibliografija važnijih radova o srpskohrvatskoj narodnoj književnosti' in V. Đurić, ed., *Antologija narodnih pripovedaka*, Novi Sad–Belgrade, 1969, pp. 420–9. More specifically, for the bibliography of V. S. Karadžić's works and their later editions see G. Dobrašinović, ed., *Bibliografija spisa Vuka Karadžića*, Sabrana dela, 1965–, xxxvi, Belgrade, 1974. For the bibliography of articles in major Yugoslav scholarly and literary journals see M. Bogavac *et al.*, eds., *Bibliografija radova o narodnoj književnosti*, i–ii, Akademija nauka i umjetnosti Bosne i Hercegovine, Posebna izdanja, xviii, xx, Sarajevo, 1972, 1974. For the basic international bibliography see D. Subotić, *Yugoslav Popular Ballads*, Cambridge, 1932, pp. 267–83 and A. Schmaus, 'Studije o krajinskoj epici', *Rad JAZU*, cclxxxxvii (1953), pp. 243–7. These can be supplemented by more up-to-date selective references in A. B. Lord's 'Notes' to his *Singer of Tales*, Cambridge, Mass., 1960, pp. 279–304. For a selective bibliography of works dealing with the ethnographical and legal background of Serbo-Croat oral epics see J. Brkić, *Moral Concepts in Traditional Serbian Epic Poetry*, The Hague, 1961, pp. 172–7. There is also a useful up-to-date selective bibliography in R. Medenica, *Naša narodna epika i njeni tvorci*, Cetinje, 1975, pp. 412–15.

I. Collections and Works Containing Epic Songs

1. *Serbo-Croat*

Baraković, J.—see Zoranić, P.
Balović Manuscript—text prepared for publication by M. Pantić, Faculty of Philology, Belgrade University.

Bogišić, V. (B.), *Narodne pjesme iz starijih, najviše primorskih zapisa* (*Glasnik srpskog učenog društva*, x, 1), Belgrade, 1878.

Broz, I. et al., *Hrvatske narodne pjesme*, 10 vols., Zagreb, 1896–1942 (vol. i, ed. I. Broz and S. Bosanac; vol. ii, ed. S. Bosanac; vols. iii–iv, ed. L. Marjanović; vols. v–x, ed. N. Andrić).

Čojković, Č.—see Milutinović, S.

Fermendžin, E., 'Prinos za životopis Gjurgja Križanića', *Starine*, xviii (1866), pp. 210–29.

Gezeman, G. (G. Gesemann), *Erlangenski rukopis starih srpskohrvatskih narodnih pesama* (Srpska kraljevska akademija, Zbornik za istoriju, jezik i književnost srpskog naroda, Prvo odeljenje, Spomenici na srpskom jeziku, xii), Sremski Karlovci, 1925.

Hektorović, P., *Ribanye i ribarscho prigovaranye*, Venice, 1568 (photographic edn., Zagreb, 1953), also in H. Lucić, P. Hektorović, *Skladanje izvarsnih pisan razlicih; Ribanje i ribarsko prigovaranje i razlike stvari ine*, ed. M. Franičević (Pet stoljeća hrvatske književnosti, vol. 7), Zagreb, 1968.

Hörmann, K., *Narodne pjesme Muslimana u Bosni i Hercegovini*, ed. Đ. Buturović, 2 vols., Sarajevo, 1976 (first edn. *Narodne pjesme Muhamedovaca u Bosni i Hercegovini*, 2 vols., Sarajevo, 1888, 1889).

Jugoslavenska akademija znanosti i umjetnosti, Manuscript iv. a. 30 (previously No. 638).

Jugoslavenska akademija znanosti i umjetnosti, Manuscript i. b. 80 (previously No. 641).

Jukić, F. I. and G. Martić, *Narodne pjesme bosanske i hercegovačke*, Osijek, 1858 (second edn., Mostar, 1892).

Karadžić, V. S., *Mala prostonarodnja slaveno-serbska pjesnarica*, Vienna, 1814.

— *Narodna srbska pjesnarica*, Vienna, 1815.

— *Mala prostonarodnja slaveno-serbska pjesnarica (1814)—Narodna srbska pjesnarica (1815)*, ed. V. Nedić, *Sabrana dela*, i, Belgrade, 1965.

— *Narodne srpske pjesme*, vols. ii, iii, Leipzig, 1823; vol. i, Leipzig, 1824; vol. iv, Vienna, 1833.

— *Srpske narodne pjesme*, i–iv, Vienna, 1841, 1845, 1846, 1862.

— *Srpske narodne pjesme*, v, Vienna, 1865.

— *Srpske narodne pjesme*, i–ix, ed. Lj. Stojanović ('državno izdanje'—'state edition'), Belgrade, 1891–1901 (vols. i–iv rpt. 1929–32; vols. v–ix rpt. 1935–6; vol. vi rpt. 1940).

— *Srpske narodne pjesme*, vol. i, ed. V. Đurić, Belgrade, 1953 (rpt. 1964); vol. ii, ed. S. Matić, Belgrade, 1953 (rpt. 1958); vol. iii, ed. N. Banašević, Belgrade, 1954 (rpt. 1958); vol. iv, ed. V. Latković, Belgrade, 1954 (rpt. 1958).

— *Srpske narodne pjesme,* i–iv, ed. V. Nedić, Belgrade, 1969 (rpt. 1976).

— *Srpske narodne pjesme iz neobjavljenih rukopisa Vuka Stef. Karadžića,* ed. Ž. Mladenović and V. Nedić, i–v, Belgrade, 1973–4.

Kašiković, N., *Narodne pjesme,* Sarajevo, 1951.

Krnjević, H., *Antologija narodnih balada,* Belgrade, 1978.

Kujundžić, L. (-Car), *Narodne pjesme* (published after World War II, no indication of publisher, place, or date of publication, a copy in the National Library in Sarajevo).

Leskovac, M., *Bećarac,* Novi Sad, 1958.

Mazarović Manuscript—text prepared for publication by M. Pantić, Faculty of Philology, Belgrade University.

Miklošić, F., *Die Volksepik der Kroaten,* Vienna, 1870.

Milutinović, S. (pseudonym Č. Čojković), *Pjevanija cernogorska i hercegovačka,* Buda, 1833.

— *Pjevanija cernogorska i hercegovačka,* Leipzig, 1837.

Nedić, V., ed., *Bugarštice,* Belgrade, 1969.

Njegoš, P. P., *Ogledalo srpsko,* ed. R. Bošković and V. Latković, *Celokupna dela,* v, Belgrade, 1951 (first published, Belgrade, 1846).

Pantić, M., ed., *Narodne pesme u zapisima xv–xviii veka,* Belgrade, 1964.

Parry, M. and A. B. Lord, *Srpskohrvatske junačke pesme,* Belgrade–Cambridge, Mass., 1953.

Pavić, A., 'Dvije stare hrvatske pjesme', *Rad JAZU,* xlvii (1879), pp. 93–128.

Petranović, B., *Srpske narodne pjesme iz Bosne (ženske),* Sarajevo, 1867.

— *Srpske narodne pjesme iz Bosne i Hercegovine,* Belgrade, 1867.

— *Srpske narodne pjesme iz Bosne i Hercegovine,* Belgrade, 1870.

Popjévke slovínské—Manuscript in the handwriting of Đ. Matijašević, J. Betondić, I. M. Matijašević *et al.,* Nacionalna i sveučilišna biblioteka, Zagreb, R. 4091.

Radičević, F., *Crnogorske gusle,* Belgrade, 1876.

Reljković, M. A., *Satir iliti divji čovik,* ed. I. Bogner, Osijek, 1974 (first published Osijek, 1779).

Rešetar, M., *Stari pisci hrvatski,* Zagreb, 1917.

Šunjić, M., *Narodne junačke pjesme iz Bosne i Hercegovine,* Sarajevo, 1915 (second edn. 1925).

Vrčević, V., *Hercegovačke narodne pjesme,* Dubrovnik, 1890.

Zoranić, P., J. Baraković, *Planine—Vila Slovinka,* ed. F. Švelec (Pet stoljeća hrvatske književnosti, vol. 8), Zagreb, 1964.

Živančević, M., *Bugarštice,* Belgrade, 1965.

354 Bibliography

2. *English, French, and German translations (listed under the names of translators or editors)*

Bowring, J., *Narodne srpske pjesme—Servian Popular Poetry*, London, 1827.

Dozon, A., *Poésies populaires serbes*, Paris, 1859.

— *L'Épopée serbe*, Paris, 1888.

Gerhard, W., *Wila*, Leipzig, 1828.

Herder, J. G., *Volkslieder*, 2 vols., Leipzig, 1778, 1779.

Kepper, S., *Die Gesänge der Serben*, 2 vols., Leipzig, 1852.

Low, D. H., *The Ballads of Marko Kraljević*, Cambridge, 1913 (second edn. 1922).

Lytton, R.—see Meredith, O.

Meredith, O. (R. Lytton), *Serbski Pesme or National Songs of Serbia*, London, 1861; published also in R. Lytton, *Orval or the Fool of Time and Other Imitations and Paraphrases*, London, 1869. Later editions: O. Meredith, *The National Songs of Serbia*, Boston, 1877; O. Meredith, *Serbski Pesme or National Songs of Serbia*, London, 1917.

Morison, W. A., *The Revolt of the Serbs Against the Turks*, Cambridge, 1942.

Mügge, M. A., *Serbian Folk Songs, Fairy Tales and Proverbs*, London, 1916.

Noyes, G. R. and L. Bacon, *Heroic Ballads of Servia*, Boston, 1913.

Parry, M. and A. B. Lord, *Serbo-Croatian Heroic Songs*, Cambridge, Mass.–Belgrade, 1954.

Petrovitch, W. M., *Hero Tales and Legends of the Serbians*, London, 1914.

Rootham, H., *Kosovo—Heroic Poems of the Serbs*, Oxford, 1920.

Seton-Watson, R. W., *Serbian Ballads*, London, 1916.

Talvj (Talvi—Therese Albertine Luise von Jakob), *Volkslieder der Serben*, 2 vols., Halle, 1825, 1826 (second edn. Halle and Leipzig, 1835; third enlarged edn. Leipzig, 1853).

Vogl, J. N., *Marko Kraljevits, Serbische Heldensange*, Vienna, 1851.

Voïart, E., *Chants populaires des Serviens, recueillis par Wuk Stephanowitsch et traduits, d'après Talvy*, 2 vols., Paris, 1834.

Wiles, J. W., *Serbian Songs and Poems—Chords of the Yugoslav Harp*, London, 1917.

II. Critical Approaches

1. *Books and Studies*

Banašević, N., *Ciklus Marka Kraljevića i odjeci francusko-talijanske viteške književnosti*, Skopje, 1935.

Bogišić, V. (B.), 'Predgovor', *Narodne pjesme iz starijih, najviše primorskih zapisa*, (*Glasnik srpskog učenog društva*, x, 1), Belgrade, 1878, pp. 1–142.

Bowra, C. M., *Heroic Poetry*, London, 1952 (rpt. 1961, 1964, 1966).

Bošković-Stulli, M., *Usmena književnost kao umjetnost riječi*, Zagreb, 1975.

— ed., *Usmena književnost*, Zagreb, 1971.

Braun, M., *Das Serbo-croatische Heldenlied*, Göttingen, 1961.

Brkić, J., *Moral Concepts in Traditional Serbian Epic Poetry*, The Hague, 1961.

Chadwick, H. M. and N. K., *The Growth of Literature*, 2 vols, Cambridge, 1936 (rpt. 1968).

Ćurčin, M., *Das serbische Volkslied in der deutschen Literatur*, Leipzig, 1905.

Đorđević, T., *Beleške o našoj narodnoj poeziji*, Belgrade, 1939.

Đurić, V., 'Srpskohrvatska narodna epika', *Antologija narodnih junačkih pesama*, Belgrade, 1973 (first edn. 1954), pp. 9–159.

Entwistle, W. J., *European Balladry*, Oxford, 1939.

Gesemann, G., *Studien zur sudslavischen Volksepik*, Reichenberg, 1926.

Golenishchev-Kutuzov, I. N., *Epos serbskogo naroda*, Moscow, 1963.

Jagić, V., 'Građa za slovinsku narodnu poeziju', *Rad JAZU*, xxxvii (1876), pp. 33–137.

Jacobson, R., 'The Kernel of Comparative Slavic Literature', *Harvard Slavic Studies*, i (1953), pp. 1–71.

Karadžić, V. S., *O srpskoj narodnoj poeziji*, ed. B. Marinković, Belgrade, 1964.

Khalansky, M., *Yuzhno-slavyanskiya skazaniya o Kraleviche Marke*, Warsaw, 1895.

Kilibarda, N., *Bogoljub Petranović kao sakupljač narodnih pesama*, Belgrade, 1974.

— *Legenda i poezija*, Belgrade, 1976.

Koljević, S., *Naš junački ep*, Belgrade, 1974.

Krnjević, H., *Usmene balade Bosne i Hercegovine*, Sarajevo, 1973.

Kostić, D., *Starost narodnog pesništva našeg*, Belgrade, 1933.

Lord, A. B., *The Singer of Tales*, Cambridge, Mass., 1960 (rpt. 1964).

Ljubinković, N., 'Narodne pesme dugoga stiha', *Književna istorija*, iv (1972), pp. 573–601; v (1972), pp. 18–41; v (1973), pp. 453–79.

Maretić, T., 'Metrika narodnih naših pjesama', *Rad JAZU*, clxviii (1907), pp. 1–112; clxx (1907), pp. 76–200.

— *Naša narodna epika*, Belgrade, 1966 (first edn. Zagreb, 1909).

Maticki, M., 'Poetika epskog narodnog pesništva—slovenska antiteza', *Književna istorija*, iii (1970), pp. 3–52.

— *Srpskohrvatska graničarska epika*, Belgrade, 1974.

Matić, S., *Naš narodni ep i naš stih*, Novi Sad, 1964.

— *Novi ogledi o našem narodnom epu*, Novi Sad, 1972.

Medenica, R., *Banović Strahinja u krugu varijanata i tema o neveri žene u narodnoj epici*, SANU, Posebna izdanja, vol. ccclxxxi, Odeljenje literature i jezika, vol. 14, Belgrade, 1965.

— *Naša narodna epika i njeni tvorci*, Cetinje, 1975.

Mickiewicz, A., *Les Slaves*, Paris, 1866 (first edn. 1845).

Murko, M., *La Poésie populaire épique en Yougoslavie au début du xx*ᵉ *siècle* (Travaux publiés par l'Institut d'études slaves), Paris, 1929.

— *Tragom srpskohrvatske narodne epike*, 2 vols., Zagreb, 1951.

Nazečić, S., *Iz naše narodne epike*, Sarajevo, 1959.

Nedić, V., *O usmenom pesništvu*, Belgrade, 1976.

— ed., *Narodna knjizevnost*, Belgrade, 1966 (rpt. 1972).

Panić-Surep, N., *Filip Višnjić*, Belgrade, 1967 (first edn. 1956).

Popović, M., *Vidovdan i časni krsti*, Belgrade, 1976.

Popović, P., 'Narodna književnost', *Pregled srpske književnosti*, Belgrade, 1932 (first edn. 1909), pp. 55–91.

Putilov, B. N., *Ruskii i yuzhnoslavyanskii geroicheskii epos*, Moscow, 1971.

Samardžić, R., *Usmena narodna hronika*, Novi Sad, 1978.

Saran, F., *Zur Metrik des epischen Verses der Serben*, Leipzig, 1934.

Schmaus, A., 'Studije o krajinskoj epici', *Rad JAZU*, cclxxxxvii (1953), pp. 89–247.

Søerensen, A., 'Beitrag zur Geschichte der Entwicklung der serbischen Heldendichtung', *Archiv für slavische Philologie*, xiv (1892), pp. 556–87; xv (1893), pp. 1–36, 204–45; xvi (1894), pp. 66–118; xvii (1895), pp. 198–253; xix (1897), pp. 89–131; xx (1898), pp. 78–114.

— *Entstehung der kurzzeiligen serbocroatischen Liederdichtung im Künstenland*, Berlin, 1895.

Stefanović, S., *Legenda o zidanju Skadra*, Belgrade, 1928 (rpt. from *Volja*, III–1 (1928), pp. 359–69, 451–68; III–2 (1928), pp. 49–61; rpt. in *Studije o narodnoj poeziji*, Belgrade, 1937, pp. 245–314).

Subotić, D., *Yugoslav Popular Ballads*, Cambridge, 1932.

Talvj (Talvi—Therese Albertine Luise von Jacob), *Historical View of the Languages and Literature of the Slavic Nations*, New York, 1850.

— 'Slavic Popular Poetry' (unsigned review of V. S. Karadžić, *Narodne srpske pjesme*, Vienna, 1833 and W. Oleska, *Piesnie Ludu polskiego i ruskiego w Galicyi*, Lemberg, 1833), *The North American Review*, xliii (1836), pp. 85–120.

Vaillant, A., 'Les chants épiques des Slaves du sud', *Revue des Cours et Conferences* (30 Jan., 15 Feb., 15 Mar. 1932), Paris, 1932, pp. 309–326, 431–47, 635–47.

Zima, L., *Figure u našem narodnom pjesničtvu*, Zagreb, 1880.

— 'Nacrt naše metrike narodne obzirom na stihove drugih naroda, a osobito Slovena', *Rad JAZU*, xlviii (1879), pp. 170–221; xlix (1879), pp. 1–64.

Zogović, R., 'Predgovor', *Crnogorske epske pjesme raznih vremena*, Titograd, 1970, pp. 7–134.

2. Articles

Banašević, N., 'Le cycle de Kosovo et les chansons de geste', *Revue des Études slaves*, vi (1926), pp. 224–44.

— 'S. Matić, Poreklo kosovskih pesama kratkog stiha', *Prilozi za književnost, jezik, istoriju i folklor*, xxix (1963), pp. 327–32.

— 'Ranija i novija nauka i Vukovi pogledi na narodnu epiku', *Prilozi za književnost, jezik, istoriju i folklor*, xxx (1964), pp. 171–90 (rpt. in V. Nedić, ed., *Narodna književnost*, Belgrade, 1966, pp. 392–416).

Barić, H., 'Netko bješe Strahiniću bane . . .', *Srpski književni glasnik*, N. S. xlix (1936), pp. 594–603 (rpt. in V. Nedić, ed., *Narodna književnost*, Belgrade, 1966, pp. 196–206).

Deretić, J., 'Struktura epske pesme "Ženidba od Zadra Todora" ', *Književna istorija*, iv (1971), pp. 207–32.

— 'Banović Strahinja', *Književna istorija*, iv (1972), pp. 395–426.

Džaka, B., 'Geneza motiva o troglavim stvorenjima u Furdusijevoj "Šahnami" i u našoj narodnoj epici', *Izraz*, xvi (1972), pp. 53–70.

Đurić, M., 'Veze Homerove poezije s našom narodnom i umetničkom epikom', *Zbornik radova SAN*, vol. x, Belgrade, 1951, pp. 165–216.

Filipović-Fabijanić, R., 'Odnos narodne pesme i pripovetke', *Rad Kongresa folklorista u Varaždinu 1957*, Zagreb, 1959, pp. 177–80.

Goethe, J. W., 'Serbische Literatur' (written in 1824, first published in the Weimar edn., 1903, pt. i, vol. 41–2), 'Serbische Lieder' (first published in *Über Kunst und Altertum*, No. 2, xv, 1825), 'Serbische Gedichte' (first published in *Über Kunst und Altertum*, No. 1, xvi, 1827), 'Volkslieder der Serben' (written probably in 1826–7, first published in the 'letzter Hand' edn., 1833, vol. 46), 'Das Neuste Serbischer Literatur' (first published in *Über Kunst und Altertum*, No. 1, xvi, 1827), *Kunsttheoretische Schriften und Übersetzungen—Schriften zur Literatur*, ii, Berlin, 1972, pp. 269–95.

Grimm, J., 'Narodne Srpske Piesme . . . ' (first published in *Göttingische gelehrte Anzeigen*, No. 177–8, 1823), *Kleinere Schriften*, iv, Berlin, 1869, pp. 197–205.

— 'Volkslieder der Serben' (first published in *Göttingische gelehrte Anzeigen*, No. 192, 1826), *Kleinere Schriften*, iv, Berlin, 1869, pp. 419–21.

Jakobson, R., 'Studies in Comparative Slavic Metrics', *Oxford Slavonic Papers*, iii (1952), pp. 21–66.

Jovanović, V. M., 'O srpskom narodnom pesništvu', *Srpske narodne pesme*, Belgrade, 1937, pp. ix–xlii (first edn. Belgrade, 1922; partly rpt. in V. Nedić, ed., *Narodna književnost*, Belgrade, 1966, pp. 16–20).

Karadžić, V. S., 'Predgovor' (written in 1823, first published in *Narodne srpske pjesme*, i, Leipzig, 1824), *Srpske narodne pjesme*, i, ed. V. Nedić, Belgrade, 1969, pp. 523–53.

— 'Predgovor' (first published in *Narodne srpske pjesme*, iv, Vienna, 1833), *Srpske narodne pjesme*, iv, ed. V. Nedić, Belgrade, 1969, pp. 363–82.

— 'Mjesto predgovora' (first published in *Srpske narodne pjesme*, i, Vienna, 1841), *Srpske narodne pjesme*, i, ed. V. Nedić, Belgrade, 1966, pp. 19–23.

— 'Predgovor' (first published in *Srpske narodne pjesme*, iv, Vienna, 1862), *Srpske narodne pjesme*, iv, ed. V. Nedić, Belgrade, 1966, pp. 9–12.

Kravcov, N., 'Slavyanskaya narodnaya ballada', *Akademiya nauk SSSR—Uchenie zapiski Instituta slavyanovedeniya*, xxviii (1964), pp. 222–46.

Latković, V., 'O pevačima srpskohrvatskih narodnih pesama do kraja xviii veka', *Prilozi za književnost, jezik, istoriju i folklor*, xx (1954), pp. 184–202 (rpt. in V. Nedić, ed., *Narodna književnost*, Belgrade, 1966, pp. 292–313).

Lord, A. B., 'Homer, Parry, and Huso', *American Journal of Archeology*, lii (1948), pp. 34–44.

Low, D. H., 'The First Link Between English and Serbo-Croat Literature', *Slavonic Review*, iii (1924), pp. 362–9.

Marković, M., 'Puškin, Merime i naša narodna poezija', *Prilozi proučavanju narodne poezije*, iv (1937), pp. 66–88.

Murko, M., 'Die Volksepik der bosnischen Mohammedaner', *Zeitschrift des Vereins für Volkskunde*, xix (1909), pp. 13–30 (rpt. in *Europäische Heldendichtung*, ed. K. von See, Darmstadt, 1978, pp. 385–98).

Nazečić, S., 'O nekim pitanjima muslimanskih epskih pjesama', *1941–1951—Izbor književnih radova*, ed. M. Marković *et al.*, Sarajevo, 1951, pp. 252–67.

— 'Epski Kraljević Marko', *Izraz*, xxvi (1969), pp. 541–59.

Nedić, V., 'Slepa Živana, pevač Vuka Karadžića', *Prilozi za književnost, jezik, istoriju i folklor*, xxix (1963), pp. 59–71.

Novaković, S., 'O ovijem pjesmama' in B. Petranović, *Srpske narodne pjesme iz Bosne i Hercegovine*, Belgrade, 1867, pp. v–xxviii.

Bibliography 359

Novalić, Đ., 'Narodne pjesme o Nikoli Zrinskom-Sigetskom i njihov utjecaj na mađarski ep "Sziteti Veszedelem" ', *Izraz*, xvi (1972), pp. 29–52.

Pantić, M., 'Nepoznata bugarštica o despotu Đurđu i Sibinjanin Janku iz xv veka', *Zbornik Matice srpske za književnost i jezik*, xxv (1977), pp. 421–39.

Schmaus, A., 'Miloš Obilić u narodnom pesništvu i kod Njegoša', *Rad X-og kongresa Saveza folklorista Jugoslavije*, Cetinje, 1964, pp. 43–54.

Slijepčević, P., 'Prilozi narodnoj metrici', *Godišnjak skopskog Filozofskog fakulteta*, i (1930), pp. 17–37.

Subotin, S., 'Adam Mickjevič i naša narodna poezija' in A. Mickjevič, *O srpskoj narodnoj poeziji*, Cetinje, 1955, pp. i–ix.

Taranovski, K., 'O jednosložnim rečima u srpskom stihu', *Naš jezik*, N. S. ii (1950), pp. 26–41.

— 'Principi srpskohrvatske versifikacije', *Prilozi za književnost, jezik, istoriju i folklor*, xx (1954), pp. 14–27.

— 'Roman Jakobson, *Studies in Comparative Slavic Metrics* . . .', *Prilozi za književnost, jezik, istoriju i folklor*, xx (1954), pp. 350–60.

Vulović, S., 'Rujno—Prilog ispitivanju epiteta u narodnoj (usmenoj) srpskoj poeziji', *Godišnjica Nikole Čupića*, vi (1884), pp. 263–70.

Žirmunskij, V. M., *Epicheskoe tvorchestvo slavyanskikh narodov*, Moscow, 1958.

Zuković, Lj., 'Vukov pjevač starac Milija', *Putevi*, xi (1965), pp. 599–612.

— 'Vukov pjevač starac Milija—Analiza pjesama', *Radovi Filozofskog fakulteta u Sarajevu*, iii (1965), pp. 273–305.

— 'O tužbalicama naročito s obzirom na ostale vrste naših narodnih pjesama', *Radovi Filozofskog fakulteta u Sarajevu*, v (1968–9), pp. 293–307.

— 'Istorijski kralj Marko i epski Kraljević Marko', *Izraz*, xviii (1974), pp. 197–232.

III. Historical and Ethnographical Background

Anon., '*Die Serbische Revolution* . . . von Leopold Ranke', *The British and Foreign Review*, xii (1841), pp. 543–82.

— 'Servia. An Historical Sketch', *All the Year Round*, N. S. xv, pt. i (20 Nov. 1875), pp. 174–8; pt. ii (27 Nov. 1875), pp. 198–202.

— 'Servia and the Slavs', *Dublin University Magazine*, lxxxviii, pt. i (Oct. 1876), pp. 385–96; pt. ii (Nov. 1876), pp. 513–22; pt. iii (Dec. 1876), pp. 773–9; lxxxix, pt. iv (Jan. 1877), pp. 140–6.

— 'Marko Kralievitch: The Mythical Hero of Servia', *Macmillan's Magazine*, xxxv (Jan. 1877), pp. 222–9.

— 'The Literature of the Servians and Croats', *The Westminster and Foreign Quarterly Review*, N. S. liii (1 April 1878), pp. 303–27.

Bakotić, P. 'Starac Milija', *Školski vjesnik*, xii (1962), No. 1, pp. 13–25, No. 2, pp. 1–23, No. 4, pp. 1–11, Nos. 5–6, pp. 23–31, No. 8, pp. 15–32.

Božić, I., S. Ćirković, M. Ekmečić, V. Dedijer, *Istorija Jugoslavije*, Belgrade, 1972.

Božić, I., and V. J. Đurić, eds., *O knezu Lazaru*, Naučni skup u Kruševcu 1971, Belgrade, 1975.

Budimiz, M., *Sa balkanskih istočnika*, Belgrade, 1969.

Cvijić, J., *Balkansko poluostrvo i južnoslovenske zemlje* (two books in one volume), Belgrade, 1966 (first Serbo-Croat edn. 2 vols, Belgrade, 1922, 1931, translation and enlarged edn. of *La Péninsule balkanique*, Paris, 1918).

Čajkanović, V., *Mit i religija u Srba*, Belgrade, 1973.

Ćirković, S., 'Dubrovačka kovnica i proizvodnja srebra u Srbiji i Bosni', *Istorijski glasnik*, Belgrade, Nos. 1–2 (1976), pp. 91–9.

Ćorović, V., *Istorija Jugoslavije*, Belgrade, 1933.

Domentian, *Životi svetoga Save i svetoga Simeona, Stare srpske biografije*, iv, tr. L. Mirković, Belgrade, 1938.

Fortis, A., *Viaggio in Dalmazia*, 2 vols., Venice, 1774.

— *Travels into Dalmatia*, London, 1778.

Gesemann, G., *Heroische Lebensform*, Berlin, 1943 (trans. into Serbo-Croat as *Čojstvo i junaštvo starih Crnogoraca*, Cetinje, 1968).

Han, V., 'Putevima narodne tradicije od srednjovekovnih fresaka do folklornih originala', *Zbornik Svetozara Radojčića*, Filozofski fakultet, Belgrade, 1969, pp. 391–8.

Hektorović, P., 'Odgovor Nikoli Nalješkoviću' in H. Lucić, P. Hektorović, *Skladanje izvarsnih pisan razlicih; Ribanje i ribarsko prigovaranje i razlike stvari ine*, ed. M. Franičević (Pet stoljeća hrvatske književnosti, vol. 7), Zagreb, 1968, pp. 241–7.

Hrabak, B. 'Dubrovnik i rodski pirati', *Istoriski glasnik*, Belgrade, No. 2 (1956), pp. 1–13.

— 'Gusarstvo i presretanje pri plovidbi u Jadranskom i Jonskom moru u drugoj polovini xv veka', *Vesnik vojnog muzeja*, Belgrade, No. iv (1957), pp. 83–98.

Jireček, K., *Istorija Srba*, 2 vols., Belgrade, 1978 (first Serbo-Croat edn. 4 vols., Belgrade, 1922–3).

Kačić Miošić, A., *Razgovor ugodni naroda slovinskoga*, Venice, 1756 (second enlarged edn., Venice, 1759).

Karadžic, V. S., *Sabrana dela*, Belgrade, 1965:
    i *Pjesnarica 1814–1815*, ed. V. Nedić, 1965;
    ii *Srpski rječnik (1818)*, ed. P. Ivić, 1966;

iv *Srpske narodne pjesme i*, ed. V. Nedić, 1975;

viii *Danica*, ed. M. Pavić, 1969;

ix *Srpske narodne poslovice*, ed. M. Pantić, 1965;

x *Novi Zavjet*, ed. V. Mošin and D. Bogdanović, 1974;

xii *O jeziku i književnosti*, ed. B. Nikolić, 1968;

xv–xvi *Istorijski spisi*, i–ii, ed. R. Samardžić, 1969;

xvii *Etnografski spisi*, ed. M. S. Filipović, 1972;

xviii *O Crnoj Gori—Razni spisi*, ed. G. Dobrašinović, 1972;

xix *Deutsch-Serbisches Wörterbuch*, ed. M. Pudić, 1971;

xxxvi *Bibliografija spisa Vuka Karadžića*, ed. G. Dobrašinović, 1974.

— *Srpske narodne pripovijetke*, Belgrade, 1969 (first edn. Vienna, 1853).

— *Srpski rječnik*, ed. P. P. Đordević and Lj. Stojanović, Belgrade, 1935 (based on second revised edn., Vienna, 1852).

Knolles, R., *The Generall Historie of the Turkes*, London, 1603.

Konstantin Filozof, 'Život despota Stefana Lazarevića', in G. Camblak, Konstantin Filozof, Pajsije Patrijarh, *Stare srpske biografije xv i xvii veka*, iii, tr. L. Mirković, Belgrade, 1936.

Konstantin Mihailović (iz Ostrovice)—see Mihailović.

Kuripešić, P., *Putopis kroz Bosnu, Srbiju, Bugarsku i Rumeliju 1530*, Sarajevo, 1950.

Lutovac, M., 'Ibarski Kolašin', *Srpski etnografski zbornik*, lxvii (1954), pp. 5–119.

McLuhan, M., *The Gutenberg Galaxy*, London, 1971 (first edn. London, 1962).

Merimée, P. (Anon.), *La Guzla; ou Choix de poésies illyriques, recueillies dans la Dalmatie, la Bosnie, la Croatie et l'Herzegovine*, Paris, 1827.

Mihailović, K. (Konstantin iz Ostrovice), *Janičarove uspomene*, ed. Đ. Živanović, Belgrade, 1966 (first Serbo-Croat edn., Belgrade, 1959).

Mihaljčić, R., *Kraj srpskog carstva*, Belgrade, 1975.

Mijušković, S., ed., *Ljetopis popa Dukljanina*, Titograd, 1967.

Mladenović, A., *Jezik Petra Hektorovića*, Novi Sad, 1968.

Montgomery, J. A., *A Critical and Exegetical Commentary on The Book of Kings*, ed. H. S. Gehman (*The International Critical Commentary*, 10), Edinburgh, 1951.

Nenadović, (Prota) M., *The Memoirs*, ed. and tr. L. F. Edwards, Oxford, 1969 (written probably after 1831 or 1833, but incorporating notes going back to 1804, first published Belgrade, 1867).

Novaković, S., *Srbi i Turci xiv i xv veka*, ed. S. Ćirković, Belgrade, 1960.

Njegoš, P. P., *Gorski vijenac*, ed. R. Bošković and V. Latković, *Celokupna dela*, iii, Belgrade, 1952 (first published Vienna, 1847).

— *The Mountain Wreath*, trans. by J. W. Wiles, London, 1930 (second edn. Westport, Conn., 1970).

Olesnicki, A., 'Turski izvori o kosovskoj bici', *Glasnik Skopskog naučnog društva*, xiv (1935), pp. 59–98.

Ostrogorski, G., *History of the Byzantine State*, Oxford, 1968 (first English edn. Oxford, 1956, second English edn. New Brunswick, N. J., 1957).

Pasternak, B., *Doktor Zhivago*, Milan, 1961.

Popović, D. J., *O hajducima*, 2 vols., Belgrade, 1930, 1931.

Radojčić, N., 'Grčki izvori za kosovsku bitku', *Glasnik Skopskog naučnog društva*, vii–viii (1930), pp. 163–75.

— ed., *Zakonik Cara Stefana Dušana 1349 i 1354*, Belgrade, 1960.

Radojčić, S., 'O nekim zajedničkim motivima naše narodne pesme i našeg starog slikarstva', *Zbornik radova SAN*—Vizantološki institut SAN, ii (1953), pp. 159–75.

— 'Kosovka djevojka', 'Zidanje Ravanice', *Uzori i dela starih srpskih umetnika*, Belgrade, 1975, pp. 237–51.

Ranke, L., *A History of Servia and the Servian Revolution*, London, 1847 (second English edn. London, 1853).

Ređep, J., *Priča o boju kosovskom*, Zrenjanin, 1976.

Ruvarac, I., *O knezu Lazaru*, Novi Sad, 1887.

Samardžić, R., *Hajdučke borbe protiv Turaka u xvi i xvii veku*, Belgrade, 1952.

Stanojević, G., *Senjski uskoci*, Belgrade, 1973.

Stanojević, S., 'Gregoras o našim junačkim pesmama', *Stražilovo*, v (1892), p. 413.

Stefanović, S., 'Nekoji podaci iz mađarske literature za datiranje naše narodne poezije', *Prilozi proučavanju narodne poezije*, iv (1937), pp. 27–35.

Szyrma, K., *Letters on Poland*, Edinburgh, 1823.

Tadić, J., *Promet putnika u starom Dubrovniku*, Dubrovnik, 1939.

Teodosije, 'Život svetoga Save', *Stare srpske biografije*, i, ed. M. Bašić, Belgrade, 1930 (first edn. Belgrade 1924).

Trifunović, Đ., *Srpski srednjovekovni spisi o knezu Lazaru i kosovskom boju*, Kruševac, 1968.

Tsuzuki, Ch., *The Life of Eleanor Marx 1855–1898*, Oxford, 1967.

Vieillefond, J. R., 'Les pratiques religieuses dans l'armée byzantine d'après les traités militaires', *Revue des études anciennes*, xxxvii (1935), pp. 322–30.

Vujicsics, D. S., 'Egy Szerb Guszlár a xvi. Szāzadi Magyarorszāgon', *A Hungarológiai Intézet Tudományos Közleményei*, iii (1971), pp. 135–9.

Wilson, D., *The Life and Times of Vuk Stefanović Karadžić 1787–1864*, Oxford, 1970.

IV. General Reference

Đordević, T. R., *Naš narodni život*, 10 vols., Belgrade, 1930–4.

Enciklopedija Jugoslavije, 8 vols., Zagreb, 1958–71.

Karadžić, V. S., *Srpski rječnik*, Belgrade, 1935 (photocopy of the edn. edited by P. P. Đordević and Lj. Stojanović, Belgrade, 1898, based on the second revised edn., Vienna, 1852; first edn. Vienna. 1818).

Kašanin, M., *Srpska književnost u srednjem veku*, Belgrade, 1975.

Kombol, M., *Poviest hrvatske književnosti*, Zagreb, 1945.

Kulišić, Š., P. Ž. Petrović, N. Pantelić, *Srpski mitoloski rečnik*, Belgrade, 1970.

Pavić, M., *Istorija srpske književnosti baroknog doba*, Belgrade, 1970.

Rečnik srpskohrvatskog književnog i narodnog jezika, Srpska akademija nauka i umetnosti, i, ed. A. Belić *et. al.*; ii–ix, ed. M. Stevanović *et al.*, Belgrade, 1962–.

Rečnik srpskohrvatkoga književnog jezika, i–iii, ed. M. Stevanović, Lj. Jonke *et al.*, Novi Sad–Zagreb, 1967–9; iv–vi, ed. M. Stevanović *et al.*, Novi Sad, 1971–6.

Rječnik hrvatskoga ili srpskoga jezika, Jugoslavenska akademija znanosti i umjetnosti, i, ed. Đ. Daničić; ii, ed. Đ. Daničić *et al.*; iii–v, ed. P. Budmani; vi, ed. P. Budmani, T. Maretić; vii–xii, ed. T. Maretić; xiii, ed. S. Bosanac *et al.*; xiv, ed. T. Grdenić *et al.*; xv, ed. J. Hamm *et al.*; xvi–xxiii, ed. J. Jedvaj *et al.*, Zagreb, 1880–1976.

Stanojević, S., ed., *Narodna enciklopedija srpsko-hrvatsko-slovenačka*, 4 vols., Zagreb, 1925–9.

Index

This index is divided into three sections. Section I lists major 'Features' of Serbo-Croat epic singing. It also includes under the heading 'battles and wars' some historical events prominent in the general epic landscape. Section II lists 'Titles of songs and literary works. It does not include references to songs when they are not discussed in their own right but merely cited under respective numbers in footnotes, mostly as sources of formulaic expressions. Such references are listed under more pertinent headings in Section I, e.g. 'formulas and formulaic language'. Section III lists 'Names' of authors, historical personages and/or major epic heroes. The singers' names are given in alphabetical order under 'singers'. References to Bogišić, Gesemann, and Karadžić are selective and mostly limited to the descriptions of their collections and their judgements on various matters. Modern authors have initials only. Main entries are in bold type.

III. NAMES